Australian Women

Contemporary Feminist Thought

Other books in this series

Australian Women: Feminist Perspectives, ed. Norma Grieve and Patricia Grimshaw

Australian Women: New Feminist Perspectives, ed. Norma Grieve and Ailsa Burns

Australian Women

Contemporary Feminist Thought

Edited by Norma Grieve
and Ailsa Burns

Melbourne
OXFORD UNIVERSITY PRESS
Oxford Auckland New York

OXFORD UNIVERSITY PRESS, AUSTRALIA

Oxford New York Toronto
Delhi Bombay Calcutta Madras Karachi
Kuala Lumpur Singapore Hong Kong Tokyo
Nairobi Dar es Salaam Cape Town
Melbourne Auckland Madrid
and associated companies in Berlin Ibadan

OXFORD is a trademark of Oxford University Press

First published 1994

National Library of Australia
Cataloguing-in-Publication data:

Australian women: contemporary feminist thought.

Bibliography.
Includes index.
ISBN 0 19 553503 0.

1. Feminism—Australia. 2. Women—Australia. I. Grieve, Norma, 1925–. II. Burns, Ailsa, 1929–.

305.40994

Edited by Janet Mackenzie
Designed by R. T. J. Klinkhamer
Cover illustration and design by Cathie Lindsey
Indexed by Geraldine Suter
Typeset by Syarikat Seng Teik Sdn. Bhd., Malaysia
Printed by McPherson's Printing Group, Australia

Published by Oxford University Press
253 Normanby Road, South Melbourne, Australia

Contents

Contributors

GILL BOTTOMLEY teaches anthropology and comparative sociology at Macquarie University, Sydney. She is the author of *After the Odyssey* (1979), *The Export of People* (1984) and *From Another Place* (1992), and of numerous articles and chapters on the subjects of migration, culture, ethnicity, gender and racism. She has also co-authored and co-edited *Family in the Modern World* (1983), *Ethnicity Class and Gender* (1984), *The Cultural Construction of Race* (1988) and *Intersexions: Gender/Class/Culture/Ethnicity* (1991).

LOIS BRYSON is currently Professor of Sociology at the University of Newcastle. She is a widely published academic researcher who has had a long-term concern with the effects of social policy on issues of equality. She wrote (with Faith Thompson) Australia's first urban community study, *Australian Newtown*, and has written on poverty, family, work, gender, sport, the welfare state and public sector management. Her most recent book, *Welfare and The State: Who Benefits?* focuses on the effects of the recent pre-eminence of economic liberalism on equality across a range of the advanced industrial societies.

STEPHANIE BUNBURY is Arts Editor of the Melbourne *Age* newspaper. She has written about film for the *Age*, *Cinema Papers* and *Scripsi,* and contributed a chapter to *Don't Shoot Darling!: Women's Independent Film-making in Australia* (ed. Blonski, Creed and Freiburg, 1986). Convinced that nothing sharpens the critical faculties so much as surfeit, she has always spent an inordinate amount of time at the movies, even before she got free tickets.

AILSA BURNS is Associate Professor of Psychology in the School of Behavioral Sciences at Macquarie University. She co-edited (with Norma Grieve) *Australian Women: New Feminist Perspectives*, and is the author of *Breaking Up: Separation and Divorce in Australia; Children and Families in Australia* and *Home and School* (both with Jacqueline Goodnow); *Don't Feel the World in Caving In* (with Rosemary Dunlop); and *The Family in the Modern World* (co-edited with Gill Bottomley and Penny Jools). A cross-cultural study of mother-headed families, *The Post-Marriage Family*, will be published in 1993 by Lawrence Erlbaum.

BARBARA CREED is a Senior Lecturer in the Division of Cinema Studies at La Trobe University. She has published in Australia and internationally on feminist film theory and cultural studies, and is co-editor of *Don't Shoot*

Darling!: Women's Independent Film-making in Australia. She reviews films regularly for *The Week In Film* on Radio National and is the author of *The Monstrous Feminine: Film Feminism Horror* (Routledge, 1993).

ANN CURTHOYS is Professor of Social History at the University of Technology, Sydney. She has been Dean of the Faculty of Humanities and Social Sciences, and Acting Pro-Vice-Chancellor, at UTS, but is now delighted to have returned to teaching and research. She is author of *For and Against Feminism: A Personal Journey into Feminist Theory and History* (Allen and Unwin, Sydney, 1988); co-editor of several books on Australian history; and author of many articles and chapters on feminist theory and Australian women's, Aboriginal, immigration, and political, media, and cultural history. She is currently engaged in two projects: one is a history of the 'Freedom Ride' protesting against discrimination against Aboriginal people in rural New South Wales in 1965; the other, with Paula Hamilton and Julianne Schultz, is a history of journalism in twentieth-century Australia.

NORMA GRIEVE is a Senior Associate of the Department of Psychology, University of Melbourne. She has co-edited two companion volumes to this collection, *Australian Women: Feminist Perspectives* (1981) and *Australian Women: New Feminist Perspectives* (1986).

PATRICIA GRIMSHAW is the Max Crawford Professor and currently Head of the History Department at the University of Melbourne, where she teaches American and Australian history, and Women's Studies. She is author of *Women's Suffrage in New Zealand*, and *Paths of Duty: American Missionary Wives in Nineteenth-Century Hawaii*, and has co-edited a number of collections, most recently *Studies in Gender: Essays in Honour of Norma Grieve.*

GILLIAN HEWITSON is a tutor in the Economics Department at La Trobe University. She has completed an honours degree in economics at Flinders University and a master's degree in economics at Monash University. She is now enrolled in a Ph.D. with joint supervision in Women's Studies and Economics at La Trobe University.

ADRIAN HOWE teaches theoretical criminology in the Legal Studies Department at La Trobe University. Her main teaching and research interest is in developing a poststructuralist and feminist approach to the problems of men's violence and masculinist education. She has recently completed *Penal Regimes: Critiques and Transgressions—Socialist, Feminist and Postmodern Approaches to Penality* (Routledge) for the 'Sociology of Law and Crime' series, edited by Maureen Cain and Carol Smart.

JACKIE HUGGINS is an Aboriginal historian and writer whose first book, a biography of her mother titled *Aunty Rita*, is currently in press. She has completed a second book, *If The Truth Be Known*, a collection of her personal essays on history, racism, colonialism and women's issues. Recently she was awarded a research fellowship at the University of Melbourne where she compiled the first anthology of Black women's writing in Australia, called *Tidda's Business*.

GISELA KAPLAN is Professor of Social Science at Queensland University of Technology, Brisbane. Amongst her major publications are *Contemporary Western European Feminism* (Allen & Unwin, New York UP, and UCL, London, 1992), and, jointly edited, *Hannah Arendt: Thinking, Judging, Freedom* (Allen & Unwin, 1989). She was born in Europe and studied at Monash University where she obtained her Ph.D. Lecturing overseas included Canada, Germany, and the USA. She has worked for refuges, for migrant and women's issues. In the Australian Sociological Association, she served on the Executive and then as its Vice President (1991) and she is currently editor-in-chief of the *Australian Journal for Social Issues*.

BEVERLEY KINGSTON is Associate Professor of History at the University of New South Wales. She wrote Volume 3 of the Oxford History of Australia (*Glad Confident Morning*) and is the author of *Basket, Bag and Trolley* (forthcoming).

VICKI KIRBY is currently a Visiting Scholar in the Visual Arts Department at the University of California, San Diego. She had a Visiting Fellowship at the Humanities Research Centre at the Australian National University in 1993, and is presently working on two books on the body and sexual and cultural difference.

MARILYN LAKE is a Reader in History and Director of Women's Studies at La Trobe University. She has published widely in the area of gender relations in Australian society, in particular on the subjects of war, sexuality, and feminism. Her forthcoming book, to be published in 1993, is a feminist history of Australia, written with Patricia Grimshaw, Ann McGrath and Marian Quartly.

SUSAN MAGAREY has been Director of the Research Centre for Women's Studies at Adelaide University since 1983 and before that was lecturer in charge of the Women's Studies program at the Australian National University. She edits *Australian Feminist Studies*, and her main research interest is Australian feminist history.

ANDREW MAY completed a doctorate in Urban History at the University of Melbourne in 1993. He is currently a Research Fellow at Monash University, working on the history of Melbourne since 1945.

ROSEMARY PRINGLE teaches Sociology and Women's Studies at Macquarie University, Sydney. She is author of *Secretaries Talk*, co-author of *Gender at Work*, and is currently writing a book about gender and medicine. Along the way she has become interested in both butchery and the funeral industry which she is also currently researching.

JILL ROE is Associate Professor of History at Macquarie University, Sydney, and a section editor (NSW) of the *Australian Dictionary of Biography*. Her most recent publication is *'My Congenials': Miles Franklin and friends in letters, 1879–1954* (1993).

PHILIPA ROTHFIELD is a Lecturer in Philosophy at La Trobe University. She has published on feminist theory, psychoanalysis, postmodernism, law, social theory and philosophy of the body. She is currently writing a book on the body which is informed by her involvement in contemporary dance.

LYNDALL RYAN has been Reader in Women's Studies at Flinders University since 1986, and was inaugural convenor of the Australian Women's Studies Association. She co-founded *Refractory Girl* as a women's studies journal in 1972. Her research interests include reproductive politics, women and the state, and Aboriginal history.

SUSAN SHERIDAN has been Senior Lecturer in Women's Studies at Flinders University since 1987. She has taught Women's Studies courses since the early 1970s at Adelaide University, University of South Australia and Deakin University. She has published widely on feminist cultural theory and Australian women writers.

CARMEL SHUTE has been an industrial officer since 1983 with the Public Sector Union and, prior to amalgamation, the ABC Staff Union. She trained as an historian at the University of Queensland and La Trobe University, but gave up academia to pursue a life of political activism. She has been a long-time activist in the women's movement and on the left. In 1974, she was a founding editor of *Hecate: A Women's Interdisciplinary Journal.* She worked on both the 1978 and 1980 Women and Labour Conferences and co-edited *Worth Her Salt* in 1982. She is currently a convenor of Sisters in Crime and dreams of having enough time to write a crime novel set in the Melbourne suburb of St Kilda, where she lives.

MARIAN SIMMS is a Senior Lecturer in Political Science at the Australian National University. Her most recent book is the second edition of *A Woman's Place: Women and Politics in Australia* (co-authored with Marian Sawer). She has published widely on women and politics and political parties. In 1993 she was the President of the Australasian Political Studies Association.

MAILA STIVENS studied anthropology at the University of Sydney and the London School of Economics. She has carried out research in Sydney on kinship in a middle-class suburb and in Negeri Sembilan, Malaysia, on gender and underdevelopment, and latterly, on the Malay middle class. A founding editor of the journal *Critique of Anthropology*, she taught anthropology at University College, London from 1977 to 1987, before returning to Australia, where she is now Director of Women's Studies at the University of Melbourne. Her publications include as editor, *Why Gender Matters in Southeast Asian Politics* (1991) and, with Cecila Ng and Jomo Sundaram, *Engendered Inequality: Malay Women and the Land* (1993).

ANNE SUMMERS is currently editor of *Good Weekend* magazine. She is the author of three books, including the best-selling *Damned Whores and God's Police* (new edition 1994). She was Canberra Bureau Chief for the *Australian Financial Review* before becoming chief adviser on women's issues to Prime Minister Bob Hawke. In 1986–7 she was North American Manager for John Fairfax Ltd, and from 1987 to 1989 was editor-in-chief of *Ms.* magazine. In 1988 she and her then partner Sandra Yates raised $20 million on Wall Street, enabling them to purchase *Ms.* and *Sassy*, thus completing the second woman-led management buyout in US corporate history. Until early 1993 she was the Women's Adviser to Prime Minister Paul Keating.

MARGARET THORNTON is a Professor of Legal Studies at La Trobe University. She has particular interests in feminist legal theory, gender discrimination and legal education. Her publications include *The Liberal Promise: Anti-Discrimination Legislation in Australia* (Oxford UP, 1990)

Acknowledgements

The authors and publisher are grateful to the following copyright holders for granting permission to reproduce copyright material in this book:
Deakin University and Jackie Huggins for her article 'A Contemporary View of Aboriginal Women's Relationship to the White Women's Movement'.
Penguin Books Australia and Anne Summers for her article 'Feminism on Two Continents: The Women's Movement in Australia and the United States'.

Introduction

Norma Grieve and Ailsa Burns

In the previous companion volume, published in 1986, Miriam Dixson, one of the foundation scholars of Australian women's history, writes of the initiation of public discourse on the gender script as 'an achievement without historical parallel'. In the 1990s, feminism has established a firm and assured place in Australian culture, and is now recognised in many quarters as one of the great and enduring intellectual movements of the twentieth century. Today, virtually all issues are women's issues, and feminists contribute not only on matters with which they have been commonly associated—such as childcare, violence against women, reproductive freedoms, women's paid and unpaid work, welfare and women and equal opportunity—but to the range of contemporary issues and debates. In the federal bureaucracy, women are now a voice at the table. An increasing number of voices has been added to the debates, as proportionally more women have taken advantage of the education and occupational opportunities now available to them.

Feminism, like many intellectual and political movements of the 1990s is explicitly concerned with diversity. A diversity of theoretical positions has always been a feature of feminism, and many feminists have within their own practice consciously taken up different positions for different problems. However, the diversity of the 1990s has more complex features: moreover, it presents the challenge of not only acknowledging and respecting difference but also *incorporating* diversity into feminist projects.

This wealth of material presents its own difficulties for a collection such as the present one. What is to be included and what not? As in the previous volumes, we are guided by the fact that our collection is directed primarily to students of women's studies. For this reason we have drawn on a range of disciplines to which feminists have made a contribution, as well as on women's studies. There have been other considerations, such as the wish to include new voices as well as the projects and interests of established scholars, and also to represent views from outside the academy. In consultation with our authors, we have asked them to address topics which have emerged as important theoretical and political issues, and/or that appear especially important for the 1990s.

We have found, as will the reader, that a valuable organising framework is provided by our first chapter, in which Ann Curthoys discusses Australian feminism since 1970. She observes a distinctive character in Australian feminist discourse, notably an openness to feminist ideas from a variety of Euro-American sources; this conclusion is echoed in Jill Roe's chapter on women and nationalism. Roe notes that since the 1890s, Australian women have been intrepid in attendance at international conferences, firstly as representatives of voluntary organisations and after 1918 often as official government delegates. She points up the discrepancy between their high international profile and their weak representation in federal and state Parliament. (Vida Goldstein's neat appearance in London in 1911 led Christabel Pankhurst to comment that perhaps that was how women appeared after they had secured the vote and no longer had to become disarranged struggling for it.) Despite this strong international emphasis, Roe concludes that there has also been an interesting relationship with Australian nationalism, which has accommodated more women than its ultra-male image suggests.

Gisela Kaplan and Ann Summers also comment on the distinctiveness of Australian feminism in political and social policy areas, as they reflect on their respective experiences of European and North American feminisms. Kaplan comments on the strangeness of the concept of femocrat to European feminist, and speculates that Australian bureaucracy has a post-colonial legacy of operating as a site of power which is unlike the more limited administrative character of European bureaucracy. European women have focused on parliamentary representation, where they are proportionally more numerous than their Australian counterparts. Kaplan also believes that multiculturalism has made us more aware of diversity than is the case in the more homogeneous European states; she notes that we, like Scandinavia, are kinder to women in our welfare policies, since we do not tie benefits to a person's occupational history, as is the case in USA and many European nations. On the other hand, European and Australian feminisms share some political and philosophical influences, in particular the Marxist and socialist feminist influences that have been evident from the beginning of Second Wave feminism in this country.

Ann Summers has for the last decade been uniquely placed to comment on the ways in which Australian and North American feminisms differ. In contrast to the political strategies of North American feminists, she observes that Australian feminists have learned to work successfully in the political mainstream, in flexible and pragmatic ways. They have developed increasing political clout, whilst North American feminists have become marginalised and faction-ridden. As she sees it, the US movement's inability to organise around a common agenda and to develop an effective electoral strategy, has meant that the 1980s saw nothing new accomplished, and some women's entitlements actually taken away. 'The Reagan and Bush years were not good for American women, but they were even worse for the American Women's Movement because it lost its perspective—and its nerve.'

A significant part of Curthoy's necessarily selective account of Australian feminisms since 1970 is devoted to questions of theory, which have assumed urgency, if not pre-eminence, at least within the academy, with the emergence of postmodern and post-colonial critiques. In fact the claim has been made that in the 1990s theory and practice are not two different faces of political feminism, but that theory is now a form of political practice. Curthoys records how various theoretical frameworks have developed, flourished, declined and endured, and in some cases been transformed, revitalised, or compromised, by the critiques of post-modern and post-structural feminist social theories.

She observes that one of the earliest theoretical frameworks employed in Australian feminist analyses, the Marxist and socialist feminist approach, has become less influential. However, readers will observe from the present collection that economic *issues* endure and more or less oblige a materialist analysis. Radical feminism, with its concern with masculinist ideologies and practices, still flourishes. The power of systemic patriarchy is still omnipresent and oppressive, and encountered by women at more sites and in new manifestations, as women and men interact more widely in the culture. Curthoys sees the continuing trajectory of radical feminist theory being altered by contact with feminist post-structuralism. This approach to social theory has developed more complex and stringent critiques of the malecentred philosophical basis of patriarchy, and in the process has detected androcentric assumptions in feminist paradigms. Another long-standing theme in feminist theorising has been generated from liberal humanism, and is reflected in continuing assessment and critique of the humanistic projects of equal opportunity. Curthoys observes that there is a dilemma within this approach. Is feminism part of humanist politics, or a powerful critic and thus part of post-modern thought? Postmodernism has, according to Curthoys, sharpened the debate concerning universality versus difference. How universal are the ideals of equality to which Western feminists have aspired? Is the struggle for the idea of universal freedoms necessarily wrongheaded since the Enlightenment project is inherently marginalising of other than Eurocentric understandings, interests and projects? Curthoys discusses these complex questions with an enviable clarity. These issues are taken up again in this collection in detailed and different ways by Vicki Kirby, Philipa Rothfield, Maila Stivens, Barbara Creed, and Margaret Thornton.

Vicki Kirby takes as her project the complex task of defining the 'vexed term' *postmodernism* and attempting to characterise its relation with feminism in general, and the specific case of Australian feminism. She asks whether feminism is undermined by postmodernism's apparent disrespect for its terms of reference, and if so, what this means for feminism's contemporary identity? The relationship between postmodernism and feminisms, she argues, is a reciprocal one. The identities of postmodernism and its apparent adversaries are not distinct. Postmodernism is 'viral'—it takes nourishment from feminisms' interrogations. On the other hand, the identity of Australian feminism, she argues, owes something to its uniquely local engagement with, and assimilation of, postmodern arguments.

Maila Stivens, as a feminist anthropologist, is at the intersection of the problems associated with the postmodern critique, and she perceives awkward relations between all three of these projects: anthropology, feminism and postmodernism. She discusses a number of possible positions that a feminist anthropology could take up in the face of criticism of anthropology as inherently Eurocentric. She notes the anxiety expressed by some feminist anthropologists regarding the depoliticising tendencies inherent in postmodernism. This is echoed in the charges made by some radical feminists that academic feminists have lost sight of the political struggle and have shown insufficient resistance to the stance of relativism. Stivens suggests that the complex problems raised by postmodernism, both for feminisms and for feminist anthropology, are far from resolution.

Philipa Rothfield focuses on the issue of universalism versus difference. She explores the problems inherent in universalistic propositions about women, but her particular contribution is to tackle the difficult issues raised by the so-called 'acknowledgement' of difference. She discusses white racism, and the theoretical and 'actual' responsibility, concern, and accountability of women in positions of relative dominance. Under what conditions may they, or indeed should they, speak for 'others' and involve themselves in issues other than their own?

Barbara Creed's exposition of the new theoretical direction in lesbian and gay coalition politics—queer theory, and the associated queer cinema—exemplifies another response to postmodern subversions, in this case the critique of hegemonic sexualities. Queer theory attempts to place a wide range of experiences of marginalisation within its conceptual umbrella. Creed cautions that the future of this new alliance will depend on 'the willingness of each group to recognise the differences of the other'.

Stephanie Bunbury considers teen movies, a genre that became big box-office in the 1980s. In these films, the narratives turn on teenage isolation and its crises. Within the plot, the boys' sphere is confused but comradely and prankish: above all, the boys have fun. The girls' sphere, where present at all, is passive and victimised, or silly and vain. Film theory holds that this is not a problem for the audience, because females identify 'up' to adopt the male point of view, as this is the view taken by the camera itself. And girls are the main consumers of teen movies. Bunbury considers the various ways in which the images presented allow adolescent girls to identify with apparently male images of freedom, jollity and autonomy.

In her account of feminisms since 1970, Curthoys identifies a number of substantive issues, of which feminism and race are given pre-eminence. Australian white feminists have had a forceful reminder of the consequences of an unthinking acceptance of the idea that their own concerns—arising out of Western white women's subordination by the masculinist patriarchy—are relevant to all women. Aboriginal women have in recent years articulated their rejection of white feminists' analysis of subordination. They have particularly abjured the anti-masculinist position inherent in white feminisms, and the feminist critique of the family, which to Australian Aborigines has been an institution they have had to fight to sustain and protect against white destructive intrusions. Jackie Huggins' chapter was written in 1990, and is reprinted here as a basic text in any attempt to understand relations between Aboriginal and non-Aboriginal women. It is an unequivocal and passionate rejection of the assumption by some white feminists that they can speak on behalf of Aboriginal women. Aboriginal women see their oppression as constituted differently from white women, and indeed they assert that white women have yet to acknowledge their complicity in that oppression. The research essays of the feminist historians Patricia Grimshaw and Marian Lake are in part a response to such criticisms.

Grimshaw and Andrew May describe the representation of women and gender in Koori culture in the mid-nineteenth century that emerged from the reports and articles of white middle-class male missionaries, protectors and 'scientific' commentators. The authors suggest that this white discourse,

> intended to be descriptive, but in fact highly racist, in turn was used as the century proceeded to justify oppressive settler behaviour and increasingly harsh public policies towards Koori women, men and children.

This research presents a shocking history of 'an imperial project of tragic proportions' in which Koori lands were usurped and 'attempts to usurp Koori culture were made by successive colonial legislators'. Marilyn Lake is concerned with a later period, the first half of this century. She attempts to recover the discursive resources of those white middle-class feminists who worked for what they saw as the independence of Aboriginal women and their assimilation into an emergent and more enlightened Australian culture. Lake suggests that 'distinctions made between white "civilised" and black "primitive" womanhood were integral to the formulation of the feminist project' at that time. She links this complicity in 'the imperial project' with contemporary manifestations of what she argues is feminism's inherently missionary politics. As then, these politics are still problematic as we try to 'reconcile general rules about human rights with the specificities and rights of cultural traditions'.

Gill Bottomley's chapter adds a further perspective to the issues of cultural tradition and 'difference' in her discussion of the debates associated with Australia's large intake of immigrants since World War II. She scrutinises the much-employed concepts of identity, ethnicity, nationalism, community and multiculturalism, illustrating some of her points from the essay by leading Australian feminist Eva Cox, 'What ethnic identity?'. In this essay Eva describes her experiences as the child of Viennese parents who fled to England when she was a baby, stayed there for seven years and then lived in Rome for a further two years before emigrating to Australia. As one who has lived through a kaleidoscope of ethnic identities, Eva sees over-reliance on those as unsatisfactory and dangerous:

> as a child of refugees, I want a world where we learn tolerance as a primary characteristic . . . where we are not looking to the tribe for identity and creating outsiders to make us feel good.

Bottomley goes on to consider the positives and negatives of ethnic and national self-identification.

A further set of questions explored in this volume concerns Australian women's relationship to the workforce. As Lois Bryson notes, women's labourforce participation has steadily increased, with the increase among married women particularly striking: from about 12 per cent in the early 1950s to over 52 per cent in the 1990s. At the same time, the participation of men has decreased, so that by 1991 women formed 41.8 per cent of the Australian workforce. Introducing these issues, Gillian Hewitson presents a feminist perspective on neo-classical economics (NCE). Hewitson notes that while the dominance of NCE among Australian economic policy-makers makes the development of a feminist critique vital, this is a task which has been as yet largely ignored. Her essay explores the concept of rational economic man (REM) whose presumed behaviour lies at the core of neo-classical economics. REM as an economic actor is a conscious, knowing, self-interested, rational being who consistently makes market decisions in line with his own individual preferences. He is taken to represent both male and female individuals: however, he has no responsibility for children, the old, the sick, or even for the maintenance of the social bonds that hold human communities together.

As Hewitson notes, this male-based formulation of human nature can lead to some conclusions dangerous for women. These include the assumption that workers do not have children or other domestic responsibilities; and justification of unequal pay as simply evidencing that 'the market' puts less value on women's work. As women now comprise more than 40 per cent of the labourforce, the power of neo-classical economics to affect their interests obviously merits feminist attention.

Hewitson's argument is strengthened by the material presented by Lois Bryson. Bryson points out that the workforce patterns of women and men have steadily converged, partly due to greater 'feminisation' of men's work (more time out of work, more part-time and contract work) and partly due to women's greater participation and potential participation (via more extended and varied education and training). The result has been that women have become more directly stratified into the class structure—in their own right as workers—rather than taking on the class position of their husbands and fathers. This shift has been paralleled in the welfare system, which through the 1980s became steadily degendered, as wives' benefits were redefined as sex-neutral spousal benefits, single mothers were encouraged to enter the workforce, and single fathers allowed to stay out of it to care for children. Bryson asks whether these changes have increased gender equality, and concludes that the advantages for women outweigh the disadvantages. But, like Hewitson, she warns of the dangers of public economic policies that could counteract the gains that have been made.

Carmel Shute discusses issues associated with another powerful agent in the economic sector—the trade union movement. The union movement has been historically a men's movement—a bastion of grey cardigans and pub-based negotiations—with little interest in women workers. However, falling membership and other factors have brought a new interest in attracting as members the women who have entered the white-collar and public sector unions. This has meant endorsing woman-friendly policies such as flexible hours, award restructuring, childcare, affirmative action and parental leave. The women officials who have developed and promoted such policies have faced and continue to face some tough battles. When first elected to the State Council of the Victorian State Public Service Federation, Kay McVey, (later to become the General President) was hissed and booed by male delegates every time she got up to speak. The women also have to deal with a 'gerrymander' by the male-dominated unions (mining, metal workers) that have lost members but retained their voting power; and with family-unfriendly hours of work, often sixty hours a week, including night and weekend meetings. She quotes one woman official's view:

> Being a union . . . organiser eats you up; it consumes you. Men can cope better with that: they have support at home. Women don't get the same buzz out of the power—for them it's much more the stress of the commitment.

Shute concludes that over the last fifteen years women have been successful in establishing themselves as a genuine force, but this has involved learning rules such as 'Don't be too polite, girls.'

While membership of the unions has declined, that of the professions has boomed. Rosemary Pringle notes for example that between 1947 and 1986 there was a 600 per cent increase in the number of lawyers in Australia. The new professionals included a large influx of women, especially into law, medicine and architecture. Pringle asks whether this represents a gain for women, or merely creates new forms of discrimination, with women confined to the lower levels of these professions. She finds that women have been well received in the lower ranks of medicine, a fact reflected in the media's replacement of 'Dr Kildare images with the [women] doctors in *E Street* and *GP*', who muddle along and are good doctors precisely because they are family women with children of their own. The specialties have been more resistant, but even so the number of women entering specialist medical training has doubled. The law is proving more intransigent, although half of today's law students are women; and Pringle discusses some reasons for this.

What is work and what is not? Lois Bryson's paper refers to the extensive debate on women's unpaid labour and its relationship to the economy. Beverley Kingston takes up a different aspect—shopping. Her witty account draws extensively on retail trade journals of 1945–70, evidently a goldmine of misogynistic and condescending articles and jokes about the illogical behaviour of consumers who failed to buy the goods that the retailers believed they should. These shoppers were mostly women—even some 80 per cent of menswear was known to be sold to women. Despite the scorn of the (mostly male) retailers, the shoppers sometimes had the last laugh. For example, an immense amount of effort went into marketing the postwar New Look and other Paris-inspired fashions. Sir Sydney Snow, founder of the giant retail firm, opined that an interest in fashion made women 'better citizens—a woman without a fashion sense and to whom the more beautiful things in life do not appeal, generally remains on the lower rungs of the human ladder'. Disregardful Australian women rejected the New Look and its ilk, opting instead for comfort, affordability, and the lower rungs of the ladder. They also moved retailers to introduce escalators specially built 32 inches wide to accommodate a mother and child side by side, since 'it had been observed that women shopping were usually accompanied by a child'. Kingston charts these and further battles between retailers, shoppers and saleswomen, the latter mostly over equal pay, hours, and access to forbidden selling areas (hardware, crockery, glassware and electrical appliances were for many years reserved for men, although women could sell 'small devotional and ecclesiastical items'). Kingston concludes that 'the underlying toughness of the modern women's movement in Australia may be [partly] related to all those years as a customer with a complaint which no-one would take seriously'.

The chapters discussed above emphasise the importance of both gender and class. A further group of chapters deals with issues where the gender divide is particularly salient. They highlight the importance of a fictive personage whom we might call benchmark citizen man (BCM). Just as rational economic man (REM) dominates the thinking of neoclassical economics, BCM provides a standard against which women involved with the courts, politics, and various other institutions find themselves measured and, being women, are often found wanting.

The first two pieces in this section discuss the operation of the law. Margaret Thornton notes the allure that legislation on equal opportunity and affirmative action has held for women workers, and the support that feminist law reformers gave to its introduction. She believes that the promise of EEO has not been realised, and in fact could not be, because of the law's failure to accept that the situation of women is different from that of 'benchmark Anglo-Celtic heterosexual able-bodied male'. The woman who believes that she has been discriminated against (and is brave enough to bring a case) must show that she has been given less favourable treatment than a similarly situated man; but since women are rarely similarly situated, it is hard for her to meet the law's requirements. Affirmative action legislation has been introduced to overcome the deficiencies of EEO, but as Thornton sees it this has so far been largely toothless, and has at best resulted in a few 'suitable' women being admitted to previously inaccessible occupations.

Adrian Howe also discusses the law's difficulty in dealing with sexual difference, in this case in respect of homicide. Some four in ten of all homicides are domestic, usually a man killing his partner, and provocation is an important defence. A recent review of homicide law by the now discontinued Law Reform Commission of Victoria concluded that the provocation defence is not gender-biased. Howe argues that this is because the review failed to analyse the content of what is presented as provocation. For the male murderer, this usually comprises evidence or suspicion of the female partner's adultery, which 'provoked her own demise' since there 'can be no greater provocation [to men] than [women's] . . . adultery'. Howe describes cases in which men who have killed their partners, and sometimes other people along with them, and have successfully pleaded that they were provoked by the wife's 'sexual taunts' or other similarly uninvasive behaviours. At the same time the law has been slow to recognise provocation in cases where a battered wife waits her time to murder a violent and dangerous man, as her action lacks the spontaneity of male homicidal rage. Howe concludes that the law's definition of what 'ordinary, reasonable man' (BCM) may be expected to do operates in this arena also so as to victimise women.

Readers interested in pursuing this topic will find the video film *Excuse for Murder* (ABC Four Corners) a valuable complement to Howe's chapter.

BCM makes an appearance again in Marian Simms' research on preselection of candidates by the major political parties. Whereas elections are exceedingly public affairs, candidate preselection is mostly a private party matter, conducted behind closed doors. The selectors and their biases thus exert a powerful influence on the makeup of parliament. Simms interviewed key figures in the preselection process (state secretaries and branch directors) regarding their ideal candidate, and was offered a happy family man who was a 'former state footballer [and] who goes to confession'. Nevertheless, the number of women candidates achieving preselection has increased, and those with media appeal are now considered sympathetically ('a newsreader or weather reader would be worth looking at'). Those women candidates who do get preselected are mostly concentrated into marginal and hopeless constituencies, where they are seen as 'flagwavers' for the party. However, an interesting development in recent elections has been the increasing presence of women in the 'gladiator' class, where a marginal seat is targeted for additional resources and media treatment by the challenging party. Simms places her research within current feminist epistemological debates. She has two projects: firstly to bring together the public and the private political worlds, and secondly to identify feminist empiricism as a viable approach to epistemological issues.

Norma Grieve continues this feminist empiricist approach. She draws on the writings of the American developmental psychologist Eleanor Maccoby, which she links with two Australian discursive analyses of gender interviews, to suggest a beginning to masculinist culture in the tendencies of preschool children to separate themselves into same-sex groups. Maccoby describes a series of ingenious child studies that explore how girls' and boys' groups develop different social rules. These rules work well enough in their own groups, but in mixed-sex groups girls find themselves overlooked and overruled. Grieve discusses the move from separation to active child-regulated segregation, which in some Australian schools has moved to sexism in the classroom and harassment of girls in the playground as the boys enact their versions of masculinity. She suggests that this formulation of male behaviour as 'boys' games' has implications for understanding many of the written and unwritten rules of adolescent and adult interactions in mixed-sex groups and for school affirmative action programmes.

Several of these chapters refer to the issue of women's double workload, which has become more salient as more women have entered the workforce. Ailsa Burns discusses the finding of Bittman and others that married women continue to do most unpaid domestic labour even when in paid employment. She asks why women put up with it, and describes a number of explanations that have been offered (including the evidence that not all women do or are expected to put up with it). Benchmark citizen man flits through these pages also, holding out his hand for a cup of tea, and leaving rings in the bathtub ('I don't know who does the bathroom; she must do it, 'cause I don't').

As this book is written primarily for students of women's studies, it concludes with a chapter describing the development of women's studies courses in Australia. The authors—Susan Magarey, Lyndall Ryan and Susan Sheridan—note that the universities have not always been hospitable to women's studies, and that in some academies gaining even a toehold has been difficult, despite student enthusiasm. They discuss the content typically taught, and suggest that in the 1990s theoretical issues concerning postmodernism, difference, race, essentialism and internationalism will be crucial, and will influence a multiplicity of debates in which feminists are involved—for example, women's work needs, and the rethinking of such patriarchally defined terms as skill and merit.

These and related issues have received considerable attention in the various chapters of this book. There are, however, many other issues that are important to feminists, but that space precludes covering in the present volume: issues in health, education, the arts, welfare, science, technology, eco-feminism and the peace movement, to name but some. As we noted earlier, the last two decades have seen such an expansion of feminist thinking that there is now virtually no issue that is not a feminist issue. We trust that this third volume in the *Australian Women* series will not only inform and stimulate readers, but also encourage them to extend the insights provided to other questions and issues.

PART I

The Context of Australian Feminism

ONE

Australian Feminism since 1970

Ann Curthoys

Is there such a thing, an 'Australian feminism' stretching back from now to then, from the 1890s to 1970? Can we recognise ourselves in the past? Is it still reasonable to characterise this entire period, as we so often do, as a feminist Second Wave, following a turn-of-the-century First Wave? Or have we in these last twenty-three years or so experienced not one but two 'waves' of feminism, a second, 'rebellious', wave in the 1970s and a third, 'self-determining', wave in the 1980s and 1990s?

The discontinuities between 1970 and now are all too evident. The world which Australian feminism addresses has changed radically, in some ways out of all recognition. There is no socialist bloc; Western Europe looks very different indeed; the politics of the Middle East and much of Africa have changed beyond recognition. The war in Vietnam, so dominant in feminist consciousness in 1970, is long over, so long over that there have been several cycles of memory and narration. The nations of Asia are barely recognisable; a number of them are much wealthier, certainly more industrialised. Closer to home, Australia has moved from a severe labour shortage to one million unemployed, and dramatically higher levels of schooling and education. Questions of post-coloniality, Aboriginality, and multiculturalism are framed and debated in an entirely different way. And as is so often noted, changes in communication technology have altered our relation to the rest of the world, culturally, politically, economically. In 1970 we had no computers, no colour television, no video, no answering machines; we also had no land rights legislation, no equal-pay provisions, few heritage or environmental legislative protections. It was a different time.

If the world in which we live has changed so fast, so also has the possible meaning of 'Australian feminism'. Our sense of what we mean by 'Australian' has changed very substantially from the largely Anglo-Celtic ideal that predominated in 1970. Continued large-scale immigration, a widely-supported government policy of multiculturalism, and increased awareness of Aboriginal and Torres Strait Islander demands for land rights and sovereignty together challenge and undermine these earlier understandings of Australianness. 'Australian' now has a notion of cultural plurality built into it, though a substantial minority resist this idea, and others, speaking from an indigenous Aboriginal perspective, question the legitimacy of the idea of an 'Australian' at all. And our sense of 'feminism' has also changed significantly, seen most easily by discontinuities in terminology, as the 'Women's Liberation Movement' of the early 1970s gave way by 1975 to the 'women's movement', or simply 'feminism'.

Yet perhaps there are continuities too. If there is one thing the last twenty-plus years have taught those who now identify as Australian feminists, it is the value of collective memory and historical consciousness. The young women who established the women's liberation groups of the early 1970s lacked any knowledge of their own history, their antecedents. As a result, they erroneously thought they were doing something entirely new, speaking out in a way no-one ever had before against a thoroughly unequal and unjust, male-controlled world. They had to learn, all over again, that there had long been a women's movement, with a range of organisations across the political spectrum. 'First Wave feminism', the women's movement of the late nineteenth and early twentieth centuries, had to be discovered (or invented). So too had the women's organisations of the decades immediately before 1970, and their major campaigns for women's rights, especially for equal pay, which had still, in 1970, to be achieved. For the women's liberationists, the political demands of Aboriginal and Torres Straits Islander women had particularly to be learned about and understood—the growing movement for land rights, employment, citizenship, and access to and control over education, health, and housing.[1]

A Very Short History of Australian Feminism

One reason for the historical amnesia of the activists of Women's Liberation was that they had not been involved in the already existing women's movement, which had become rather respectable and staid. Younger women, if politically active, were more likely to be involved in the movement against the Vietnam War and attracted by the associated ideals of the 'counter culture', stressing participation and collective consciousness, and a critique of competitive, rationalist, technology-driven Western civilisation. Isolated by a generation gap from organised feminism, and finding themselves to be second-class citizens within the New

Left, the women in the New Left proceeded to invent a new form of feminism for themselves.[2]

Their inspiration came from the US. Information about a new and growing movement called 'Women's Liberation' came to Australia at the end of the 1960s, at first through overseas journals, then from Americans migrating to Australia, and Australians returning from visits to the US. Women's liberation groups emerged in each capital city, earliest in Sydney and Adelaide, later in Melbourne, Brisbane and other cities, formed by and large by young women who had been active in the anti-war movement. Each group went through a 'consciousness-raising' period, where discussions were held on women's difficulties and problems, the point being to draw out the ways in which problems experienced individually were in fact common problems, socially produced. All over the country women's houses appeared, newsletters and magazines were started, and demonstrations were held around immediate political issues, especially women's right to abortion.[3]

Feminist ideas spread through word of mouth, the media, consciousness-raising, and the literature produced by the movement itself. The new women's movement had an impact on parliamentary politics with the establishment of the Women's Electoral Lobby (WEL) in February 1972, with direct emphasis on attempting to achieve change through pressure on the existing political parties. Its participation in the federal election campaign of that year placed feminist demands on the wider political agenda.[4] Despite hostility from sections of the media, from politically organised men, and from conservative women's groups, feminist ideas have continued to gain ground fairly steadily from that time. Although Women's Liberation had initially arisen from the New Left, it very quickly drew support from way beyond it.

There were many sources for this widespread female rebellion. There had for at least a decade been growing contradictions: between the increasing numbers of women with higher education, and the restricted range of, and low pay for, the jobs those women could enter; between the need for female labour in the expanding tertiary sector of the economy, and the social stigma against married women working; between ideals of sexual permissiveness and the 'sexual revolution', and a sharply defined 'double standard' of sexual morality; and between the demographic trend to shorter periods of childbearing and rearing within a woman's life cycle, and the continuing social assumption that a woman's role was indeed 'in the home'. All this laid the basis for an enormous groundswell of female discontent.

As a consequence of the conjunction of an active women's movement and a new and reforming Labor government, there was a period of rapid change in relation to the feminist agenda in the years 1913 to 1975. Equal pay was granted by the Arbitration Commission's decision of

December 1972. The new government's policy of providing funds for community initiative in setting up new community services, including those sought by feminists—refuges for battered women, health and rape crisis centres, and so on—provided a sudden opportunity to gain government funds for feminist projects.[5] Expenditure on childcare rapidly increased; with the establishment of Medibank, and legal changes in some states, abortion became both legally accessible and cheap. So fast was the pace of change that a new set of bureaucratic structures had to be established: a Women's Affairs section (later to become the Office for the Status of Women) was established in the Department of Prime Minister and Cabinet, and advisory units within other departments.

The women's movement continued to grow in strength through the second half of the 1970s and through the 1980s, though the fall of the Labor government in November 1975 slowed the frenetic pace of change and reform at federal level that had characterised the previous three years. The pattern emerged that the women's movement made most headway under Labor governments, either state or federal, and, while experiencing some setbacks when Liberal governments came in, was able to maintain and at times extend gains even under less sympathetic governments. Government support for childcare provision, and for equal employment opportunity, generally grew during the 1980s; support for childcare became a major election issue in the 1993 election campaign.

A major change during the 1980s was the growing importance of women in the politics of the peace movement, the environment, and parliament. The peace movement peaked in the 1980s,as concern spread over the very real possibility of nuclear war, and huge demonstrations reaching up to 80,000 people or more were held in most major cities and towns. Women were very active in this movement, and not only in the peace marches: they provided the spearhead of many of the more militant actions, such as the peace camps outside American bases. During this same period, women were prominent in the growing environmental movement, often becoming spokespeople for campaigns such as those against logging and woodchipping in south-eastern Australia. On the basis of these and similar political experiences, women during the 1980s became slightly better-represented in politics, even as ministers and premiers.

Both the peace and environmental movements, however, faltered in the early 1990s. With the end of the Cold War as the 1980s came to a close, the fear of nuclear holocaust, and with it the peace movement, rapidly declined. The very high rates of unemployment have dampened support for environmentalism, as policies of 'development' to create jobs gain greater support. Challenging the peace activists and the environmentalists have been conservative women and women's organisations; they have opposed many feminist victories, particularly the right of access to abortion, and defended the traditional nuclear family against feminist critiques.[6] Partly on the basis of political experience in these women's organisations defending traditional values, some strong individual females have emerged as conservative political figures. Defence of the rights and interests of women can be heard these days just as easily within a conservative as a radical or liberal rhetoric.

Producing Feminist Theory in Australia

These, then, are some of the general configurations of the recent history of 'Australian feminism'. For the rest of this chapter, I want to concentrate on the history of Australian feminist *theoretical* debate: in terms of its processes of production, institutional locations, and substance; and in terms of the ways in which the concerns we can trace through this near quarter-of-a-century of feminist theorising in Australia indicate the influence of international intellectual movements and shifts on the one hand, and of local politics on the other.

Australian feminist argument and debate occurred in the early 1970s in a range of small political groups, Women's Liberation, WEL, and the older women's organisations. The Women's Liberation groups of the early 1970s read avidly, especially American pamphlets and newspapers and books such as Kate Millett's *Sexual Politics*, but also expatriate Germaine Greer's *The Female Eunuch* (1970). Soon, the Australian groups were producing their own pamphlets, printed conference papers, magazines like *MeJane*, *Mabel*, and *Girls' Own*, and journals such as *Refractory Girl* and *Scarlet Woman*. None of these theoretical writings were produced within the academy, though most of the early contributors and editorial collective members of *Refractory Girl* were graduates, and some were graduate students.

Very gradually, imperceptibly even, the intersection between feminist theorising and the academy grew stronger. Feminists entered the academy and scrutinised it, one discipline after another. At the same time, with access to higher education sought by ever-increasing numbers of people, and by proportionately large numbers of women, 'the academy' became a larger part of Australian women's educational and occupational experience. In response to these various trends, the demand for university courses on feminist theory grew. Through the 1970s and 1980s interdisciplinary women's studies programmes, and subjects and classes focusing on women and feminist theory within the established disciplines, emerged all over the country.[7] Journals were accordingly established by academic feminists within an academic framework of style and production, such as *Hecate* (since 1975), and *Australian Feminist Studies* (since 1985), while specialist feminist disciplinary journals also emerged, such as *Lilith* in history, or the rather fugitive *Olive Pink Society Bulletin* in anthropology.

Not only did feminist theoretical debate in Australia emanate increasingly from the academy; it also began to relate differently to international debate. From 1970 to 1985, the pattern was very much one of Australian feminists reading overseas debates, especially American, French, and British, and then discussing this 'overseas theory' in the light of immediate Australian political concerns and particular Australian intellectual traditions, all the while considering and arguing over problems of feminist theory. The journals and books which carried this Australian debate were rarely distributed or known elsewhere; one Australian feminist whose work *is* known internationally, Meaghan Morris, refers generally to 'all the internationally unread and unavailable Australian texts that I would wish to be able to take as "read" '.[8] The Oxford University Press sequence of Australian feminist collections, of which this present volume forms a part, is likely to provide no exception. In other words, there has been, till recently, a one-way flow of ideas: Australian feminists have known all about feminist debate in Euro-America, but feminists there have known virtually nothing about us. And the intersections with non-European feminist debate have been minimal.

There were and continue to be many reasons for this one-way intellectual traffic. On the import side, Australian intellectuals and political thinkers have long looked to Britain, America, France, and Germany for ideas. On our inability to export Australian debate, there is the obvious problem that Australian concerns matter little to feminists elsewhere. While Aboriginal and Torres Strait Islander peoples appear as scarcely known and therefore (especially, it seems, to the French) rather exotic, 'white' Australians tend to appear to Northern Hemisphereans as pale and uninteresting reflections of themselves. As Morris, again, says, 'Americans and Europeans often also assume that we are abstracted, like a footnote from *their* history'.[9] There is another reason too: the economics of publishing, with its relatively restricted domains of circulation. While British and American books and journals are frequently distributed throughout the Anglophone world, publications emanating from Australia, New Zealand, Canada, and South Africa are rarely distributed outside their country of origin. Feminists writing in these countries know little about each other, and know too that their own work remains unknown anywhere else.

Since the mid-1980s, though, cracks have begun to appear in this wall, constituted by indifference and economics, surrounding Australian feminist theorising and debate. The work and writing of Australian feminist theorists has begun to percolate through to European and North American audiences, especially work by the aforementioned Meaghan Morris, together with people like Carole Pateman, Elizabeth Grosz, Sneja Gunew, Pauline Johnson, Moira Gatens, Sophie Watson and Rosemary Pringle, Marilyn Lake, and others.[10] Australian feminism, then, has become less isolated than it was, and a little more confident. There appears to be a growing appreciation overseas of the distinctiveness of Australian feminist discourse, in its openness to feminist ideas from a variety of sources, English, French, German, American. Yet the path to participating in an international feminist debate is not smooth; Meaghan Morris has complained, for example, that her use of distinctive Australian expressions and terms is edited out in overseas journals. It remains to be seen whether Australian feminism will be able to enter into international debate, in the way that British and American feminisms do, on its own terms and in its own modes. Or perhaps it will always be an Other to Anglo-American or Euro-American 'normal' feminist discourse and language.

Feminism and Marxism

The early Australian Women's Liberation pamphlets incorporated a Marxist interpretation of American capitalism and imperialism, made prominent by the left wing of the anti-war movement. This Marxist influence on early Women's Liberation led to much discussion of the value of housework for capitalism, and of women's paid work as 'cheap labour'. Women were oppressed because the family, which kept them in a dependent and subordinate position, was essential for the capitalist system, and was thus extremely difficult to overthrow. Only by changing the entire social and economic system could women's demands for equality and social justice be met.

Yet early Women's Liberation theory, though drawing on Marxist concepts and concerns, was not confined to them. A Marxist interest in the value of women's labour was combined with an argument that women as a group were oppressed by sexist ideology, based on biological determinism. Further, women's oppression came to be seen not merely as an additional kind of oppression, analogous to that of the peoples of the Third World, but as the most basic kind of oppression, on which all other oppressions were modelled and built. There was a tension within this Women's Liberation theory between an awareness—derived from the Marxist and New Left influence in the movement—of the class differences between women, and a feminist assertion of their unity in oppression. This tension provided a focus for theoretical debate over the next decade, as socialist feminism went ever more deeply into problems of the relationship between women's oppression, or patriarchy, and capitalism. Influenced by the ideas of Louis Althusser, a French structuralist Marxist, some socialist feminists attempted to see how women's oppression was functional to capitalism, exploring theories of women's labour, domestic labour, and the role of the state.

These problems, it turned out, were not soluble within the terms in which they had been posed. If either 'class' or 'gender' were conceived as a fundamental ordering principle in society, then each term did seriously undermine the explanatory power of the other, however much particular theorists might have wished otherwise. In any case, the concept of 'class' began to be used less and less certainly in both political and theoretical debate. By the early to mid-1980s, the socialist feminist tradition had become very much a minority strand within the women's movement, and the attempt to put together the ideas of feminism and Marxism, as advocated by English Marxist feminist Juliet Mitchell in 1970, seemed to have failed. In 1976 an American, Heidi Hartmann, in a much discussed article 'The Unhappy Marriage of Marxism and Feminism', declared the union a failure; over the next ten years, most former socialist feminists came to agree, many concluding that Marxism was a gender-blind and male-centred theory.[11] Already weak, the socialist and Marxist feminist tradition more or less died at the end of the 1980s, when socialism itself collapsed throughout Eastern Europe.

Feminism and Post-structuralism

Radical feminist theory had a different, and more enduring, trajectory. In the early 1970s it quickly shook off the Women's Liberation concern with Marxism, class, and capitalism, and concentrated on the notion (shared with socialist feminists) of 'patriarchy', the name given to the universal social and ideological system through which men oppressed women. Radical feminist attention focused on issues such as women's physical exploitation and vulnerability; on domestic violence and rape; and on questions of sexuality, female and male, lesbian and heterosexual. One strand of radical feminism saw lesbian separatism as the only acceptable course, given the strength of its critique of men, masculinity, and male sexuality. What constituted it as radical, rather than liberal or socialist feminism, was its belief in the priority and immutability of the gender divide, the difference between male and female, men and women. Other forms of division, such as class or race, nation or ethnicity, might be acknowledged to varying degrees, but only as secondary forms of social differentiation. One of the strongest exponents of this position in the 1980s was Judith Allen, whose historical work, and polemical essays, relied on a very strong male/female antinomy, a tale of the oppression of women by men.[12]

Radical feminism in Australia was revitalised and altered in the second half of the 1980s by its contact with French post-structuralist feminist theory. Such French-influenced feminism followed in some ways from the ideas of radical feminism developed in the 1970s, especially in the way the distinction between men and women was so firmly drawn, but it had a stronger philosophical critique of existing theory behind it. Elizabeth Grosz emerged as a leading Australian interpreter of a form of feminism based on the theories of power and subjectivity associated with names such as Lacan, Foucault, and Derrida, and of the work of French feminists such as Luce Irigaray and Julia Kristeva. Her papers and books did a great deal to present such theories to an Australian, and then an international, audience.[13] This body of work emerged from philosophy and cultural studies, and developed a notion of 'woman-centred theory', based on a critique of male-centred, or 'phallocentric' theory. It criticised previous feminist theory for being caught within the paradigms of the (sexist, patriarchal, or phallocentric) theory it opposed; for remaining, that is, too close to established male theoretical ground.

Post-structuralist feminism focused attention away from the 'productionist' concerns of Marxist-influenced feminism, and back towards the body and bodily difference. In an influential essay titled 'A Critique of the Sex/Gender Distinction', published in 1983, Moira Gatens attacked the long-standing feminist distinction between 'sex', as denoting the realm of biologically-given sexual difference, and 'gender', as indicating socially constructed male–female difference. The distinction had been formulated to indicate that biological sexual difference did not necessarily entail the different social roles for men and women that currently existed; in other words, that women's social inferiority was not a natural or necessary consequence of biological imperatives, such as childbearing, or lesser muscular strength. Gatens pointed out, however, that in developing this form of defence against sexist biological essentialism, feminists had ended up with a conception of the body as a non-cultural ahistorical phenomenon. 'There is', she wrote, 'no neutral body, there are at least two kinds of bodies; the male body and the female body . . . the subject is always a *sexed* subject . . . Gender is not the issue, sexual difference is.'[14] In a later article, Gatens argues that, far from taking the body as a biological given, we must now ask why and how it happens that we understand it in this way.[15] Elizabeth Grosz subsequently took the argument further, using Foucault to argue that, in contrast to many earlier feminist arguments, power functions not through 'ideology' but directly on bodies by means of disciplinary practices. The body is both the primary object of power, and a site of resistance to regular, systematic modes of social organisation.[16]

Feminist philosophers' interest in developing a philosophy of the body stemmed largely from their interest in French post-structuralist theory and its meaning for feminism. The tremendous interest their theory aroused, especially amongst younger university women, may have a lot to do with the continuing salience of bodily sexual difference in the face of rapidly changing social relationships. Women have made certain social gains, but the importance of sexual bodily difference remains undiminished. Naomi Wolf's *The Beauty Myth*, an American book which itself owed nothing to post-structuralism, was a best-seller in 1992, both because of the importance of the issues it raised for so many women, and because her book was so powerfully written, so evocative of the psychology of so many women today. In the late twentieth century, she argues, we find underneath women's gains a 'dark vein of self-hatred, physical obsessions, terror of ageing, and dread of lost control'. The ideology (as Wolf puts it) of beauty is the last one remaining of the old feminine ideologies that still has the power to control women; as the rest is challenged, the beauty myth is left intact. The more women win on the legal and economic front, the 'more strictly and heavily and cruelly images of female beauty have come to weigh upon us'.

Feminism, Humanism and Anti-humanism

The question of how freedom for women might best be pursued continues to perplex feminist theory. From its beginnings feminism relied on the Enlightenment ideal of the citizen, supposedly universal, free, and equal; the point was to refine this ideal to include women as well as men. As Simone de Beauvoir argued in *The Second Sex* in 1949, woman must be considered first as a human being, rather than continuing to live in a world where men compel her to assume the status of the Other. In modern Australia, liberal feminism has used this humanist ideal to provide the arguments against unequal treatment and access which underpin anti-discrimination legislation and the provision of women's services. Now, however, it is less clear whether feminism is indeed a form of liberal-humanist theory, or whether it has instead become its most powerful modern critic. A major strand of feminist theory now sees universalist ideals as false, positing a common humanity while retaining an ideal of the individual as male.[17] It has lost its earlier belief in the possibility of universality and gender-neutrality. As Pauline Johnson points out, modern feminism has played a crucial role in the development of philosophical critique of the claims to universality made on behalf of a Western conception of human reason.[18]

In recent years, the debate over universalism versus difference has been sharpened by the rise to prominence of postmodernism. Against what it sees as the Enlightenment's illusory universalism, postmodernism stresses difference, of ethnicity, culture, identity. Feminists have found the claim to impartial universal reason to be a sham, a universalising of distinctively male discursive power. Should we therefore abandon the Enlightenment commitment to the cause of reason and truth, or, more cautious now, nevertheless remain committed to Enlightenment ideals of equality and universality? That is, does the failure of Enlightenment thought so far to live up to its own project necessarily mean that the whole project was and is wrongheaded?

Pauline Johnson, an Australian feminist philosopher writing in the British journal *Radical Philosophy*, provides a spirited defence of Enlightenment ideals, asserting their continuing relevance for a feminism which today seems so inclined to reject them. Johnson is influenced by German and Central European philosophical traditions, especially the work of Habermas. She argues that those feminists (and postmodernists) who reject Enlightenment ideals altogether rest their case on a caricature of the historical Enlightenment, based more on seventeenth-century rationalism than eighteenth-century anti-dogmatism. In addition, she argues, we can rescue Enlightenment ideals if we see them not as having been tried and found wanting, but as constituting an unfinished cultural project; 'feminism's current critique of Enlightenment formulations appears as another vital episode in the unfolding of the Enlightenment project itself.[19]

Johnson's attempt to rescue the Enlightenment for feminism is an important one. Yet if those feminists who use a postmodernist critique of the Enlightenment rely on too *narrow* a definition of the Enlightenment, Johnson seems to err in the opposite direction, relying on such a broad conception that the Enlightenment is identified with history itself. Countervailing critiques, particularly those stemming from long-standing Romantic traditions or more recent anti-colonialist perspectives, are somehow construed as critiques from inside, rather than, as they might well be, from outside the Enlightenment tradition. Any project of rescuing the Enlightenment as history's telos, the project of modernity, runs the risk not only of marginalising all other discourses and intellectual traditions, but also of Eurocentrism. For all that, the debate over the relevance to feminism of Enlightenment ideals of equality and universal rights is not concluded.

Feminism and Liberalism

Where feminist philosophers have focused on questions of the body, reason, and truth, feminist political theorists have been concerned with the specifically *political* dimension of Enlightenment thinking, the question of liberalism. Carole Pateman has been the most powerful proponent of the argument that liberalism cannot be made compatible with feminism. A key figure in feminist political theory internationally, Pateman left Australia for the US in the late 1980s. Her major works, notably *The Sexual Contract* (1988), do not refer in detail to Australian feminist debates, and very little of her work has appeared in Australian feminist journals or has been published in Australia. Yet her work does bear the influence of Australian feminist experiences, with its insistent concern with the question of how feminists might argue for the possibility of change through the agency of government. And her ideas have certainly been influential within Australian feminist discussion of liberal theory and the state.

Pateman argues that liberalism, being grounded in a fraternal, exclusively male, social contract, cannot provide a basis for women to take an equal place in a patriarchal civil order. In refusing bodily and other difference, liberalism cannot generate the conditions for women's freedom. As a result, while feminism has often been seen as a continuation of liberalism, an extension of liberal principles and rights to women as well as men, it inevitably challenges liberalism itself. In Pateman's argument, the social contract of liberal theory was made not by individuals, as usually supposed, but by brothers, a fraternity, by men who share a bond *as men*. In short the contract guarantees the rule of men over women; through it the brothers appropriate women's ability to give birth. Women, Pateman maintains, are still excluded from the central category of 'the individual', the bedrock of contractarian doctrine. Her solutions are for women and men to address sexual difference politically, rather than repress it in the name of a hypothetical non-sexed individual. The achievement of legal equality and freedom becomes then not the end of feminism but rather the precondition for the development of women's autonomy, where women become free as women, rather than as like men.

Pateman's argument has some difficulties for Australian feminist debate. The form of liberalism she is addressing is closer to that of the American individualist nation than to the corporate 'new liberalism' which underlies both the Australian welfare state and modern Australian liberal feminism.[20] In addition, her argument rests on a unitary conception of women, an 'autonomous femininity', a set of definable female interests and demands that will be different from men's. A key question confronting feminists seeking political change—will the reforms they seek benefit women generally, or some at the expense of others?—cannot be addressed in this binary framework. While questions of class and race are from time to time noted in Pateman's work, they are not seen as having relevance in the sphere of sexual difference and sexual relations.

Feminism and Race

Within Australian feminism, critique of both radical and socialist feminism came during the 1980s and 1990s (and in some cases earlier) from groups of Aboriginal and immigrant women. They saw many of its demands, its anti-male flavour, and its critique of the family as all indicating the particular concerns of white, Anglo-Celtic, Australian-born women. For migrant women, as they so often said, the family was important in the traumatic processes of displacement and migration; it was something to be protected and valued, however critically, rather than attacked. At first, Anglo-Australian feminists responded to immigrant women's critiques by acknowledging them as especially oppressed, at work, in marriage, in the family. This was little better. As Sneja Gunew put it in a 1991 article, 'ethnic and migrant women are sick of being characterised by feminist analysts as kitchen-slaves, mute factory-fodder, baby-machines whose lives are supposedly totally dominated by their patriarchal husbands'.[21]

If ethnic and migrant women found Australian feminism to be unthinkingly attempting to assimilate all women to the specific experiences of Australian-born Anglo-Celtic women, Aboriginal and Torres Strait Islander women found it even less relevant to their concerns. For Aboriginal women, the anti-male style of the women's movement was generally out of place: they felt greater solidarity with their own men than with European-Australian women proclaiming universal sisterhood[22]. Aboriginal families were so historically under attack from a white racist society, even to the point of systematically removing Aboriginal children from their parents, they were something Aboriginal women generally wanted to defend and protect, not attack. Most Aboriginal and Torres Strait Islander women were therefore wary of the white women's movement, but did increasingly take opportunities to address it, especially at conferences. The Women and Labour conference in Brisbane in 1984 was torn apart by critiques from Aboriginal women asserting that white middle-class feminism promised nothing to them; but later conferences, such as the 1987 Socialist Feminist Conference and the Women/Theory/Australia Conference in 1989, saw more amicable exchanges, as white feminists, very gradually, began to take the point.[23]

Some European-Australian feminists tried to incorporate Aboriginal women's issues into their feminist theory by developing a concept of 'double oppression', where women's and black oppressions were added together (if class were added, this became 'triple oppression'). The idea was to keep the focus centrally on gender, with race as an additional source of social difference and conflict. It was hard to accept that Aboriginal and Torres Strait Islander issues challenged some of the theoretical foundations of feminism, particularly white Australian women's construction of themselves as members of an oppressed group. Most had great difficulty in accepting that white women had historically been party to the processes of racism and colonialism, wanting to see women always as the victims of any historical situation. Part of the problem is indicated in the subtitle of *Damned Whores and God's Police*, Anne Summers' pathbreaking feminist history text, first published in 1975: 'The Colonisation of Women in Australia'. The analogy of colonial invasion, exploitation, and dispossession is used, metaphorically, theoretically, and rhetorically, to describe the experience of white women. In so doing, it blurs and undermines the possibility of recognising that white women were themselves colonisers, part of the invading society which dispossessed and exploited Aboriginal and Torres Strait Islander women and men.

Feminism and History

It was a sign of the depth of the problem that, throughout the 1980s, feminist histories continued to be written which barely acknowledged the questions of racism and destruction of Aboriginal and Torres Strait Islander society. Feminist historians have been remarkably successful in challenging and changing the historical profession, yet their key dilemma remains the gap between their endeavours and the writing of the history of colonial conflict between the indigenous and incoming peoples. There is still relatively little real interchange between these very different discourses—'feminist' and 'post-colonial'.[24] Women's and feminist history still too often continues in its daily practice to write a history of gender conflict located wholly *within* non-Aboriginal Australian society rather than a gendered history *of* colonial contact and conflict.

These problems are now being confronted in the burgeoning discussion of gender and national identity. Feminist historians have entered the long-standing debate on national identity, hitherto largely male territory. The 1890s remain a crucial site for feminist historians and literary critics, just as they continue to be for the male scholars they critique. Marilyn Lake, in an influential article in 1986, defined the 1890s search for an Australian identity as a masculinist quest, based on a militant assertion of anti-feminist principles, and a yearning by city-based journalists and writers for what they thought was the free, unencumbered, yet convivial lifestyle of the itinerant outback white single male.[25] This idea has generated great interest, though there has also been considerable debate as to whether the links between nationalism and anti-feminism were as close as Lake suggests.[26]

In some of this debate, there is a tendency to forget women's own search for national identity, their complicity in desires for an all-white, racist, true Australia. Nationalist history, for example, is sometimes presented in feminist discourse as entirely male.[27] Similarly, militarism is examined as a product of masculinity, with the high levels of female support for militarism and war left unexplained. Nevertheless, the frequent complicity of women and feminism in white Australian racism is at last, slowly, beginning to be explored. There is growing attention to the significant feminist political support for (and, let us not forget, in some important cases critique of) the ideals of White Australia, in the work of people like Kay Saunders, Susan Sheridan, and Marilyn Lake.[28]

Aboriginal and Torres Strait Islander demands present to non-Aboriginal Australian feminists a challenge to our view of the world far more profound than previously understood. There have, of course, always been different political positions on Aboriginal-feminist issues. Non-Aboriginal feminists have disagreed sharply over how to respond to gender-based conflict within Aboriginal communities, but perhaps the most common approach amongst non-Aboriginal feminists has been one of attempting to understand the specificity of Aboriginal women's demands *within* an overall conception of redressing the wrongs of women generally. The Supreme Court's 1992 Mabo decision on land rights was a landmark, and there has been the growing though uneven acceptance by non-Aboriginal Australians of their responsibilities for the past (dispossession itself, brutality, murder, exploitation, institutionalisation, family break-up). Feminists are slowly starting to realise that Aboriginal and Torres Strait Islander demands cannot be contained within the existing feminist framework, and that the entire political framework within which feminists operate is under question, and liable to change. The declaration of the UN Year of Indigenous Peoples proved a stimulus to some deeper reflection; significantly the International Women's Day Marches in March 1993 were in some cities led by groups of Aboriginal women.

Conclusion

A brief survey like this can only be partial, and I am all too conscious of the important areas of debate I have not covered. That I must exclude so much is a tribute to the productivity and fertility of Australian feminist debate. One line worth exploring would be the continuing feminist concern with psychoanalytic theory, especially evident in feminist film theory and film-making; another, the huge area of debate surrounding women's writing, feminist literary criticism, and semiology; yet a third, the vast debate within and beyond political science around feminist engagement with the state. But it is time to conclude, and to return to my initial question. Can we, indeed, conceive of an Australian feminism, stretching from the present back at least to 1970? While the decline of Marxism and the rise of postmodernism within feminist debate represent major shifts in direction, and in ways of posing feminist questions, we can nevertheless detect important continuities. There has been a persistent attempt to recognise, theoretically and practically, what (if anything) it is that women have in common, and what (if anything) it is that divides them. Australian feminists are having to work through the paradox that women are constantly at once construed as a group, as difference, as species being; and at the same time as differentiated, in conflict, disjoined.

TWO

What Has Nationalism Offered Australian Women?

Jill Roe

A recent history of changing attitudes to nationalism in Australia is entitled *A Nation at Last*? The title echoes Henry Lawson's welcome to Federation, 'I hear our country's a Nation at last!' It also highlights the fact that, although Australia today is a highly nationalistic society, the emergence and consolidation of a nationalist sentiment has been a slow process. It has also been uneven, and is still incomplete. Much the same might be said of what the leading Australian feminist of the interwar years, Bessie Rischbieth, optimistically envisaged as 'the march of Australian women'. This chapter examines some key encounters between women and nationalism in Australia over two generations. It is concerned mainly with links between the ending of colonialism and the changing status of women in Australia, from the surge in nationalist sentiment a century or so ago to about the 1940s.[1]

The relationship between women and nationalism has seldom been straightforward. With the sudden collapse of international socialism and an apparent weakening of other forms of oppositional politics since the 1980s, it is now attended by a sense of anxiety and urgency. This seems only appropriate. Nationalism may be the great survivor of the nineteenth-century 'isms'; but its contemporary image is often far from attractive, due in part to the recurring barbarisms committed in its name in modern Europe, and also to certain well-known exclusions of race and rigidities with respect to gender in nation-state development elsewhere. Yet there is also a widespread sense that the time has come to re-examine nationalist premises, and there is a need for new perspectives.

In these circumstances it is significant that, in Australia at least, nationalism has long been regarded as a normal if not wholesome sentiment, and the study of gender relations has been primarily concerned with the national ethos. Miriam Dixson's resoundingly nationalistic title *The Real Matilda* (1976), a study of 'woman and identity in Australia, 1788 to 1975', is a reminder that in this country the relationship between women and nationalism has been under continuous and critical scrutiny since the first books on women's history appeared in the 1970s. What follows takes up issues specific to an earlier period of feminism which have been overlooked in theoretical debates so far. These issues have arisen as the rather worn literary evidence which has dominated nationalist discourse is reviewed and re-evaluated in the light of recent research, especially biographical research, much of it under the auspices of the *Australian Dictionary of Biography*.

As may be anticipated, this approach casts the story of women and nationalism in a somewhat different light. In colonies of recent settlement such as Australia, the nationalist dream of self-determination has offered women a space—sometimes. At other times the alternative of internationalism has seemed more promising. In the twentieth century, it will be suggested, Australian women have oscillated between nationalist and internationalist strategies in an ongoing struggle for enhanced status.

An important aspect of the argument overall is that from time to time, Australian nationalism has created space for women abroad as well as at home. Not much, perhaps, but some. Australian women's expatriatism probably increased during the period under consideration. Nevertheless, women began attending international forums in the 1890s, and there was a new development in the 1920s. Whereas previously participation abroad had been mainly via informal networks and the voluntaristic alliances of the age of empire, from the 1920s leading Australian women increasingly fixed their sights on official—that is, national—accreditation, in London and Geneva.

There has been a strong formal preference for internationalism over nationalism in modern feminism. This chapter acknowledges the strengths of that preference. But it also observes that the juxtaposition of nationalism and internationalism has become increasingly unreal. Not only have both national and international idealisms taken a terrible battering in modern times, but as nation-states have increased in strength, they have more and more become the effective basis of internationalism. Plainly too, the old distinction between domestic and foreign policy becomes ever more blurred. These trends suggest that, especially for remote places like Australia, over time nationalism may have become more useful to women than hitherto appreciated. On the other hand, like other nationalisms, Australian nationalism has often been a snare and a delusion, for as German historian George Mosse puts it, 'The dynamic of modern nationalism was built upon the ideal of manliness.'[2]

It sometimes seems as if there is more space for women at the beginning of social movements. This is a tricky inversion of perspective; it may sound implausible, given the apparently 'masculinist' character of the 1890s in Australia. But it is well attested in other instances, for example in the history of spiritualism and socialism; and it highlights the fact that in the late nineteenth century nationalism was a new and dynamic social movement. So was feminism. Both were great mobilisers. Not only that, both movements were forward-looking. In Australia, and maybe in most places in the late nineteenth century, they overlapped and interacted in variously productive ways.

A key component of nineteenth-century Australian nationalism was the belief in the emergence of a superior Australian type, female as well as male. The Australian girl was admired for her independence, even in that compendium of all chauvinisms, the *Bulletin*. From the late 1880s to her untimely death in 1897, 'Sappho Smith' was probably the *Bulletin's* most widely read columnist. Scourge of the Sydney social round, she was sketched at the head of her column as a disapproving dowager, complete with lorgnette. In real life, 'Sappho Smith' was a bright young thing from Paddington called Alexina (Ina) Wildman. As a schoolgirl she presented herself and her poems at the *Bulletin* office and joined the staff soon after. When she died aged twenty-nine, editor J. F. Archibald mourned the loss of 'the incomparable Ina Wildman'. Ina Wildman had not excluded the foibles of feminism from her column, and Archibald was no friend of feminists, or aspiring women poets for that matter. But there was room on the *Bulletin* for a lively and like-minded girl. There were many such women in Australian journalism at the time, Mary Fullerton in Melbourne for example. Wildman was followed at the *Bulletin* by Louise Mack (author in 1898 of *Girls Together*), and her sister Amy edited the women's pages of the *Sydney Morning Herald* from 1907 to 1914.[3]

Thus by the late nineteenth century the Australian girl might speak for herself. When she did, it was discovered that she had a thoroughly modern, very Australian mentality. Stella Courtland, heroine of South Australian Catherine Martin's popular novel *An Australian Girl* (1890) is an advanced thinker, of remarkable moral integrity. Judy, the wild girl of 'Misrule' in Ethel M. Turner's *Seven Little Australians* (1894) did not live long enough to develop such characteristics. But she too is vital, courageous and self-sacrificing. And when *My Brilliant Career* finally appeared in 1901—it had been completed in 1898—with its wonderfully rebellious heroine Sybylla Melvyn, the 21-year-old author Stella Maria Sarah Miles Franklin became famous overnight—the Olive Schreiner, the Marie Bashkirtseff, of Australia, they said. Some said *My Brilliant Career* was the first truly Australian novel.

In contrast, the journalistic image of the adult Australian woman was far from flattering. She was thin and mean, unable even to sin with zest.

Her teeth were bad, and in the novel *Such is Life* (1903)—'bias offensively Australian'—Joseph Furphy predicted she would have a moustache. Fortunately women had to be taken more seriously when they obtained the vote, first in South Australia in 1894, then in Western Australia (1899), and nationally with the achievement of federation, in 1902. Not only did the electorate double, but for a brief moment—women were enfranchised in Finland in 1906—on this as on some other issues Australia (and New Zealand) were 'leading the world'.[4]

Votes for women reflected well upon the young nation. Perhaps inevitably, since the legislation had to be passed by all-male assemblies, men took the credit. For women the very fact of enfranchisement was a source of pride, and their subsequent behaviour at the polls was proof that it was justified. Available electoral evidence backs up Miles Franklin's positive picture of the first women voters in *Some Everyday Folk and Dawn* (1909), a post-suffrage romance set in Penrith, New South Wales, in 1904. The new women voters are portrayed as capable and responsible, self-respecting too. The vote was a great boost to women's self-esteem.[5]

Some Everyday Folk and Dawn is dedicated 'To the English *men* who believe in votes for *women*', a reference to the militant suffragette campaign, by then well under way. Franklin's gesture points to another strengthening effect of the suffrage. Enfranchised Australian women found themselves in demand in suffrage and other reform campaigns all around the world. Thus in 1902 Vida Goldstein went to Washington to the founding conference of what became the International Woman Suffrage Alliance (IWSA), and served as its secretary. Likewise, much interest was shown at conferences of the World's Woman's Christian Temperance Union (World's WCTU) in the efficacy of the woman's vote in Australasia, especially in support of local option laws. Other suffragists pointed with pride to Australia's early achievement of non-contributory old-age and invalid pensions (1908–9).[6]

More will be said later about participation in international conferences. One point belongs here, however. Probably the greatest contribution made by the newly enfranchised Australian woman to the cause of progress beyond Australia was simply that she was so *respectable.* Even the most vigorous and outspoken Australian feminist could seem the model of neatness. Writing home from Chicago after a trip to London in 1911 where she met up with Vida Goldstein, then an organiser for the Pankhursts' Women's Social and Political Union, Miles Franklin reported what a contrast Vida was to the generally untidy suffragettes. To which charge, she adds, Christabel Pankhurst replied 'perhaps that was an example of how women appeared after they had secured the vote and no longer had to become disarranged struggling for it.'[7]

In 1903 Vida Goldstein was among the women who availed themselves of the right to stand for the new federal parliament, granted with the vote in 1902. Neither she nor any other woman was successful until 1943, when Enid (later Dame Enid) Lyons was returned; and it became notorious that although South Australian women had had the right to enter parliament since 1894, none actually did so until 1959. When Edith Dircksey Cowan became the first woman elected to an Australian parliament (Western Australia) in 1921, women had already been elected in Finland (1907), Denmark, the United Kingdom and the Netherlands (all 1918), Germany, Austria (both 1919) and Czechoslovakia (1920). When Miles Franklin visited Australia in 1923–4 after nearly twenty years in Chicago and London, it was obvious to her that Australian women were no longer 'leading the world'.[8]

The explanation may lie partly in the passing of the first generation of Australian feminists. Pioneer South Australian campaigner Mary Lee died in obscurity in 1909. Catherine Helen Spence, known affectionately in her lifetime as 'the grand old woman of Australia'—Australia's first female political candidate—died in 1910, and was soon forgotten. Then the Great War 1914–18 brought not only the political demise of Vida Goldstein and her kind of anti-war feminism, but a severe challenge to all forms of feminism.[9]

The fate of anti-war feminism in Australia during and after the Great War is well known. Anti-war activists were abused and marginalised, and the great feminist hope that women would be predisposed to peace faltered and faded away. For those women who supported the war effort however, new spaces seemed to open up. To some, the new opportunities for participation encouraged hopes of a realignment of feminism and nationalism after the war. If anyone could have brought it off, it was Dr Mary Booth, in Sydney.

Mary Booth was an early graduate of the University of Sydney. She obtained her medical training at the University of Edinburgh and in Dublin, and when she returned to Australia in 1901 took rooms near Macquarie Street; but like most early women doctors she experienced difficulty in obtaining access to hospitals, and before the war was probably best known for hygiene lectures in girls' schools and her work in establishing school medical services. She was also a founder of the Women's Club. War brought her real opportunities—not that she participated directly, and not for want of trying to. Her offer to serve in Egypt was rejected. The only women required were trained nurses. Undeterred, Booth turned her mind to voluntary work in Sydney. It soon became full-time. As early as November 1914 she organised the Babies' Kit Society for babies in Belgium and Britain. She became a prominent advocate of conscription and Prohibition during the war. After the war, in 1921, Prime Minister William Morris Hughes bestowed on Booth and her fellow volunteers the right to call themselves the Anzac Fellowship of Women, a unique accolade.[10]

Booth's first major initiative was the Soldiers' Club. In March 1915, shortly after the third convoy of troops sailed from Sydney, she noted that there was nowhere central for recruits from the country or men on leave from Liverpool Camp to 'meet friends, leave parcels, read, write, smoke, have a wash and partake of light refreshments'. Canvassing support for the proposed club she wrote, 'We want to do all we can to keep our men fit and happy until they leave us to take part in the terrible struggle that demands the best that the Empire has to give.' The District Commandant agreed that something should be done to keep the men off the streets and out of the pubs.[11]

The Soldiers' Club, opened on 3 June 1915 in the old Royal Hotel, George Street, was a great success. Though no alcohol was allowed, there were 1500 men on the books in the first week. Public support was forthcoming also. On the first Violet (button) Day on 13 August 1915, nearby Rowe Street was turned into an Eastern Bazaar, complete with letterwriters to send messages to the troops; and 1500 pounds were raised for the club. By 1916 it was claimed 1000 men a day passed through its doors, including many returned men.[12]

Booth and her helpers, mainly girl volunteers, conducted the Soldiers' Club from 1915 to 1920. With the club as her base, in August 1915 she established the Centre for Soldiers' Wives and Mothers, for women in difficulties due to their dependence on absent soldiers, for example because of non-receipt of allotments (the dependant's allocation from married soldiers' pay). The centre seems like a good idea, but remained small, perhaps because there were so many war charities in Sydney, and its administration soon passed to Dr Booth's sister, Miss Bay Booth.[13]

Booth's next initiative was more telling. On the first Anzac Day, 25 April 1916, she instituted a women's service of remembrance at Woolloomooloo, opposite No. 2 wharf where the troops embarked. Women distributed rosemary and laid wreaths on the gates, and there was an open-air religious service led by the archbishop of Sydney; it was followed by lunch and a concert in the Lower Town Hall at which Nellie (soon Dame Nellie) Melba sang. Later a memorial fountain was erected opposite the gates by the Soldiers' Wives and Mothers—it is now relocated on the footpath nearby—and inscribed 'To commemorate the place of farewell to the soldiers who passed through these gates opposite for the Great War 1914–1918.' One reference to subsequent services, held yearly until 1958, records that 'Women, old and young, stand before the gates and weep.'[14]

On Anzac Day 1921 Dr Booth and her helpers reformed as the Anzac Fellowship of Women. The first object of the fellowship was to promote the comradeship of women who had been engaged in war work during the Great War. Other objects were to foster the spirit of Anzac Day, have regard for the welfare of returned soldiers and the bereaved, and to welcome British immigrants. In fulfilment of these objects, during the interwar years the fellowship established an Empire Service Club, a (British) Ex-Service Women's Club, a hostel for immigrants at Miller's Point and, from 1931, an Anzac Festival committee. For many years the festival committee ran a cultural competition in schools to foster the spirit of Anzac and a concert on Anzac Eve where the prize poems and songs were performed.[15]

Dr Booth was awarded an OBE in 1918. Citing her war work and the needs of women and children, in 1920 she stood as an independent feminist candidate for the North Shore, the first election for which women could stand for the New South Wales parliament. (Women became eligible to stand in New South Wales in 1918.) She was unsuccessful. Again in 1922, now supported by the liberal/nationalist Women's Reform League of New South Wales, she tried and failed to enter national politics.[16]

This was probably the most substantial attempt to link women and nationalism in the 1920s. But it was a dead end. After Prime Minister Hughes, no political support was forthcoming for the fellowship; and there is some evidence of competition, from the New Settlers' League for example. Sooner or later all the Booth projects faltered. Younger women like Miles Franklin felt Dr Booth was living in the past. Having attended a Woolloomooloo wharf ceremony in the late 1920s, what Franklin recalled was 'a number of ageing and battered women decorated with rosemary . . . who wept anew at the thin platitudes gargled by the parson', yet whose spirits arose at the beauty of incoming warships. Later Miles would serve rather despondently as judge for one of Dr Booth's Anzac Festival competitions. It seems the version of nationalism which emerged from the Great War was a burden for women.[17]

After the horrors and folly of war—Miles Franklin came to call it 'our war', meaning the war which destroyed the idealism of her generation of feminists—they quite rightly feared another. A second generation had grown up in the shadow of the militant suffrage campaign in Britain and with the new, economic angle on oppression, as in Olive Schreiner's analysis of 'parasitism' in *Woman and Labour* (1911). The 1920s brought a new emphasis on internationalism.

Franklin's own position was at once strongly opposed to war and increasingly committed to cultural nationalism. Living in London after the war she was probably closest to what I call 'empire feminism'. When she arrived from Chicago late in 1915—like Dr Booth she preferred to participate somehow—two notable empire feminists, Harriet Newcomb and Margaret Hodge, were among those who took her under their wing. Newcomb and Hodge had been co-principals of Shirley College and friends of Rose Scott's in Sydney before the war. In London, Franklin was close to radical Liberalism and the liberal imperialism it espoused through her friend and mentor, Lady Byles. Very likely Lady Byles was one of those she had in mind when she dedicated the first of her 'Brent of Bin Bin' books, *Up The Country* (1928), to the 'Old Hands'. The accompanying Author's Note reads: 'Thus to the Old Hands at home and abroad—old enough to be cultured by contact either with nature or with humanity's stored knowledge—this yarn is an offering.'[18]

About 1914 Newcomb and Hodge toured the Dominions to strengthen the bonds of friendship within the empire by linking women's groups to the British Dominion Woman Citizen's Union. It was through the Dominion Woman Citizen's Union that Australian women were affiliated to the International Woman Suffrage Alliance, which they attended as part of an empire delegation. Rischbieth's account of these developments has the Dominion Union and another empire friendship league, the League of Women of the Empire, as precursors of the British Commonwealth League of Women, of which she was a founder in 1925, and which was for decades a base for women of the best circles at the heart of the empire. Not much is known of its other work. What it seems mostly to reflect, however, is the exclusive, conservative cast of Australian nationalism after the Great War already encountered by Dr Booth.[19]

With the Treaty of Versailles in 1919 and the League of Nations, established in Geneva in 1920, came genuine internationalism. This had a dual relevance for Australian women. First, Australia was a signatory to the treaty, and so far as the League was concerned, an independent nation-state. (Dominion status within the empire was not fully articulated until the Balfour Declaration of 1926). Second, whereas women in Britain and America were rewarded for their war work by the vote (or in the British case, some were), Australian women, long since enfranchised, gained no particular reward. Indeed, they suffered a deterioration in status. Inevitably, the needs of the returned soldiers were paramount; and numerous social and political obstacles remained to women's full participation in public life. But the new international organisations could be expected to address many of the issues relevant to the woman citizen's continuing subordination; the Covenant of the league explicitly stated that 'All positions under and in connection with the League . . . shall be open to men and women.'[20]

Australian women have been intrepid with respect to international conferences. Whenever the causes dearest to their hearts held conventions, congresses, assemblies, etc., great efforts were made for someone to go. One of the first was Catherine Helen Spence, who attended the International Conference on Charities and Correction at the Columbian Expo in Chicago in 1893 as representative of the South Australian State

Children's Council. Another was the president of the Australasian Woman's Christian Temperance Union, Elizabeth Nicholls, who was sent to the World's WCTU convention in Edinburgh in 1900 as rest and reward for her hard work.[21]

The war put a stop to all that. Afterwards there was the inconvenience of obtaining that newfangled device, the passport. The numbers of conference-goers increased nonetheless. Large delegations set off from Sydney in the early 1920s for the annual conventions of the Theosophical Society in India, for example. Likewise the Soviet experiment would entice enthusiasts like Katharine Susannah Prichard and Betty Roland to Russia. It is hardly surprising, therefore, that in 1922 women waited on Prime Minister Hughes to press for representation in the Australian delegation to the League of Nations in Geneva. Later that year Mrs Marguerite Dale became the first woman delegate (alternate) to the League of Nations.[22]

Here the difference between international conference participation before and after the Great War emerges. Before the Great War, attendance was generally on the basis of personal accreditation by voluntary organisations. (An exception was Dr Booth, who represented the Commonwealth government at a conference on infant mortality in London in 1913.) Under the changed circumstances of the postwar world, which made Australia in effect a dominion and to that extent altered the meaning of British citizenship, national accreditation would often be needed or desired. Henceforth it would often not suffice to be a representative Australian woman. With Marguerite Dale the Australian woman representative made her bow.

Accommodation to the new internationalism occurred at speed, too fast for some in fact. In 1920 Vida Goldstein and Elizabeth Nicholls attended the first postwar conference of the International Woman Suffrage Alliance in Geneva, held concurrently with the first Assembly of the League of Nations. They reported the need for national accreditation in future. As current president of the Women's Service Guild in Western Australia and a committed internationalist—she had been a theosophist since before the war—Bessie Rischbieth saw the point immediately. A year later what became the Australian Federation of Women Voters (AFWV) was formed, with Rischbieth president and Nicholls vice-president. (And so another round of triennial conferences began, for the first time in Australia.) Interestingly, the organisations from which the federation began came mainly from South and Western Australia, the two earliest suffrage states, where the principle of non-party women's organisations was probably strongest. Elsewhere the constituent organisations seem to have been rather flimsy, part of Rischbieth's personal network, as in the case of New South Wales stalwart Emily Bennett, an organiser for the previously mentioned Women's Reform League immediately after the war. It was indeed Rischbieth's Federation of Women Voters and the Women's Service Guild which in 1922 waited upon Hughes to send a woman to Geneva; and, as it happened, Marguerite Dale was a member of the federation in New South Wales. The federation also gained the accreditation to the International Woman's Suffrage Alliance, much to the annoyance of the old National Council of Women. In 1923 Rischbieth led an AFWV delegation of nine to the ninth triennial congress of the alliance in Rome, assembled at the invitation of the newly installed premier, Benito Mussolini, who opened the congress surrounded by Blackshirts (Fascist guards). 'It may be imagined,' wrote Rischbieth, 'with what mounting excitement the nine Australian delegates waited to catch a glimpse . . . of the first Dictator of modern times.' The next day, following a suffrage procession, the Australian delegation was the first alphabetically to shake Mussolini's hand. At the next alliance congress, in Paris in 1926, Rischbieth became a member of the board, a position she retained until 1939.[23]

Rischbieth remained president of the AFWV until 1942. In 1928 she led a large Australian delegation to the first Pan-Pacific Women's Conference in Honolulu. In 1935 she became the thirteenth woman appointed by the Commonwealth government to the Geneva delegation. Her prestige and success stand in striking contrast to Booth's nationalist activities in the interwar years. The extent of real policy-oriented success is another question, the answer to which depends on further research. But two things stand out. First, Australian women were extensively organised before the war, but mostly on a state basis; these state organisations were generally affiliated directly with headquarters overseas, in England as in the prewar League of Women of the Empire, or in America. Some older women's organisations were transnational, Australasian like the WCTU. But there were few federally-based organisations. War and the new internationalism compelled leading women to think nationally. Second, the time was ripe for a national approach to the many outstanding issues affecting the status of women. For example, the problem of married women's citizenship was everything *but* a states question. Women who married aliens lost their nationality rights, not to mention advantages and protection, in a world where the rights of married women and their children were far from universally endorsed; this problem was not resolved until 1948, when new nationality and citizenship legislation was passed in both Britain and Australia. (This was in fact the first Australian nationality and citizenship legislation; previously Australians were imperial—that is, British—citizens.) Thus there was an international and an imperial context to the question, and it was ultimately only resolvable at the national level.[24]

By the 1940s a new wave of women's organisations with a new nationalist focus—the United Associations, the Women's Charter, Women for Canberra—had emerged to take on these and other questions. They in their turn were to derive immense support from exploiting the tension between the international and the national status of Australian women. In 1946 Jessie Street became an actual (rather than alternate) delegate to the new United Nations Organisation in San Francisco. In that year also there were four women in the Australian parliament (in 1947, five). A new chapter in the history of women and nationalism in Australia had begun.

Today there are many more women in public life, and Australia is represented abroad by women in numerous capacities. Both Australia and its relations with the wider world have been transformed since the days of Mary Booth, Bessie Rischbieth and Jessie Street, who died in 1970; and since the 1970s a third generation of Australian feminists has emerged. It seems the strategy of national and international affiliations according to circumstance may still be relevant. In 1992, ninety years after enfranchisement, only sixteen women had ever sat in the House of Representatives in Canberra, and perturbing levels of expatriatism among skilled women again obtain. The career of Elizabeth Reid, first adviser on women's affairs to the Whitlam government and later international bureaucrat, may be suggestive. Who now is in a position to represent Australian women?

THREE

Women in Europe and Australia: Feminisms in Parallel?

Gisela Kaplan

Feminism has consciously attempted to transcend cultural and historical differences by arguing that the oppression of women is universal. There is no doubt that feminism now represents a substantial social and intellectual force. In this chapter I intend to relate the Australian and European feminist experiences and to compare women's status on either continent. What does Australia have in common with Europe that will permit me to argue that Australian feminism may be well contextualised by turning the limelight on Europe? Is Europe, in particular, capable of making a discrete contribution to Australia's situation and debate? In the context of these debates, what does it mean to speak of feminisms in Europe and in Australia? What benefits can be derived for Australian women in the 1990s and beyond from such comparisons; what lessons, if any, can be learnt; and what allegiances, if any, can be claimed? To ask questions of this kind is to open a Pandora's box of searching definitional, conceptual, cultural and psycho-social issues.

Australia and Europe: Definitions and Connections

The first, most basic, observation to be made is that Australia is an English-speaking country. The second observation is that in European (and American) eyes Australia is an island continent in an awkward geographical position, tucked away, as most maps of the world show, on a far-away southern edge 'down-under'. The former has proven a distinct advantage for women, the latter an important disadvantage.

To dwell a little on the advantage: those who lay the strongest claims for the internationalism of feminism are generally located within a discourse of English-language feminism. English language feminism, with a hegemony of the USA, may include the British Isles, and even Canada, Australia and New Zealand. Canadian feminism tends to be relatively marginalised within that discourse[1] but in this context Australian feminism has made a substantial contribution. Via the route of a world lingua franca, it has broken into an international debate of sorts, one that we might call an English-language 'Northern Hemispherism'.

Australia's geo-political position is another matter. The historical and theoretical debates of the 1980s have made it more than evident that Australia is an anomaly in world history.[2] Up until now it has been popular to divide the world into north and south. Northern Hemispherism, to an extent, left Australia out in the cold. There is no corresponding 'Southern Hemispherism', and there is little evidence that such a worldview is likely to develop in the near future. Equally, the division of the world into First, Second and Third World nations has always left an uncomfortable indecision in Australian minds. There are examples of Australia being treated as a Third World country by First World countries, such as the dumping of unsafe substances which have long been banned in the First World. The Australian standard of living is, however, very comparable to industrialised nations of the First World. The term 'Western industrialised nations', to which we have grown accustomed, is yet another anomaly in the Australian case. That location has long been identified as Western European and Northern American. However, in political terms, 'Western' denotes political institutions and cultural traditions to which Australia certainly has a strong claim.

There are more than superficial reasons for the argument that Australia and Europe have substantial historical links. Indeed, modern *white* Australia is a European creation. Significantly, its creation occurred after the French Revolution, and largely built on ideals and experiences of the Industrial Revolution and the failed European revolution of 1848. Even when the young Australian nation reacted against, or just differently from, the 'mother' country, it still reacted within the context of certain aspects of European culture and traditions. The recent 'discovery' that Australia is geographically located in a region of Asian and Pacific nations has raised new questions about Australia's responsibilities towards these 'newly discovered' neighbours and the economic opportunities derived from them. There are questions to be asked about what is contiguous, coeval or merely coexistent.

It is this realisation of geographical position which has contributed to the criticism that Australia was 'Eurocentric' in the past, taking its cues from Europe and choosing as its reference point European affairs and values. The recent shift away from Australia's so-called Eurocentrism was simultaneously accompanied by a realisation of Australia's Aboriginal history, sometimes producing a sense of ambivalence about the European invasion and the appropriateness of transplanting European values, systems and institutions to the faraway island continent. In the late 1980s, it was noted that politics in Australia 'still involves debates about national identity'.[3] In the early 1990s, one needs to replace 'still' by 'once again'. Even within Australia's own history, Australian scholarship has undergone periods of identification and repudiation,[4] suggesting an uncertainty as to a claimed Australian heritage and identity.

I would not regard the Australian feminist debate as 'Eurocentric'—in contrast to what I will term Northern Hemisphere debates. Northern Hemisphere debates must not be mistaken for a discourse with Europe.[5] English-language feminist debate has largely been confined to itself, with scant evidence of a discourse with other European nations. Too often, 'Europe' was ultimately meant as a reference to English writing, geographically located in the British Isles. By contrast, *Australian* writing often betrays strong European intellectual roots.

The Australian Women's Movement

The Australian women's movement after World War II had little direct connection with Europe. European influences were minimal and usually insignificant. Rather, Australian feminists followed US models and strategies, and largely related to writers from the North American continent (including Canada). US leadership in the so-called Second Wave movements is incontestable. Most European countries were also guided or influenced by feminist writing from the USA;[6] they adopted strategies of protest in tune with their own culture, temperament and philosophy, but these activities remained little known in Australia until many years after the events.

If there were similarities between Australia and European countries, they must have emerged in parallel and without any communication. There are some similarities, and they have to do with the ideological roots of the protest. For instance, Curthoys suggests that the early part of the women's liberation movement in Australia followed an anarchist tradition of political organisation.[7] Anarchist traditions were very strong in Italy and in Spain, and hence the arguments, the organisation, the strategies of those groups were correspondingly similar. Likewise, the Marxist-Leninist groups and writers in Australia had much in common with writers of this political background in Europe because they drew on the same texts for their analyses, again suggesting deep roots in European intellectual traditions.

Miriam Dixson argued some years ago that socialist feminism had a far greater influence on the Australian movement as a whole than nearly anywhere else in the Western world. She has attributed this to the belief in the legitimacy of work and to the Australian ethos of the right to work.[8] Socialist feminism could become so influential in Australia partly because of the socialist tradition within the ALP and a general political tradition of 'fair play'.[9] Building on her views, it is worth nothing that socialist feminism was, and still is, a strong force in Europe. In the First Wave movement (from the 1880s onwards) Germany had taken the lead in international socialist feminism. Clara Zetkin (1857–1933) was a household name amongst radical women of the 1880s. Her book *The Women Workers and Women's Question* (1889) was not only an influential text at that time, but it formed the basis for a women worker liberation movement in Italy in the 1970s. While imprisoned, the German socialist, August Bebel, wrote a book *Women and Socialism* (1879), which became one of the most widely read works of socialist literature. It was translated into fifteen languages. Then there was the widely influential democratic socialist Rosa Luxemburg (1871–1919) who was assassinated in Berlin. The Russian activist and writer Aleksandra Kollontai (1872–1952) devoted her life to women's and workers' issues. As a prolific writer, she retained substantial influence well after her death in the Second Wave movements across Western Europe.

My point here is that not just socialism but socialist feminism has a well-established European tradition, is well organised and distinctly transnational, with a presence especially in the Netherlands, Denmark, Spain, Italy and Germany. Together with radical groups from France and other countries, socialist feminism created a network across Europe with which Australian feminism found strong affinities and forged personal and group links. In what is broadly defined as radical theory, Australian feminism has also become very receptive to French feminism. But these events happened in the late 1980s rather than at the time of the onset of the Australian women's movement.

The involvement, if somewhat belated, of the Australian trade union movement in promoting key feminist objectives[10] equally finds some parallels in Europe (rather than in the USA). In particular France, Italy, Iceland, Sweden and Denmark have a long history of unionisation and union action in which women were and are participants, although the Australian experiences of women workers with unions have been more negative than in some of the European counterparts.[11] It is interesting to glean union attitudes to women's issues by focusing on women's participation in union elites. The data of Table 3.1 were obtained in the early 1980s.

Table 3.1 Percentage of women in union elites in selected countries

Country	%	*Country*	%
France	25.5	Austria	8.1
Italy	15.9	West Germany	7.8
Iceland	15.5	UK	6.9
Denmark	12.9	Switzerland	3.0
Australia*	11.0	Belgium	2.8
Sweden	9.4		

Source: Information 6. Women's Representation in Trade Unions, European Trade Union Institute, 1983.

*These Australian figures are only estimates and refer to union officials at all levels. In 1985, there was only one woman on the ACTU executive out of 31, or 3 per cent (see Jenny Doran, 'Unions and Women', in B. Ford and D. Plowman, *Australian Unions: An Industrial Relations Perspective*, 2nd edn, Macmillan, South Melbourne, 1989, p. 200). Hence, the figures may be an overestimate when all major unions are considered.

Nevertheless, there are perhaps two elements of the Australian women's movement which are unique to Australia and find few if any parallels in Europe. One, more akin to US events, was the movement against the Vietnam War by which the Australian women's movement was strongly influenced. Another concerns Australia's 'ambiguous pluralism'. Within their specific social contexts, European feminisms were never particularly equipped to conceptualise the idea of an 'ambiguous pluralism'. Most European countries in the 1970s were still relatively homogeneous, at least by Australian standards. Australia, as one of the most multicultural countries in the world, had begun to think in terms of the diversity of its population and the legitimacy of different communities of interest. The combination of these two unique aspects in Australia created a particular style of feminism that perhaps has no equivalent anywhere else in the world.

In the process of the consolidation of feminism in Australia and in Europe there are few issues that have not been debated, often hotly. In the attention given to, say, abortion, family planning, childcare, rape, women's refuges, education and training, and a million more areas of social and intellectual concern, I find no substantial difference between Australia and the various European countries. The two aspects that deserve more than a mention are women and work, and women in politics. Women and work has been the single most prominent issue in Australian feminist debate. The role of women in politics has been the most prominent issue of analysis in Europe. I shall therefore highlight those two areas here.

Women, Work and Family

Scandinavian countries are generally credited as the creators of the modern welfare state. The point of the 'welfare state', and one of the main reasons for its success at the time, so Logue explains, was to create not welfare but equality.[12] This notion lies conceptually at the heart of social policy development and, likewise, it presupposes a specific understanding of democracy as *social* democracy.[13]

The Scandinavian models, especially Sweden, were widely discussed in Australia. The idea of egalitarianism has always appealed to Australians, although for a long time this appeal was based largely on criteria of class, not of gender. As Shaver pointed out recently, a paradigm shift in social services from a gender politics of difference to one of 'equality' took a long time.[14] In Australia and in Scandinavian countries alike, the notion of social citizenship has been reflected in the social security system. The conceptual and economic consequences of this view are therefore profound. In Australia and in Scandinavian countries (except Finland), entitlements and benefits are a *social right* rather than a *concession.*

It is interesting to note here that neither the Scandinavian countries nor Australia in general suffered from the severe setbacks brought about by fascism in many Western European nations from the 1920s or 1930s on. Hence, in Australia the reforms towards a more equitable and just society were never rescinded, revoked or seriously challenged. Nevertheless, in the Scandinavian countries, as well as in Australia, reforms and social infrastructure development proceeded slowly. Between 1901 and 1968 there was no single noteworthy reform on women's issues taken in Australia,[15] and the few rights which women had acquired were rarely used (see below); but at least these could build on existing reforms.

In Australia, in some Scandinavian countries and in the Netherlands, the establishment of need and of the right to claim assistance is divorced from the employment history (or lack of it) of the individual. This point cannot be made too strongly[16] as it impinges on gender issues in important ways. To elaborate briefly, the participation of women in the labour force has increased substantially in all industrialised nations over the past twenty years but there has been a substantial increase in women employed in part-time work, with all the typical drawbacks of this work status. This is true of nearly all Western industrialised countries. In most countries, including Germany and the USA, no benefits accrue to the housewife, the casual employee, the part-time or the seasonal worker, and hence no claims for benefits can be made. The most radical example of the principle of tying benefits to stringent requirements of a previous work-history can be found in the USA. In the USA, only 17 per cent of all the unemployed receive direct unemployment benefits because of the specific requirements set for the characteristics of such a history.[17] Even when such requirements are set at a more generous level, the nexus between full-time work and the right to claim benefits has been broken in only a few countries, Australia belonging to the few in the Western world.

The cutting of the nexus between employment and benefits is an important ideological shift away from the Protestant work ethic and from implied notions of the deserving and undeserving poor. It also signals a broadening of the concept of work itself. The latter is of particular interest to women. As latest Australian studies and European statistics have shown, women continue to spend an inordinate proportion of their lives in unpaid labour.[18] The fact that it is 'unpaid' is no longer an argument for claiming that it is therefore no longer 'labour' and can be ignored.

Australia has experienced problems in its labour history similar to those of Europe, although here they were more pronounced and lasted longer because of the different geo-political conditions. The battle for equal pay, for instance, was ultimately fought not just nationally but supra-nationally in European summit meetings. The Treaty of Rome of 1957 saw regulation of pay across the member states as an important criterion for setting reasonable standards within a competitive economic context of the various countries. Not so in Australia. Here, the fight for equal pay became one of the longest-fought, bitterest and most wearing battles for women in Australian industrial history.[19]

Australian labour law and the social security system in general have so far largely failed to enshrine gender-specific rights and issues in their overall concepts, unlike the Scandinavian countries. Concerning maternity leave, for example, generally Australian *practices* (as distinct from policies, guidelines, and pockets of implementation) are far behind European countries. I cannot think of any Western European example where women in any work sector are not allowed some paid leave for childbirth. Moreover, some countries such as Sweden, the Netherlands, Germany and including Portugal have shifted the onus of childbirth and childcare away from women. These laws now permit parental leave, allowing the father of a child (who need not be the husband of the mother) to take substantial leave for the sake of childcare, again on full pay and without loss of position.[20]

Significantly, in Finland, which has the highest rate of women in full-time employment (75 per cent) anywhere in the Western industrialised world, parental leave provisions are the best in the world. Here, leave extends to 158 working days (or eight months), five months of which may be taken by the father. During the period of absence from work, 80 per cent of the last full wage is paid. If a woman is not in the labour force at the time of her confinement, she is paid a basic income by the government. Leave arrangements in Finland can be extended to three years, as leave of absence without pay.[21] Where there are childcare expenses, a couple may use these as tax-deductible items. In some Australian work sectors and in some states similarly positive rules may apply; but in practice these remain, to date, privileges for a few women and men rather than a right for all.

Even more enviable is the array of services for children in some Scandinavian countries. These have been developed in the context of ideas of equality, social justice, and hence of employment opportunities for women and men alike.[22] In Denmark, over 60 per cent of children under the age of six can be assured of day care, leaving the parents to pursue a career and maintain full employment.[23] It may be true that Australian government funding of community-based childcare far exceeds that in Britain or the USA, but the habit of the Australian media, the politicians and many spokespersons of making 'international' references only to English-speaking countries has thoroughly distorted the picture of practices in the Western world. Much political mileage for women's issues could be gained by comparing Australian standards with the *best* practices overseas, not with the worst.

Of course, the provision of social services is tied to spending, and more than indirectly to taxation and even to employment levels. Sweden is one of the most highly taxed countries in the Western world and, up to now, it had one of the most tightly knit social security nets and amongst the lowest unemployment. There are signs of changes for the worse. Since 1990, Sweden has suffered its worst economic crisis since World War II. GDP declined, unemployment doubled in two years (from 1989 to 1991) and is said to be above 5 per cent. At the elections in 1991, the new prime minister of Sweden, Carl Bildt, announced his intentions to foster privatisation, lower taxes and decrease social services. Presumably, if taxes were maintained, social services would not need to be decreased. The sceptics say that Sweden is bankrupt and can no longer afford its lavish social service programmes. I have always doubted that simple belief that social service is a luxury item for good times. Much of what is social service in the widest sense is preventative, and therefore ultimately cheaper for a society.

Overall, I am inclined to argue that much of Australian thinking is more readily comparable to that of the more conservative Western European nations, such as Germany, not to the most progressive such as Scandinavia, despite the earlier similarity to Scandinavian reforms. This is reflected in percentages of women in leading positions, in universities, in politics and in the workforce generally, as well as in other conceptual similarities. The definition and treatment of families within the legal, health and taxation system is a case in point. In Sweden and the Netherlands, for instance, the concept of 'family' has been successfully challenged; recognition is given to 'cohabiting partners', who may or may not be married and may or may not be heterosexual. Australia has yet to grapple with conceptual issues of this kind in order to ascertain how present conditions might disadvantage women.

Women and Politics

The study of European feminism, of women's status in many countries and of the women's movements in Western Europe reveals a surprising set of statistics as far as politics is concerned. The English-speaking countries, with their much avowed establishment and inheritance of a democratic tradition, also have the lowest participation of women in politics of all Western industrialised nations. Figure 3.1 shows the similarity of the Australian and the British figures. Here, then, a comparison of Australia with Europe reveals the dramatic, but not surprising, Australian indebtedness to the British system. Surveys conducted in the United Kingdom more than ten years ago showed that even then the population at large was very much in favour of women's participation in politics.[24] These attitudes, however, were rarely translated into practice. No similar survey was conducted in Australia, but I would not be surprised if attitudes in Australia were similarly favourable.

Figure 3.1 Percentage of women in national legislatures in European and English-speaking countries.

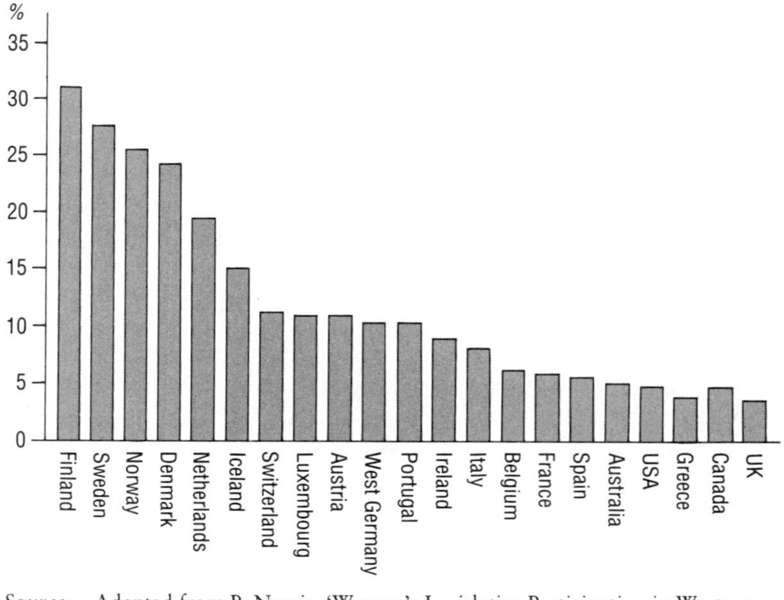

Source: Adapted from P. Norris, 'Women's Legislative Participation in Western Europe', *West European Politics*, 8, 4, 1985, p. 90.

In Australia, the low participation rate of women in politics at all levels of government is even more surprising than in Britain. South Australia was far ahead in enfranchising women in 1894. Encouragingly, by 1992, the average participation rate of women in politics in Australia had risen to 14 per cent,[25] but this remains low when compared to nearly 40 per cent in Scandinavian countries. Australian women's groups have been relatively tardy in lobbying for greater participation of women in politics. The first wave of efforts in this direction occurred around the time of Federation itself; the second took shape in the 1970s under the leadership of the Women's Electoral Lobby; and, in 1992, a new campaign was launched by a coalition of women's groups in NSW who adopted the name Women Into Politics.[26]

This latest campaign is commendable and noteworthy, but one needs to ask why it is about twenty-five years behind similar campaigns in Scandinavian countries. This question has intrigued me because the legislation of Scandinavian countries was often so similar to Australian policies before World War II. Iceland, a country largely living off its primary industry, sparsely populated, is an island country like Australia, claiming to be egalitarian in essence. Iceland produced a rather remarkable women's movement which started at about the same time as that in Australia. Unlike the Australian women's liberation movement, however, the formal organisation (Kvenna Frambothid, or KF) abolished itself within a year (1982) when it decided to enter politics. Today, Iceland's president is a woman (Vigdis Finnbogadóttir). When will the two major parties in Australia preselect women in winnable electorates, move women from the backbench, and allow more women in cabinet?[27] When will Australia have its first woman prime minister?

This fast transition from social movement to political interest group was unique even within Scandinavia.[28] It was not atypical of women in Scandinavian countries, however, to focus attention on direct political intervention for the sake of gaining influence if not political control. Norwegian women have been remarkable in their single-minded focus on female representation in politics. From the very beginning of the feminist campaigns in the late 1960s, one of the chief goals was to get women into politics. Norwegian women succeeded rather quickly in this goal. By the mid-1970s, most Norwegian parties had succumbed to the demand for a 40 per cent representation of either sex in parliament. Moreover, in Norway women were catapulted to power rather suddenly. By the late 1980s, nearly half of all ministers were women, as was the prime minister, Dr Brundtland.

The Australian campaign of 1992 called Women Into Politics sounds strangely familiar to that of Norwegian women in the 1960s. But why the delay and the difference? Both in Norway and in Australia the feminist lobby fought bitter battles. In both countries, socialist, Marxist-

Leninist, and radical feminist groups operated. Both countries were rather conservative, guided by a constitutional monarchy; both had enfranchised women in 1901–2; and in both there had been a marked delay between the formal acknowledgement of women's rights and the actual use of those rights. Even in its political history, there are a few seeming common denominators. Norway had suffered the indignation of sovereignty of another country. It was under Danish or Swedish rule for centuries. As an independent country, signalled by the election of its own king in 1917, it has had a brief history. Norwegians were the ruled, not the rulers. It is the same for Australians.

This comparison certainly has substantial flaws, and it is easy to pick glaring examples of its inadequacy. After all, Norwegian society was and is a homogeneous group, unlike Australian society. British rule in Australia has also left its mark by producing a colonised society in ways typical of British colonial *administration*. There is no comparison here with Norwegian society, first in terms of the extent of control of another sovereign power and second in terms of the historical propensity of such developments. British-style colonial bureaucracy was set up to rule. It was originally designed simultaneously to obfuscate the source of power and to embody the maintenance of power. I venture to claim that Australia may be unique amongst Western industrialised nations in having inherited such a bureaucracy which, on one hand, appears to serve the same functions as any Western-style bureaucracy but, on the other, may still carry characteristics of the vested powers of colonial bureaucracies. Hence, in order to gain influence, shape policy and work for social change (within the limits that such a system can bear), it may be as useful in Australia to enter bureaucracy as it is in other Western countries to enter politics.

It is probably symptomatic of this phenomenon that only in Australia has the association of women with bureaucracy attained any positive connotations. The term 'femocrat', especially when used approvingly, generally leaves European and US feminists speechless, because in most European countries bureaucracies are perceived as cumbersome and mechanistic appendices of government, not as being in themselves an expression of or a seat of power. There is no dearth of Australian publications mentioning 'bureaucratic feminism' and 'femocrats'; despite sceptical accounts, there is often more than faint praise associated with the evaluation.[29] One would be hard-pressed to find publications with such a slant anywhere in Europe, notwithstanding the fact that the greatest expansion of women's employment in Europe has occurred in the public sector.

If Australian women of the 1990s suddenly feel that women ought to get into politics, this indicates another shift in Australian political reality.

I am suggesting that a comparison of statistics between Scandinavian countries or, for that matter, European countries and Australia, may be misleading. To be sure, Australian feminists enjoyed their short honeymoon period with the Whitlam government. So did Greek women when PASOK (the Panhellenic Socialist Party of Greece) was voted into office in 1981.[30] In both countries, for different reasons, such bliss was short-lived, and so was the experience of public debate in either country. Bureaucracy is not usually associated with public debate. The forum for public debate lies in politics.

There is a further point to be made. Both in Europe and in Australia, there was from the onset of the women's movements of the early 1970s a strong radical feminist element which argued forcefully, and in its way convincingly, that revolutions 'from within' a given system were a conceptual and political impossibility. Ultimately, reformism was incapable of challenging existing norms and, therefore, incapable of initiating change. It was therefore essential, so radical feminism argued, to stay away from organised mainstream (male) power.[31] In other words, those women did not *want* to engage in the lobbying for greater representation of women in politics.

However, the argument can be made that we need fair representation of a multiplicity of views in all decision-making bodies of government. Women, and minority and special-interest groups, need to be in places of power and of decision-making. Most Scandinavian countries have long argued that *social* concerns have to become *political* and part of public life. Clearly, having women in politics will not by itself produce a 'multiplicity of views', as the example of the former prime minister of Britain, Margaret Thatcher, has admirably demonstrated. What we need is an assurance that different representations will result in a multiplicity of views. The Irish president, Mary Robinson, is an example of the new kind of leadership.

In Australia, I can see no Aboriginal people in government, far too few women, no-one who is overtly representing homosexual interests, or those of ethnicity, disability, or old age. Social democracies have a different concept of the mandate and of representation. Most Scandinavian countries and the Netherlands have already understood that a multiplicity of views promotes the democratic process. Even in the USA, there has been a gradual change in composition of government. Only the very conservative parliamentary democracies, of which the British Westminster system is one and Germany is another, believe that representation of interests and pressure groups works against the democratic process of fairly elected governments and of a fair and objective exercise of that mandate. Our governments are as yet almost hermetically closed to 'interest' representation, as if a politics of pluralism could not be trusted.

Conclusion

Feminism has been extremely uncomfortable for established political traditions, social conventions and vested interests. Amongst the new wave of 'conscientious objectors' to feminism are the extreme right-wing lobbyists of the USA and Europe, who glibly argue in favour of a supposedly limitless 'freedom of speech' against an alleged 'political correctness'. Feminism is as yet anything but politically 'correct', socially accepted or culturally understood. It remains still one of the most disputed but best-articulated points of view which threatens left and right orthodoxy.

I would argue that the issues of the 1990s for women are again basic ones, particularly having regard to the backlash (sexist and racist) throughout the Western world, especially in mainland Europe. These concern the right to be heard, *and* to be different,[32] the right to work and to be justly rewarded for that work; the right to assemble and to participate in decision-making despite and *because* of this difference. In these important basic principles, there is indeed very little difference between the Australian and the European experience. Simone de Beauvoir was once asked why she had become a feminist and she answered, 'I understood the unfathomable depth of women's oppression'.[33]

FOUR

Feminism on Two Continents: The Women's Movement in Australia and the United States

Anne Summers

The more than two years I spent as editor-in-chief of *Ms.* magazine (1987–1990) gave me an unparalleled vantage point from which to assess the workings and accomplishments of the American women's movement. I went into the job taking for granted, as I am sure most Australians would, that the United States represented the pinnacle of the achievements of Second Wave feminism. I very quickly learned how wrong this assumption was. Many of the entitlements which Australian women take for granted, such as federally funded childcare, mandated (if unpaid) maternity leave or the existence of women's policy advisers at every level of government, simply do not exist in the United States. Even more surprising, but seemingly related, was the low number of women holding elected office, especially in federal politics.

In 1988, my first full year at *Ms.* and a US Presidential election year, there were only twenty-five women in the entire US Congress, a mere 4.7 per cent.[1] I made political coverage a top priority of the magazine; in the United States women register and vote in greater numbers than men, and we published figures which showed that in the previous election, in 1986, the 'gender gap' (women's different voting patterns to men's) had delivered the margin of victory to a significant proportion of the winning contenders.[2] So it seemed self-evident to me that, as in Australia, women's votes would be solicited and that a feminist magazine which for the first time was treating electoral politics seriously would be in for some serious wooing by candidates. Not so, as it turned out. The major party candidates were courteous; they answered our monthly questions on policy issues; but they evidently felt there were no advantages, and perhaps some negatives, in getting too close to *Ms.* magazine. The biggest surprise was the calculated contempt shown to us by Democratic contender Michael Dukakis. He had agreed to pose along with his senior campaign staff, many of whom—including his campaign manager—were women, for the cover of our October 1988 issue. Right at the last minute, after our photographic team had already flown to Boston, Dukakis cancelled. 'Scheduling difficulties' was the official explanation. Cold feet was the truth.

I was amazed at the seeming impotence of the women's movement, its inability to influence or even be part of the campaign debate, and the fact that politicians could so easily disregard it. Ultimately I became convinced that at least part of the responsibility for the movement's political frailty lies with the movement itself, especially the national leaders. They have no political strategy whatsoever and seem incapable of putting together a pragmatic plan to force the political system to deliver to American women the social and economic equity long promised by the movement's rhetoric. It can perhaps be postulated that the Reagan–Bush era is responsible for the movement's failure: that twelve years of feminist-unfriendly Administrations in Washington left the movement battle-scarred and exhausted. If that is the case, the exhaustion appears to be near-terminal, since the advent of the feminist-friendly Clinton Administration has not produced anything remotely resembling the kind of partnership which Australian feminists have managed to forge with government. Indeed, early in 1993 there seemed almost to be an air of hostility towards President Clinton, and a strange ambivalence by many feminists towards Hillary, his high-profile and policy-active wife.

During his first few weeks in office Clinton reversed one after another of Reagan and Bush's restrictive abortion measures. Instead of the joy and appreciation one might have expected from feminists, there were complaints and even outright opposition from women's movement leaders who claimed the changes did not go far enough. After more than a decade of fighting to preserve abortion rights, the National Organisation for Women astonishingly opposed Clinton's proposed Freedom of Choice Act, a measure which would give the right to abortion a federal legislative base and remove it from the vagaries of judicial review. Their opposition stems from the view that it is not sufficient to keep abortion legal; the proposed law should make abortion easily accessible by forbidding states to impose any restrictions, such as the need for parental consent for minors.[3] American feminist leaders will not settle for anything less than purist perfection and, as a result, they mostly end up with nothing. Rather than entrench even a few basic rights which can be built on and expanded later (as Australian feminists did with the Sex Discrimination Act 1984), women's movement leaders—as distinct from their frustrated and apparently impotent members—would rather fight than win. This is what happened with the Equal Rights Amendment in 1982, when the refusal of feminist leaders to compromise on substance or tactics left American women without a constitutional guarantee of equality.

Why is this the case? Why has the movement which brought the world the Second Wave of feminism proved incapable of delivering the political agenda it originally mapped out? Movement leaders have a tendency defensively to blame the media, blame the politicians, blame anybody in fact rather than engage in self-reflection that might provide some answers. Movement leaders will protest that the Powers-that-be are afraid of the 'F' word—feminism—when in fact the movement has its own 'F' word problems: it is too dominated by Fame, Factionalism and Fuzzy-thinking to provide American women with the representation they are entitled to—and so badly need.

The American women's movement is no different from American society in general in its obsession with fame and celebrity. The movement has its own celebrities, and the famous American feminists are very famous indeed—women like Gloria Steinem, Betty Friedan, Kate Millett, Susan Brownmiller and Bella Abzug are known to millions of people across the globe. This phenomenon does not exist in the women's movement anywhere else in the world, and certainly not in Australia, where a much greater egalitarianism prevails. Nor have other national movements surrendered much of their political agenda to the fads of the famous. Far from being able or willing to resist this national fetish, American feminism has become so dependent upon celebrities that the movement's credibility and effectiveness have been damaged.

The women's movement uses famous people to raise money, to make political statements, and to march in the front row of political demonstrations. The rationale is that the presence of a Jane Fonda, a Glenn Close, a Whoopi Goldberg or a Cybill Shepherd will attract the media and result in both better coverage of the event or the issue, and a greater chance of 'ordinary' people paying attention. In practice it means that a tremendous amount of effort goes into persuading famous people, especially movie stars, to lend public support to women's causes and events. This gives American feminist events a very different character to those in Australia. I attended the star-studded dinner in Washington, DC, the night before the massive pro-choice abortion march in April 1989, and was struck by how elitist and alien it was. The movie stars did some mingling at the after-dinner reception (naturally, you had to pay extra for the privilege of such propinquity), and each celebrity immediately attracted a cluster of star-struck women who pushed past bodyguards to have their brief encounter with fame. The next morning the stars—wearing their Distinguished Guest sashes!—were closeted in a special VIP tent until the march began.

The sight of feminists fawning over movie stars is something to behold! Especially if the particular star's recent roles have been ones feminists would not want to review favourably. (Glenn Close and *Fatal Attraction* was a current case in point.) But this is usually overlooked if the star is willing to lend her celebrity to a pro-feminist statement or event. The presence of Fame seems to blunt the critical faculties of the non-famous, who simper and gush and otherwise demean themselves. The inequalities involved are more extreme than those between women and men; indeed if any woman grovelled towards her husband or boyfriend the way some feminists kowtow towards the rich and famous, we would feel we had not progressed very far.

American feminism's dependence on fame, and the famous, seriously weakens the women's movement. Time and energy that could be applied to political struggle—lobbying politicians to get legislation passed for instance—are diverted to selecting, seducing and then servicing the celebrities. (Don't think these people stop being temperamental just because they are donating their services to a worthy cause!) Perhaps even more important, the movement has surrendered control of its political agenda. In a sense, it has become captive to the ideological whims of the celebrities. Such people usually have strong feelings (publicly, at least) only about issues involving personal life-style choices such as abortion. It is almost unheard of to have famous names lending their support on economic issues: they are too complicated, too difficult. Maybe this is why these subjects are so neglected by American feminism. Yet it is issues like equal pay and job opportunities that affect the daily lives of most women and are of more immediate, urgent and continuing relevance than the more fashionable subjects which Hollywood stars feel strongly about.

No political movement is free of factionalism, and the women's movement is no exception, but only the American women's movement would conduct so many of its fights, and especially the feuds between famous feminists, in the media. This of course does nothing to improve the impression of unity amongst feminists, and thus weakens the movement as a whole.

The most famous feminist feud, between Gloria Steinem and Betty Friedan, author of the 1963 classic *The Feminine Mystique*, seems to have started in 1970 when Steinem formed the Women's Action Alliance in apparent competition with Betty Friedan's brainchild, the National Organisation for Women.[4] Two years later, Friedan reacted to the founding of *Ms.* magazine by issuing a press release stating that Gloria Steinem 'was ripping off the [women's] movement for private profit' and that 'no one should mistake her for a leader'. Steinem retaliated by telling a reporter: 'If I have a lot of problems about my being a leader of the women's movement, I'm sure *she* has even more about me being a leader of the women's movement.'[5] The willingness of both parties to perpetuate, and escalate, their hostility via the media would horrify most Australian feminists; they would see it as a betrayal of the principles of sisterhood to denounce one another publicly in this fashion.[6] Nor would Australian feminists publicly trash other women for having the temerity to offer alternative views of reality, especially of feminism, as American feminists do, seemingly without hesitation. In 1991 Steinem described *Washington Post* journalist Sally Quinn as a 'water bug' (a critter Australians know as a cockroach) for an article which questioned the political achievements of the women's movement. Robin Morgan used her editor's letter in *Ms.* magazine in 1993 to describe combative author Camille Paglia as 'a publicity-obsessed, intellectually bereft, rather pathetic person trying to revive the lie that women want to be raped'.[7]

This fractiousness between individuals repeats itself in organisational animosity. The major women's groups find it difficult to agree on a broad common agenda, and are surprisingly fuzzy in their thinking about issues and strategy. It should not be a dauntingly difficult task to identify the three or four key issues that, once won, could transform the live of millions of American women. Such a battle-plan would command respect from women and from legislators, and might oblige candidates for office to become more responsive to the political demands of the women's movement. But the sad reality is that, prior to the election of President Clinton and his promise to protect abortion rights, that was virtually the only issue which movement leaders could agree upon—and even then there were plenty of disagreements about tactics. The frenetic political activity around abortion rights in the late 1980s and early 1990s actually helped disguise the extent of disagreement within the movement. Most grassroots members of the major organisations are probably unaware of it. Yet the movement's inability to organise around a broad-based agenda, and to link it to a tough-minded electoral strategy, has meant that American women have endured a decade where nothing new was accomplished, and some entitlements (federally funded abortions for poor women, for instance) were taken away. The Reagan and Bush years were not good for American women; they were even worse for the American women's movement because it lost its perspective—and its nerve. The movement has always had a tendency to dwell on single issues, especially those of a personal or cultural nature, at the expense of the economic issues. The movement spent the 1980s preoccupied with abortion, pornography, sexual abuse (especially of children, including present-day adult 'survivors') and, after the Senate hearings concerning Clarence Thomas and Anita Hill, sexual harassment.[8] While these are all important subjects, for most women job protection and pay equity loom larger as day-to-day imperatives. For the women's movement to do justice to American women, it needs to be out there fighting on a broader front, forcing the political system to deliver economic justice to women so that they have real choices about their lives. The woman who cannot afford to leave a violent husband because she has only a low-paying job will probably not be overly impressed to see Jane Fonda in the front line of an abortion rights march. For no number of famous faces could hide the fact that the American women's movement entered the 1990s without a strategy for improving the lives of American women. The contrast with the Australian movement, which has a clear and articulated agenda, could not be greater.

FIVE

Living across Difference: Connecting Gender, Ethnicity, Class and Ageing in Australia

Gill Bottomley

The first section of this chapter will briefly scan some of the work of social scientists who have written about gender, ethnicity and class in studies of Australian immigration and settlement.[1] My purpose here is to develop multiple and relational perspectives that include these three categories as well as that of age. The second section will scrutinise recurrent concepts such as identity, ethnicity, community and multiculturalism. Through these critiques, I will suggest a framework that might avoid essentialisms by concentrating on the *practices* of what I describe as 'living across difference'.

Australian Research

Studies of immigration to and settlement in Australia have usually had a strong policy orientation, concerned mainly with who should be allowed in, and what to do with them once they are here. Immigrants have thus been constituted as something of a 'problem', and the wider implications—e.g. of social and cultural life and identity in a highly diverse nation—have been rather neglected. This tendency has accompanied a compartmentalising of interests and a drawing of boundaries that continue to frustrate attempts to develop a more multifaceted understanding of this highly diverse society.

In many of the earlier studies, 'migrant women' were habitually glossed as the families of migrants. The assumption was that immigrant workers were men, whose families/women would help to maintain ethnic traditions and stabilise the private sphere of life—clearly separate from the public sphere of work and politico-economic processes. The interaction between the wider society and familial and cultural forms, including those created by class and gender, was rarely examined. Some of the more ethnographic studies paid attention to women—and were often undertaken by women.[2] These studies indicated that particular forms of economic activities had specific consequences for migrant families; in other words, the public and private were interrelated. Such interrelations were apparent in research I undertook among Greek Australians in the early 1970s. For example, those women who participated in the ownership and management of small businesses had greater 'leverage' in family decision-making than the women who were entirely dependent on their husbands' earnings. In another paper based on fieldwork in Sydney, I discussed some of the effects on wives and mothers of the centrifugal tendencies of industrial cities, compared with the more centripetal mode of the villages that these women had left behind. Mothers especially had lost their centrality and a degree of control over the lives of their children and the activities of their families.[3]

The latter paper received a critical response from another wave of writers, who focused intently on women as *workers*, at the risk of neglecting the profound significance to many women of kinship and cultural practices. This has been the main focus of work about migrant women in Australia, and has resulted in useful and important studies that have revealed the widespread exploitation, especially of women from non-English-speaking backgrounds, in poorly paid jobs, with inadequate childcare and language-learning facilities, as well as working conditions that would not be acceptable to Australian-born workers. These conditions and their consequences have now been well documented in studies indicating the ethnic and gender segmentation of the workforce, and the growth in outwork.[4] More recently, the decline in manufacturing has created high unemployment among immigrant women, especially those previously employed in the clothing and footwear industries.

Not surprisingly, these conditions of labour have created widespread difficulties beyond the workplace—such as health problems, concerns about childcare, fatigue and strain—that strongly affect what we call 'private life'. The extra dimensions of sexism and racism (neither of which is necessarily confined to the Anglo majority) often create a formidable range of exploitations of women with relatively little power. A number of writers have analysed these compounded oppressions in detail, and they are the subject of continuing action by groups such as the Migrant Womens SpeakOut, various Ethnic Affairs Commissions, the Federation of Ethnic Communities Councils, several trade unions and the ACTU, among others.[5] Nevertheless, the deeply entrenched and highly structured aspects of sexism and racism, compounded by class position, present an intricate network of interconnections and reinforcements.[6]

I mentioned earlier that writers who focused on ethnicity tended to ignore class, or even to suggest that class was irrelevant in Australia.[7] The research on workforce segmentation demonstrated not only that class is relevant, but that class relations are defined by gender and ethnicity or 'race' in specific ways. In 1984, several writers published a collection of papers that employed a triple perspective of ethnicity, class and gender in delineating Australian.[8] Two authors focused specifically on 'migrant women', a portmanteau term that obscures wide diversities. In her chapter, Jeannie Martin stressed the high workforce participation of women who were also wives and mothers, entailing 'a tension between production and social reproduction', compounded by expectations from countries of origin of the central significance of women's tasks. Martin noted that the dichotomies production/consumption, public/private and work/non-work falsify the constant interaction between these supposedly separate spheres.[9]

The other chapter about women, which I wrote, took up a debate about the participation of women of non-English-speaking background in politics, including feminist activities. This responded to a paper written by three women from FILEF (the Federation of Italian Workers and their Families) countering culturalist claims that Italian women were apolitical and/or confined to the house by sexist oppression. They pointed to the workforce-based and domestic constraints on the time and energy of many Italo-Australian women, and to the political activism of women in Italy, especially in the strong and courageous feminist movement. Agreeing with this argument, I referred to the women's movements in Greece, which, like their Italian counterparts, had been closely linked to liberation movements and especially to left-wing political parties. Not only are these political structures not available in Australia in the same way, but political activities among immigrants have generally been discouraged.[10]

Clearly, all these factors are important if we are to understand specific situations. People's actions and adjustments are defined by disadvantages, such as language, work, family responsibilities. They are also defined by other circumstances that can be understood culturally, such as the centrality of mothers, and the historical participation of women in liberation and other political movements in places like the Mediterranean. The editors of *Ethnicity, Class and Gender* have continued this linking of structure and culture, subjective and objective, in a more recent collection titled *Intersexions: Gender/Class/Culture/Ethnicity* (1991).[11]

Intersexions draws on feminist and post-colonial discourses concerned with issues of representation, but attempts to go beyond criticism and to offer some alternative ways of proceeding: for example, by combining comparative and specific analyses; by examining our own positions as commentators; and by including the voices of some of the people 'being represented'. It also crosses several boundaries, including that of geography: it draws material from Vanuatu, Indonesia, India and Bangladesh. Genres are also blurred in the inclusion of literary work by Aboriginal, Greek-Australian and Vanuatuan writers.

Obviously, what has happened here is that questions about 'migrant women' have been increasingly related to wider issues about women in society, ideological forms, cultural transformations and resistances. In this development, feminist perspectives and debates have been extremely important in questioning the boundaries set up around legitimate knowledge. For example, long-standing assumptions about the separation of public and private spheres are challenged by the linking of domestic and paid work. Cultural distinctions based on class, gender, even rural or urban origin, are seen as salient—in other words, 'culture' does not equal 'ethnicity'. What I intend to do now is to discuss the possibility of conceptualising the interconnections described above together rather than separately. This section will suggest a framework for avoiding essentialisms by concentrating on the practices of living across difference.

Multiplicity and Interweavings

In one of his *Six Memos for the Next Millennium*, Italo Calvino focused on 'multiplicity', invoking with approval the work of another Italian novelist, Carlo Emilio Gadda, who, according to Calvino,

> tried to represent the world as a knot, a tangled skein of yarn; to represent it without in the least diminishing the inextricable complexity or, to put it better, the simultaneous presence of the most disparate elements that converge to determine every event.[12]

In universities, we are expected to untangle complexities, but we need to recognise the illusory quality of this untangling. Aspects of people's lives are socially and culturally always under construction, in relation to each other.

However we conceptualise their interrelation, gender, ethnicity and 'race' are commonly regarded as relatively fixed features of human beings—i.e. as distinguishable by particular attributes. But these features are extremely variable, and the supposedly biological underpinning of gender and 'race'—and sometimes ethnicity—is constantly contested. Even the concept of class has not entirely escaped the claims of 'natural hereditary inferiority'. These concepts, therefore, hover above fields of bitter dispute, fields full of knots and disparate elements! While dispassionate untangling sounds like an admirable aim, it can only be attempted with a recognition of some of the political implications of such terms.

This observation highlights another, perhaps obvious, but important aspect of the tangle. All of these terms are enmeshed in politicised discourses as well as being the subjects of intellectual concern. For example, the debate about whether Women's Studies should be described as Feminist Studies faces this dilemma.

Several of the chapters of *Intersexions* directly address this question of politics and knowledge. One is Margaret Jolly's chapter 'The Politics of Difference: Feminism, Colonialism and Decolonisation in Vanuatu'. Recognising ethnic and class differences between women 'as a starting point for feminism, rather than as an embarrassing afterthought' (p. 53), Margaret points out that gender, race and class are 'structurally complicit', demonstrating this complicity in colonial and post-colonial Vanuatu. She concludes her paper with the hope 'for a feminism which starts from difference, and which is equally concerned about racial, class and women's oppression' (p. 74).

The main points to recognise at this stage are: (a) the contextual aspect of ethnicity and gender and their interrelation; and (b) the effects of this socio-historical context on the constitution of gender and ethnicity in what is often described as 'identity politics'. I intend to return to a more detailed consideration of the concepts of identity and ethnicity, as promised. Before doing so, and by way of illustrating context and interweaving, I want to refer to a recently published book entitled *Who Do You Think You Are?*, written about and by 'second-generation immigrant women' in Australia.[13] One particularly impressive chapter is Eva Cox's 'What Ethnic Identity?'. Eva's story begins with her departure from Vienna in 1939 as a baby in the arms of her Jewish refugee mother. The next seven years of her life were spent in straitened circumstances in wartime England, where her mother-tongue, German, was regarded as 'a filthy language'. The following two years were lived in Rome, in a flat with 'five bedrooms, three bathrooms and a maid', but Eva identified with the neighbouring Italian children rather than her American schoolmates. Then, an Anglophone child with Italian as a second language and the lingering 'execrable German', Eva became a New Australian. 'But', she recalls,

> I was not allowed to belong: I was still defined as a reffo and a Jew and I wondered what it all meant, as my main sense of identity by now was as an outsider. [p. 63]

When multiculturalism arrived, it allowed some degree of freedom, but developing an ethnic identity was a problem for someone whose state of birth had left her and her family stateless. A Jewish identity could not be denied, because Eva had been persecuted and labelled as a Jew. But Eva believes in no god, and asks,

> So what is ethnic identity? A valuing of diversity and an appreciation of the value of difference makes sense, but within an understanding that we are still part of societies with dominant cultures. [p. 64]

Eva also strongly objects to tribalisms, patriotisms and nationalisms. In her words,

> As a child of refugees, I want a world where we learn tolerance as a primary characteristic, with responsibility and respect rather than competing rights, where we are not looking to the tribe for identity and creating outsiders to make us feel good. We need to see in others a diverse reflection of self. [p. 65]

A number of important points are made with great economy in Eva's story. We will examine three of them:

1. Our location in social, geographical and historical space is completely contingent in nature. In his aptly named study of nationalism, *Imagined Communities* (1983), Benedict Anderson reveals what he calls 'the magic of nationalism', which transforms chance into destiny and contingency into meaning.[14] In these transformations, nationalism can inspire love and self-sacrifice, partly because of the transcendent quality of identification with past centuries of ancestors and the timelessness of language. Anderson also suggests a sense of contemporaneous community in language, especially in the chorusing of national songs and ceremonial poetry. He points out that such choruses can be joined, that we can learn languages, become 'naturalised' or have children whose nationality differs from our own. But in some countries—and Germany is an important example—the primordialism of ethnicity is defined by *blood,* not language or customs, and the contemporaneous community of nationalism can become a fortress (or a prison).

So we are all pre-written to a great extent, born in a specific place, to specific parents, within a specific historical context, with particular physical characteristics. We have no control over these accidents, yet they preform our life trajectories—and I use that verb carefully. I make this point in order to emphasise some of the ways in which accident is transformed into destiny, and to explore the degrees of freedom within this highly structured contingency. As Eva's story demonstrates, there are also built-in contradictions. In her case, her native tongue was the tongue of a terrifying enemy; her religious affiliation linked her with a state whose nationalism recalls that enemy, but it might also have provided her with an internationalism that 'does not privilege place of birth or language' (p. 65). Certainly, Eva confirms the importance of considering structural factors as well as the more psychological or individual aspects of what she describes as 'identity'.

2. Ethnicity, nationalism, religion, and to some extent gender and class intersect and interweave in this story. Her emphasis is on the former themes rather than the latter; but she notes that, as a woman, she is 'colonised by male culture in the same way as all Australians are colonised by Anglo culture'. In her words, 'it's about power and who defines the values' (p. 64). All aspects of what Erikson (1968) describes as psychosocial identity are mediated through patterns of dominance. Erikson refers to Freud's description of his own 'clear consciousness of inner identity', an ability to do without agreement with 'the compact majority'—in his case, a range of majorities who have persecuted and excluded Jews. Psychosocial identity anchors our transient existence, but Erikson points to the danger of imagining a 'pseudospecies' based on a communal identity that is not questioned or relativised.[15]

3. Eva's story shows the negative aspects of ethnicism and tribalism. While recognising the importance of shared respect for an ethnic heritage, we also need to recognise that ethnicism can form the basis for the kind of vicious regression that manifests itself in racism. Such a regression requires a negative valorising of an imagined Other in order to delineate a supposedly homogeneous 'We'—as in the 'ethnic cleansing' currently being carried out in what used to be Yugoslavia, and, of course, during the Nazi Holocaust. What Anderson calls the 'deep horizontal comradeship' of identity can require a terrible cost.

The concept of identity is based on the exclusion of difference, on a presumption of homogeneity. The word identity is derived from the Latin *idem*, meaning 'the same'. Similarity is an innocent enough notion, which can form part of the process of what is called 'identity', seen as a combination of self-identification and identification by others. In other words, the term indicates who one feels similar to, and who one is categorised together with. This process, however, largely takes place below the level of consciousness, and within structured layers of power relations. Assumptions of natural identification—defined by shared ethnicity or gender—obscure the complexities of these layers, despite the strategic significance of collective experiences.

Readers might complain that all I have done so far is to point to some of the knots in this particular skein of yarn that includes gender, ethnicity, nationalism, racism and class. But I am arguing for a socio-political approach to these knots that recognises their interconnectedness. As we have already seen, binary oppositions prioritise one term and subordinate the other. Identities as homogeneities block alliances across lines of race/ethnicity, gender/sexuality, class and generation. Feminists have theorised multiple inscriptions that allow for cross-cutting affiliations. But it remains difficult to conceptualise this cross-cutting, and even more difficult to recognise that all psychosocial identity is constructed *across* difference, and to develop a politics of difference.

Part of that difficulty lies in the fact that much of our pre-structuring remains below the level of consciousness. Consciousness-raising therefore is likely to have minimal effect. Nevertheless, practices like consciousness-raising or critiques of 'legitimate knowledge' can not only challenge relations of symbolic power, but offer alternative ways of understanding experience. In her book *Etrangers à Nous Mêmes* (1988), Julia Kristeva confronts racism in this way, partly through a historical account of the notion of 'foreigner' and partly through an explication of Freud's concept of the 'unhomely', that which is strangely disquieting and remains hidden in the unconscious. Foreign-ness, she argues, is the basis of identity. Only a universalism (what she calls a 'cosmopolitanism') capable of incorporating rather than excluding difference can meet the practical exigencies of an increasingly heterogeneous world.[16]

In a more recent interview, Kristeva reiterates her position, speaking of 'a democracy of the multiple . . . in seeing individual differences, singularities' and resisting homogeneities. Clarke and Hulley, her interviewers, take care to distinguish between Kristeva's concept of the individual and that which forms the basis of 'the American subject of history' (p. 154). For Kristeva, the individual is already positioned in language and ideology and therefore in history—and 'subjectivity is always constituted within dialogue' (p. 155).

One of the major contributions of feminist writers—and other minority writers—has been in placing themselves (ourselves) within the discursive frame and thereby challenging forms of representation. Kristeva has done this in *Etrangers à Nous Mêmes*, speaking of some of the difficulties of being a foreigner in France, but also arguing that polyglots can unsettle the certainty of the ethnocentric ('one needs a disequilibrium to hear discord').

These brief observations cast another light on the frequently posed question, 'who speaks'? We might also ask 'who listens?' and 'what do they hear?' Apparently, Mandarin Chinese has a verb that means 'one listens and hears' and another that means 'one listens and fails to hear'. In the words of the novelist Gish Jen, 'people hear what they can, see what they can, do what they can, that's the understanding . . . everywhere there are limits'.[17]

This brings me back to my earlier questions about understanding. My own framework of understanding owes a good deal to the work of Pierre Bourdieu, which I have used over the past decade or so. Bourdieu has always criticised the dichotomy between subjective and objective, and the use of categorising as an excuse for thought. He also outlines three levels of knowledge, all of which need to be considered. The first is the subject of phenomenology, the level of immediate experience; the second objectifies that experience; and the third level objectifies that objectification, reflecting on the conditions of construction of what we call 'objective knowledge'.[18]

As we have seen, the third level is especially problematic, requiring a reflexivity that goes much further than self-reflection. The questions of 'who speaks', 'who listens' and 'who hears' are all implicated in this third level of knowledge. A sociological view must therefore reflect on the particular conditions that produce speakers and listeners. Bourdieu has elaborated the idea of *habitus*, 'the embodiment of history', which incorporates the multiple perspectives that I have been discussing, as a set of structured and structuring dispositions. Hence, people who share similar positions in a social field also share schemes of perception and similarities that both arise from, and create, continuing distinctions. This means that gender, class and ethnicity are experienced as natural attributes: they manifest themselves in language, in techniques of the body, in the organisation of time and space, and in what become 'natural' attitudes.

In a recent paper, Toril Moi employs Bourdieu's concept of 'social field'— as 'a competitive social space'—in relation to *habitus*, (p. 1021), to construct a relational view of gender behaviour.[19] She traces de Beauvoir's life in terms of what Bourdieu describes as social, symbolic and cultural capital, and demonstrates the social variability of gender. However, Moi goes further; she reanalyses Helene Cixous's essay 'The Laugh of the Medusa', which was first published in a special issue of the literary magazine *L'Arc* dedicated to Simone de Beauvoir. In Cixous's essay, there is not one reference to de Beauvoir, despite the fact that this is the only essay that explicitly discusses women's writing. 'Reading with Bourdieu', Moi perceives this as a snub to Beauvoir and a bid for control of legitimate knowledge within the field of French feminism. Cixous thus casts Beauvoir as conservative, as a representative of male-dominated discourse, while herself using the very rhetorical strategies of that discourse. Her field therefore is the French intellectual field in general, and her practice partly explains the success of her essay in 1975.

I mentioned earlier that *habitus* is manifest in practice. The social world operates in terms of practices: the interaction between *habitus* and specific social fields is conceived as dynamic; these terrains of struggle can only be explored through this sort of empirical and ethnographic method. The defining logic of practice, according to Bourdieu, is 'polythetic', literally 'many positions', capable of sustaining a multiplicity of contradictory meanings 'because the overriding context of its operation is practical'.[20] Because, as we have seen, we are usually implicated in contradictory situations, practices are usually logically 'fuzzy'. To the questions of who speaks, listens and hears, I would like to add the more inclusive question of practice—what do people *do*? This question also demands detailed empirical work, as well as sensitivity to context.

In Australia, in theory and to some extent in practice, multiculturalism can encourage an openness towards difference, perhaps even to the unhomely or uncanny.[21] But this possibility is limited by the presentation of multiculturalism within a political framework of pluralism, of parallel and homogeneous differences that serve to emphasise certain aspects of ethnicity and ignore others. Beyond these limitations, the multicultural has the potential to challenge imagined communities, a potential that has been most clearly recognised by a number of staunch defenders of Anglomorphism. Despite their energetic drawing of boundaries, the social—and even the biological—reality of the Australian population is one of heterogeneity and hybridity. At the last count, 67.3 per cent of the population described their ethnic origins as mixed English and something else. Ethnic purity, therefore, is increasingly illusory; the same can be said of cultural purity. Ideas, beliefs and practices that delineate particular ways of life are being transformed and renegotiated in different contexts, and reassembled within specific social fields.[22] Remembering that these fields are terrains of struggle, it is still possible to maintain some optimism about practices of living across difference in Australia.

I would also urge some optimism about gender relations in Australia, both on the grounds of heterogeneity and on the grounds of considerable achievement which we often fail to recognise. This is by no means to deny ongoing oppressions, but to evaluate and contextualise sources of strength. The competition for hierarchies of oppression often leads us to misrecognise both our strengths and our privileges.

Before I conclude, I want to return briefly to one of the social categories that I mentioned at the outset. That is the category of age. The question of ageing is remarkable for its absence from most feminist literature, although Germaine Greer has recently made a major contribution to the study of menopause, and Ursula Le Guin wrote her wonderful piece 'The Space Crone' in 1976. (This publication is not mentioned by Greer, despite its relevance to her own argument. Perhaps this kind of omission speaks to the problem that I canvass here.)[23] Both Greer and Le Guin were motivated partly by their own menopauses, and this subjective aspect of feminist writing probably accounts in part for the neglect of ageing. The earliest feminist activists, of course, would never have mentioned such matters, but they were certainly old enough to have done so—in other words, older women have not always been regarded as marginal to feminism. However, those feminists were also well endowed with cultural, and usually material capital; as we have seen, class, as well as ethnicity, has been backgrounded by the perspective of white, middle-class, Anglophone feminist writers. But the absence of elderly women is remarkable, given that we all have mothers—at least—and that we are all likely to age. Some of the hostility of younger women, including feminists, towards older women strongly challenges notions of sisterhood—

and daughterhood. Toril Moi's analysis of the obliteration of the Oedipal mother is pertinent here, as is the possibility that older women evoke fear and rejection of ageing as a condition of relative powerlessness.[24] Some of the feminist discussions about bodies and Bourdieu's work on *habitus* can, however, direct attention to ways of questioning cultural constructions of bodies that can include age, ethnic and class cultures as well as gender.[25] If we consider the embodiment of social conditions, we can note that the increasing physical inflexibility of ageing is accompanied by a form of cultural immobility: an exclusion from social and sensual pleasures considered more appropriate for younger people. The social memories of the elderly are deemed irrelevant to those concerned with technocratic know-how, speed and material production. As a result, older people tend to be marginalised and rendered socially silent.

At the same time, ageing is increasingly a feminist issue as both later life and, by association, poverty are increasingly feminised: three-quarters of the aged poor in Australia are women, largely because of their experience as unpaid or poorly paid workers.[26] For the elderly, as for women generally, the various forms of capital described by Bourdieu are of crucial importance. This applies especially to material capital, but also to cultural and symbolic capital, including the status of motherhood and the social recognition of wisdom and experience.

Studies that interrelate ethnicity and ageing provide some evidence of the balancing of these forms of capital. Blakemore (1989) suggests that race, ethnicity, class and gender may represent stronger influences on the experience of old age than membership of an age cohort.[27] The authors of an extensive survey of American studies on ageing and ethnicity also urge that ethnicity be seen in interaction with these factors as well as that of sex.[28] Their comparison of Blacks, Hispanics, Native Americans and those of European origin indicates that the pervasive emphasis on subjective evaluations of well-being obscures the significance of relative disadvantage among the elderly. In their view, gerontologists must also examine the broader economic and political processes, i.e. both the objective and subjective. These conclusions echo some of the themes traced in this chapter, especially the need for relational perspectives that emphasise the interweaving, and include the intractable tangles, of various ways of living across difference.

SIX

A Contemporary View of Aboriginal Women's Relationship to the White Women's Movement

Jackie Huggins

As women we have all been subject to divide and rule socialisation, and racist and sexist ideologies. However, the overwhelming evidence and experience of Aboriginal women points to the fact that they remain discriminated against due to their race rather than their gender. For example, a cosmetically apparent Aboriginal woman is regularly stereotyped on the basis of being a boong, coon, nigger, gin or abo far in excess of being a 'woman'. The lack of recognition and real understanding of this political difference is a major issue still to be resolved by the white women's movement.

Aboriginal women fight not only the material but also the cultural pressures which have sought to construct them according to someone else's mould. Western theory, language, academia—to name a few—are foreign constructs in which Aboriginal women do not fit. Therefore an oppressive society controls and manipulates Aboriginal women and in turn dictates how they should behave, think, learn, speak, write etc. White feminism and women's studies are white cultural products which have been guilty of all of the above. With this in mind much of the following therefore will be written in Aboriginal terms of reference—a genre which, like full-blown bourgeois intellectualism, may tend to alienate the readership of 'others'. This style is used deliberately as the author's political statement and preference in order to elevate the powerless and to negate the superiority of the powerful.

To analyse the relationship between Aboriginal women and white feminists, it is necessary to look at the history of contact between these two quite distinct political groups. In the late 1950s and 1960s, much of the Aboriginal movement's focus shifted to the national level and links were made between Aboriginal women in many states through bodies like the Federal Council of Aborigines and Torres Straits Islanders (FCAATSI) and One People of Australia League (OPAL), during the campaigns to change the federal Constitution and end the assimilationist denial of Aboriginal culture. This campaign, in which Aboriginal women played vital political roles, had a great moral victory in the 1967 Referendum to have Aborigines included in the census and to have the Commonwealth assume responsibility for Aboriginal affairs. Aboriginal pressure then intensified to turn this into a real commitment in terms of new policies and particularly land rights, and so the Aboriginal movement was a very obvious element on the political scene by the early 1970s.

It was under these circumstances that the emerging Women's Liberation Movement met the Aboriginal movement. In their enthusiasm to be anti-racist, white women simply invited Aboriginal women to join their movement, with little apparent recognition of the full horror of racism in australia, nor of how it continued to damage Aboriginal men as well as women. In asking Aboriginal women to stand apart from Aboriginal men, the white women's movement was, perhaps unconsciously, repeating the attempts made over decades by welfare administrations to separate Aboriginal women and use them against their communities. While there were Aboriginal women who were deeply aware of the politics of sexism, many reacted with anger at the limited awareness of racism shown by the white women's movement.[1]

Aboriginal women insisted that the Women's Liberation Movement recognise that the conditions they faced were different. The white women's movement argued, for example, that compared to men, women in australia were poorly educated and worked in poorly paid jobs. Yet Aboriginal women were better educated than Aboriginal men, and when they were able to be employed, they worked in better-status jobs than Aboriginal men. The white women's movement was at that time concerned with sexuality and the right to say 'yes', to be sexually active without condemnation. For Aboriginal women, fighting denigratory sexual stereotypes and exploitation by white men, the issue was more often the right to say 'no'. Where white women's demands to control their fertility were related to contraception and abortion, Aboriginal women were subject to unwanted sterilisation and continued to struggle against the loss of their children to interventionist welfare agencies. While Aboriginal women insisted on their rights to have access to full medical services, including information about contraception, their demands to control their own fertility were related to the right to have as many children as they wanted.[2]

The Women's Liberation Movement learnt such lessons slowly and somewhat painfully, as it grappled with issues of class and race over the next two decades. A more diverse and complex white women's movement has continued a relationship with Aboriginal women which at times has been tense and distant, but at other times has allowed close personal support and productive organisational alliances.[3] Tensions persist, however, because Aboriginals are still concerned that the white women's movement does not appreciate how racism shapes sexism, nor the needs of Aboriginal women to be supported in strengthening their whole community and ensuring their children's futures.[4]

Australian historiography has been notably silent about relationships between white women and Black women and, in particular, female employers and their Aboriginal servants. It is imperative that any discussion of race and gender includes the issue of oppression of Black women by white women, however. Indeed, given the effort devoted to feminist consciousness-raising and the quest to expose oppression of women by men, it is ironical that white women have usually excluded such a critical analysis from their purview. In white feminist writings, a wall of silence invariably has been maintained on this issue. The focus has been on 'women' as an entity as constituting the oppressed. Yet this literature has never raised the question of whether women themselves are oppressors. Instead, there has been a tendency to equate the situation of white women with that of all women. When the complex factors of race and gender are considered, however, white women's activities have to be seen as a part of the colonisation and oppression of Black women. Certainly, sisterhood was not powerful enough to transcend such racial boundaries.

There is a growing body of evidence which describes how Black women were treated by their white counterparts. In several recent works, Aboriginal women authors have begun to expose the gross inequality of female inter-relationships, and the dynamics of the oppression of Black by white. Such oppression was most pronounced in the domestic servant sphere. When Aboriginal girls and women were sent into domestic service, they found that the 'boss' was almost invariably a female. White female employers also designated their white domestics as unequal, but Black workers were held in even lower regard. At times, close bonds did develop between white and Black women, but the boundaries of the unequal relationship were clearly defined by the former along the lines of class and race. Furthermore, in many situations Aboriginal women were subject to quite brutal treatment by white women.[5]

In *Wandering Girl*, Glenyse Ward describes at length how she was mistreated by her female employer.[6] Her story illustrates that the domination of Aboriginal women by white women has a very recent history. Ward has shown how white women in the 1960s displayed all the characteristic notions of racial superiority in their treatment of Aboriginal employees. As Kathy Willetts's review states:

> Mrs. Bigelow's sneering references to 'my Black servant' indicate a deeply felt racism, metonymic of the racism of the bigoted country Australians of the time . . . Told in stark and simple language, the account Ward gives sets up a series of readily decodable signs which offer a preferred reading of the text in support of Aboriginal claims for redress of violently oppressive conditions imposed on them until as late as the 1960s.[7]

Kathy Willetts's critique is apposite; it sets the precedent for Aboriginal women to review other Black women's books, thus creating Black perspectives of Black perspectives—a promising new departure in australian literary criticism.

Clearly the issue of oppression of Black women by white women is a contentious issue, requiring far more attention in the future. Yet the work of Black writers and their experiences illustrate that race and gender relations cannot be considered in isolation, one from the other. Myrna Tonkinson observes:

> The virtual absence of friendship between Black and White women in colonial Australia, at the same time as sexual relationships between Black women and White men were widespread, is an apparent paradox. Yet, it makes sense in the logic of colonial relations. In all colonial relations there is an assumption by the colonisers that they are inherently superior to the colonised . . . Since friendship is founded on notions of affinity and equality between individuals, it is not a condition to which colonial settings are conducive.[8]

These comments about the colonial era are still relevant today. White feminists' continued attempts to impose their politics onto Aboriginal women despite Aboriginal women's clear rejection is most certainly an attempt at intellectual colonisation.

Aside from the domestic servant sphere, the oppression of Aboriginal women and children by white women was also extreme in the fields of welfare and education, and this situation continues today. Many Aboriginal children have suffered brutally at the hands of white women who have always known what 'is best' for these children. White women were and are still a major force in the implementation of government policies of assimilation and cultural genocide. As welfare workers, institution staff, school teachers, and adoptive and foster mothers, white women continue to play major oppressive roles in the lives of Aboriginal women and children.

Racism in the welfare and education systems continues to be a major focus of Aboriginal women's political struggles today. These are the issues which Aboriginal women activists often see as priorities rather than those taken up by white feminists. The stealing of Aboriginal children is one of the greatest political concerns of Aboriginal women today. Unfortunately, it has too often been white women responsible for tearing Black children from their mothers' arms and placing them in the care of other white women who often abused them. Whilst this practice is allowed to continue, there can be no peace or true political alliances between Black and white women in this country.

It is no excuse to say that white women are not the ones who make oppressive government policies: they have played crucial roles in the support and implementation of these policies, in both paid and unpaid capacities. In this sense, white women cannot be seen as powerless in the face of male power as they are in fact collaborators in the use of white (male) power against Black people. When Aboriginal women, either as mothers or community workers or political activists, challenge the racist abuse of their children, they too often find themselves struggling against a white women who is defending individual or institutional racism. Generally Black women feel no relief to find that they are dealing with a white woman instead of a white man in these matters. Many say they prefer to deal with white men because they then escape the missionary-style zeal that some feminists employ in their belief that because they are feminists they are experts on *all* women and that Aboriginal women need 'raising up' to their level of feminist consciousness. And so we see that colonialism is alive and well in the women's movement. Some feminists behave just like the missionaries' wives who wanted to raise Aboriginal women to the lofty heights of white women's sex roles and christianity, too arrogant to realise that Aboriginal women's traditional social, political and spiritual roles gave them a far better position than white women could ever imagine.

White feminists, generally using middle-class privileges, have successfully challenged the male power structures of governments and now have significant input into policies and practices affecting women and girls. It is vital that they also challenge their own inherent racism, both individually and collectively, in analysis, policy and practice. Otherwise, as white women become empowered through the women's movement, their roles as oppressors of Aboriginal women and children will be multiplied and reinforced rather than dismantled. Aboriginal women may therefore find themselves more opposed to white women than previously. The increasingly powerful role of femocrats in government structures opens up areas where white women might share with Aboriginal women the benefits gained through the women's movement—if Aboriginal women's demands are respected and the politics of difference is understood. These possibilities are clearly evident in the fields of education and welfare policy development. However, given white women's general lack of analysis and real *understanding* of racism both within the movement and society in general, Aboriginal women continue to be extremely sceptical that 'sisterhood is powerful' in a *positive* sense in relation to white women. It seems we are still saying 'sisterhood might be powerful' in a positive sense. So far, white women have been very powerful in relation to Aboriginal women—unfortunately, in an unforgettably and at times overwhelmingly negative sense.

The politics of representation is another matter of concern for Aboriginal women which white women do not consider important enough to come to terms with. Aboriginal women's demand that they have the right to choose their own representatives in interactions with the women's movement is still opposed by some white feminists. White women do not appreciate the group cohesiveness and communal nature of relationships inherent in Aboriginal society: the connectedness which determines who actually does what, who has responsibility for what, who takes responsibility for saying things to whom, who does the saying, who does the writing. Women's position in Aboriginal culture, both traditional and contemporary, situates them within a powerful network of female support. This means that Aboriginal women put into practice the ideal which white feminists refer to as 'sisterhood'. This concept was borrowed by feminists from the Black civil rights movement in america, and is yet to be fully understood by white women, who still suffer the legacy of a patriarchal culture which divides them.

This powerful relationship between Aboriginal women has been practised since the Dreaming. It has been absolutely vital to the Aboriginal struggle to survive the attempted genocide since the invasion, and certainly will not be done away with for the sake of protecting white feminism! Some white women display a complete lack of respect for Aboriginal women's cultural values and political structures in their attempts to create divisions between Black women to serve the purpose of their tokenism. Despite this, Aboriginal women's unity remains strong at community, state and national levels, reinforced by the need to stand united against any form of racism.

White women do like to decorate their audiences with a few Black faces, exploiting Aboriginal women to protect themselves against charges of eurocentrism, but this only amounts to a special brand of feminist tokenism. When it comes to who represents Aboriginal women, an easy and accessible option for white women is to ignore (even after they have been directed about) these necessary structures which Aboriginals have ethically established in order to protect themselves against a usually ignorant and racist audience. Instead feminists tend to recruit Black women whom they acknowledge as 'safe', uncritical of them and hopefully espousing their ideals of womanhood and sisterhood. This practice reinforces white supremacy and is one of the lowest forms of maternalism.

On top of this, some white feminists still continue the racist practice of supporting white 'experts' to speak and write about Aboriginal women, thus maintaining their role of misinterpreting and misappropriating Aboriginal women's culture and history and undermining their politics. This practice reinforces the exploitative roles of 'expert' from the dominant colonising culture and 'subject' from the colonised and oppressed group. Aboriginal people would probably be one of the most researched groups on earth. Anthropologists, sociologists, criminologists and historians are some of the social scientists who have attempted to unravel the milieu of Aboriginal existence in australia. Male anthropologists who entered the field failed to recognise that their work operated within the limitations of their own gender biases as well as the gender restrictions within Aboriginal and Torres Strait Islander societies. So do white female researchers operate within certain limitations and expectations relating to both indigenous cultures and their own cultural realm. Black women are acutely aware of this and do not welcome uncredentialled researchers into their lives as much information has been misconstrued, abused and misused by some unscrupulous persons irrespective of gender.

White women's attempts to silence or control Aboriginal challenges to the inherent racism in feminist theory and practice of course serve to reinforce Aboriginal women's criticism that white feminists still do not recognise their own racism. White women are still not prepared to step outside their culturally determined frameworks or forgo their privileged positions of being part of the dominant culture. Unfortunately, some recent interactions between Black women and radical feminists have only increased the Aboriginal community's feelings of anger at the women's movement, reinforcing the sense of alienation which serves to drive the wedge in further to what was already a tenuous relationship. Whilst white feminist theory may espouse the *ideals* of sisterhood and solidarity, feminist practice continues to damage the possibility that this rhetoric is translated into *action*.

What white women do not realise is that, despite the general diversity of opinions in Aboriginal society, the strong stance that Aboriginal women take against the white women's movement remains universal. In evidence for this there has not been in australia to date, one published document by an Aboriginal or Torres Strait Islander woman who avidly supports the women's liberation movement. There is certainly no discussion of support for it either in Aboriginal community circles.

The commonality in views about the movement has led Aboriginal women to participate in inquisitively piecemeal ways at white women's conferences; but they become detached and again placed on the peripheries when challenges are made to a eurocentric agenda, to insensitive and offensive content matter, or they become excluded due to some valid concerns or goals which white feminists often overlook.

When attending these gatherings Aboriginal women are usually seen in several limited and oppressive ways. Foremostly as tokenistic, if we are at all articulate then we are exceptional, assimilated—too white to be

Black and too Black to be white, sharing and participating in white beliefs and values, angry, hostile, threatening and subversive to white women's interests, agendas and goals.

These perverse perceptions indicate that white women continue to regard Aboriginal women as inferior to them and will therefore insist on treating Black women accordingly. Due to ingrained racism Black women are not respected as women due to the temporary amnesia that persists, obscuring that we are, in fact, women too and not just Blacks. Black women experience a series of multiple simultaneous oppressions continuously.

Until there is a real understanding of racism in this country and genuine moves made toward racial equality, many Aboriginal women will not be prepared to talk publicly, to audiences of 'others', about the oppression they suffer through sexism. White feminists' interference in this issue is unwelcome, as to date it has only reinforced racist stereotypes of Aboriginal women, men and culture. However, in the meantime white women should not forget they do not exclusively 'own' feminism.

The often pathetic excuses given when Aboriginal women are not in attendance at women's conferences are that 'we don't know of any who would be interested', 'no-one came even though they were invited', 'but the Black american and Maori women are really into theoretical debates in their countries, why aren't the Aboriginal women here in australia?'. Well, perhaps they're just too smart to enter into yet another alien discourse and institution designed by and for whites without any consultation with Black people in the first place, a process which would simply repeat the whole history of Black–white relations since the invasion of this land.

It is also apparent that Aboriginal women are viewed as the 'other' based on a menial or sexual image: as more sensual but less cerebral, more interesting perhaps but less intellectual, more passive but less critical, more emotional but less analytical, more exotic but less articulate, more withdrawn but less direct, more cultured but less stimulating, more oppressed but less political than they are.

The reasons why Aboriginal women do not participate in the white women's movement are complex from the outset. Aside from the points already covered, other issues are:

- a closed women's movement which has never addressed the needs of Aboriginal women;
- exclusion of Black women, without conscience;
- the need to acknowledge our struggle as Blacks first;
- lack of understanding of the fact that race is imperative in any kind of gender analysis;
- unfamiliarity with, and dismissal of the process of colonisation and how it has affected all Aboriginal people, i.e. non-support of Aboriginal children and families;

- lack of consideration of our position with Aboriginal men and our extended family and communal networks;
- elitism and subordination of subjects and objects; and
- use of alienating and culturally insensitive theoretical discourses.

Without recognition of the above, there is no point in Black and white women entering into or continuing discussions together.

Many Aboriginal women view their incorporation into the white feminist movement with contempt and suspicion and as being equivalent to the old, patronising governmental doctrines of integration and assimilation. As with the assimilation process, which never worked anyway, we have no desire to be white so why bother; we have too many other barramundis to fry which concern our whole community and not just half. Our needs are too urgent to be addressed with anything except top priority and we cannot afford to educate and 'hang around' for white women to evolve. Instead of alleviating the burdens for Aboriginal women, white women usually add to them.

The challenge for women's studies today is that it needs to construct attractive and viable courses relevant to 'other' women, including Aboriginal and women from non-English-speaking backgrounds. Unless this is done it will not enable diversity and richness as women in the creative expression of their own experiences. There needs to be a constant theme of feminist politics of difference interwoven throughout every class interaction giving rise to the empowerment of students as women.

To acknowledge our differences as creative and to respect those differences for what they are, not what they appear to be, places women in a unique place. So much can be achieved in this way. Yet, without this realisation, there is no point in working out and continuing our struggles together. If these foundations are not laid, then a recipe for disaster awaits us and serves only to divide Black women and white women further. The failure to include Aboriginal women in terms defined by them is to construct culturally insensitive, alienating and inadequate feminist theories and policies. To universalise the experience of only white middle- and upper-class women is nonsensical, engendering massive and serious implications not only in women's studies but in the movement as a whole. Without a race analysis within the women's movement, Aboriginal women will always be on the margins and consider it an unnecessary and irrelevant social movement in which their voices will never be heard. The white women's movement in australia needs to implement some revolutionary zeal which overcomes oppression *per se* so that all women may benefit.

Aboriginal women are not prepared to engage in discussions with white women until meaningful and anti-racist discourses are constructed which transcend the barriers which separate us. At present Aboriginal women's experiences with white feminists prevent them from seeing dialogue as anything but a naive and tokenistic beginning, as race is finally surfacing on the agenda but still yet to be understood. On those occasions when there is collaboration between white and Black women, meaningful representations and negotiations with mentally and spiritually evolved white individuals or groups must occur in order to empower Aboriginal women and to address and work on their concerns. This might then mean that white feminists become part of the solution instead of the problem.

SEVEN

Between Old World 'Barbarism' and Stone Age 'Primitivism': The Double Difference of the White Australian Feminist

Marilyn Lake

Feminism's great animating insight lies in the recognition of the systematic nature of men's power over women; its concomitant blindspot is the frequent failure to see that the sisterhood of women also involves systematic relations of domination between women. This chapter is concerned with the domination that was at the heart of an emancipatory project.

For many years, critiques within and without feminism have pointed to the privileged position of middle-class and white Western women and challenged the right of such women to speak on behalf of all women. The case was made, for example, that the priorities and interests of middle-class, white, women were not the priorities and interests of working-class, black, women.[1] Analyses that assumed the importance of the private/public distinction to women's lives or critiqued the family as wholly oppressive were said not to be so relevant to poor Third World or immigrant women.[2] Aboriginal women have argued that the white feminist emphasis on abortion rights and birth control did not speak to a community concerned with the survival and rebuilding of families.[3] The priority accorded to gender as a category of social analysis was also a problem for many non-Western women, whose subordination could not be explained with reference to the narrowly sexualised category of 'women'.[4] Racism and political repression affected men as well as women; racism, it was observed, 'doesn't play favourites'.[5]

More recently, a body of writing that is variously termed Third World or post-colonial has begun to point to the fact that the feminist project was not white, Western and middle-class by accident. There were good reasons for its character and complexion. First, feminists tended to be white and middle-class, because they were not oppressed on account of their colour or class. Second, feminism could be seen as the product of a particular historical moment and context, the European 'woman movement' acquiring its meaning and metaphors in an imperialist world. Historical and anthropological investigations are beginning to suggest that feminist ideology and practice were shaped by 'the social, economic and political forces of imperialism to a far greater extent than has been acknowledged'.[6] In a study that explores the ways in which British feminists of the Victorian period 'constructed "the Indian woman" as a foil against which to gauge their own progress', Antoinette M. Burton has argued that an acknowledgment of 'the impact of empire on the British women's movement is one of the most urgent projects of late-twentieth-century Western feminism'.[7] The feminist goal of the 'advancement of women' was frequently explained with reference to the 'backwardness' of 'other', 'coloured' or 'primitive' women. The goal of the independence of women was both an emulation of the imagined condition of Western white men and a condemnation of the 'sex slavery' or 'chattel' status of women in 'backward' societies.

In an essay advocating the 'liberation of women' in 1915, Ada Holman, a socialist and feminist and 'for years a prominent worker in political and other organisations', declared: 'Let us, once for all, cast off the shackles of primitive woman and passionately demand, as it is ours to demand, the creation of the superwoman.' Primitive women were characterised by their 'specialisation as females' in the service of men: liberation meant women's accession to the status of independent non-specialised human beings. Moreover, the 'meek women must be saved in spite of themselves'.[8]

The imperial/colonial mentality enshrined 'whiteness' as a dominant value; feminism was not and is not immune to this racial ordering of the world. In a well-known 'reply' to Mary Daly's *Gyn/Ecology*, Audre Lorde criticised the text for its tendency to locate women's power and strength in white Western communities and traditions, while seeing African and Asian women only as 'victims and preyers-upon each other'.[9] Chandra Talpade Mohanty has drawn attention to the continuing centrality of 'Third World Difference' to contemporary Western feminist analysis. The representation of the 'Third World Woman' as the veiled, powerless, victim of barbaric religious and cultural practices underpins Western women's self-presentation as 'secular, liberated and in control of their own lives'.[10]

Post-colonial criticism has, then, produced an interrogation of feminism's complicit relations with Western Imperialism and pointed to the constitutive role of white supremacy in the intertwining of imperial and gender relations. Race is seen to be just as relevant a category in understanding the history and politics of white women as it is for black women. White gendered subjectivities and reformist political programmes are found to be formulated in explicit or implicit racial terms. In her pathbreaking work *Beyond the Pale*, Vron Ware traced 'ideas that have historically constructed definitions of white womanhood and to ask how these ideas have been formed either in conjunction with or in opposition to feminist ideology' (p. 24).

In this chapter, I suggest that distinctions made between white 'civilised' and black 'primitive' womanhood were integral to the formulation of the feminist project in Australia in the first half of the twentieth century, at a time when nation-builders were self-consciously constructing a White Australia. In settler colonies such as Australia and New Zealand, whiteness became a crucial marker of boundaries and status. Concerned to differentiate themselves from other (coloured) colonised peoples, white Australians stressed their common racial identity as Britishers. Yet white settler subjects occupied an ambiguous position as colonisers and colonised both. Subjugated and derided as colonials, white Australians were also heirs to the imperial project: internally in their occupation of Aboriginal lands and destruction of Aboriginal culture and languages; and externally in their role as administrators of Papua New Guinea.

A post-colonial framework helps us to see Western feminism's conceptual dependence on and contribution to imperial relations, even as it sought to challenge them. But, like the post-structuralist project to which it is sometimes allied, the logic of a post-colonialist stance may pose a profound challenge to the very viability of a feminist politics. As Micaela di Leonardo has observed, 'there is no place for any morally evaluative or politically committed stance within the disintegrating logic of post-structuralism'.[11] Yet feminism is surely inherently evaluative and judgemental, involved in making universalistic pronouncements about the good of women. Arguably, feminism is also inherently a missionary politics, concerned to rescue women from oppressive conditions, committed to saving women. How we reconcile general rules about human rights with the specificities and rights of cultural traditions is one of the vexed issues to be addressed by feminists and others in the 1990s. One way out of the apparent impasse has been opened up by black and Third World feminists keen to formulate their own versions of feminism—to reconceptualise ideas of resistance, community and agency in the contexts of their own cultures. Asian Pacific women need to 'affirm our own culture', writes Mitsuye Yamada, 'while working within it to change it'.[12]

'Black women's liberation also must be part and parcel of the whole liberation movement of black people in this country', asserted Lilla Watson, the Aboriginal activist.[13] What distinguishes Third World feminism, argues Chandra Talpade Mohanty, is this inextricable link forged between feminism and political liberation movements.[14] Such an alliance would seem to be the appropriate response to Western feminism's traditional dalliance with imperialism.

In April 1932 Mary Montgomery Bennett, a feminist advocate of the cause of Aborigines in Western Australia, wrote rapturously to Bessie Rischbieth about her work in training Aboriginal women in the skills of spinning and weaving:

> Ever since I have been here I have been longing for you to see this place and the development of the work which particularly appeals to me—an Australian woman's work for native women. It is grand, beautiful! an inspiration![15]

Mary Bennett's account of her work rested on a taken-for-granted distinction between 'Australian women'—white like herself—and 'native women'. As a feminist, Bennett believed in the necessity of economic independence for all women as the basis and precondition of their emancipation. The Aboriginal women with whom she worked earned income from the sale of articles, such as raffia brooches, which they themselves had made. The enterprise would not reap great profits, but 'it is enough that the women and girls can be self-supporting and are self-supporting. Economic dependence is the root of all evil.'[16]

Mary Bennett was working at the Mt Margaret Mission, managed by Pastor R. M. Schenk in an area near Laverton in southwest Western Australia. There she worked as a teacher to Aborigines, exploring novel teaching techniques, using craft as her medium. She came from a wealthy pastoral family and had been widowed in 1927. In 1930 at the age of forty-nine she published *The Australian Aboriginal as a Human Being*, a plea for Commonwealth responsibility for Aboriginal affairs. She became involved with the Women's Services Guilds in Perth, through which she established a close working relationship with Bessie Rischbieth. Widowed in 1925, Rischbieth, like Bennett, enjoyed an independent income that supported her work as a feminist activist in Australia and overseas.[17] President of the Women's Services Guilds between 1920 and 1922, Rischbieth was also a founder of the Australian Federation of Women Voters, which was formed to provide a national voice for Australian women in federal politics and international forums, such as the League of Nations. Feminists in affiliated bodies such as the Women's Services Guilds in Western Australia, the South Australian Non-Party Association and the Victorian Women's Citizens Movement were active in the 1930s in promoting the status and welfare of Aboriginal women.

Bennett and Rischbieth recognised the importance of an independent income for women. They joined with other feminists of their time in a critique of 'sex slavery' that understood prostitution as the paradigmatic female condition. Oppression of various kinds was often theorised as 'slavery'—the socialist critique of 'wage slavery' had been anticipated by feminists' identification of 'sex slavery' and later, 'white slavery'. Whereas 'sex slavery' frequently referred to prostitution and/or marriage, white slavery referred to the abduction of women, especially white women, by Old World slave-traders for the use of men in all parts of the world. All three terms operated as metaphors diverting attention, as all metaphors do, from the original term: the trade in black bodies. Metaphors operate as disappearing acts, but the rabbit does not really vanish. In denunciations of 'sex slavery' and its significant derivative 'white slavery', the blackness of 'real slaves' was an absent presence. I have argued elsewhere that when Australian feminists gave priority to the goal of 'independence' rather than equality in the early twentieth century, they did so because of an engagement with a socialist tradition which had long critiqued capitalism's imposition of a condition of dependency on the proletariat.[18] There is, however, another dimension to feminism's espousal of independence which will be explored here. Feminism's emphasis on independence as the proper condition of women was underpinned by understandings of the status of whiteness and a primitivist discourse on the natural condition of native women.[19] The advancement of women—white Western women—was predicated on the backwardness of other women.[20] Feminism was thus inherently imperialistic. The investment in feminism's civilising mission was reinforced in Australia when feminists in Western Australia and South Australia came face to face with 'other' women. The 'independence of women' gained its meaning in contradistinction to dependence as the natural condition of primitives and natives. 'As we care for, or neglect, the welfare and development of this dependent race,' advised the Association for the Protection of Native Races, in 1933, 'so the honour or dishonour rests upon every man and woman of the British race in Australia.'[21] Natives were placed in Protectorates; they were wards of the state and the dependants of the white man. In claiming independence, feminists were asserting their status as white, and claiming the rights of self-government enjoyed by white men. And in working towards the 'independence' of Aboriginal women, feminists were enabling them to become 'white' as well.

This paper suggests that the feminist project in Australia in the first thirty or so years of the twentieth century relied on a primitivist discourse that was fundamental in constituting the feminist identity as inherently imperialistic. The assumed backwardness of primitive Aboriginal society shaped feminist ideas about the way forward. Feminists' work with Aboriginal women was 'coloured' by their preoccupation with sex slavery and (white) Australian women's ever imminent fate—or so the propaganda suggested—of white slavery. When Australian feminists looked at Aboriginal women they saw, in a terrible moment of misrecognition, themselves. 'The plight of the native woman is pitiful', said West Australian feminist Ada Bromham. 'If we can do nothing for them, how can we hope to protect our own women?'[22] In rescuing Aboriginal women, they were saving themselves.

They were also forging a national identity. The broader context of Australian feminism can be located in feminists' double identity as colonial settler subjects positioned as both colonisers and colonised. Subject to the humiliations of being treated by the British as 'colonials', white Australians responded by asserting their status as white subjects and by redefining the meaning of Australian. In his novel *The Melbournians*, Francis Adams has his protagonist Susie MacGhie, recently returned from a trip to London, exclaim:

> I don't see why Australians shouldn't be proud of being Australians, and not be ashamed of owning it, as they are in England. One woman asked me once if I wasn't a Kaw-lonial, just as if you'd asked if you weren't a Haw-tentot or a Esquim-maw. I said no; I was an Aw-stralian.[23]

In order to distinguish themselves from other (coloured) colonised peoples—from Hottentots and Eskimos—Australian settlers attached special significance to the status and meaning of 'whiteness'.[24] Furthermore, in order to rebut the inferiority attributed to Australians as 'Kaw-lonials', Australian radicals and feminists reworked the distinction between civilised and non-civilised as a distinction between the democratic New World and the non-democratic Old World. In so doing they invoked Havelock Ellis' observation:

> The growth of a high civilization seems to be so closely identified with the economic freedom and independence of women that it is difficult to say which is cause and which is effect.[25]

It was within this conceptual framework that Australian women, already enfranchised, condemned the British government's 'barbaric' treatment of the suffragettes, with one Adelaide woman suggesting a petition from 'the free women of Australia' to be sent to the British prime minister deploring the infamous 'Cat and Mouse Act'.[26] A letter addressed to the Pankhursts from the 'Enfranchised Women of Australia' expressed appreciation of their struggle and pride in the knowledge that 'we are of your blood and race'. They compared their easier situation in a country 'where prejudices have not had time to crystallise so solidly as is the case in older lands longer under the sway of tradition and convention'.[27] Australian women's freedom would be defined in terms of the 'unfreedom' of both British and Aboriginal women.

As colonised and colonisers, Australian feminists shaped their New World identity in opposition to the 'Old World barbarism' of Britain and the older 'primitive barbarism' evident to them in Aboriginal society. The first differentiation is evident in an assessment by New South Wales labour activist Lilian Locke-Burns of women's comparative progress:

> In no other part of the civilized world as far as one can ascertain is so much being done by the state in the way of providing for mothers and children as in the Australian Commonwealth. In Great Britain and some other countries which lay claim to some share in democratic reforms, the mothers are only protected (if protection it may be called) under some form of social insurance. In the American states also very little has been done so far in this direction beyond some attention to delinquent children and the usual institutional efforts that we find in most countries which have evolved beyond the barbaric stage. Neither in England or America do we hear of any such humanitarian provision as the Australian Maternity Allowance.[28]

In this assessment of women's achievements, Locke-Burns was redefining the meaning of Australian in terms of a dichotomy between New World civilisation which treated women well and Old World barbarism which treated them poorly; at the same time, she cast some doubt on the older countries' claims to be really civilised. One of the most telling indictments against the Old World was its tolerance of that 'dark shadow' white slavery:

> The White Slave Traffic—that dark shadow that hangs over all the older countries of the civilised world—that huge octopus whose tentacles reach wherever in the crowded town of the Old World is a fair young girl without influential friends to protect her.[29]

White Slavery was always characterised as a phenomenon of the Old World, its agents coming across the seas to invade Australia.

In the Old World 'fair girls' were at risk. In the New World they would come into their own as independent—self-supporting, self-reliant and self-governing citizens. The Victorian feminist journal *Woman Voter* cast women's advancement in matching temporal and geographical terms:

> [In the] old order women were regarded primarily as sex creatures . . . to be chosen by men as sex mates, not primarily even as mothers of the race but as outlets for the sexual impulses and alleged needs of men . . . this was the old chattel idea of things.

In the 'new and sweeter order' brought about by 'woman's rebellion against exploitation of her body in and out of marriage, women would attain a greater degree of independence, marriage would be placed on a higher plane and self-restraint would prevail'.[30] The temporal distinction had a geographic analogue. In its support of White Slavery, the Old World was no better than 'primitive' societies: they were all distinguished by their commitment to 'the old chattel idea of things'.

By the early 1930s, a number of Australian feminists had become active in Australia and in Britain in publicising the deplorable treatment and conditions of Aboriginal people. In the southern states, a group of women organised around Bessie Rischbieth, Mary Montgomery Bennett, Mrs Tennant Cooke, Mrs Britonarte James and Mrs Edith Jones. They became politically active in the interests of Aboriginal women, as they saw them, lobbying parliamentarians and other women's groups on issues such as constitutional change to effect Commonwealth control, land rights, citizenship rights, education and sexual exploitation—the 'almost universal traffic in our unfortunate native women and children'.[31] Bennett and Rischbieth considered that as it was men who perpetrated and benefited most from the exploitation of Aborigines, it was up to women—white women—to change the situation. Moreover, as advanced, enlightened women, they had a responsibility to do so: 'We free women are responsible for the continuance of these evils, because we are not sharing our light with our Aboriginal fellow women.'[32] Feminism was clearly imbued with a missionary project: as feminists, they had a special responsibility to share their light; as women, they had special capacities. In 1933 representatives from thirteen women's groups, including the Woman's Christian Temperance Union, the National Council of Women, the Country Women's Association and the Labor Women's Organisation, wrote letters to the Western Australian government requesting that at least one woman be appointed to the forthcoming Royal Commission on the treatment of Aborigines in that state: 'psychologically it is only women who can measure up the needs of the native woman who are the key to the position'.[33] 'Native women' were the key to the position of Aboriginal people because of their use and abuse as 'sex slaves'—by both Aboriginal men and white men. Here was the problem of woman and man in black and white: dependent women open to exploitation by lustful men. The native women must attain independence; the white man had to practise restraint and self-control. All women had to be protected from men.

Mary Bennett—white woman, feminist and determined activist—gave much thought to the position of Aboriginal women, and put her extended analyses into speeches and writing.[34] In a speech to the British Commonwealth League in London in June 1933, she detailed her experiences in the southwest region of Western Australia, where she found Aboriginal women in a 'borderland of transition' between the 'wild life' of 'native culture' and 'white civilisation'. The passage between the one and the other had produced a 'terrible crop of evils', but there was no future in a return to 'native culture' because in that 'primitive' world: 'All power is vested in these older men, and their rule, as with all primitive cultures, is hard on women.' In Bennett's assessment, women in Aboriginal society were 'first and last, just "property" at patriarchal disposal', and the property status caused 'women and children to suffer also the evils of infant betrothal, child marriage, polygamy and *wife-lending*' (her emphasis). 'Civilisation' had not improved Aboriginal women's lot, however. In fact 'their conditions [had] become very much worse'. On the one hand, dispossession had led to slow starvation; on the other, women had been forced into 'wholesale prostitution'—'originally property, they have now become "merchandise" '. Bennett recommended the allocation of land rights—'adequate territories where the natives can live in communities of their own, unmolested by whites, and learn to grow their own food'.[35]

The 'molesting whites' whom Bennett had in mind here were men such as the police officers who regularly fathered 'half-caste' children. She, like other feminists, believed that for women to be free they needed to 'advance' beyond their condition as 'creatures of sex'—to live on a 'higher plane'. On the new reserves Aborigines would not resume their 'patriarchal' tribal life, but rather be incorporated into civilisation, rendered more civilised by feminist monitoring. In reporting on her textiles work with Aboriginal women to Bessie Rischbieth, Bennett had recounted the story of Linda, a 'fine capable girl, with an instinctive passion for purity'. Linda was 'betrothed in infancy to an old man, a witch doctor, and a dirty old man at that. She loathes him but some years ago he took her, and there is no escape . . .'[36] Bennett herself seemed to evince a particular loathing for older men's sexuality. Through her feminist lens, Aboriginal elders appeared as 'dirty old men'—from whom Aboriginal women needed to be protected. 'Patriarchy' in the literal sense of rule by older men was thus particularly repugnant. Having 'committed the crime of being born *girls*', Aboriginal girls were 'foredoomed to give their clean little bodies to dirty old men in the bush who can claim them by native right'.[37] But younger democratic white men were just as bad. The continuing sex slavery of women was civilisation's one great contradiction: on the new reserves Aboriginal women would have access to education and 'all the other rights that are founded on education'. If this scenario excluded 'molesting' police officers, it depended entirely on the intervention of white teachers and instructors such as Bennett herself.

Primitivist discourses cast black women as rampantly sexual, uninhibited in their desires.[38] The terms used to refer to Aboriginal women in Australia—gin, black velvet, lubra—denoted their primary sexual identity, which in turn established their difference from white women. Reformers recognised the power of words in shaping a reality. Professor

A. P. Elkin of the anthropology department at the University of Sydney was asked if he could, in his capacity as new president of the Association for the Protection of Native Races, assist in deprecating the use of the term 'lubra': 'people seem to think that it is not so heinous an offence to maltreat or mistreat a Lubra or a Gin, as it is to hurt a Girl or a Woman'.[39] Central to Mary Bennett's feminist project was the attempt to counter the stereotype of the native woman as naturally lascivious by insisting that she had an 'instinct for purity'. Aboriginal women could be like white women: 'the women, intrinsically, are fine, and ready for a position of respect and independence'.[40] As in the case of white women—degraded in white slavery, prostitution and marriage—their salvation was thought to lie in an independence won through work and citizenship.

Progressive reformers, men and women, all imagined the advancement of Aborigines in assimilationist terms in these years. At its most radical, the vision of integration had Aboriginal and non-Aboriginal Australians learning from each other, with an emergent Australian culture adopting the best from both worlds. 'A Native Policy for Australia', promulgated by a member of the Aborigines' Protection League, insisted that 'there are other kinds of civilisation and other kinds of democracy than the Anglo-Saxon type'. The solution to the exploitation and oppression of Aborigines by whites was

> for each race to live as citizens in its own community until such time as the disparity shall have been bridged, by one race giving up its extreme competitiveness and the other race giving up its extreme communalism and by educational advance.[41]

Neither progressive men nor women had much time for extreme communalism, however, and the interdependence, collectivism and reciprocity that characterised traditional Aboriginal society were profoundly at odds with the independence championed by feminists.

When progressive men imagined an assimilated community they usually advocated one of two strategies. One was 'biological absorption': the putting aside of racial prejudice to enable free inter-marriage.[42] This 'absorption of blacks by the whites' did not envisage Aboriginal men embracing white women. Rather, white men were the active parties here, their semen acting as a bleaching agent. The other strategy incorporated black men, providing them with decent wages to enable them to emulate white breadwinners:

> Employed natives should be attracted to service by good conditions, like employed whites, and they should be enabled to save their wages with a view to improving the position of their family.[43]

In both scenarios, Aboriginal women were cast in the role of wives—of white or black men.

To feminist activists, Aboriginal women were the quintessential sex slaves—an object lesson in the consequences of dependence. Prostitution and the 'half-caste problem' both resulted 'very largely from the same cause—their dependence'.[44] Feminist interaction with Aboriginal society reinforced their account of the world. They advocated neither biological absorption nor marriage. Their idea of salvation was, however, no less assimilationist. They sought to dissolve the distinction between Australian and native by invoking the sisterhood of all women, united in their passion for purity. The solution, like the solution for white women, was independence. In the words of a 'Call to the Women of Australia to Demand an Honourable Native Policy', the most fundamental reform of all was 'the right of women to the sanctity of the person'.[45] But as a politics caught up in the dynamics of colonialism, feminism engaged in an emancipatory project predicated on white domination and the refusal of difference. Feminists shut their eyes to the critique of independence implicit in Aboriginal culture. In their preoccupation with independence, feminists were complicit in the Western masculinist mythology of the self-made man, a myth that stigmatised dependence as 'parasitism' and served to deny human interdependence, in particular men's dependence on women.

What did the Aboriginal women, who were the objects of the feminist rescue mission, think? It is, of course, difficult to know, but some records remain. In 1933 some self-styled 'half-caste women of Broome' petitioned the members of the Royal Commission enquiring into the conditions of Aborigines. Their plea was that they be classified as whites, not natives, because then they would not be subject to the regulations of the 1905 Aborigines Act: 'we ask our freedom, so that when the chance comes along we can rule our lives and make ourselves true and good citizens'. This demand for self-rule was prompted not by the desire for independence but for marriage: 'the chance to marry a man of our choice'.[46]

In her book *Gone Primitive*, Marianna Torgovnick notes that Western discourse on the primitive is not just outer-directed, but 'inner-directed—salving secret wounds, masking the controller's fear of losing control and power' (p. 192). When Australian feminists such as Mary Bennett looked at Aboriginal women, they saw their own worst fears realised. Women were bartered like a 'bale of wool' or 'taken by a claimant'.[47] Women lacked self-possession and self-government. The 'dark shadow' cast by white slavery threatened to engulf 'fair women' too. Australian women and girls were constantly warned against white slave agents in their midst, agents dispatched invariably from London. White men's lusts—their perversely primitive sexual urges—threatened not just the sanctity of women's bodies, however, but white civilisation itself. In succumbing to the primitive, white men became degenerates: they lost their qualities proper to their race and forfeited their place in the world. In losing sexual control, the white man would lose political control. In 1934 Mary Bennett—descendant of pastoral pioneers—wrote in distress to Bessie Rischbieth of the 'madness' of her fellow whites:

> I cannot see how white supremacy in the Pacific can last out this decade even. We, I mean white supremacy, is in the most imminent danger and everybody is blind. In my view, our only chance of survival is to put our 'spiritual' house in order and do it mighty quick.[48]

Such were the dimensions of the challenge as defined by the colonised and colonising feminist.

EIGHT

'Inducements to the Strong to be Cruel to the Weak': Authoritative White Colonial Male Voices and the Construction of Gender in Koori Society

Patricia Grimshaw and Andrew May

On 10 May 1854 Edward Parker delivered a lecture in the Mechanics Hall in Melbourne to the John Knox Young Men's Association, on the chosen topic 'The Aborigines of Australia'. Parker had served as Assistant Protector of Aborigines in Victoria (known as the Port Phillip district until 1851) as part of a British colonial effort to contain the devastation of Koori lives on this imperial frontier. An evangelical Christian, Parker had a record of offering Kooris assistance in numbers of ways, including at times public advocacy for their interests. In 1840 he had angrily summarised the Kooris' plight as white settlers flooded across their lands in this style:

> to be beaten back by the 'white man's foot'—to be excluded, perforce, from lands which they unquestionably regard as their own property, and from scenes as dear to them as our own native homes to us—despoiled—denied the rights of humanity— classed with and treated as wild dogs—I can entertain no other expectation but that they will be driven to more frequent depredations, and exposed to more rapid and certain destruction.[1]

His condemnation of the British imperial project in Victoria was a far cry from other colonial characterisations of the expansion of empire in Australia, and one that set Parker apart from most of his peers.

We isolate a detail from his wide-ranging lecture. At one point Parker attempted an energetic refutation of an error which had become widely believed: that there was a crucial difference between Aboriginal women and European women in reproductive capacity. In 1839 the explorer Count Strzelecki had originated the belief that once an Aboriginal woman had sexual relations with a European man and bore a child to him, she lost the ability to conceive a child with a man of her own race. We might point to sterility arising from venereal disease. Strzelecki's intention was otherwise, suggesting that there were genetic differences between Aborigines and Europeans. Parker gave Strzelecki's statement an unqualified and indignant denial—indignant, he said, because its source lay in a denial of 'the Scriptural statement that man has one, common parent, and that God has made of one blood all nations upon earth'. [2]

Parker's effort to assert the shared humanity between Aborigines and Europeans went unrewarded in this instance. Robert Brough Smyth, a scientific administrator and member of the Board for the Protection of the Aborigines, took this fiction up again in his 1876 publication, *The Aborigines of Victoria*. Smyth painstakingly cited specific examples of Koori women who had borne children successively to European and then Aboriginal fathers. There were no grounds, said Smyth, to believe Aborigines to be different from any others of the human species, yet repetition of Strzelecki's error provided 'the text of some lay sermons intended to elevate the white man at the expense of his darker brother'. He expressed the hope that those, whose habit till now had been

> to dogmatise on questions of so much importance may enquire and investigate before they promulgate opinions which are likely to retard the advance of science, embitter the relations between races whose interests are conflicting, and offer inducements to the strong to be cruel to the weak.[3]

In the 1880s James Bonwick was, however, reiterating in print the same biological lie, and so the error continued.[4] Colonists, it seemed, were keen to discover such clues as part of a spurious search for inborn differences between the two groups of people confronting each other at this site of conflict.

Both Edward Parker and Robert Brough Smyth demonstrated some acuity in their real sense of the ways in which the public statements of self-styled white experts on Aborigines could enter a political discourse—one that was very damaging to Aborigines—at a level sometimes far broader than their authors' specific intentions. In this instance Parker and Smyth demonstrated a consciousness of the ways in which those people who asserted knowledge claims, shaped definitions of Aboriginality. These definitions were critical for oppressive white settler conduct towards the indigenous people of the colony. What they seemed unaware of was the extent to which they themselves, and a number of other men who were similarly placed in relation to Kooris, voiced observations that, while denying the fiction of biological difference, stressed cultural difference in ways also highly problematic for Koori fortunes. These very white men, many of whom proposed themselves as advocates for Koori interests, were bounded by their own conceptions of normative behaviour, and were exposed to brief, fragmented moments of the lives of Kooris. Yet they nevertheless made self-confident truth claims that said as much about their own cultural values as they did about the realities of Koori lives. The information they spread through their speaking and writing, whether based on first-hand observations or on evaluations of others' observations, had as much margin for erroneous and destructive impact as did Strzelecki's.

It was white men rather than white women who, by virtue of their hegemonic hold on positions of power, were able to define Koori culture in public ways. White women found other means within public and private arenas of establishing social distances along racial lines. In this instance it is to certain white men that we have turned our attention. There were various issues on which they focused their gaze. One focus common to all was of vital significance for definitions of Kooris, and hence more broadly for their contribution to a white imperial discourse: their representation of gender in Koori society, of Koori women's life experiences relative to those of Koori men.

In recent years numbers of feminist post-colonial scholars have drawn attention to the crucial role of colonial representations of gender in non-Western societies in the legitimation of the imperial project. Where indigenous women could be portrayed as oppressed by men of their own group, the destruction of the traditional culture through western appropriation of indigenous resources and political systems could be made to appear moral. Lata Mani, for example, in describing British reactions to *sati* (or suttee) in colonial India, declared the situation more complex than 'we came, we saw, we were horrified, we intervened'. The existence of the practice of *sati* 'provided ground for the development of other agendas', cherished by British officials and missionaries, that were vastly more far-reaching than the apparent chivalrous endeavour to 'rescue' indigenous women from harm.[5]

This chapter similarly examines the discursive practices of certain colonial men who appropriated the right to define the position of women and the nature of gender relations in Koori society. It is not the information about Koori women and gender which these men purported to set forth which interests us, but the discursive practices the men employed to define their 'otherness'.[6] We suggest that here, too, the highly negative style of this discourse, intended to be descriptive but in fact highly racist, in turn was used as the century proceeded to justify oppressive settler behaviour and increasingly harsh public policies towards Koori women, men and children.

The men whose writings we examine here who played a crucial part in public construction of Koori society and culture based their right to speak on various claims.[7] There were the Protectors and Assistant Protectors of Aborigines, of whom Edward Parker was one, who in the 1840s were appointed to make some efforts, poorly supported by colonial authorities, to moderate the harsh impact of white invasion. Ostensibly humanitarian, their project was essentially to segregate Kooris spatially and thus collude in the settlement process. There were the first missionaries who shared the protectors' agenda of introducing Kooris to Western ways of living and Christian religious beliefs. Such men wrote for colonial officials, church authorities and local church audiences. A few others—the squatters Edward Curr and Charles Griffith and the draftsman and artist George Haydon, for example—took a personal interest in Kooris in the early phase of white presence; they asserted knowledge claims, and wrote to sell their accounts to a British readership avid for exotic news of their far-flung empire. As with protectors and missionaries, their stance towards Kooris was problematic—Curr himself in his early bush days clearly showed a readiness to murder Kooris—and they shared much in outlook with the philanthropists and missionaries, even if they were less explicit in their moral condemnation of Koori culture.[8]

There were also men who engaged in an interest in Koori society through the path of new sciences. They usually had concerned themselves with many aspects of Victoria, giving European names and qualities to climate, vegetation, rocks and soil. They moved with similar brashness, at times bordering on callousness, to a chronicle of the lives of Kooris, the first users of the terrain. In the 1870s and 1880s, men such as Robert Brough Smyth and Alfred Howitt (Curr joined their ranks) compiled their own and others' retrospective observations of Kooris, drawing often on information supplied by the men who had had early contact.[9] By these decades small groups of the fifty or more original Koori clans remained, and most lived on missions and reserves; but the men of science had few qualms about establishing the facts, as they saw them, of Koori culture. These men of science, like the rest, spoke from the subject position—albeit sometimes unstable and shifting—of the white middle-class male of mid-nineteenth-century British, Christian cultural background: all ethnocentric at best, and racist at worst.

These men who claimed authority to speak about Koori society in nineteenth-century Victoria knew, and made it clear they knew, that the reason for the desperate straits within which Kooris found themselves revolved around two points of tension between invaders and the invaded: over white settlers' access to Koori lands, and over white male settlers' sexual access to Koori women. A travel diary kept over the space of a few months by George Augustus Robinson, who was appointed Chief Protector of Aborigines in the late 1830s, makes this point forcefully, and may usefully establish something of the specific historical context within which the so-called experts' construction of Koori culture began to take shape.

George Augustus Robinson made a tour on horseback and foot through the Western District of the Port Phillip District from May to August in the year 1841. His brief was to gather information for the lieutenant governor, Charles La Trobe, on Koori numbers, their physical condition, and the treatment they were receiving from the white settlers who had rushed to occupy land since the first squatters established a foothold in the mid-1830s. The detailed journal kept by Robinson during his journey must be read as the product of a white Christian man in a position of some power who was colluding with those bent on appropriating Koori lands: the British authorities were offering sufficient philanthropic gestures to salve their consciences. Robinson personally, at the same time, evinced more sympathy with the Kooris' difficult situation than the majority of his countrymen. When asked by English settlers what 'the natives' would possibly do with the land if whites did not cultivate it productively, Robinson would reply: 'The answer is plain—they could live upon it and enjoy the pleasures of the chase as do the rich of our own nation.'[10] Robinson's account introduces graphically the sites of contestation surrounding white appropriation of Koori lands and white oppression of Koori women.

Robinson noted with surprise that already whole tracts of land in the Western District of Victoria, described by the explorer Major Mitchell less than a decade earlier, were by 1841 sadly devoid of Kooris. Looking down the valley of Koroit, he found its beauty greatly diminished, he said, by evidence of this depopulation. He found this distressing.

> Sheep and cattle had supplanted its original occupants. The numerous native fires, seen by Mitchell, no longer darkened the air with smoke; not a solitary smoke of a native fire was to be seen. Nor do the original inhabitants roam in freedom and at will over the green hills and valleys of the Wannon as recorded by that traveller.[11]

Only two of the Koori clan who had lived around Portland Bay remained alive, and just one solitary old man from the district where the township of Portland was built. Robinson was not slow in facing the need to confront the reasons for this massive depopulation. One morning the squatter Edward Henty rode up to his camp in the company of a local Police Magistrate, James Blair, to report that a Koori had murdered one of Henty's fellow squatters, and the squatter's shepherd. Both Henty and Blair were greatly agitated, and in fear and rage expressed the terrible view that *all* the Kooris of this tribe should be exterminated. If Blair were governor, he would send soldiers to demand the murderer, and if this did not succeed, send in the soldiers to shoot the whole tribe. He himself could not seek out the murderer without taking at least twelve police, 'for he should have no power to restrain the settlers from shooting the women and children'.[12] Edward Henty had no doubt that settlers were 'dropping' (that is, murdering) Kooris: indeed, 'if a black was to lift a spear or attempt anything at him he would, if he had a gun, drop him, if the rope was ready to be put round his neck the next minute'.[13]

But there were other settlers not pretending to wait for 'provocation' to act in similar style. Whites more sympathetic to Kooris told Robinson that for every white man killed, twenty Kooris were shot. The squatters, the Winter brothers, had a swivel gun mounted at their home station: many homesteaders were well stocked with guns and ammunition. There were squatters who encouraged their men to shoot Kooris wherever and whenever they could 'because, thereby, they would the sooner get rid of them'.[14] Further, such squatters, rather than employ recent migrants, preferred emancipated convicts as workers; 'in other words, the conscience of the latter are seared and they will meet their wishes in destroying blacks'.[15] When a frightened young Koori woman appeared at Robinson's camp one evening to tell how three Kooris, 'Mary', 'Kitty' and 'Piccaninny Jenny', had been enticed by the promise of damper to approach some white men and then were shot, Robinson recorded: 'This through [threw] the tribe into grief and the cold indifference manifested by the white people horrified me.'[16] The young woman, an eyewitness to the crime, was too terrified to lodge a formal account, and in any case, Robinson's hands were tied because under the current law the evidence of Kooris was not admissible in court. Squatters and their men were bent on destroying remaining Koori hunting places, he found, such as groves of trees where Kooris caught birds; white men rode furiously through Koori camps, destroying and pillaging as they went, on the pretence of searching for stolen stock. 'Where are the natives to go?' asked Robinson. 'Where are they to procure food? Or are they to live?'[17]

There were those other brutal encounters, sexual ones, that Robinson noted in his journal. On one occasion he met two very young girls whom he believed were encouraged to stay in a particular area 'by the nefarious disposal of the white men—for improper purposes'. His suspicions were confirmed during the evening when he overhead the girls' conversation, in a context as appalling to readers in the 1990s as to Robinson in the 1840s:

> these two children were sitting by themselves and conning over to themselves obscene, scurrilous and blasphemous language—with the most

> perfect indifference, apparently quite unconscious of what they were repeating. Some of the words were: well done fuckumoll, go it fuckmoll, good night fuckmoll. Fuckmoll and fuckumoll was often repeated.[18]

They had learned these words, thought Robinson, in a hard school.

On one occasion Robinson noted a Koori woman's resistance: she apparently complied with a rendezvous with one of the squatter Tulloh's men, only to attempt to trap him. She followed the hutkeeper into the bush, where a Koori man was hidden in the bushes, waiting to protect her. Earlier, this hutkeeper had called his dog off the Koori woman. Frustrated and enraged, he now expressed the wish that he had allowed his dog to tear out her entrails: 'damn her eyes, black bitch, she deserved it for telling lies', was the vicious response.[19] Other Koori women were raped, or submitted to sexual entreaties because of fear of starvation. On many occasions he encountered shepherds who were obviously bribing Koori women to stay near their huts for sexual purposes by offering them food. With Kooris near starvation, the white men would kill sheep on the pretext that the sheep were dying. They even gave over part of their own rations of tea, sugar and flour to encourage Koori women to stay.

Robinson observed the continual painful hostilities between Koori men and white men over these sexual liaisons. One night white men came to the Robinson camp, pushing and shoving the Aboriginal men who accompanied them, all the while swearing at them. They were trying, of course, to provoke a fight, and therefore an excuse to retaliate by taking away the Koori women. Koori men told of many earlier occasions when white men shot at them and then forced women to accompany them. Robinson entered in his diary another incident. A squatter found that a Koori man had injured one of his hutkeepers severely with a waddy and had the man shot. The cause of the Koori man's anger? (Robinson's articulation of the interchange is of course a crude one.)

> The hutkeeper agreed with the man to leave his gin [*sic*] 3 days at the end of which time he would give the girl a blanket and the man a blanket. He kept her two days, beat her and turned her away.[20]

Robinson saw or heard many such heartbreaking stories, brief as was his trip. They undoubtedly could be multiplied hundreds of times over. Others who had the opportunity, like Robinson, to observe at first hand interaction between settlers and Kooris, whatever their insight into the complexities of these situations, were certain that in the context of the continuing British dispossession of Koori lands, this other appropriation of Koori women's sexuality played a critical role in the instigation of violence and bloodshed. Edward Parker wrote to Robinson of his own futile efforts to persuade the young Koori women 'to resist the importunities of the white man', and to prevent Koori men likewise from living near the stations, but he knew they were near starvation, and that he himself had insufficient food, clothing or shelter to offer them.

The results of the casual sexual couplings of white men and Koori women, continued Parker, were 'disease, jealousy, brutal quarrels both with whites and blacks, and rendering the condition of the natives more deplorable, and the property of the colonists more insecure'.[21] Two years later Parker expressed his conviction that 'nine out of ten of the outrages committed by the blacks may be traced up directly or indirectly to such circumstance . . .'.[22]

What was appalling for these observers was the distress caused by the venereal diseases spreading among Kooris as a result of this sexual intercourse. Another Assistant Protector, James Dredge, found it extremely difficult, he wrote, to convey the intensity of the problem: syphilis now affected Kooris of both sexes, 'originating in every instance—as far as my observation goes—in their intercourse with white men'.[23] His fellow Assistant Protector, William Thomas, predicted that unless the spread of the disease was arrested, the outcome would be 'the total defunct of the whole'.[24] A doctor, Wilmot, described the horror of the course of syphilis, which presented on the thigh, perineum or scrotum as small sores that 'rapidly coalesce and degenerate into foul ulcers terminating ultimately in a warty excrecense; in a few weeks it spreads very widely'.[25] Near one station virtually all Koori women were so badly affected that they could scarcely crawl about; a white worker on the station, whom Kooris thought the main culprit, had recently died of syphilis. Even so, the women's personal pain and suffering was only the beginning of their misery. Parker described Koori mothers' grief as within days or weeks of their birth, 'their poor children become covered with a syphilitic eruption, and speedily perish'.[26]

That the protectors like Robinson, Parker, Dredge and Thomas could display genuine sympathy with the terrible situation in which Kooris were placed was clear. But as they established details of white men's greed and cruelty, another layer of meaning was present in all they said and wrote, condemnatory of Koori cultural gender practices and in effect attributing to them a vital part in their own tragedy. Of Koori mothers with syphilis, Parker wrote: 'it is melancholy to witness the effect of their wretched conduct in their offspring'.[27] Thomas referred sardonically to the venereal disease 'which civilized man spreads from shore to shore', but added: 'The awful depraved habits of themselves adds much to put a barrier to arrest its progress . . .'.[28] In similar vein Dredge wrote: 'it is extremely difficult to convey a correct report of the awful amount of disease amongst both sexes, of every age, resulting from illicit and promiscuous intercourse with the whites, and with each [other]'.[29]

The protectors, in other words, presented Koori women as contributing to their plight because they appeared to have within their own cultural system sexual practices which deviated from those British Victorian practices which the protectors upheld as proper behaviour. There was an elision between their description of white oppression, and their description of the ways in which indigenous cultural practices interacted with white aberrant behaviour to bring about tragedy. Such assertions could only make it easier for white settlers thereafter to disregard their own cruel and unthinking dispossession of Kooris, in order to concentrate on the perceived disorder of Koori social behaviour. Some first commentators offset their negativism about Kooris with attempts to bring them also into a shared humanity through a language stressing familiarity. As Edward Curr wrote:

> But notwithstanding many differences between the Black and the White man, their sympathies, likes and dislikes were very much what ours would have been if similarly situated . . . This fact only gradually dawned on me, as I had somehow started with the idea that I should find the Blacks as different from the white men in mind as they are in colour.[30]

Other, more callous colonists were impressed by the differences in Koori culture that these men claimed the authority to know and reveal, and failed to share any searching evaluation of their own contribution to Kooris' difficulties. Increasingly it was the exotic, not the familiar, that was emphasised, and the exotic in this case could be made unpleasant reading for readers devoid of notions of cultural relativism, and arrogantly certain of their own superiority. Authoritative male voices joined into a chorus of lament at Koori women's position, viewed within Koori organisation of sexuality, work, family life and childrearing.

No formal attempt has been made to write an ethnohistory of Koori society before the 1860s, and we have no way of gaining access to the voices of the Koori women and men described by the white settlers. Yet to offset these colonial men's claims to privileged knowledge, we might appropriately turn to the writings of twentieth-century anthropologists and historians of Aborigines whose lives adhered to traditional practices and beliefs. Recent Australian historians and anthropologists, non-Aboriginal and Aboriginal, have discovered Aboriginal women within pre-colonial societies to have possessed considerable influence and autonomy in a society sharply divided on lines of gender. They suggest that women increased their status over the course of their life cycle, from the relatively powerless period of girlhood to a respected older age; that women were integral and important to the material survival of the entire clan and were valued accordingly; that women were important within their family of origin as well as within their new kinship affiliations through marriage, and derived status and strength from this. The issue of women's overall power remains contested territory, with a debate concerning Aboriginal women's social status revolving around the nature and degree of their economic, spiritual and childrearing roles, but the overall image, particularly in the work of feminist scholars, is a positive one, suggesting mutual respect between women and men.[31]

While one would scarcely anticipate that mid-Victorian gentlemen would read Koori culture with the eyes of modern scholars, at the same time nor can they be readily relieved of responsibility for their obtuse and opiniated condemnation. The dominant racist nineteenth-century narrative which they did so much to create was as harsh and negative as it was often blind to the context of negative changes in Koori lives engendered by the incursions of the colonisers themselves.

'The Government of the Aborigines is strictly Patriarchal';[32] 'The position of the women is one of great degradation';[33] 'The women . . . are generally a most miserable and truly pitiable race of beings, over whom the men exercise a cruel and tyrannical despotism';[34] 'as regards the females, they must obediently serve their masters in every season and under all circumstances'.[35] Writer after writer offered views in this mode, impervious to sources of women's power or to restrictions on male autonomy, meanwhile constructing a massive case for Koori women's oppressed status. As writers provided instances to give substance to their generalisations, their emphasis on the structural underpinnings of this situation could shift from Koori women's relationships to sexuality, to their work in reproduction, to their labour and to the distribution of resources resulting from that labour. Their readings of all elements of gender organisation revealed more about white cultural prejudices than the realities of Koori life.

Most writers provided graphic illustration of women's presumed oppression in a misreading of sexual practices. Some simply proclaimed women to be the sexual property of all men of a tribe. Alternatively: 'There is no such thing as marriage, in the proper sense of the word . . .', wrote Smyth with spurious glibness.

> The acts which precede matrimony are certainly not entitled to be regarded as rites. Men obtain wives by a convenient system of exchange, by conquest sometimes, and sometimes a woman is stolen. By what mode soever a man procures a bride, it is very seldom an occasion of rejoicing for the female.[36]

Haydon attempted to effect a crude jocularity in his estimate that 'another instance of the ignominy' to which Koori women were subjected was the action of the young man procuring a wife:

> having seen a woman whose sable charms overcome him, he first asks her to run away with him, if she refuse when opportunity favours, he inflicts a blow on her head with a heavy waddy or club which stuns her, and then carries her off to his own home, where she spends a life of drudgery and misery . . .[37]

Thomas, ignorant of the careful intricacy of betrothal arrangements, described the existence of marriages of young girls to older men as 'infant conubiancy' as he set his face against it in his adopted district.[38] Parker saw women oppressed by the 'gross sensuality' of Koori men, manifested in the institution of polygamy:

> one great point of ambition in the Australian native was to get a number of wives. I have known as many as six appropriated to one man. Two were common among the middle-aged men. The unfortunate women had no voice in their own disposal. They were considered the property of their nearest male relative . . .[39]

But what was worse, he continued, the men could dispose of their wives as they wished: 'the strongest mark of friendship that could be displayed by one man to another, was to present him with one of his superfluous wives'.[40] Meanwhile, thought some, the wives fought jealously with each other to obtain their husband's favour. If the wife attempted to escape, so this disastrous tale went, 'the probability is that she would be speared or beaten to death for her pains'.[41] The physical violence of Koori men towards wives was displayed as an image of Koori men's violence towards other Koori men, seen often to be based in conflicts over women and marriages.

This misrepresentation of Koori life led to this outcome: it made Koori women into victims, it made Koori men into vicious oppressors and gave legitimacy to white male attempts to 'protect' Koori women. That male violence occurred within Koori society—as in most societies—prior to white contact is well established, but the controls on it were also strong. Now fact and fiction, in this context of alienation, became dangerously confused. Story after story was told, with scant regard to the source or interpretation of evidence, of Koori men's violence towards women. Just one report by Parker gave details of a series of events, half-understood, but unambiguously reported, of women's oppression. One elderly man beat and burned his wife for opposing his wish to take a young woman, 'a common prostitute evidently from her own choice', as his second wife. The wife, however, subsequently begged Parker with tears in her eyes not to put her husband in jail. Another man speared two women, one in the back and another in the thigh, for offending him. When accosted and locked up, this man, according to Parker, offered to allow his own wife to be speared to expiate his crime.[42] Such crudely observed and arrogantly described accounts were legion. Women could scarcely have been shown in a worse situation. Men could scarcely have been shown more cruel.

So authoritative European males represented Koori women as the sad and powerless victims of their men, who lacked the capacity for affection. What was worse in their construction of Koori culture was the assertion that the men were lazy, and oppressed their wives further by keeping them hard at work. 'The man, regarding them more as slaves than in any other light, employs them in every possible way to his own advantage. They are obliged to get him shell-fish, roots and eatable plants',[43] went a typical interpretation of the gender division of labour. Or, 'the great value of a gin to one of these lazy fellows' might be best judged by considering 'the industry and skill of their gins and wives . . . in making nets, sewing cloaks, mussel-fishing, rooting, etc.'.[44] The men, said Dredge, principally monopolised the animals, reptiles, birds and fish, while the roots, grubs and ants were the women's lot;[45] or, as Haydon put it, for her services, a wife was 'usually rewarded with the part of any food which the husband cannot gourmandize'.[46]

Haydon, in line with many writers, noted negatively that when clans moved about the women carried the groups' material possessions. He had observed 'these poor enduring creatures':

> toiling on a burning hot day through the bush, laden with a heterogeneous assemblage of pots, blankets, rugs, bags containing charms, etc., skins, baskets, and perhaps mounted on all these articles will be a child from three days to six years old, and this is not for a walk of an hour but probably for the whole day.[47]

The shifting of the clan and the carriage of goods, others noted, was not delayed if a woman had a newborn baby, whom the woman had to halt her journey to suckle at frequent intervals.

Motherhood, they said, oppressed Koori women in further ways. Insufficient concern and respect was shown the woman at the time of birth, or immediately afterwards. (We might otherwise say, of course, that Koori women, until smitten with European diseases, were strong, active, healthy and bore childbirth stoically.) Even worse, and terribly, numerous writers portrayed the women as forced to kill their young if new babies were seen as a threat to the clan's mobility. The 'will of the tribe' demanded it. Within Koori laws, wrote Smyth, 'infanticide is a necessary practice, and one which, if disregarded, would, under certain circumstances, be disapproved of; and the disapproval would be marked by punishment.'[48] Infanticide was first assumed, and then, once again, ascribed to male callousness. For Koori women were portrayed as very affectionate mothers indeed. The death of a child was a time of fearful distress: 'It has been an occasional custom . . . for the mother to carry about for weeks the body of her lost one.'[49] Again,

> stronger than the maternal love of the tigress or the lioness is that of the Australian Aboriginal woman for a favourite child. She will die in an effort to preserve it, and as willingly suffer the pangs of hunger, and the prolonged misery of hard travel to secure it from injury.[50]

Wrote another:

> they never desert their children; as soon as they are able to walk the mothers endeavour to induce them to look out for their own food ... and never think of leaving them for any length of time until well able to provide for themselves.[51]

This apparent praise, of course, for the women's mothering qualities was once again constructed to contrast the cruelty of the men.

Koori women might well love their offspring, but the burdens of births and childrearing took their toll under the conditions of life which the writers constructed. And the result? The appearance of these very women was portrayed in the most appalling terms, by men who not only were unused to confronting female nakedness, but who drew their comparisons from racial stereotypes of degraded physical countenance and inferior mental capacity. Just as the British nineteenth-century urban poor were depicted by the middle class as savages and 'a race apart', Koori culture felt the full force of racial prejudices.[52] 'If the men are ugly, the women are hideous,' wrote Griffith. He foreshadowed a link between non-white races and animals that would become prominent in nineteenth-century racialist discourse. The women's appearance was in part, he said, because they became mothers so early; 'their hands, arms, feet, and legs being more like the paws and claws of the lower animals'.[53] Thought Parker: 'Brutal treatment, frequent privations, and too early marital associations, combine to impoverish and deteriorate the constitution of the aboriginal female.'[54] Describing elderly women, Haydon was even more crass: 'The old women are withered and decrepid, presenting a disgusting appearance, closely resembling an ouran-outang.'[55]

It would be a mistake to assume that the subject position from which these self-appointed authorities spoke was always a stable one. When describing specific women, specific events involving women, their descriptions could acknowledge more favourable contexts although drawing on sexist rather than racist stereotypes. 'The female Aborigines have their amusements as well as the males, and simple and innocent they are,' conceded Thomas of young Koori women:

> they are particularly fond of dancing in the Spring and Autumn especially . . . they decorate their heads with flowers, and round their wrists like bracelets and round the ankles, and very gay the black lasses look, they dance away as merrily as our country girls round the May Pole, they chase their own leader who is young like themselves.[56]

Alfred Howitt wrote of Gippsland Kooris: 'In affairs of moment the women have a voice, and it is not without weight.'[57] Of travelling Koori parties, another wrote 'the women stayed close to their men, who supported them when descending gullies or climbing hills, either by the arm or by the whole body'.[58] And yet another: 'Men show strong affection towards each other; they love their wives; women are faithful, and die on the graves of their husbands . . .'.[59] On a man who grieved for his dead wife: 'we subsequently inter his faithful lubra . . . the old man wept bitterly, the kindness of all around to this lubra would scarce be credited'.[60] Again: 'they have great natural affection'. In many respects, wrote Thomas, 'in the bush' they were a well-ordered, affectionate community: 'there is no complaining in the streets of a Native Encampment[;] all partake of the fortune of the day and share among each other what providence has been pleased to give them'.[61]

In the course of George Robinson's tour of the Western District he met a Koori woman, sixty to seventy years of age, sitting by a small fire with a young man and two small boys. Robinson asked their names and to which country they belonged. The man, with some emotion, struck the ground, saying ' "Here is my country, *deen deen*—here here",' whereupon the elderly woman:

> who had chronicled in memory the long long history of her country took up the theme and waving her hands reiterated what her fine formed son had stated and in a garrulous strain enacted a variety of events connected with the history of her country which had happened in their primitive [*sic*] state. And then in a dejected and altered tone deplored the loss of her country and its original enjoyment.[62]

Like so many of the women depicted in Robinson's journal, she was far from the oppressed and miserable figure of the Koori woman of the dominant voice in the white male texts. What was more, this woman knew very well the source of their current plight: their loss of land, the exploitation of Koori women, the depression they felt. As 'Billibellary', a senior Koori man, said to William Thomas in 1843: 'Blackfellows all about say "that no good have them Pickaninneys now, no country for Blackfellows like long time ago".'[63]

As protectors, missionaries and amateur ethnologists recorded the additional devastation that alcohol brought to Koori society on top of dispossession, sexual appropriation and disease, they created simultaneously a representation of Koori traditional society, and in particular of the place of Koori women within it, that was increasingly powerful in the evolving discourse of white imperial domination.

These men of authority viewed Koori women's position embedded in the context of Koori organisation of sexuality, work, family life and childrearing in negative terms which provided justification for the deaths of Kooris as individuals, for the wiping out of Koori culture and society, whether abruptly or, as settlers phrased it, in the course of time. The representation of Koori social disorder underwrote racial and cultural segregation including the surveillance, marginalisation and eventual dismantling of Koori culture. Just as in spatial terms government policy mercilessly took possession of Koori lands and directed colonial protectors Robinson, Thomas and Parker to enforce spatial surveillance and segregation by dissuading Kooris from frequenting the streets of Melbourne town and their traditional riparian camps along the adjacent river systems, and to confine them to outlying reserves and mission stations.[64]

Unwittingly, perhaps, but unerringly, these white men's representations of women and gender became, indeed, 'inducements to the strong to be cruel to the weak'. These men's words assisted in destroying, in the eyes of white colonists and colonial authorities, the moral core of Koori society, thereby facilitating the usurpation of Koori lands, and attempts to usurp Koori culture, by successive colonial legislatures. They had participated in an imperial project of tragic proportions.

PART II

Producing Feminist Theory: Difference and Complexity

NINE

A Narrative on the Limits of Theory

Philipa Rothfield

> The story happened to someone else. More precisely, it happened to someone else's mother. To the mother of Isaac Bashevis Singer, the writer, the American writer, the American Jewish writer, the American Jewish writer who came from Poland and writes in Yiddish which is translated into English. I could tell you a lot more about him, but that would take up a lot of space and I want to get to the story which is part of a whole lot of stories . . .
>
> Michelene Wandor, *Guests in the Body*

Problems within Problems

This chapter is a phoenix which has risen from the ashes of two pieces I have written on feminist theory and female identity.[1] Those pieces explore the following issues. First, the nature of female subjectivity: how to theorise the interrelated character of the elements which comprise women's identity. Second, the nature and breadth of feminist theory: its character, range and content.

I call this piece a phoenix because I have had a change of heart regarding my whole approach. To explain, my concern in relation to female subjectivity was to theorise the various elements which comprise it, whether conjunctively, disjunctively or incommensurately. It is not enough, for example, to *add* race to gender; one has to look at the ways in which these elements *interact* with one another. Furthermore, such elements may combine differently in particular localities, situations and historical milieux. My problem was to find a way of writing about the various aspects of female subjectivity; to find a means to theorise their coalescence. Australian people have their own varied set of qualities—Koori, Anglo-Celtic, Vietnamese, Cambodian, Greek, Italian, Turkish, country, city, outback, lesbian, heterosexual, to name but a few. How do collections of these and other elements combine in the one person? Is there a general way of stating this?

The issue of subjectivity has a microscopic focus. From a macroscopic point of view, a related question arises regarding the scale and character of the second issue, feminist theory. The problem here concerns the place of *generality* (all women) and its capacity to deal with *specificity* (particular women). The question can and has been put whether or not feminist theory should deal in universals, that is, speak of a universal class of women: all women.[2] For example, is it a good thing to speak of women in Africa, women in Europe and in the USA as constituting the one group, women? Is it appropriate to speak of all the women of Australia as a single group? There is a degree of overlap between the two concerns, subjectivity and theory. If one decided to curtail universalisation, one would be loath to develop a universal position regarding subjectivity, for a theory about all women will purport to speak of each and every woman.

Universality has come to be viewed with suspicion in two senses. One is more formal, and arises from postmodern theory. The other ground of suspicion is more obviously political. We will deal first with the political criticism. There are those who have been spoken for by the purported totality of the universal form.[3] Historically, it has been possible to make use of universality to speak or write on behalf of everybody. It is still possible: politicians do it all the time. But not everybody is able to do so. Hence, one of the charges coming from women, 'minority' ethnic groups, people of colour, and of the Third World, is that only those in a position of relative dominance can impose a universalising face of knowledge. Donna Haraway calls such an act the 'God trick' namely, the attempt to take a God's-eye view of the domain of discussion.[4] By pretending to be God, one is able to exempt oneself from the field of discussion.[5]

The political point is that only some people can play God. It is easier to espouse objectivity and neutrality as a WASP male academic than as a working-class woman of colour struggling to gain access to some means by which to represent herself. And here is the contrast: those who have been rendered marginal in relation to a particular sphere of discussion have had to struggle to gain the recognition that they have not been adequately represented.[6] Part of that struggle inevitably involves the need to assert a group's difference from the universalising norm. The marginalised group has to take up, if not create, a position of difference in order to gain some form of acknowledgment. For example, in the USA women of colour have had to speak *as* women of colour in order to challenge the hegemony of white feminism, whereas white feminists have not had to identify themselves as white because in that context white functions as the unacknowledged norm. Within feminism, this issue has been whether the term 'all women' necessarily sets up a narrow sense of woman. A political consequence of the above is that the unacknowledged norm (e.g. white) can readily purport an inclusive and universal theoretical range. In contrast, those who have had to assert their difference from a given norm cannot also claim universality. Given these asymmetries, the question can be put whether it is a good thing to theorise about all women. This is especially so when such an act is performed by those women in positions of dominance over other women, for it is liable to become an asymmetric *speaking for* all women.[7] That is one end of the double critique of universality.

The second critique of universalism and universality comes from postmodern theory. The view there, as initially expressed by Lyotard, is that universal forms of theory no longer have the same credibility or sense of legitimacy as they once did.[8] There has been quite some exchange between feminists over whether the postmodern critique has anything to offer feminism; whether it is possible to retain an adequate sense of the political within a feminist postmodernism; and whether postmodernism has anything to offer women who do not take up positions of dominance within feminist discourse, for example, women of the Third World, women of colour, and working-class women.[9] There are those who enlist the support of postmodernism in order to combat hegemonic feminism, and those who are critical of its potential political losses.[10]

I mention feminism and postmodernism because each area has had something to say about the status of the universal within feminist theory. These two sources come together in questioning the universal claims of feminist theory. However, the problem of universality and feminist theory is not one of theory: it is one of *domination*. The presumption that some feminists can write on and about all women has come under scrutiny because those women who have been excluded, silenced or marginalised have struggled to articulate their critique of forced and false universality. By forced universality I mean the imposition of universal claims upon an entire class or group, or the presumption that a particular characterisation stands for an entire category.[11] The possibility of such an imposition depends upon differential relations of power.

It is this last point that relates to my change of heart. At its most abstract, the shift has to do with the relation between theory and politics. More specifically, it relates to the following point made by a woman of colour in the United States, Maria Lugones:

> The second trick that racism played/plays on white women theorists is conceiving this lack of noticing us *as a theoretical problem*, which they label the 'problem of difference' . . . But white women theorists seem to have worried more passionately about the harm the claim does to theo-

> rizing than about the harm the theorizing did to women of color.[12] [my emphasis]

Lugones is right. Speaking as a feminist theorist, as one who writes feminist theory, it is true that somewhere within there is a desire to find a solution to the problems of difference in writing, that is, within theory. Lugones' point is that white women may appear to respond to problems and issues of difference, but that the response may be felt more on a theoretical plane than in terms of culpability, responsibility, concern, even guilt.

A number of questions arise here regarding the distinction between theoretical and actual responsibility. How is it possible to distinguish between a 'non-real', theoretical acknowledgement of responsibility and an actual concern? Lugones suggests that the difference is that the worry is directed to different areas. Her point is that attention ought to be focused upon (or at least not eclipse) concrete harm. White women must address the ways in which women materially suffer from racism: in economic, social and cultural terms; in relation to work, education and personal life.

Lugones' point seems to privilege practice over theory. For the moment I think such a privilege ought to stand. This is what I mean by describing this as a problem *between* theory and politics. It is not about the conjunction of theory *and* politics but about the tensions that exist in between, and that tension is felt most fully in the realm of practice. The issue is this: the tendencies of theory are such that political practices and concerns can become eclipsed. All the more so when the theorist is clearly in a position of privilege, that is, is favourably located within a network of relations of domination.

Lugones writes of the USA, which is not the model for all things Australian. Nevertheless, I think her criticism of white feminists has some relevance for Australia. Whether this is so or not depends upon whether, and how, white Australian theorists have dealt with or ignored questions of racism and of difference; how white feminists acknowledge their (our) complicity in forms of racism; and what kinds of theoretical response have been formulated. In the USA, there has been a history of criticism and critical dialogue between some women on these matters. In Australia, perhaps more recently, there has also been both criticism and critical exchange between white women, and Aboriginal and Torres Strait Islander women; and between Anglo-Celtic women, and women of non-English-speaking backgrounds. But also, there are many critical exchanges which have never occurred because inequalities of speaking position mean that all women do not exist together within the one communicative domain. Women of different backgrounds do not necessarily speak the same language, speak in the same forums, nor even exchange words.

The subtlety of Lugones' remark is that white feminists can both 'deal' with problems of difference and yet fail to confront them at the same time. This reminds me of Chogyam Trungpa's work, *Cutting Through Spiritual Materialism*, where Trungpa identifies the ways in which a spiritual orientation can function as an obstacle that stands in the way of genuine spiritual growth.[13] Trungpa's point is that people can be incredibly busy being spiritual (adopting its trappings) without actually developing in any genuinely spiritual sense. This is the spiritual materialism to which he refers. Its relationship with Lugones' point is that it is possible to acknowledge a problem and appear to deal with it, and yet to avoid it at the same time.[14] The possibility arises because of the differences between theory and the concrete: in Lugones' case, the question of *actual harm* to women of colour can be overshadowed by the concern to find a theoretical solution. But this is a possibility which is not open to all, for the question of harm can be avoided only by those who do not suffer its effects.[15] In this context, avoidance is a possibility which is open only to white feminists.

There are further problems for white feminists who are concerned with the politics of difference and domination. Let us accept the claim that a desire for theoretical mastery can eclipse a sustained recognition of racism's concrete effects. How should these effects be acknowledged?[16] For a white feminist, there are two possible answers. One is to address the concrete harms to which Lugones refers; the other is to address the racism of white feminism. The first possibility has an outward focus; it can be seen as a response to the elisions of theoreticism. The second possibility is inward-looking; it is an attempt to characterise the ways in which domination is able to occur. As I see it, there are dangers in each answer.

The danger which attends the first possibility relates to the politics of speaking and representation. If addressing concrete harm amounts to *telling* an oppressed group what they suffer, real problems arise. There are also problems if the acknowledgment of harm amounts to speaking *on behalf* of an oppressed group. The point is to address the harms that women suffer, not to speak on behalf of them nor to tell them what they experience. It is likely that listening would be a first stage, including the responsibility to create the opportunities for listening to occur. Furthermore, women will be positioned differently in relation to that harm depending upon whether they are suffering it, complicit in its production, or something else. Thus, the question of addressing harm has to be determined in relation to who is doing the addressing.

Narcissism is the danger which attends the second possibility, the inward-looking means of addressing white racism. On the one hand, it is obviously crucial that women in positions of privilege study and critique that privilege: why should the marginalised do all the work?[17] On the other hand, it is important that their self-concern does not replace or occlude concern for the other. Much depends upon how their self-concern is elaborated, keeping in mind the reason for it: to address and combat racism at its source.

Perhaps I have characterised these two directions in too solipsistic a sense. Problems of domination are problems of relationship. Privilege is also a relational term. It is necessary to determine the problems, the responses, and the strategies which white or privileged feminists should, and could, adopt. These matters ought to be determined in relation to the concerns of those who have been correlatively oppressed. Lugones writes of interaction, others of accountability.[18] The point is that domination cannot be undone in formal terms alone (that is, purely on the level of theory). Formality can even occlude its undoing, and white feminists need to find ways of becoming accountable to those whose oppression is ostensibly their concern.

Political accountability is not built into the structures of the academy, where individualism and mastery currently prevail. Lugones speaks not only of theory but also of the investment that white feminist theorists have in its ascendancy. In another context, Jane Gallop has written on the phallic illusion of mastery and its manifestation in the 'subject presumed to know'.[19] The notion of subject here is that of the person. In this context, the subject who knows is the academic subject, the academic person who occupies a position of knowledge. The presumption of knowledge, to which Gallop refers, is an attempt to shore up a position of authority from which to speak. It is no wonder, then, that those whose very esteem depends upon assuming a position of authority are attached to the presumption of knowledge. How is it possible to be both authoritative *and* accountable, given that accountability seems to suggest a form of vulnerability?

Although theorising requires a certain degree of authority, there is no virtue in assuming an authority one ought not to have. White feminists do not necessarily have the authority to speak on behalf of those sisters to whom they stand in a relationship of domination.[20] They may be *asked* to, but that is different. The notion of authority has two senses, and the difference between them is instructive. In one sense, authority is *individualistic*. It refers to the legitimacy of the subject's speaking position; that is, whether the subject has the knowledge, even the power to speak as an authority on a matter. 'Experts' are often interviewed by the media as authorities on a particular subject. The other sense of authority is *relational*. It has to do with being given the authority to speak. The subject becomes an agent for others. In this latter sense, authority consists of being authorised to speak (on behalf of). The difference between these two senses is that the first is individualistic—being an authority, assuming such a position—whereas the second alludes to authority arising from the will of others. More often than not, academic authority is seen to be an individual's right, rather than one which derives from a community source.[21]

It is authority in the latter sense that white feminists could seek. In turn, this authority can arise only from an interactive relation of accountability. The vulnerability mentioned earlier follows from the fact that on occasion white feminists may not be entitled to assume the mantle of authority in relation to the politics of difference and domination. In other words, our authority might legitimately be challenged by others. Vulnerability is not unknown in the academic world. It occurs every time someone offers his or her ideas for academic criticism and discussion.[22]

In sum, then, my change of heart is over whether answers can be found in theory alone. I have no intention to rubbish theory—this is not an anti-intellectual exercise. It is rather one about the place of politics within theory, about its ability to disrupt theory.

Let me conclude this section with a reference to a discussion between Foucault and Deleuze on intellectuals and power. According to Deleuze, there was a time when practice was the instantiation of theory, and another time when the opposite was true, when practice was what provoked theoretical developments. Now, he claims, the relation is neither totally one thing nor another. Instead:

> from the moment a theory moves into its proper domain, it begins to encounter obstacles, walls, and blockages which require its relay by another type of discourse . . . Practice is a set of relays from one theoretical point to another, and theory is a relay from one practice to another. No theory can develop without eventually encountering a wall, and practice is necessary for piercing this wall.[23]

The notion of a relay between theory and practice is important. Not only does it reject a total opposition between the two terms: it recognises the *movement* between the two. And perhaps this is my stalemate: any attempt to solve the problems of feminism and its repertoire of privilege and domination cannot remain in the realm of theory alone. Although there is a sense in which feminist theory is a form of practice, it is not so in the relevant sense. A theoretical concern within feminism over its relation to the underprivileged will have to engage with those spheres of practice in which such domination occurs.

Jockeying into Position: The Politics of Place

The previous section contains a litany of problems, complaints and inadequacies. It makes no offers of solution, except in the attempt to prise loose the grip upon feminist theory maintained by white feminists. In the spirit of the above, then, let me try to negotiate some of these problems in relation to my own place and time of writing: Australia in the 1990s. What follows is not a comprehensive statement by any means. It is an attempt to rehearse the problems of identity in relation to my own perspective and position, and to indicate certain indeterminacies that arise in the process of articulation.

Let me begin by saying that Australia has its own relations and histories of privilege, invasion, domination, colonialism and neo-colonialism. Some of these relate to colour, and indigenous (Aboriginal and Torres Strait Islander) peoples; others relate to class, sexual difference, ethnicity, migratory and cultural origins, and religion. Our class relations are specific, as are the particular histories which inform them. It is not appropriate to take the USA as a paradigm. For example, in Australia, the privilege of being a white woman has to do with being white in relation to Aboriginal women (and men) in the context of Australian colonial, and neo-colonial, racist oppression. As Jackie Huggins points out, class relations interpenetrate relations of domination.[24] Relations of race and class are so oppressive that Huggins argues that Aboriginal people, men and women, are virtually 'fighting for the same things'. She depicts substantial differences between white and black women in Australia, especially as they are felt in class term.[25] For Huggins:

> Without question, it is easier for a black woman to consider herself first as a human being, second as Aborigine, and only third a member of the female sex.[26]

Clearly, this remark arises from the Australian situation. It is not a comment about race and gender for all contexts, though it may relate to other situations.

'White' is not the only signifier of privilege in Australia. There are other relations of privilege and domination between women, particularly those stemming from ethnicity, cultural difference, and migration. Jeannie Martin writes that there is a feminist emphasis upon the plurality of struggles as one way of responding to differences between women; nevertheless,

> given the structural marginality of disfavoured NES [non-English-speaking] migrant groups in Australia, such strategies could merely augment marginality, especially given the structural privilege enjoyed (in this case) by Anglo feminists.[27]

In such a context, Anglo feminist is a term of privilege.

Australia has had specific, and distinct waves of migration: the invasion of first settlement; the gold rushes; before World War I; after World War II; and since the 1960s. The current and relative position of migrant groups is markedly different, depending upon where people came from, how long they have been in Australia, and who they are. The way in which a group is identified is also a substantial question. Stuart Hall writes:

> Cultural identities are the points of identification, the unstable points of identification or suture, which are made within the discourses of history and culture. Not an essence but a *positioning*. Hence, there is always a politics of position, which has no absolute guarantee in an unproblematic, transcendental 'law of history'.[28]

Hall describes the points of identification as mobile and unstable; he locates them within a discursive context of history and culture. The struggle around their mobility is always staged within a material and symbolic setting. How a group is identified, and how it represents itself, are political matters. By way of example, I may want to write about the variety of peoples who have come from South-East Asia, Indo-China, the Indian subcontinent and around the Pacific rim. But the word 'Asian' is a levelling term, one which effaces difference and has been used to construct a category for racist purposes, whether in the context of debates around migration or more nakedly.[29] Like the homogenised oriental so well depicted in E. Said's work, *Orientalism*, 'Asian' is a term one cannot readily use because of its 'material and symbolic setting' within Australia.[30] If one were to question what purposes identifying a group within Australia as Asian might serve, one would need to look at the material and discursive conditions which support and enable the description. These include histories of migration, the cultural presence of various communities, their standing and reception in Australia, and their economic position. I often hear people described as 'Asian Australian', whereas Anglo-Australians are just called 'Australian'. For a long time, the Australian identity was believed to be British. The marking out of Asian—or Greek, or Irish—Australians is what Hall calls a *politics* of position. It is unstable and historical.

Let me turn now to my own sense of cultural identity as an Australian Jew. One reason to select this aspect is because I feel I can speak with authority as an Australian Jew; that it is somehow less problematic than to speak of others' cultural identities. Of course, many of the Australian Jewish community would be horrified to think of me speaking 'on behalf' of them on such matters. Perhaps I speak only for the few; or perhaps this illustrates that all *speaking for* is dangerous, that the issue of authorisation is complex. My other reason for pursuing one aspect of my own identity is to enunciate my own speaking position on matters of privilege in Australia.[31]

What is it to be Jewish? I am not religious, so being Jewish is not that. I am not an Israeli national, nor do I represent Israel as my actual or symbolic home nor as my imagined community. I do not have a single origin, a nationality from which my diasporic history (*qua* Jewish) originates. At university in the 1970s I felt inadequate when certain of my Anglo-Celtic friends were constructing ancient Druidic genealogies for themselves, for what did I have? A father who is Scottish-born, before that English, Russian, then it becomes uncertain. And an Australian-born mother, of Palestinian parents, who were of German and Ukrainian–Lithuanian parents and, again, it becomes uncertain. The only thing I know for certain is that many European Jews were killed by the Nazis in World War II, a rather painful source of self-identification. Being an Australian-born Jew differentiates me from Jews born elsewhere; even in Australia there is a diversity of family origins amongst Jews: Polish, Hungarian, Spanish, Iraqi, Egyptian.

Phillip Roth writes of his being Jewish as a form of ethnicity.[32] Whether this is so depends upon how one regards ethnicity: whether as an imagined community, a social construction, a cultural group, or a region of peoples.[33] Gayatri Spivak notes that:

> Culturally, of course, there is talk of ethnicity which is strongly endorsed by ministries of culture. But practically speaking what these spaces want is access to proper names, for which there is in fact no literal reference . . .[34]

A brief visit to Israel is enough to persuade me that there are great differences between Israeli Jews. If Jews are an ethnic group, it is unlike other more 'coherent' ethnic groups.[35] Perhaps it would make more sense to characterise Australian Jews, Russian Jews, Ethiopian Jews, but there have been too many waves of migration for this to be entirely successful. For example, the recent arrival of Russian Jews in Australia clearly differentiates them from the Russian Jews who arrived before, and even after, World War II. Russia has changed a great deal during the century, as has the Australia to which these Jews have emigrated. Also, the patterns of Jewish movement around the world are extensive and long-standing.[36]

Although Jews are not all bound by a singular imagined community, there is nevertheless a fairly robust sense of actual community. If I meet a Jew in Melbourne, I expect to know at least some members of his or her family, and my mother or father is usually able to tell me about people's family background. Some secular Jews in Australia have taken it upon themselves to construct their own sense of identity, history, and culture.[37] Such a project is, of course, much more fractured—that is, less coherent—than this might suggest. An example of its fractured nature is apparent in Barrie Kosky's staging of *The Dybbuk*.[38] A dybbuk is a creature who invades the body of a human being. Sol Anski's *Dybbuk* is a Yiddish play based upon a tale of bodily possession and exorcism. Kosky's production did not remain faithful to the play, nor did it fully use it. The production invoked images of Kabbalistic mysticism, superstition, vaudeville figures of Yiddish theatre and songs. It moved between the play's narrative, references to actors who performed Yiddish theatre in Vilna, and mystical, religious reference. The play itself was staged in what is usually a motor workshop in the middle of a Jewish-populated suburb of Melbourne, St Kilda. The audiences themselves, many of whom knew each other, also tell a story of Jewish presence in Australia.

The physical setting of Kosky's production, its oil-stained concrete stage, the *shabbat* candles lining the stage, and its fractured character gave it a specific embodiment which tells a complex story of Australian Jewry. Kosky has said of his own work that there is no one 'message' which the audience is meant to 'get'. So it is with this aspect of cultural and historical identity, Jewish Australian. As Stuart Hall notes, and as the above discussion illustrates, there are always plays of difference within forms of identity.[39] I have referred to Kosky's production of *The Dybbuk* because it is a Melbourne-based representation of Australian Jewry which is both fractured and coherent; and because it supports Hall's claim that cultural identity is always unstable. It is also an important piece of work on cultural identity by a Melbourne Jew of my generation.

One of the issues of complexity for an Australian context is to discern between and within ethnic groups, Aboriginal peoples, and class relations. Actual people may be in positions of privilege in one sense and not in another. Teresa de Lauretis describes a form of feminism which acknowledges this complexity, one which theorises multiple axes of oppression. De Lauretis depicts three forms of analysis: single, parallel and multiple.[40] The singular model posits a single axis of feminism, whether women's oppression or gender/sexual difference. Its singularity can be understood in terms of totalisation wherein one axis applies to all situations, whether pertaining to gender, class or race. All oppression is subsumed into one category. One way of acknowledging the existence of other factors of oppression is by changing the metaphor from one axis to several parallel axes. De Lauretis describes these as co-equal terms of analysis. Parallel axes symbolise a number of universal categories—e.g. race, class, gender. These are added one to another in a simple arithmetical fashion.

The difficulty with the concept of parallel axes is that there is no sense of *interaction* between them. The notion of multiple axes represents a logical and epistemological shift. Multiple axes are layered, 'interrelated' and 'co-implied', so that any set or section of them is heterogeneous and 'multiply organised'. The single axis of feminism postulates a unified feminist subject. But the multiple axes of feminism act upon each other to produce a subject who is not so coherent; who may, indeed, embody contradictory features:

> So that the feminist subject which was initially defined purely by its status as a colonized subject or victim of oppression, becomes redefined as much less pure—and *not unified or simply divided* between positions of masculinity and femininity, but *multiply organized* across positionalities along several axes and across mutually contradictory discourses and practices.[41]

That lessening of purity, as De Lauretis puts it, yields a consciousness of 'ideological complicity'.[42] My own ideological complicity pertains to my position in Australia as a white feminist. Although a child of first- and second-generation migrant parents, I cannot equate my situation with that of other migrant women. This is also a class question. As an academic, I occupy a position of privilege in relation to, for example, NESB female textile workers. I mention this not only to specify my position of privilege but also to raise the problem of representation as raised in the previous section. How am I to represent these women? To what extent should I? Do I have an obligation to speak for these women, given that my ability to speak is in part made possible by their labour?

If one moves beyond the dichotomy between silence and speech (whether to speak at all or to remain silent) and into the *problematic of representation*, some particular problems arise. It is possible to distinguish between *speaking about* a group and *speaking for* a group.[43] There are two senses of representation (like those of authority, discussed above) which can at least be conceptually distinguished. In practice, however, the two are not so distinct. In this context, to speak of Aboriginal women is to move perilously close to speaking on behalf of them. At this point in time, it may be crucial for Aboriginal women to articulate for themselves their concerns, to pursue their differences of viewpoint, and to develop their own forms and terms of representation. That said, Trinh makes the point that this need to make space is no reason for women in positions of relative dominance to excuse themselves entirely from the fray:

> at least the danger of speaking for the other has emerged into consciousness. But it is a very small step indeed, since it serves as an excuse for their complacent ignorance and their reluctance to involve themselves in the issue.[44]

This is where accountability comes in. Women of privilege in Australia (whether total, partial or mixed) are undoubtedly going to tread on some toes, or more likely, fall over their own feet, in trying to 'deal' with these matters. Forms of racism and ethnocentrism are not transparent, especially to those who benefit from their distortions. The point is not so much to be in the right, as to move towards eradicating domination. I hope that in the above I have been able to explore some of the difficulties in trying to make such a move.

TEN

Viral Identities: Feminisms and Postmodernisms

Vicki Kirby

The recent proliferation of the term 'postmodernism' in journal articles, book titles, and conference programmes is a decidedly curious phenomenon. It becomes even more curious if we consider the extraordinary diversity of postmodernism's confection of arguments and styles. No doubt the word's ubiquity has a lot to do with marketing strategies in the publishing industry, where an enhanced modernity continues to promise 'the new' and 'the now' in commodified form. However, the 'post' in postmodernism can also be read reflexively. Cast in this way, it marks modernism's critique of itself, a sign that modernism's narrative of infinite renewal and progress can no longer be sustained. In this paper I want to suggest that postmodernism is parasitic in nature. Moreover, I argue that the difficulties which complicate the identity of postmodernism also afford us some understanding of how feminism is similarly compromised.

As an intellectual phenomenon, postmodernism is a critique of Reason that examines the status of what constitutes knowledge and 'the knowing subject'. Although often glibly identified with a cluster of French proper names (Roland Barthes, Julia Kristeva, Michel Foucault, Jacques Derrida, Luce Irigaray, Jacques Lacan, Gilles Deleuze etc.), the debates that are incorporated under this generic term belong to a diverse range of intellectual fields and locations, stretching from science and philosophy to the arts.[1] In these debates, which cover a period of nearly thirty years, a common feature is the attempt to displace our understanding of the knowing subject as the author of his or her actions. For example, psychoanalysis and semiotics both argue that the subject is ventriloquised by very particular historical and cultural regimes of signification, regimes that can be likened to language systems. The subject of postmodernism is consequently 'spoken through' by this inherited force field, and in such a way that the subject's sense of self-certainty, or intention, is always exceeded and subverted. The subject does not precede historical and cultural systems of representation but is rather produced within them. Nothing lies outside these systems, not even sex and sexuality.[2] In short, although our conventional understanding of 'subjectivity', 'knowledge', and 'power' is not abandoned by postmodern theorising, it is certainly provoked and complicated.

The modern era is marked by an investment in the corrosive power of objectivity, truth and rational argument. Reason has been reified as the ultimate goal of our pedagogical experience; the warranty that tautologically insures our arguments against ignorance, prejudice and error. However, in recent decades this conceptual legacy has been scrutinised more. Matters of fact have become questions about faith, and the grounds of knowledge are increasingly perceived as shifting and unstable. Consequently, the conventions of logic and reason that would otherwise guide our comprehension are now an integral part of the puzzle, and this makes it all the more difficult to understand the nature of the postmodern riddle.

This is why the uninitiated reader may be somewhat confused by postmodernism's arguments and strategies. It is easy to become lost in the maze of a logic that is both caught in, and indebted to, the same conceptual inheritance that it interrogates. Postmodernism is difficult to define because it is necessarily dispersed and parasitic; dependent upon, and complicit with, whatever it defines itself against. According to the conventions of political analysis, however, complicity is regarded as an act of treachery akin to sleeping with the enemy. For some feminists, to describe the relationship between the modern and the postmodern as complicit is to suggest that an improper exchange has taken place and that the resulting breach requires restitution and atonement. Yet this disapproval misunderstands the paradoxical nature of the postmodern challenge. Put simply, any appeal to law and order is quintessentially proprietorial: its foundational reasoning legislates what 'properly' belongs to whom. This is the same foundation that supports the political and conceptual underpinnings of modernism, in both its liberal and Marxist traditions. So we can begin to understand why a modernist assessment of *post*modernism often becomes a territorial dispute with very high stakes. The modernist need to 'hold the line' against postmodern incursions understands both its own identity, as well as the more general application of what identity entails, as something akin to property; a discrete space whose limits and borders can and should be defended from invasion.[3]

Postmodernism is, however, viral in nature. The comparison is apt because a virus possesses the ability to inhabit and even to take nourishment from its adversaries. A virus is peculiarly lifeless without a host. Biologists describe a virus as 'a packet of information'; it can reproduce itself only with the support of a host cell. The respective identities of both host and parasite become confused during the strange information exchange that ensues, with each mistaking the other for itself. For a virus, infection is life.

This biological metaphor allows us to think about the nature of identity in a slightly different way. If we grant the analogy, then the mere rejection of postmodernism is no prophylactic against contamination. Whether we like it or not, the infection has already taken place. But what happens to politics within this implication? Is feminism undermined by postmodernism's apparent disrespect for its terms of reference, and if so, what will this mean for feminism's contemporary identity? In other words, how is the familiar shape of political contestation changed by postmodernism, and is this something about which we should be particularly concerned? In this essay I want to suggest that feminism's interrogation of the inherent masculinism within Western thought is an integral part of the postmodern moment. Or, to put this another way, feminism's protean ability to mutate its identity in different contexts can be read as a specific example of the unstable nature of identity in general, and of modernity in particular.

As I have already suggested, postmodernism is a vexed term, deployed by a broad range of cultural critics with heterogeneous and often contradictory effects. The meaning of the word is elusive and always compromised, because any approach to postmodernism is a particular and interested perspective drawn from an array of vying theoretical interpretations. Given this caveat, what I want to do here is survey just some of the provocations within this elastic category that have special relevance for feminism. And I want to begin with a brief explication of the concepts 'logocentrism' and 'phallocentrism'.

For all its diverse expression, feminism is a movement whose recent history and aspirations have been thoroughly enmeshed within the modernist project. The logic of Cartesian reason (anchored in the self-certain, unified subject) and the goals of the Enlightenment share an epistemological foundation with feminism's raison d'être.[4] The desire for liberation from oppression, the privileging of knowledge over ignorance, and the assumption that a better future can be engineered from an imperfect past, are all expectations that fall well within our humanist inheritance. Accordingly, the feminist struggle for sexual equality is heavily invested in notions of consciousness-raising, progress, emancipation, and the rights of the individual. And the realisation of these entirely modern political ambitions does indeed seem eminently reasonable and possible.

Yet feminism can also be explained as a movement whose very struggles testify to modernism's routine betrayal of such hopes. The ability of patriarchal power to balance its concessions with recuperative inventiveness is sad evidence of the bitter-sweet nature of many feminist achievements.[5] The value accorded to a woman's body, to the significance of her life, and to the worth of her labours, continues to be measured against a masculine norm that finds her wanting. Within this logic, 'the feminine' becomes synonymous with a deficiency. Many feminists have argued against the assumption that this lack, or deficit, belongs naturally to woman. Instead, they have focused their attentions on the patriarchal representations through which woman's demeaned value is reckoned, discovering a political terrain of hierarchy and prejudice within the very tissue of this account. And these effects are not confined to language.[6] Within the grain of representation (whether by this we mean spoken or written language, visual images, gestural movements, indeed, any differential marking), the male subject is privileged over the female. A metonymy of attributes is understood to be properly aligned with masculinity, just as their opposite characteristics line up to provide femininity with its due counterbalance. But what are these oppositions whose meanings are so sexually alive and whose balancing 'copulation' generates this asymmetry?

Binary Oppositions and Sexual Difference

We can extrapolate from Ferdinand de Saussure's study of signs to suggest that an economy of value inheres within *all* forms of representation. The word 'economy' is appropriate here because value is hierarchically organised and produced through an implicated series of binary exchanges that oppose presence to absence, positive to negative, and so on. Saussure argued that all meaning is produced relationally that is, differentially. And his representation of difference is instructive in its political implications. Saussure describes the generative energy of meaning production that occurs within the matrix of the language system as 'absent' from the actual product (e.g. the meaning of a word) that it produces. This need to sever the process of production from its product has familiar resonances with conventional understandings of human reproduction. A woman's body is granted no value in actually producing a child, but is instead conceptualised as a mere vessel through which (male) value passes. The worth of the actual labour of production, whether it is provided by the body of the language system or the body of woman, are negated when they are described as 'absent' from their respective products. Interestingly, the implications of Saussure's larger thesis about language actually refute his own description here. Hence the perceived relevance of Saussure's work for feminism is that it goes some way to explaining how meaning is both en-gendered and en-gendering. However, the notion of difference is deceptively complex, and we might well continue to wonder how specific differences are actually generated.

One way to approach this complexity is to ground it in an example, and as modernity and rationality are importantly connected, it might be fruitful to interrogate the concept 'Reason'. How, then, do we determine that an argument is reasonable? One response might be to assume that Reason is something whose powerful self-evidence overwhelms its opposition. According to this view, Reason is self-defined, possessing an autonomous existence which is independent of what we might call 'non-Reason'. In a sense, Reason declares itself in such a way that it lacks nothing. It requires nothing more, not even explanation. Yet the power of a reasoned argument actually depends upon its ability to take its distance from its opponents, to declare its difference from them, and to enforce the purity and autonomy of its identity claim by dint of this separation. That is to say, distance makes all the difference. However, it seems that a strange contradiction resides at the heart of Reason. Reason's claim to autonomy is indebted to the connection it shares with its declared opposite, since the identity of Reason consists of its own differentiation through comparison.

When we think of binary oppositions such as knowledge/ignorance, mind/body, culture/nature, man/woman, and so on, we tend to assume that each of these terms or notions is independent, having a discrete and autonomous meaning that can safely be partitioned off from the other. After all, isn't man a completely separate and therefore different entity to woman? Within the broad embrace of postmodern critique however, the relational connection between these pairs has come under closer scrutiny. For example, although a binary appears to be composed of two independent terms, the asymmetrical status of presence to absence, or positive to negative, binds their differences through comparison and contrast. Woman is defined according to her difference from man. Consequently, there can be no equity between these terms. One term is understood to be self-defined (self-present, or self-evident); the other term marks the absence, or lack, of the first term. The latter is a shadow term, a mere negative image of the more valued term. In a sense, we might say that the negative term's very existence is compromised.[7]

At the risk of belabouring a point, I want to dwell on the subtle complexities that attend the workings of binary oppositions. They deserve an extended discussion because their implications are ubiquitous within postmodernism's labyrinthine logic. They also resurface as one of the foundational problematics through which contemporary criticism engages the political and ethical difficulties that surround the representation of sexual and cultural difference.

We gain a little purchase on some of these issues if we think of a binary as an operation that works in much the same way as the gestalt in a line drawing of a figure against a background. We are all familiar with the central image of an outlined candlestick that suddenly disappears to reveal the perfect symmetry of two faces in profile. The difference between these two images is so opposed that the presence of one entirely negates the other. Although there are two potential images here, only one has positive expression at any particular moment in time. One image is present, surrounded by an absence. When one image is positively figured, the other is negatively emptied out, and vice versa. But as we ponder a logic that interprets difference through the on/off violence of A/minus A, we should be aware that the notion of 'absence' is quite inadequate to the complexities of this relationship. What is thought to be an empty space, a hole, a blank, a nothingness, is obviously pregnant with an energy that is itself generative. This 'absence' actually sustains any image's visibility. It is the condition of possibility that figures forth the image's very legibility; the condition of possibility of perception itself.[8]

If the notion of 'absence' is now seen to be quite misleading, then so too is the notion of 'presence'. 'Presence' implies that an entity, whether it be a thing, a concept, or a person, is self-defined and autonomous; in other words, its value derives entirely from within itself. But this positive sense of an independent identity represses the fact that its claim to autonomy is actually produced, and therefore dependent upon, what it excludes as 'other'. 'Logocentrism' is the word used by Jacques Derrida to conjure the battery of presuppositions that accompanies this notion of 'presence', a notion whose legacy is endowed in the very structure of Western thought.

Let us return to the image of the figure and background to tease out a few more of these ramifications. The postmodern critique of presence confounds our conventional understanding of identity by concentrating upon the processes through which identity comes to be defined. The relational nature of identity as a production effect means that what appears to be unified is actually fractured and divided from itself, and what appears to be separate is actually conjoined. One implication of this concerns 'the knowing subject' who is supposedly unified by self-certainty. As the Saussurean schema divides all identity from itself, it also divides subjectivity. The subject of postmodernism is therefore described as a divided, or decentred subject, because it cannot know (that is, make present to itself) the extraordinary complexity of its own being.

Many critics who are aware of the hidden political agenda within binary logic try to get off the slippery slide that unravels 'one-ness', and, by extension, 'two-ness', by resorting to the stability of a third term. In a binary opposition, this can be represented by the bar that divides the terms. Just as with the figure and ground, it is located in their defining outline. Yet the structure of a binary opposition entails more than superficially meets the eye. It is not something that can be escaped from, although it can be differently inhabited.

I can explain this last point by again returning to the figure/ground image. If we trace the 'third term' of its dividing outline, we realise that the nature of identity is complicated. What divides is also divided. For we can describe the line as an entity in itself, as what defines and therefore gives identity to both faces, and also as something that is integral to the perception of the candlestick. The line's internal ambiguity also extends outward into the very frame of the image, posing the question of identity between inside and outside all over again. The movement between these different perceptions takes place within the identity of the line, but in a way that suggests that what is outside the line already inhabits it. Identity is therefore always fractured by the very differences that produce it.[9]

To summarise the puzzle so far, a binary pair cannot be understood as oppositional in any strict sense if the two terms are also internal to each other: there is 'something more' to binarisms than is at first apparent. The critique of logocentrism (the economy of presence) is important for feminism because the nuanced violence of logocentrism is also phallocentric. This means that the sexual inflection of the presence/absence split that underpins all dichotomies routinely denigrates 'the feminine' and privileges 'the masculine'. For example, we grant that knowledge overcomes ignorance, just as light penetrates the dark recesses of the unknown. The mind comprehends the body in a way that is presumed irreversible. Man penetrates woman just as Culture comes to dominate and subdue the forces of Nature. In other words, the ineluctable march of Reason and Progress through which modernity is figured has a masculine 'morphology' that lends agency to *certain* concepts by feminising others and rendering them passive. Woman is then defined *as* passivity and her identity is thereby explained and naturalised through these terms.

The violence of this logic is immediately legible when we think of the way in which woman's sexual difference is conceptualised. Woman is made the ground upon which man erects his sexuality, just as the ground that produces the apparently self-defined figure of the candlestick is then made to disappear. For example, the very word 'vagina' is Latin for 'sheath', a word whose status as mere repository is granted only a minimal sense of existence by that which fills it. The word 'clitoris' is similarly compromised, deriving from the Greek word for 'hidden'. But we might ask, from whom is this organ hidden? From the touch of the woman for whom it is part? Or is this sense of its concealment determined by an external gaze that views the differences between bodies only in terms of his own?

Jacques Lacan's re-reading of Freud via the Saussurean analysis of language specifically investigates this production of sexed subjectivity. Subsequent feminist engagements with psychoanalysis also intervene in this story that casts woman as a hole or lack, an absence whose negative status can be summarised as 'not man'.[10] Through the critique of this binary logic, postmodern critics are able to analyse its restrictive effects in order to reinscribe this textual economy with other meanings and other, different subjectivities.

Nevertheless, the space between so-called binary oppositions has remained necessary to the conventions of Reason and logic upon which all of us continue to rely. Binary oppositions provide the temporal and spatial separability that allows us to use such notions as cause and effect or origin and end; they secure the moral basis for judgements that turn around good versus evil; and they anchor our political agendas that presume to distinguish right from wrong, or better from worse.

When I began this discussion, I argued that feminism was a political movement that relied on the same assumptions that inform modernism. For the subject of feminist emancipationist rhetoric is the same unified subject who uses masculinist dualisms that devalue 'the feminine'. The question is then, how do we proceed against the violence of phallocentrism when, as feminists, we seem entirely dependent upon modernism's constructs?

I have tried to anticipate this question in a way that will hopefully make the displacement of its terms a little easier. It will be remembered that I originally argued that postmodernism is, ultimately, inseparable from modernism: its identity is viral. Postmodernism re-members its history and has a protean ability to 'morph' through a variety of often contradictory identities. Clearly, there is nothing particularly sacred about the notion of identity within this parasitic format. One of the paradoxes within this logic is that modernism, for all its political ills, should be understood to generate its own critique. Similarly, feminism is not 'the other' of patriarchal repression, if by that we mean that feminism has an autonomous political will of its own. The political force field that is phallocentrism also produces the specificity of what we call feminism. This irony does not mean that feminism is subsumed to phallocentrism. Rather, it implies that there is more to phallocentrism than its binary articulation reveals—the phallus has a hole in it! And further, it implies that the political grain of representation entails a complexity that both constrains *and* produces; it inhibits and constitutes in the same movement. In their very different ways, both Michel Foucault and Derrida argue that power is overly simplified when its effects are described through a negative vocabulary of denial, control, oppression, and domination. Yet to say that power has constitutive force is not a reversal of this negative. The critique of binaries 'enlivens' and reconfigures the very terms positive/negative.

Representation and Reality—What's the Difference?

As I try to explain what might be involved in rethinking 'the political' (because when you get down to it, that is what all of this is about), I can hear protests from the reader with whom I am having this imagined dialogue. She is becoming increasingly impatient with all this abstract analysis of language and representation, and is waiting to be convinced that these esoteric theoretical debates can make any significant difference to the lives of real women. The assumption here is that political realities in the concrete world do not survive for very long in the rarefied air that only Theory can breathe.

It is difficult to answer the sobering pragmatism that such appeals to 'the Real' invariably command: the persuasive self-evidence of its logic seems irrefutable. Unfortunately, my response in this context, bound as it is by the constraints of space, can only be a shorthand one. But this unquestioning faith in the *self-evident*, an absolute faith in what presents itself as beyond question, can be misleading, as the above discussion has tried to convey. (We might take a little courage here from feminism's own, insistent interrogation of the battery of self-evident and previously undisputed 'givens' that prescribe women's lives.) The question of what will constitute evidence is very much in dispute here, as is the conventional understanding of 'the Real'. However, this does not mean that either notion can simply be dispensed with by postmodern critics. The argument, rather, is over the complexity of these terms and over what their use is supposed to guarantee.

If we take 'the Real' as an unproblematic category, then it must be something which is universally held in common. This is an assumption insufficiently questioned by the discourse of Anthropology, a discourse which reads global diversity in its own image. It is clear that the subject who is born into a language, culture, and history that is foreign to the West may well be politically disenfranchised on both a national and global scale. The West comprehends 'otherness' through developmentalist narratives of separation and distance; a temporal 'before' or a spatial 'elsewhere'. The West thereby secures itself in a 'here' and 'now' that measures the difference from its 'self-present' referentiality as an absence.[11] In other words, ethnocentrism is enacted through the same logic as phallocentrism.

Postmodern theories of representation engage the political ramifications of this ethnocentrism in ways that can alert us to our prejudices. For example, if the body is always a specific body, inscribed and informed by cultural and historical significances that are not universally legible, then how do women in the West presume to adjudicate the meaning of a practice such as clitoridectomy? Can we assume that pleasures and sexualities are ahistorical, and that departures from a Western set of values deserve Western intervention? Can Western women insist on the right of control over their own bodies and yet claim that 90 million women in Africa should not have that same right because, from our perspective, they seem to abuse it? Can we glibly continue to claim that these women *lack* something (namely our knowledges, our sense of self, our cultural values) when the politics of feminising 'the other' as 'lacking what I am' constitutes the very logic of phallocentrism? Must we always measure difference as a deficit? These are difficult questions, and I do not want to suggest that an attention to the representational complexities of these issues can deliver an easy answer. However, there is surely an ethical imperative for feminists to acknowledge the ethnocentrism of representations that universalise 'Woman', because, just as with phallocentrism, the violent effects of these discourses are material.[12]

For many feminists and cultural critics who work with psychoanalysis, semiotics, and discourse theories, the importance of their practice is not diminished by comparison with other, more conventional forms of political intervention. Clearly, one does not preclude the other. In fact, the binary logic that conveniently separates theory from practice, or representation from Reality, is precisely what is being contested here. Although the nature of the relationship between representation and Reality is intensely debated, most postmodern feminists working on this problematic agree that there *is* a relationship and that its effects are lived.

A deconstructive reading that destabilises Reality's status as concrete origin and ground, also interprets the representation/Reality split as an enmeshed textile of relational differentials. According to this view, what we take to be Reality involves something more, a much more complicated and implicated density of 'forces'. Moreover, these 'forces' are *political* differentials in that their expression is hierarchised and sexualised. Real men and real women do not precede this political 'textile'; they are produced within its weave. However, this is not to suggest that the knit of this material cannot be recast to different effect. Indeed, this is the object of a postmodern feminism.

Australian Feminisms and Local Consumption

My attention to the politics of difference has tried to address the erasure of specificity. When the masculine subject ascends to the heavens in order to assume the advantage of a god's-eye view, the result of this all-seeing gaze is presumed objective: the Truth. Of course, to achieve this universal perspective, with its claims of impartiality, the observer must transcend the mortal 'sheath' that is the matter of his body. The body encumbers Truth by locating it; by insisting that perspective is always particular, partial, incomplete. When we ask questions about the specificity of woman within this disembodied fantasy, we do more than redress an account that both essentialises and elides woman's existence.

We also return man to a corporeal 'place' that situates him and begins to give some account of the knowledges he produces. In other words, masculinity is as much a feminist issue as the body of concerns traditionally associated with women.

I want to move from this discussion of the specificity of woman to ask a question about Australian feminisms. Given the historical and cultural specificity of our location, how do Australian feminists represent their particular perspectives on a global stage? How do we articulate our differences from the hegemonic narratives of Anglo-American feminisms? Does our relative isolation from a world that has the power to describe us as 'down' and 'underneath' make a difference to what postmodernism might mean within an Australian context?[13]

As mentioned above, the violent economies that interpret sexual difference through a logic of the Same (phallocentrism), belong to a mode of accounting that also measures cultural difference through Western frames of reference (ethnocentrism). We are perhaps used to analysing systems of representation that organise the 'otherness' of the Third World into feminised legibility. The critique of epistemology, together with the increasing attention to the fact that anthropology and other humanist discourses have constitutive force in representing 'the other', have become important sites of postmodern criticism.[14]

However, my question about the specificity of Australian feminisms concerns the heterogeneity of the West. I am referring to the 'otherness' or difference *within* a Western perspective. This difference must be repressed in order to discover 'otherness' elsewhere. The way in which Australian feminisms are represented can tell us something about the violent nature of Western representations of difference on a 'local level', and why their global export incurs such cost. In short, we have to question whether we are able to replace pretensions to universal truths with the specificity of our situated knowledges.[15]

By privileging local knowledges over their global generalisations, we acknowledge that specific knowledges are indeed different from universal ones. However, when we presume to redress the latter's neglect by reversing the binary, we interpret this difference as something which is defined by its isolation, or distance, from a universal. In doing this, we confuse the notion of specificity with autonomy, and completely erase the constitutive nature of binary relationships. We cannot escape the effects of binary logic in this way. For example, in order to talk about the peculiarities of Australian feminisms, we *need* to use those same hegemonic discourses that render our differences invisible. This need cannot be limited through the qualification of 'strategic use', as some cultural critics would hope, because we simply have no alternatives. Specificity is constituted within and through the violence of universal knowledges; it is not outside their inscriptive force. This means that when Australian feminists read Anglo-American feminisms, the resulting 'inter-text' reinscribes the difference between producer and receiver, writer and reader, agency and passivity. To read, to make sense of something, involves an act of re-cognition: reading performs a very specific historical and cultural conjunction that is necessarily and always transformative. If we animate the notion of reading to include this sense of historical and cultural *re-inscription*, then the complexity of what it is to read involves much more than we can comprehend. Consequently, 'specificity' is not 'something' that can be represented in any definitive way because it is always in the abrasive process of becoming.

I have concentrated on the vexed nature of identity because I think that there is something in postmodernism's interrogation of identity—an irreverence for the limit—that is quite self-consciously played out within Australian feminisms. With some significant exceptions, Anglo-American feminisms routinely identify postmodernism as something 'other', as something 'outside' the boundaries of its political practice. Against this, Australian feminisms have been immersed in writing, interpreting, and recycling these exotic imports into vernacular relevance for nearly twenty years.

Many young Australian intellectuals made the almost obligatory journey abroad during the 1970s and returned to translate a number of foreign texts into local usefulness. Through such broadsheets and journals as *Gay Liberation Press*, *Working Papers*, *Feral*, *Local Consumption Publications*, *Intervention*, *Art & Text* and others, Australians were alerted to the relevance of many thinkers whose work is today gathered under the banner of postmodernism. The point is, the debates that surrounded these texts were *never not political*. In Australia, feminists, Marxists, and gay liberation activists were all enmeshed in discussing and contesting how these texts could be taken up. And as I have tried to explain above, this 'taking up' was never a faithful reception of American, English, or for that matter, French receptions.[16]

I want to stress the importance of feminism to postmodernism's identity in Australia, and vice versa, because the recipe that turns such thinkers as Baudrillard, Lacan, Irigaray, Kristeva, Foucault, Derrida, Cixous, le Doeuff and Deleuze into antipodean nourishment is made up of local ingredients. These ingredients make for a different understanding of both postmodernism and feminism to that which is usually found in Anglo-American readings of the same literature. This grafting and recycling of foreign texts for domestic consumption has meant that Australians have made critical use of male-authored texts in order to articulate *feminist* critiques. The political efficacy of a theoretical approach is measured not so much by an assessment of its origin as it is by an engagement with how well it can be put to work. In other words, reading, or interpretation, is a performative and political act of transformation.

As Anne Freadman has described her own practice:

> My major methodological presupposition will be that any text is a rewriting of the field or fields of its own emergence, that to write, to read, or to speak is first of all to turn other texts into discursive material, displacing the enunciative position from which those materials have been propounded. I mean that 'use' can always do something a little different from merely repeating 'usage'.[17]

Freadman's summary provocatively suggests that feminism is first and foremost a critical reading practice. If we understand that the labour of re-reading effects a re-writing, and that a 'text' is only sometimes a book, then we differently inscribe what we mean by both 'politics' and 'representation'. We also begin to liberate feminism from the containment of its patriarchal definition. Through this re-writing, the subject of 'woman' is inter-related and implicated with absolutely everything else, indeed, with the general business of knowledge production itself. As a result, there is no subject that is not properly of interest to feminism. All knowledges are therefore of feminist concern, including those knowledges conventionally given over to men. And if feminism's identity seems strangely solvent within the generalised stretch of this politics of representation, we might now read this ubiquity as a sign of feminism's increased pertinence rather than of its dissolution.

ELEVEN

The Gendering of Knowledge: The Case of Anthropology and Feminism

Maila Stivens

This chapter looks at some of the issues involved in beginning to unravel the gendering of knowledge in anthropology. A central concern is the difficult relationship between Second Wave feminist understandings of 'gender' and the epistemological and political dilemmas in researching and writing about so-called 'non-Western', 'peripheral' or 'Other' societies. That there is an awkward relationship between feminisms and anthropology has been acknowledged by a number of writers in the field.[1] This uneasy relationship has also been the focus of at least one international conference, in Amsterdam in 1988. The main issue that came out of that meeting was how feminist anthropologists might hold on to what they have often seen as their emancipatory project in a postmodern world marked by extreme intellectual fragmentation and a retreat from totalising theories. Central sources of unease have been the differing relationships which feminists and anthropologists have to audience, positionality and accountability.[2] Many feminist anthropologists have found themselves awkwardly and ambiguously placed on the margins of both Western feminisms and anthropology, amidst a growing awareness of the inherent Eurocentrism of much contemporary Western feminist theory-making.

Both Western feminist thought and anthropology share some similar intellectual dilemmas. Both are regarded by their respective practitioners as being in crisis or at least facing an impasse. Feminisms have been in a quandary about their theoreticians' turn towards the psychoanalytic and postmodern; anthropology has been facing a wholesale undermining of its legitimacy because of its colonial history. Both have inherited some of the contemporary disarray in social thought, especially the difficulty of having an object outside the terms of 'normal' Western discourse. Feminist anthropologists have attempted to unravel the categories of their home discipline's thought in the context of a meeting of Euro-American and 'peripheral'/'Third World'[3] political and scholarly practices; but this has been only the beginning of a series of intellectual difficulties, a source of perhaps unresolvable tensions.

Feminist anthropologists' critiques of their discipline emerged in the late 1960s during a period of considerable political unrest, both within and outside the discipline. Critics had already forced acknowledgement of the problems arising out of anthropology's colonial genesis as the handmaiden of colonialism. In its strongest versions, this critique implied no future at all for a discipline hopelessly mired in its role as an agent of colonialism and neo-colonialism. Even critical anthropology, however, was attacked by feminist anthropologists for its consistent failure to address feminist concerns. As Lorraine Nencel and Peter Pels point out, early feminist critics of anthropology found themselves in a complex position, sharing objectives with both leftist politics and classical anthropology, but dissatisfied with both:[4] feminist anthropology's relationship with the rest of the critical movement has often been a tense one.[5]

Anthropology as a discipline emerges into the 1990s as a set of often unstable and contested practices. There is a continuing perception of crisis among many practitioners, with repeated critical attacks on empiricism, positivism, neo-colonialism, androcentrism, orientalism and latterly, suggestions of a perhaps terminal stalemate among various fractions of the anthropological enterprise. The critics themselves can appear to even the most sympathetic observers as a squabbling array of neo-Marxists, feminists and postmodernists,[6] who relate to the growing ascendancy of culturalist anthropology in varying ways.[7] To attribute present developments solely to a postmodern assault on metanarratives, however, overlooks the history of critical and reflexive initiatives within the discipline.

There are probably many understandings of 'postmodern' in these debates. Nencel and Pels, however, see this allegedly postmodern turn towards the literary within anthropology, especially a rapprochement with the current flowering of post-colonial literary criticism,[8] as merely a modernist experimental moment. They argue that the so-called New Ethnography is in fact a positivist attempt to reclaim the lost authority of the realist, fieldwork-based ethnography.[9] They are suggesting, therefore, that the apparent postmodern turn appears to be little more than a way of dressing up the long-term practices of anthropology, in particular positivist claims to produce a real and true picture of supposedly 'other' cultures, in new clothes.

Although feminist anthropology has played a central part in the deconstruction of 'traditional' anthropology, many feel that it equally faces a crisis of anthropological legitimation, a realisation that it cannot speak for the oppressed, nor continue to claim the power to define problems and solutions.[10] But as Nencel and Pels point out, continuing feminist challenges to both institutional and critical anthropology have often been closed off through various devices which prevent practitioners from accumulating the academic capital of tenure, publications, and reputations.[11]

The relationship between 'Western' feminisms and anthropology in the heady days of the early 1970s was a warm one. Anthropology was a robust contributor to feminist challenges to the prevailing paradigms of social science, with newly qualified practitioners fresh from the feminist front enthusiastically criticising their discipline. Young would-be-feminist anthropologists in London, where I was at the time, gathered into groups to dissect the androcentric heritage. They met some hostility from the anthropological establishment, even from older, established women. This reception, however, only hardened the resolve of many of the young enthusiasts.

The history of the uses made of anthropology in Second Wave feminist writing would be a study in itself,[12] but could well be summarised by the more pessimistic as one of progressive withdrawal by Western feminisms. It seems likely that the early would-be-feminist knowledge was received very positively because its cross-cultural project was seen as undermining claims about women's subordination's being 'natural'. The comparative approach of anthropology was seen as providing evidence for a radical critique of Western gender arrangements. But it was this very comparative perspective that led to the unravelling of the relationship.

Let me relate my own experience with matriarchy study groups. A number of these sprang up in London, and they rang around the universities looking for anthropologists to come and talk to them about matriarchy. As I had experience of the Minangkabau of West Sumatra, one of the most famous 'matrilineal' societies in anthropology textbooks, and was researching its daughter society in Malaysia, Negeri Sembilan, I was co-opted.

I talked about how, in my view, female property ownership probably did give women some 'autonomy' (a problematic concept, nonetheless, with roots in Western liberal humanism). I suggested that female-centred kinship was also a great help to women, but that Minangkabau and Negeri Sembilan society did not constitute matriarchies, and there probably had never been any matriarchal societies as far as the archeological record told us. My audience, who had invited me to display my anthropological authority, became very quiet and rather sad at my (no doubt disappointing) academicism and positivist pronouncings on 'matriarchy'. The invitations to myself and others to address such meetings slowly stopped, although the matriarchy study groups continued to flourish and do so up to the present day; in California and increasingly elsewhere they explore the power and the spirituality of the Goddess. I do not think the audience's reaction to my and other contributions was simply a case of disappointment at our being unable to shake ourselves free of academicism. The ambivalence had other, more profound roots, in my opinion, roots in a basic clash of paradigms between different feminist practices. As the attachment to ideas of the essential feminine grew within some branches of the Western movement, the historical and comparative approach of anthropology was less and less welcome.

This clash continues to the present, although it has manifested itself in different ways at different times. Many radical feminists clearly felt and continue to feel that feminist anthropologists, like other academicians, have not only lost sight of the political struggle but have also undermined alternative mythologies with their insistence on looking at history within a comparative—indeed, some would argue, relativist—stance. It is notable how little anthropology features in a great deal of contemporary feminist writing, unless it is invoked in discussions of the challenges to Western feminisms coming from and on behalf of Third World women and other women of colour. But that invocation has been complicated by recent post-colonial critiques of Western knowledges: these see all the projects of the 'Western' Enlightenment as irremediably tainted by colonialism and by the false universalism of the Western subject position. Attached as they often are to the modernist emancipatory projects of the Enlightenment, feminisms are confronted with immediate dilemmas by these post-colonial critiques. But the hostility of some literary critiques of anthropology as a colonial enterprise, while no doubt accurate, often displays very little knowledge of the history of anthropology's own internal critiques.[13] The cynical might see this as a claim for 'territory' once clearly legitimated as anthropology's.

The reasons for the progressive withdrawal of some feminist interest in anthropology warrant some examination. First, this withdrawal seems to me to be symptomatic of trends in some Western theorising, which continue to resist the noisy, numerous and increasingly 'fashionable' attempts to point out its own 'othering' practices. Bell hooks, for example, points to the ways that transatlantic feminist writing continues to fail to acknowledge its own racism.[14] Thus Western feminisms have concentrated on theories drawing on (presumed universal) language and psychic structures; this concentration has operated within a field occupied by scholars who have until recently rarely questioned their location within an unreflected, unreconstructed and indeed essentialised 'West'.[15] The demise of anthropology in its critical mode within feminism might be seen simply as a rejection of its awkward and embarrassing insistence on exploring difference within the category 'woman'; but it might also be seen as part of a general cultural abandonment of the exotic Other as a vehicle for messages about 'our' society within the centres of transatlantic theory-making. As Marcus and Fischer suggest, anthropology and feminism have at different times functioned in the European imagination as sources of cultural critique of domestic concerns, the cultural domain of the 'feminine' more recently displacing the earlier 'exotic'.[16]

The reception of feminist theory within anthropology has been equally problematic. There have been the same kinds of institutional resistance as in other disciplines. Degrees of continuing marginalisation are evidenced in such collections as Clifford and Marcus's *Writing Culture*;[17] there feminist anthropology scarcely (and by now notoriously) receives a footnote, and is excluded from any discussion of experimental ethnography. For feminist anthropologists themselves, redressing the sins of omission and commission of anthropology in its treatment of gender has proved more complex than the earlier feminist critics had hoped. It was soon realised that adding a few women would have little effect, unless their addition disrupted a few paradigms. Incorporating 'women' into anthropology was only to be achieved at the analytical and theoretical level,[18] with a recasting of social theory. It was not enough to 'add women to the existing paradigms and stir': instead, the recognition of the gendered nature of much knowledge derived from the Western Enlightenment should enforce a recasting of those paradigms.

Feminist anthropologists, then, faced certain problems in trying to reconstruct anthropological knowledge. There were, first, some difficulties with the critiques of bias within anthropology. It was hard to allege that women had been totally ignored: the founding classics contained a great deal of material about aspects of gender, for kinship and marriage were the centrepiece of the whole anthropological enterprise. It was rather a question as to how women had been represented in that body of work.[19] In particular, a number of feminists and others (e.g. Schneider in his more recent writing about anthropology's continuing fascination with 'kinship'),[20] have alleged that a great deal of this writing projected Anglo-American notions of family, gender, woman, man and domesticity on to its objects. This projection informed the whole cast of discussions of male–female relations, when they did surface, for example as 'sexual segregation' and 'sex-antagonism'; it also informed postgraduate instruction in the central anthropological rite, 'doing fieldwork', when the appropriateness of male or female ethnographers was debated.

Feminisms' political attachment to the central concept of universal 'woman' has provoked particular anxiety among feminist anthropologists about essentialism. As Linda Nicholson and Nancy Fraser have argued,[21] although feminists offer robust conceptions of social criticism, they have often tended to lapse into foundationalism and essentialism. In pointing to the problems with 'foundationalism'—that is with the 'modern' ideas that philosophy and theory in general can function to *ground* political and social criticism—Nicholson and Fraser were acknowledging the lure of feminism's roots in the large theories, the 'grand narratives' of modernity.[22] Second Wave feminisms of various varieties have been premised on basic and highly political assumptions: that there is an underlying actual or potential identity between all women; that there is a unitary body of women's interests; and that feminism depends for its cohesion—whether potential or actual—on women's shared oppression. Such (essentialist) assumptions lie behind the concepts of sexual politics, sisterhood, and other ideas about a shared solidarity among women. The historian Rosalind Delmar sees such assumptions as feminism's greatest problem.

> Women, in a sense, are feminism's greatest problem. The assumption of a potential identity between women, rather than solving the problem, became a condition of increasing tensions. Of these tensions, not the least important is the intellectual tension generated by a crisis of the concept 'woman' with feminist thought. As a concept 'woman' is too fragile to bear the weight of all the contents and meanings ascribed to it. The end of much research by feminists has been to show the tremendous diversity of the meaning of womanhood across cultures and over time.[23]

These sentiments have been echoed by Susan Bordo, who similarly suggests that the category 'gender' itself has become so fragmented by racial, class and historical particularity as to self-destruct as an analytical category.[24] I would argue with Henrietta Moore and many others that what the category *woman*—or, for that matter, man—means in any given context has to be investigated and not assumed: it is always culturally and historically specific. The concept *woman* cannot stand as an analytical category in anthropological enquiry, and consequently there can be no analytical meaning in such concepts as the position of women, the subordination of women, and male dominance when they are applied universally.[25]

Feminist anthropologists' current disquiet at the preoccupations of some feminist theory-making no doubt has its roots in the now discredited practices of speaking for one's colonised subjects. But these anthropologists are part of a chorus of Third World and other voices raised against the imposition of Western feminist agendas on the Third World.[26] Clearly, Western feminist scholars have faced enormous difficulties of their own in having to deconstruct much of the analytical equipment with which previous analyses had operated, but it is widely felt that they have to face up to further dimensions of difference. The inheritance of Western political thought and popular discourse within feminism has had profound effects in limiting the approach to difference, in spite of feminist rejections of these traditions and their limiting categories of analysis. In my view, a great deal of 'Western' feminist theorising has simply failed to move beyond its own intellectual and geographical boundaries.

There has been some recognition recently of the ways in which Western feminisms have often explicitly marginalised in discourse all those outside their implicit object—the North Atlantic woman—even while arguing for diversity.[27] But the contemporary trinity of 'race, class and gender' as the keystones of a new diverse feminism all too frequently represent an attempt to deflect the immediately confronting political challenges of women of colour in the US or Britain. Women beyond the Western centres of knowledge production are still often constructed as the subordinate part of the conceptual couple Western/Third World, and thus rendered invisible in Western feminist politics. As many have argued, the concept of difference itself is often made to refer to various versions of an irreducible essential feminine different from the male, not to explore the differences among women.

Inserting Third World scholars into existing research arrangements is no answer to these difficulties. An Algerian anthropologist, Marnia Lazreg, has put the dilemma of Third World scholars researching themselves very well when she asks, 'How can an Algerian woman write about women in Algeria, when her space has been defined, her subjects objectified and her language chosen for her?'[28] The fundamental analytical categories derived from the Western Enlightenment have constructed Third World women in terms of colonial paradigms from which women have been unable to escape. As Edward Said has pointed out, the very terms of the debates in which these issues are explored, the essentialised 'West' counterposed to an equally essentialised 'Third World', are a central part of the problem.[29]

Some Third World women, constructing themselves as bearers of 'authentic' counter-hegemonic discourses, present themselves as the better analysts of their own societies. They may, as they have done in Malaysia, challenge visiting scholars like myself about their right to speak. Some post-colonial commentators, however, argue that the claims of Third World intellectual women to be the political bearers of such authentic discourses do not necessarily stand up to close scrutiny.[30] To assert such a claim, to oppose Western representations of themselves as victims of capitalism or patriarchy in a pan-cultural subordination, these women have little choice but to operate a 'Western' modernist discourse about individual rights. In empirical terms, their own position as intellectual elite women can undermine such claims in any case. Such critics have to distance themselves from debates about the nature of their own practice, asserting an essentially innocent idea of authentic knowledge. They are often, of course, members of a middle-class intelligentsia tied into a global scholarly enterprise, although we might debate on what social and political terms they enter that global enterprise, lacking as they do access to the centre's knowledge-making institutions such as publishing and tenure. Moreover, such critics may be silenced, closed off by positivist orthodoxies about the 'outside observer's' supposed objectivity. Nonetheless, they will be only too well aware of the layers of past political experience constructing the meetings between 'local' and 'expatriate' scholars.

There is a further important issue here, one that preoccupied the subalternist scholars of India:[31] that is, whether and in what form counter-discourses can develop. Does the colonial and post-colonial hegemony of thought, of representation, 'permit' counter-discourses that are not still entrapped within the dominant discourse? Can Third World or 'peripheral' knowledge-production centres generate frameworks of knowledge about themselves that do not continue to reproduce all the categories of thought from the West that are part of the processes subsuming the non-West? Can we/they escape from the dominant victim/subject couple, which merely reinscribes another dualism? As Lata Mani has argued, women's agency, while a central concern, remains poorly theorised.

> The discourse of woman as victim has been invaluable to feminism in pointing to the systematic character of gender domination, [but it can leave] us with reductive representations of women as primarily beings who are passive and acted upon. In other words, we are left with that common figure of Eurocentric feminist discourse, the Third World woman (in Mohanty's 1988 phrase) as 'always, already victim'.[32]

Kalpana Ram has taken up this theme, suggesting that we need to bring dominance and resistance into the same account, rather than viewing them as mutually exclusive.[33]

Conclusions

I have, then, highlighted some of the issues involved in unravelling the gendering of anthropological knowledge, pointing to the complexities of the meeting of 'First World' theories and 'Third World' objects. As I have noted, many feminist anthropologists hoping to develop emancipatory knowledge-making ponder therefore the future of their project—however that is defined. Many feel marginalised by both anthropology (androcentric, increasingly reflexive) and feminism (Eurocentric, post-structuralist and/or postmodernist). They feel under attack from local political-economist activists as well for being expatriate colonial scholars. One of the ironies surrounding such debates is that feminism, with thoroughly modern origins, a product of Enlightenment-led modernity, is now claimed by some as a postmodern philosophy and practice.[34] That claim is itself a cause of anxiety to some feminist anthropologists: while highly sympathetic to calls for the recognition of the historical and political situatedness of knowledges, they are uneasy about the implications of some postmodern critiques of Western feminist 'foundationalist' narratives.[35] A rising anthropological chorus has gone into print, counselling against the depoliticisation inherent in postmodernism.[36] The concern with postmodernity is perhaps ironic, given that we might well ask how complete the modernist project is outside the North Atlantic axis. That perhaps partly accounts for the decidedly ambivalent response of many feminist anthropologists to the postmodern, literary turn in anthropology. A number clearly share the widely quoted suspicions of Elizabeth Fox-Genovese and Nancy Hartsock about postmodernism:

> The retreat from the modern, the proclaiming of the death of the author, looks very suspicious coming at a point when the white male cultural elite was beginning to have to share its status with the women and the peoples of other races and cultures.[37]

On the other hand, many of even the most pessimistic and marginalised feminist anthropologists will admit that the assault on paradigms, the 'po-mo' deconstruction with all its inherent dangers of depoliticisation, is also in many ways necessary to any attempt to reconstruct a feminist social theory, even though it may be uncomfortable, difficult and perhaps politically dangerous. Peripheral feminisms and those who speak for them render the unified political projects of Western feminists problematic by challenging their universality. In particular, I suggested that the central political concept of 'woman' as an undifferentiated category can become increasingly unsustainable in the face of the insistence on historical particularities. The deconstruction of 'woman' as a coherent political identity—and the deconstruction of gender—was unavoidable and necessary. But the process has left us with serious difficulties—both epistemological and political. Many Western feminists leave these difficulties to Third World women to resolve, as if it were their problem. Of course, we could call in the *deus ex machina* of postmodernist thinking about marginality to solve some of these dilemmas: the marginal Orientalised Other woman could thus become the central defining subject of a new feminism.[38] As Lazreg remarks for Algeria, the challenge is to move beyond deconstruction, beyond difference as *indifference*:

> History has dealt these women a hard blow. It held them hostage to colonial or imperial ventures and delivered them to travelers, chroniclers, painters and anthropologists. Now they are in a position from which they could recapture the dispersed fragments of their selves and put them back in combinations that the motley crowd of their observers may not suspect. The task is enormous but necessary.[39]

TWELVE

Neo-classical Economics: A Feminist Perspective

Gillian Hewitson

Economic discourse has come to dominate political debate and to direct economic and social policy decision-making in Australia. The figure of the competitive individual, the 'free market' ideology, and the constant recourse to the efficiency imperative, derive from neo-classical economics (NCE) which is the dominant school of thought within the economics discipline.[1] Not only has the language of NCE become 'naturalised', but NCE has invaded the subject matters of other social sciences and humanities, including politics, sociology, geography, anthropology, law, and women's studies.[2] The pervasiveness of NCE, its discursive authority, and its power to shape the institutional environment require the development of a feminist perspective on its assumptions and implications. Yet, while most social sciences and humanities disciplines have been subjected to such feminist interrogations and found problematic, NCE has been largely ignored.[3]

This essay employs the 'sexual difference' approach to analyse neo-classical microeconomics. After a brief description of this approach, the key assumptions of NCE are delineated, with particular attention to those which construct 'rational economic man' (REM). These assumptions have many implications, two of which are examined: the masculinity of REM and the instrumental and benign 'community' he creates; and the economic analysis of the private sphere which was pioneered by Gary Becker and named the 'new home economics' (NHE).[4] Finally, the essay explores the failure of NCE to address the specificity of women in the paid labourforce.

As noted, NCE is to be examined from the perspective of sexual difference. An approach based on sexual difference highlights the social and political meaning given to biological difference, and problematises the sex/gender distinction.[5] The sex/gender distinction relies upon the mind/body split, one of a series of dualisms or binary oppositions organising Western philosophical thought. It is therefore linked to other dualisms such as culture/nature and public/private, terms which are not sexually neutral.[6]

The mind/body split, or the positing of mind as logically independent of body, intersects with the 'sexual equality' approach. The agenda of this approach is equality for women based on the identification of a universal human essence, an essence common to both women and men. This approach recognises the differences between female and male bodies, but believes that they are politically irrelevant. Carole Pateman has summarised the appeal of, and the problem with, a 'sexual equality' approach:

> it is easy to suppose, in the face of the long history of assertion that women's capacities necessitate our exclusion from public life, that the only appropriate response is to insist that sexual difference is irrelevant. However, this line of argument leaves intact the sexually particular characterisation of the public world, the individual and his capacities. . . . [this approach] implicitly denies that birth, women's bodies and the feminine passions inseparable from their bodies and bodily processes have any political relevance.[7]

A sexual equality approach therefore limits feminists' demands to 'equality' with men, which requires the impossible demand that women 'become' men. Women must 'become' men because implicit in the various universal essences which define 'humanness' are characteristics constructed as masculine.

To emphasise sexual difference is not, however, to engage in an ahistorical appeal to biology; that is, it is not a claim that biology predetermines the sexual structure of society or the social positioning of female and male bodies. Rather it recognises that biology is never unmediated, or, in other words, that the meaning given to sexed bodies is always a social construction: 'the human body and sexual difference are always *lived in culture*, mediated by its values, its oppositions and its discourses'.[8]

The sexual difference approach exposes problems in many of the assumptions employed by NCE. NCE is constantly expanding—it is not a unified and fixed monolith.[9] However, there is a core of fundamental assumptions which construct REM, the subject of NCE. REM is the 'conscious, knowing, unified, rational' subject associated with liberal theory.[10] This economic actor is an important aspect of NCE's production of the world in its own image. The assumptions underlying this production will now be briefly outlined.

1. Economic scarcity is a key concept in NCE, created by the assumption of unlimited desires for goods and services on the part of individu-

als. These infinite wants mean that resources are always *relatively* scarce. An implication of this is that 'all individuals are to some extent in conflict or competition with one another for the commodities which can be made available'.[11] The reconciliation of conflict occurs through markets via the price mechanism, transforming competition as rivalry into the benign competitive market structure which constitutes the ideal market form in NCE.[12]

Economic scarcity is the basis of a widely used definition of NCE: it is 'the science which studies human behaviour as a relationship between ends and scarce means which have alternative uses'.[13] Underlying this definition are three necessary assumptions: that individuals maximise utility; that market equilibria exist; and that preferences are stable through time.[14] On the basis of these assumptions, Becker has claimed that the method of NCE provides a unified framework for understanding all human behaviour, and indeed, the non-human biological world as well.

2. NCE is methodologically individualist, seeking to explain all social and economic outcomes on the basis of the decisions of individuals. In traditional NCE, individuals undertake voluntary exchanges within the context of natural and monetary constraints, such as time and income. Impersonal market forces are taken as given, and since they cannot be controlled by humans they affect all individuals in the same neutral way.[15]

The neo-classical individual interacting with others through markets is the province of microeconomics. NCE also provides the 'microfoundations' underlying mainstream macroeconomics. These microfoundations describe how the household interacts with the economy, as a provider of labour and consumer of products. These interactions are part of the public sphere, while the internal workings of households constitute the private sphere. Until the advent of NHE, economists had been largely uninterested in the private sphere. NHE, while maintaining the division between the public and private spheres in some ways, breaks down the division in terms of the continuity of self-interested behaviour on the part of radically separate individuals.

3. Individuals are instrumentally rational. Economic rationality has two requirements, one regarding the ends and one the means. With respect to ends, an individual is rational if, when faced with a choice between A, B and C, he consistently chooses A over C if he prefers A to B and B to C. With respect to means, a rational agent will choose the most efficient (minimum cost) method of achieving a given end. This predictability of behaviour, given possession of sufficient information, supports the claim that economics is a science.

4. Self-interest in the narrow sense of selfishness is taken as the norm. However, 'caring' behaviour (altruism) is not excluded. Altruism is recast,

within the framework of instrumental rationality, into self-interested behaviour; the agent is merely maximising utility derived from a set of preferences which includes the utility of other individuals.[16] Even so, altruism is the 'other' which must be explicitly studied as different from the norm. The title of Becker's article, 'Altruism in the Family and Selfishness in the Market Place',[17] indicates the perceived need for an explanation of behaviour which takes others into account. Since neo-classical economists perceive altruism as a necessary condition for an economic explanation of the family, they needed to construct a special model for its analysis.

5. NCE relies upon the concept of possessive individualism: an individual is assumed to relate to his person as if it were property which can be the subject of contractual arrangements. With this assumption, NCE is able to examine employment, prostitution and family-related contracts in the same way as it examines contracts for non-corporeal goods and services, such as those for apples or the services of a machine.

6. NCE claims universal application. In so doing, it defines itself as 'natural', its 'laws' operating and its categories and relationships existing before the discipline itself. The economic agent which itself is constituted by neo-classical discourse is said to have existed through all time and in all situations. NCE takes as universal various features of human nature; these include the desire for property from which others can be excluded; unlimited wants; and the 'sexual needs' of men.[18] The definitions do not confine the analysis to capitalist economies, nor to goods which are exchanged through explicit markets.

7. There is a reliance on the epistemological distinction between theory and facts, and that between theory and facts on the one hand and the observer on the other. Of course, the use of models which are more or less simplified representations of the 'real world' means that economists acknowledge the truncations involved in their analyses. Nevertheless, the claims to objectivity and to access to a given and transparent reality remain. In short, the world they describe and the desires and possibilities of individuals are alleged to have existed before the discourse. Statistical techniques are used to falsify those hypotheses which are inconsistent with the facts.

The positive–normative distinction also plays an important role in NCE. This distinction differentiates between those statements which are factual (value-free) and can be empirically tested, and those based on the observer's tastes. Economic science claims to be concerned only with positive statements.

These assumptions create the economic actor. As a universal phenomenon, this actor allegedly represents both male and female individuals, who are characterised by a universal human essence.[19] From a sexual difference perspective, however, REM cannot represent the two sexes. Rather, REM is the Cartesian subject, a masculine subject who is characterised by the privileged terms in a series of binary oppositions; he is autonomous, active, rational, self-knowing and self-made. This transcendence of the subordinated, feminine characteristics (the 'not-A' terms) is also seen in his overcoming of the particular, his transcendence of the inter-relationships of human beings, seen most obviously in the mother–child relationship, but also evident in the dependence of the old, the young, the sick, the feeble, and the disabled on human care. As Ross Poole has noted, it is these relationships which in part construct the meaning of femininity.[20]

Radical separation from others, and a self-interested and instrumental approach to others, follow from the rationality integral to REM. Poole, in his paper on the masculinity of 'means/end' rationality, argues that 'instrumental rationality presupposes abstract [disembodied] individuals as its subjects'. Each individual must have 'a capacity to abstract [himself] as an agent from the particular social relationships in which [he] exists, from specific others, and even from [his] own activities'.[21] REM is a logically asocial being; his relationships in no sense define him, being simply instrumental in the achievement of his self-defined ends.

This instrumental use of others provides the basis of an exchange- or market-based theory of community. As Nancy Hartsock has argued, 'In the market, the Other's status as Other is maintained. . . . the community is only the *by-product* of actions directed at disparate ends.'[22] But non-instrumental community bonds are an integral part of the workings of human societies. Communities are maintained by the unacknowledged work of women in the private sphere. As Julie Nelson has argued,

> The male's 'transcendence' of nature and society [social connectedness] is made possible only through the subjection of the female to full-time maintenance of the social and physical connections that are, after all, indispensable for human existence.[23]

Hartsock has also discussed the impoverished account of power presented by exchange theories of community. Power disappears under the assumption of free and equal individuals voluntarily interacting on the basis of self-interest.[24] Chris Weedon makes it clear that the disappearance of power relations results from the assumptions concerning the individual in exchange theories:

> The liberal-humanist assumption that the individual subject is the source of self-knowledge and knowledge of the world can easily serve as a guarantee and justification of existing social relations. The structural and institutional oppression of women disappears behind the belief that if I as rational sovereign subject freely choose my way of life on the basis of my individual rational consciousness which gives me knowledge of

> the world, then I am not oppressed. Oppression is ultimately reduced to a subjective psychological state—feeling oppressed.[25]

Thus power relationships, of the repressive type, cannot be recognised in NCE, where maximising agents only voluntarily enter into exchanges.[26]

The view of all human interaction as mutually beneficial voluntary exchange has led to some odd conclusions in NCE, demonstrating the difficulties of explaining family dynamics in the neo-classical model. Mother is assumed to act in her own self-interest, while the patriarchal head of household is assumed to be altruistic. Mother nurtures the family so as to avoid alienating her husband's altruism. Mother's care for the children thus becomes the subject of an exchange between the parents, this care being 'payment' for Mother's access to the husband's labour-market earnings. The specificity of the relationships between parents and children is not addressed; children are commodified. That mother's 'self-interested' actions are derived from an institutionally subordinate and economically dependent position has already been excluded by the framework of 'mutual gains from voluntary exchange'.

Unlike most neo-classical analyses, Becker's investigation of intra-familial market interactions recognises, necessarily, that the human race is comprised of two sexes. Nevertheless, his work denies political significance to the socially constructed meaning of sexual difference. In analysing the (patriarchal) family, Becker assumes that the household head is altruistic, while the spouse and other beneficiaries such as children are self-interested. Becker calls the household head 'h' and the spouse 'w', and uses the masculine pronoun for 'h' and the feminine pronoun for 'w'; disingenuously, he claims that he does so simply to 'distinguish the altruist from the beneficiary'.[27] But a reversal of the sex roles is incomprehensible in Becker's analysis. In his account of the sexual division of labour, sexual roles are based in part on women's biology,[28] and in part on the comparative advantage which women's commitment to household duties gives them. While women's bodies are deemed to be biologically suited to domestic and childrearing duties, men's bodies are alleged to make them suitable for 'hunt[ing], soldier[ing], farm[ing], and . . . other "market" activities'. Becker concludes that households which allocate women to household duties and men to the labour market are more efficient in producing household commodities.[29] Becker's extension of neo-classical analysis into the private sphere of the family does not, therefore, invalidate the sexual division of labour and power.[30] The division of labour which supports the split between public and private is seen as 'natural', and so too is the structure of paid work. Becker's analysis can be distinguished from that of 'sexual difference' feminists who argue that, far from being a natural outcome of biological imperatives, these structures are socially organised and maintained in the interests of men.

We now turn to look explicitly at these socially organised work structures. When equal pay for women was on the political agenda in Australia, employers argued that unemployment for women would result. This argument required the belief that women were already being paid their productive value; an increase in their wages would constitute 'overpayment', and hence employers would substitute more productive (male) workers for women. In neo-classical terms, women were alleged to be earning their marginal productivities.[31] Wages which emerge from the markets for different skills are seen as objective assessments of the value of those skills.

During the previous hundred years, the issue of comparable worth has often been raised by feminists, who have argued that the valuation and hence remuneration of skills are contingent upon the sex of the worker. Michelle Pujol has outlined the difficulties faced by economists contributing to the debate on equal pay for equal work in England at the turn of the century. While various explanations of the systematic gap between women's and men's wages were put forward, most participants assumed both a male standard and the usefulness of the competitive market in attaining an equitable outcome. That is, the wages of men were assumed to reflect their marginal productivities, while freely operating competitive markets were assumed to be capable of bringing about this result for women, should women's wages be below their marginal productivities. However, much of the discussion also centred on the subsistence needs of women; many pointed to women's lower wages as a reflection of their lower needs. As Pujol says, this 'presents a strong challenge to the validity and universality of the neoclassical theory of wage (and price) determination'.[32]

This debate is also present in current feminist writings. Alice Kessler-Harris argues that the comparable worth argument threatens to make clear the particular interests being served by traditional (gendered) notions of equity, justice and fairness.[33] For example, in the past it was considered equitable to pay men a 'family wage' on the assumption that a man supports a dependent wife and children. While NCE does not advocate or support such wage-setting procedures, it fails to recognise that free-market outcomes cannot be objective, and that the values supporting the 'family wage' continue to result in lower valuations attached to 'women's jobs' and women's skills. This has led to unsuccessful attempts in economists' empirical work to explain the male–female wage differential as a legitimate reflection of the relative value of women's skills.[34]

Mary Hawkesworth has also discussed the impossibility of recognising socially constituted values attached to women's work within a framework grounded on the atomistic conception of the individual.[35] The particular problems which women face as women are ruled out by the assumptions of NCE, which construct a universal (masculine) actor. The male standard implicit in the capitalist structure of paid work and careers is revealed by the fact that only those without childcare and other household responsibilities are able to offer continuous, 'full-time' service and build a career. The 'worker' is a masculine subject whose identity is constituted in opposition to the private sphere and the 'housewife' who maintains him.[36] Of course, women have participated in the paid labourforce since its inception, and indeed their participation rate has increased throughout this century. But, as has been well documented, women's domestic responsibilities and the valuation placed upon them tend to be replicated when they enter the paid workforce.[37]

Sidney Webb was a participant in the debate on equal pay for equal work discussed by Pujol. He pointed to the incorporation of women into the labour market not as unsexed, universal individuals, but as women whose bodies carry particular socially constructed meanings and valuations, when he said that 'it is impossible to overlook the effect of the fact that the woman has something else to sell besides her labour'.[38] Lionel Robbins characterised the 'services' of prostitutes, the 'something else' referred to by Webb, as the scarce means to be applied to the end of 'satisfactions of a sensual character'.[39] But prostitution, another example of women in paid labour, can only be understood in NCE as the mutually beneficial satisfaction of given ends. Rather than a value-free analysis of ends, means and markets, this view embodies (but suppresses) a set of assumptions about male and female sexuality which operates to support the commodification and sale of women's bodies.

There are two aspects of the supply side of the market for prostitutes which are problematic. Firstly, unlike the employment contract, the sexual characteristics of the buyers and sellers become integral to the exchange in the markets for women's bodies.[40] The anonymity of competitive markets is waived since, as Pateman argues, 'the capitalist has no intrinsic interest in the body and self of the worker, or, at least, not the same kind of interest as the man who enters the prostitution contract'.[41] Secondly, the myth of a universal individual relating to his body as property is required. Again unlike the employment contract, it is the ability of the prostitute's body to be used for sex which is assumed to be 'property'. However, in a world made up of female and male individuals rather than disembodied (sexless) individuals, sexuality and the self are integrally connected. Neo-classical economists must reject the colloquial expression of prostitution as women who 'sell *themselves*'; rather they allege that prostitutes sell services. But, because individuals' identities are always sexed, 'when a prostitute contracts out the use of her body she is selling *herself* in a very real sense'.[42]

The demand side of the market also requires a particular understanding of the sexuality of the buyer; prostitution is only possible with a certain construction of masculine sexuality. Martha Vicinus has noted that the dominant paradigm for sexuality is overwhelmingly male and heterosexual. The 'hydraulic' model defines sexuality as 'an independent force or energy disciplined by personal or social constraints. Sex is always something to be released or controlled; if controlled, it is sublimated or deflected or distorted.'[43] Clearly this view of male sexuality justifies, 'naturalises', the public availability of female bodies. Male sexuality is understood as a need or want which creates a market demand as a function of the income and preferences of male consumers. Male sexuality, then, is capable of being appeased by the commodification of women's bodies. The interaction of demand and supply determines the market price, and the invisible hand has apparently worked again. However, biology is never unmediated: particular needs and wants are not 'natural', but can only be understood in a social context and as created by particular discourses. In the neo-classical understanding of prostitution, we see the intersection of the hydraulic model of male sexuality and the produced subject of NCE discourse. These discourses support what Pateman has called the public affirmation of the law of male sex-right.[44]

The classification of feminisms into liberal, Marxist, and others, which characterises many women's studies introductory texts, indicates the frameworks initially adopted by feminists. The problem was women and how to account for women's position in terms of extant theoretical systems. More recently, however, attention has been focused on 'theory' itself as the problem. Part of this questioning process is to refuse to accept NCE at its own valuation as an objective and universally applicable theory of behaviour. The hidden use of a masculine subject, and the implications of this, must be made explicit. NCE constitutes an androcentric discourse, with a particular rather than an objective view of the world; this view privileges the masculine, and actual men, at the expense of the feminine, and actual women.

THIRTEEN

Queer Theory and Its Discontents: Queer Desires, Queer Cinema

Barbara Creed

All the world is queer
Save thee and me
And even thee's a little queer.

My grandmother was a very lovable and very proper woman. As a child I was intrigued by the above words, which she had framed and sitting on top of the fridge. Why did she feel a need to announce to the world from her kitchen that no-one was 'normal', and then neatly exclude herself from the proposition? Did this mean she wasn't queer but my grandfather was? Not until I grew up did I understand that the poem was a sardonic comment on the idea that the individual always thinks her/his viewpoint represents the norm. At first the idea that all the world was queer meant no more than 'different', 'oddball', 'quirky'. But as I grew older and discovered my sexual desires were 'different', I eyed the poem from a new perspective. Was my grandmother telling me something? Did she know about me? If she were alive today, what would she think about the latest entry to the field of sexuality debates—queer theory? I suspect she would say that she had known about it for a long time. She didn't need an elaborate theoretical paradigm to justify what was obvious to anyone with eyes in their head.

It is not surprising that queer theory has arisen (or is it a revisitation?) at this particular historical moment. After nearly two decades of heated debates on sexuality, something was desperately needed to break the theoretical impasse. It is a measure of the times that, after only a few years, queer theory is being taken very seriously—and not just by queers. At one extreme, it has even found its way into the contents pages of a few academic textbooks, where it sits a little oddly. What is queer theory? Is it more than just a queery, another question mark thrown into the current mix of meta-theories? I hesitate to proceed because in answering my question, I will inevitably give queer theory an academic respectability that it basically eschews. But perhaps it might be a good thing if the Academy turned a little queer.

Definitions of Queer Theory

The idea of a new approach, a queer theory, derives from the establishment of Queer Nation in New York in April 1990. Factors which helped create a more militant mood amongst lesbians and gay men were the increasing number of attacks on lesbians and gay men in the East Village, and a growing homophobia brought about by public response to AIDS. Act Up was established as the militant arm of Queer Nation. 'Queer is meant to be confrontational—opposed to gay assimilationists and straight oppressors while inclusive of people who have been marginalised by anyone in power.'[1] With its 'in your face' attitude, queer is deliberately provocative; it aims to root out the 'vanilla' in everyone.

Queer is now most commonly used to designate same-sex desire, either lesbian or gay male, without specifying whether the desire is between women or men—although, given the history of the term [2] and its association with male desire, this may prove problematic for some lesbians. In the past we have drawn on a number of terms which were gender-specific—'lesbian theory', 'lesbian feminist theory', 'gay male theory'. 'Queer' functions as an umbrella term that incorporates all of these—and more. It provides us with another way of thinking about sexual desire, a way that resists theoretical pigeon-holing. It allows us to expose the problems of gender-specific terms, such as 'lesbian feminist' and 'gay male'; some of these have been and still are associated with inflexibility.

For instance, these terms fail to take into account the growing diversity of the gay male and lesbian communities. In the 1970s, lesbian feminists believed that 'feminism was the theory, lesbianism the practice'. It was thought that once a woman had 'come out', lesbianism would constitute her central identity. Differences such as those of class, race, colour were all too often ignored or subsumed under the overriding factor of sexual preference. Differences such as those of sexual practices and styles of dressing were completely subsumed. As Arlene Stein writes:

> The once clear connection between lesbianism and feminism in which the former was assumed to grow naturally out of the latter, is not all that clear today. Gone is the ideal of a culturally and ideologically uni-

> fied Lesbian nation. A series of challenges, largely from within lesbian communities themselves, have shaken many of the ordering principles of lesbian feminism.[3]

By the 1990s, the dream of a Lesbian Nation has been overtaken by that of a Queer Nation—a space/place where identity is no longer seen as more important than difference.

Queer theory challenges identity politics, opting instead for diversity, plurality. Questions of class, colour, race and ethnicity are crucial. Another equally important area relates to questions of sexual desire. Queer theory addresses a range of practices, including bisexuality, sadomasochism, cross-dressing, transsexuality and transvestism. Some extend this even further to include—or at least allow—the possibility of discussing, although not necessarily condoning, all forms of sexual desire that fall outside the vanilla pale—such as fetishistic, coprophiliac, and even bestial desires. The problem with extending the term 'queer' to include a range of perverse desires is that not all proponents of queer theory would necessarily support such a stand. Some do not want to identify queer theory with desires that are not lesbian or gay and are clearly associated with more socially shocking forms of sexual behaviour.

Historical Origins

The term 'queer' was first used in an academic context to describe a conference which was held in New York in 1989, and entitled: 'How Do I Look? Queer Film and Video'.[4] Its aim was to discuss gay and lesbian theory. The conference had grown out of a reading group which had no set agenda but addressed a number of different areas. The group

> moved more or less at random from the writings of Michel Foucault to lesbian-feminist philosophy, from Freud to Freud's commentators and critics. We read recent work on identity, homophobia, AIDS, sex work, and lesbian sadomasochism.[5]

Discussing the cultural and historical origins of queer theory is problematic, largely because recent theoretical articles tend to concentrate on the influence of contemporary movements, such as feminism and postmodernism, and ignore the crucially important political events of the late 1960s and early 1970s—events which in my view constitute the beginnings of queer as a political force. These movements were centrally concerned with identity politics, often ignoring the voices of difference. The gay liberation movement, which originated in the Western world in the late 1960s, belonged to a group of radical movements, including women's liberation, black power, and the peace movement. The catch cries of 'gay is good', and 'out of the closets and into the streets' were heard throughout the capital cities of the Western world. The gay liberation movement, as it became known, consisted primarily of marches, zap demonstrations, public talks, and conferences, as well as a mushrooming of gay groups and publications with their own social and political agendas. Gay politics were deliberately confrontational and aimed at giving gay people a pride in their new-found identity while forcing community recognition. Gays, from now on, would be vocal and visible.

In the early years of the gay liberation movement in Australia, women and men worked together within their different gay groups for social acceptance and reform. Although the gay movement consisted primarily of lesbians and gay men, there was a great deal of interest in other forms of sexual practices including cross-dressing, transsexuality, bisexuality and celibacy. Individuals espousing these various positions were active members of the gay movement. I do not wish to give the erroneous impression, however, that all forms of difference were happily tolerated. On the contrary, these minority groups were criticised by some who wanted to impose their own view of sexuality. Hostility was expressed towards the idea of bisexuality, cross-dressing and butch–femme role playing. Some thought bisexuality was a cop-out; some argued that butch–femme simply copied the dominant heterosexual model; others resented seeing men dressed as women. The period was characterised by a tension within the movement around the question of different sexualities. In my view, this was a healthy state of being because it generated much debate.

The statement by the 1975 Melbourne Homosexual Conference Collective reflects this tension. It also voices similar concerns (see above) stated nearly two decades later by Queer Nationals in their call to accept all forms of difference within Queer Nation.

> In the past homosexual rights groups have often alienated our base of support in the homosexual community. For instance, the university-oriented new left radicalism of Gay Liberation resulted in imposition of a highly moralistic, dogmatic ideology on the homosexual community . . . We must seriously consider the needs of the homosexual community. We need to constructively examine diverse lifestyle possibilities.[6]

Gay liberation publications such as *Gay Liberation Press* and *Camp Inc.* also regularly published articles about effeminates, transsexuals, transvestites, drag, sexual objectification and butch–femme role-playing. In America, gay liberation demonstrations were led by street transvestites. Dennis Altman documents the role played by transvestites in *Homosexual: Oppression and Liberation*. He points out that demonstrations brought together the various groups within gay liberation, breaking down some of the tensions between them.

> There was an erosion of at least some of the tension between various groups in the movement, and more significantly, the continued acceptance of the street transvestites as a key part of the gay liberation movement, an acceptance symbolized by the formation of a new group, the Street Transvestite Action Revolutionaries, made up, largely, of street people.[7]

Lesbians, in particular, debated the politics of celibacy, non monogamy, serial monogamy, bisexuality and butch–femme. The proposed establishment of Amazon Acres (the beginnings of a Lesbian Nation?) on the east coast of Australia gave rise to heated debates about lesbian separatism, and gay men joked half-seriously about setting up Tarzan's Strip on the neighbouring mountain. These debates gradually changed direction in the mid-1970s as many lesbians left the gay movement in order to join forces with the women's movement. This did not mean that work on gay identity automatically halted. On the contrary, it continued, but its directions now reflected the concerns of two mainly separate groups: on the one hand, lesbians and heterosexual women in the women's movement and, on the other hand, gay men and a small number of lesbians in the diminished gay movement. With the emergence of queer theory in the 1990s and the development of coalition politics, lesbians and gay men have once again begun to communicate. Whether or not this new alliance will ultimately succeed will, as queer theorists argue, depend on the willingness of each group to recognise not only the differences of the other but also the differences within, as well as the existence of other minority groups such as those of transsexuals and transvestites. The crucial shift has been from an identity-centred politics to one that recognises plurality, diversity, difference.

I have mentioned these events to emphasise firstly, the strong diversity of the gay liberation movement in its early years; and secondly to show that queer theory did not emerge suddenly from nowhere. In a sense, queer theory has reactivated debates about sexual diversity which were central to gay theory of the 1970s. What is new is queer theory's emphasis on the importance of difference and on the illusory nature of identity and subjectivity. In particular, queer theory draws on three new areas of thought which have influenced the academies in the last two decades. These are the work of Michel Foucault, the Lacanian pyschoanalytic revolution and postmodernism.

Michel Foucault

If the work of any one individual theorist is to be taken as central to queer theory, it is that of Michel Foucault—specifically his writings in the first volume of *The History of Sexuality*.[8] Here Foucault sets out a theoretical framework for understanding the way in which sexuality is constructed in the individual subject through various social discourses, such as those of medicine and psychiatry. He sees sexuality not as a given, a natural fact of life, but as a construct, an effect of various discourses. His de-naturalising view of sexuality unsettles the dominant view that sexuality is an objective phenomenon, a truth, that can be intellectually known. Rather, sexuality is a discursive effect; it is constructed in the body, in behaviour and in social relationships. Sexuality and its power relationships are diverse, fragmented, and complex. Many factors must be considered: race, class, gender, sexual desire, sexual practices. Furthermore, power does not simply flow from oppressor to oppressed; those in a lesser power position still exercise power. Power relationships—and sexual ones—are extremely complex.

Foucault's approach challenges the view which, while acknowledging that power is socially constructed, maintains that lesbians and gay men would be liberated if only they could dismantle male heterosexual power structures that pervade and dominate their everyday lives—those structures which 'repress' their true desires. This model of power relations is also held by those feminists who argue that women would also be free if they could simply destroy the patriarchal power basis of society. This view of power which sees lesbians and gay men as passive objects of heterosexual male power structures is not only utopian; it also denies the various ways in which homosexuals already exercise power and autonomy and are engaged in social transformation.

Foucault also attempts to shift emphasis away from 'repression' as the dominant concept invoked when we study the relationship between sex and power. In fact, he is critical of political struggles which are based in identity politics (radical feminism, gay liberation) and argues for the importance of desexualising the political struggle. In his view, medical discourses control deviant groups (homosexual, transsexual, sadomasochistic) through the processes of observation and classification. In this way, sexuality actually becomes a means of controlling the individual who is reduced to her/his sexual desires. Sexuality is seen as a given, an essence, a coherent whole, rather than as constituted by a series of practices, discourses and social relations. Queer theory seeks to explore sexuality in relation to the latter.

Jacques Lacan

Lacanian psychoanalytic theory has been exhaustively documented over the past two decades;[9] it is primarily his attack on the notion of the unified subject that is relevant to this discussion. In Lacan's view, the child does not develop a coherent ego or sense of self; rather, the subject's sense of possessing a coherent identity is seen as illusory. While the subject may yearn for a sense of self that is coherent and unified, this will always remain outside her/his grasp. The subject's desire to become/identify with a more perfect image has been used to explain[10] the powerful attraction of the cinema and the institution of stardom.

Drawing on the Lacanian critique of the unified ego, queer theory seeks to challenge the idea that there is a unified or set concept of lesbian or gay male identity. As discussed above, it was this notion of identity—of the ideal lesbian and gay male self—that was central to gay liberation identity politics of the 1970s. The gay liberation critique of the cinema was based on the fact that films did not present such an image, that it was censored or repressed by the dominant heterosexual interest groups. Queer theory argues that there is no single, acceptable, normal lesbian or gay male identity. It is somewhat ironic that over the past two decades, during which lesbians and gay men fought to have their sexual desires recognised and accepted, that we now find ourselves wanting to challenge the notion of identity that has become publicly acceptable. This notion is that the homosexual is a 'normal' upright member of society (middle-class, professional, yuppie) who also practises her or his own version of missionary-position or vanilla sex. Just as feminist theorists[11] have recently begun to critique heterosexuality—particularly the belief that masculinity constitutes an unproblematic category—lesbian and gay male theorists have begun to critique homosexuality and other 'deviant' sexual practices which seek refuge in the notion of an ideal, set identity.

Queer theory has emerged in response to this critical re-evaluation and in so doing has acknowledged a range of sexual desires and practices, such as sado-masochism, fetishism, transsexuality and transvestitism. How far one extends this range is a controversial issue. But it seems to me that if queer theory seeks to question the notion of a unified, discrete homosexual identity, it must take into account *all* of the forms of desire that exist, not simply those that have found acceptability within the lesbian and gay male communities. The current controversy over lesbian sado-masochistic practices highlights the difficulties opened up by the notion that we live, not in a gay, but in a queer world.

The same holds true for the heterosexual world, but it is not yet prepared to acknowledge that heterosexuality might include a range of practices. Rather, the latter are marginalised as 'deviant' or 'abnormal'. Yet heterosexual practices include sado-masochism, paedophilia, bestiality, fetishism, necrophilia, and so on. Further, the heterosexual community, being much larger than the homosexual, engages in 'deviant' practices to a significantly greater degree. The recent BBC series on masculinity, *The Big Picture*, made it clear just how 'abnormal' so-called 'normal' heterosexual practices are.

Postmodernism

Postmodern theory has also influenced the direction taken by queer theory. While postmodernism seems to have been espoused by many different voices—from Madonna to Baudrillard—which at first sight appear to have nothing in common, postmodern theory does proceed from a set of clearly established positions. I will discuss those which are most relevant to an understanding of the origins of queer theory. Postmodernism supports the view, advanced by Jean-François Lyotard, that there is a crisis in the function of narrative: that the Great Narratives of the West no longer speak with any authority. There has been a crisis of faith in the kind of thinking that inspired a belief in the inevitability and ultimate success of Western progress, imperialism, science and technology. As Lyotard has stated:

> One can note a sort of decay in the confidence placed by the last two centuries in the idea of progress. The idea of progress as possible, probable or necessary was rooted in the certainty that the development of the arts, technology, knowledge and liberty would be profitable to mankind as a whole . . . . After two centuries, we are more sensitive to signs that signify the contrary.[12]

What this means is that there has been a questioning and rethinking of the philosophical agenda—Man, Truth, History, Politics. Postmodern practice critiques the notions of Truth, Beauty and Goodness with its use of parody and pastiche by which it displays a deliberate irreverence for the Past. As I have argued elsewhere,[13] the postmodern critique of the master narratives of the West, which is ultimately a critique of male mastery, has its origins in the feminist critique of patriarchy—a crucial fact which is rarely acknowledged.

In her book, *Gynesis*, Alice Jardine argues that in France recognition of the collapse of the master narratives amongst theorists has led to a rethinking of philosophy and to

> reconceptualisation of that which has been the master narrative's own 'non-knowledge,' what has eluded them, what has engulfed them. This other-than-themselves is almost always a 'space' of some kind (over which the narrative has lost control), and this space has been coded as *feminine*, as *woman*.[14]

Essential to the new postmodern forms of writing has been a valorisation of the feminine. Jardine argues that theorists such as Lacan, Deleuze and Guattari, Baudrillard, Kristeva and Foucault have all referred to a 'space' outside the dominant discourses which they code as 'feminine' in some way, and which they argue is essential to new postmodern ways of speaking and being. These spaces refer to the unknown, the improper, the profane, the oriental, the feminine—all that which lies outside the dominant male discourses of the past. This is the space that a number of male theorists, such as Derrida with his 'invaginated text', want to speak, but only in the name of the male subject. This however does not mean, paradoxically, that woman, the biological subject, is most suited to inhabiting these spaces, to speaking the 'feminine'. Man is better at 'becoming woman'. Jardine refers to the writings of Deleuze and Guattari where they:

> refer to Virginia Wolf as having incorporated the process of what they call 'becoming woman' (*le devenir femme*) in her writing—but 'not to the same extent' as Henry James, D. H. Lawrence, or Henry Miller.[15]

Once again we witness an act of colonisation in which the subject—male and female—speaks from a masculinist position. There is an attempt to appropriate the notion of 'woman as other' in order to construct a new form of phallocentric discourse.

Queer theory represents/is the space of the other, the spaces that Jardine argues are 'not attributable to *Man*, the spaces of the *en-soi*, Other, without history—the feminine'.[16] Queer theory speaks about itself from within. Unlike the master discourses of the West, it does not position its subject as 'other'; it is the other. Queer theory situates otherness—a range of identities—as more important than the notion of a singular identity.

In his analysis of postmodernism, Lyotard calls for the abandonment of all Truths and the provisional adoption of short narratives which the dominant discourses have attempted to silence. Queer theory seeks to open up a space in which these narratives, these spaces of the other, can speak. It also seeks to demonstrate the inter-relatedness of all positions. The *en-soi*, the Other, is and always has been contaminated by the Subject. But, because the kinds of desire being spoken are viewed by many as unknown, terrifying and monstrous, queer theory's project may prove an extremely difficult one. The queer theorist may balk at speaking her/his own queerness, but rather take the queerness of others in order to protect her/himself via the mechanisms of projection and displacement. Confronting the 'otherness' within oneself is a formidable task.

Queer Theory and Queer Cinema

A significant number of books and articles on queer theory address the cinema.[17] This may well be because the cinema—perhaps more than other cultural practices—mobilises the individual viewer's engagement in relation to a wide range of sexual desires and practices: lesbianism, male homosexuality, bisexuality, cross-dressing, transvestitism, sadomasochism, paedophilia, necrophilia, fetishism and so on. In particular, sexual difference theory was taken up by those working within feminist film theory. This happened specifically in England, where the French psychoanalytic revolution exerted a profound effect. Drawing on Freudian and Lacanian psychoanalytic theory, feminist film theory has explored a number of related concepts: the formation of subjectivity in language, the Lacanian Imaginary and Symbolic, male castration anxiety, woman as lack, penis envy, the phallic women, fetishism, the male gaze, masochism, sadism, hysteria. Given the variety and deviant status of these concepts, it is amazing to see how feminist debates about sexual difference safely negotiated this minefield of desire without self-destructing. Feminism did so by anchoring discussions to the relatively 'safe' realm of heterosexuality and its attendant desires. Only at a later stage did feminist film theorists begin to explore more risky areas such as the lesbian in film, the lesbian viewer, and the representation of lesbian sadomasochism on the screen.

Much of this discussion has centred on the issue of spectatorship. Influenced by Laura Mulvey's important article, 'Visual Pleasure and Narrative Cinema', feminist film theory argued that in the classic narrative film, woman functions as object of the look, man as its subject. If mainstream Hollywood cinema is addressed primarily to an ideal male spectator, where does this leave the lesbian viewer? If the gaze of the lesbian spectator seeks to eroticise the image of woman on the screen, does this mean that she is a surrogate male or do we need a new theory, a queer theory, to theorise the lesbian spectator? If the male protagonist of the film narrative is subject of the look rather than object, does this mean that the male body resists the eroticised look of the homosexual male viewer? Such questions are central to recent articles on queer cinema.

Like queer theory, queer cinema also has a history; it has arisen out of the practice of lesbian and gay film-making which has historically belonged to the independent, avant-garde tradition. In recent years, the Melbourne Lesbian and Gay International Film and Video Festival has brought many of these films together for public screening. At the major festivals in England, Holland, Canada and the United States, 1992 proved a crucial year. A new kind of gay film-making emerged: festivals attracted record-breaking audiences and queer film-making became commercially viable. A number of these new queer films were screened either at Australian film festivals or at commercial cinemas. These include: Tom Kalin's *Swoon* (1992); Derek Jarman's *Edward II* (1991); Todd Haynes' *Poison* (1990); Jennie Livingston's *Paris Is Burning* (1990) and Gus Van Sant's *My Own Private Idaho* (1991)

In her pioneering article, 'New Queer Cinema', which presented an overview of this new movement, B. Ruby Rich analysed the reception of queer cinema at the Gay and Lesbian Film Festivals in Amsterdam and San Francisco; the Festival of Festivals in Toronto; the Sundance Festival in Park City, Utah; and the prestigious New Directors/New Films Festival in New York. She argues that although the new queer films and videos do not share the same 'aesthetic vocabulary or strategy or concern', they do share 'a common style':

> Call it 'Homo Pomo': there are traces in all of them of appropriation and pastiche, irony, as well as a reworking of history with social constructionism very much in mind. Definitively breaking with older humanist approaches and the films and tapes that accompany identity politics, these works are irreverent, energetic, alternatively minimalist and excessive. Above all, they are full of pleasure. They're here, they're queer, get hip to them.[18]

With her reference to 'irony and pastiche' Rich points to the postmodern concerns of queer cinema, while her comment that these films break with the older humanist tradition indicates the influence of the Lacanian theory of subjectivity on queer cinema—two recent theoretical movements I discussed earlier as central to the emergence of queer theory.

For lesbians, however, the shortcomings of this new *commercial* queer cinema are clear: the films are almost exclusively about male desire. Lesbians are also making films which are new and different; predictably, however, they are not as commercially viable as films about male desire. New lesbian queer films are screened almost exclusively at festivals and include: Cleo Uebelmann's *Mano Destra* (1987); Monika Treut's *The Virgin Machine* (1988); Monika Treut's and Elfi Mikesch's *Seduction the Cruel Woman* (1985); Cecilia Barriga's *The Meeting of Two Queens* (1992) and Jane Cottis' *Dry Kisses Only* (1992). These films share the same concerns with parody, pastiche and a critique of subjectivity as do the films about male desire. Australian women exploring these issues include Vicki Dunn with *Can't You Take A Joke*? (1989) and *Red Label*, (1987) and Leonie Knight with *In Loving Memory* (1991) and *The Father is Nothing* (1992).

Even when an opportunity arises to explore lesbian desire in a mainstream film, such as *Fried Green Tomatoes* (1991), censorship intervenes. All suggestions of lesbian desire, apparent in the novel, have been removed. The lesbian love scenes were cut from *Basic Instinct* (1992), a film which has also been criticised by those lesbians and gay men who want to see only 'positive' images on the screen. In viewing mainstream cinema, female viewers must 'read between the lines'. At the end of *Thelma and Louise* (1991), the two women laugh and kiss each other on the lips just prior to the magnificent scene in which their car hurtles them into space in an orgasmic burst of unstoppable energy. The women head for the skies, choosing each other over the cohort of angry men on the ground, guns poised and ready, but with nothing to shoot at. Friendship explodes into passion, but only in the final shot when it is too late to explore this new direction in the women's relationship. The end of *Thelma and Louise* recalls the ending of the classic male buddy movies, such as *Butch Cassidy and the Sundance Kid* (1969), in which one or both members of the male couple died at the end before the narrative was forced to recognise the homoerotic desire that existed between them. Mainstream films about female buddies (*Outrageous Fortune* (1987), *Fried Green Tomatoes, Mortal Thoughts* (1991), *Antonia and Jane* (1991), *Thelma and Louise*), are now at the stage that the male buddy genre has left far behind. Amy Taubin argues that the new queer male directors are really 'the sons of Scorsese', whose films are particularly memorable for the way they eroticise their male stars for the homoerotic male gaze.[19] She is pointing to a tradition and history of film-making that has excluded women—both as directors and as stars. It will be interesting to see if the emergence of a commercially viable queer male cinema influences the renewed interest in female buddy films. Will lesbians appear in mainstream films, rather than art-house films such as *Salmonberries* (1992)? Or will lesbian queer cinema retain its marginal status?

One important aspect of queer cinema—lesbian and gay male—is its critique of conventional modes of representation. This has been taken up in two main areas. The first relates to the 'positive image' approach to filmic representation of character. Those who adopt this approach argue that cinematic images of lesbian and gay men should always be positive; that is, the characters should be morally upright, good characters who provide worthwhile role models for audience identification. Queer cinema takes issue with positive images by refusing to represent gay characters only as 'positive' or heroic figures. This is evident in a number of texts, including *Swoon, Edward II, Poison, Seduction the Cruel Woman*. *Swoon* re-examines the notorious Loeb–Leopold murder case of the 1920s, in which the thrill killers were two young homosexual men. *Poison* and *Seduction the Cruel Woman* represent the main characters as caught up in sado-masochistic desire. In particular, Tom Kalin has been criticised by some members of the gay community for making *Swoon*, on the grounds that gay film-makers should represent homosexual men on the screen only in a positive light. But to present only good lesbian and gay male characters on screen signifies as much a manipulation of reality as presenting only negative stereotypes. Furthermore, if negative images are excluded, lesbian and gay male characters will end up bland, one-dimensional caricatures incapable of invoking the tragic elements of character, let alone appearing in full-blown tragic narratives. The mood of queer cinema also breaks a more subservient response to the straight world; queer cinema is no longer interested in having straight approval if it means having to deal only in positive images. In this sense queer cinema reactivates the confrontational approach of the gay movement in its early years.

The debate about positive images is related to another controversial area of representation—the depiction of sado-masochistic lesbian sexuality in film and video. Lesbian sado-masochism has been hotly debated within the lesbian/feminist community. It has also been explored in a number of films; two of the more notable have been Cleo Uebelmann's *Mano Destra* and Monika Treut's and Elfi Mikesch's *Seduction the Cruel Woman*. The former, which speaks directly about lesbian bondage and domination, explores the significance of anticipation in a lesbian sado-masochistic relationship; a woman is continually tied and untied as she waits for her tormentor/lover to appear, but all she hears is the sound of approaching footsteps. The latter tells the story of Wanda, a paid dominatrix who runs a performance theatre where people come to have their sexual fantasies enacted. While Wanda treats all of her sexual encounters as theatre, her lovers—Caren, Justine and Gregor—want them to be real. *Seduction the Cruel Woman* has been criticised by some for even suggesting that women might desire pleasure from pain, while others have praised it for depicting women as 'powerful and seductive . . . capable of acting out fantasies and shaping their own sexualities'.[20]

Those who oppose lesbian sado-masochism in film—and in reality—argue that women who enjoy such fantasies are in thrall to a patriarchal ideology and are likely to be 'harmed' by viewing sado-masochism on the screen. In an ideal feminist world there would be no relations of submission and domination, not even in the unconscious; these are male inventions designed to keep women in a state of submission. The critics of lesbian sado-masochism argue that if women cannot stop themselves from having ideologically unsound fantasies, then they should stop fantasising altogether.[21] Presumably, films which depict such fantasies should be banned. Certainly feminists should stop viewing such films, even if they are made by other women.

The contrary position argues that relations of submission and domination are not 'male' but intrinsic to human nature; individuals should be free to explore these darker aspects of human relationships in any way they please as long as they are not literally harming another individual against her/his will. The viewing of films about lesbian sado-masochism provides an important means for such an exploration. In her discussion of this issue, Julia Creet makes an interesting observation that those women within the lesbian/feminist community who censor other women's behaviour are effectively taking a male position.[22] They are setting themselves up as representatives of a maternal law in the same way men uphold and enforce the so-called law of the father.

Queer theory argues for plurality and multiplicity. It asks us to rethink the nature of sexual identity; to pay attention to the borders and margins; to accept difference within the lesbian and gay world, including other marginalised positions: bisexuality, transsexuality, transvestitism and sado-masochism. Queer theory argues for the importance of lesbians and gay men acknowledging the differences between them; such a recognition is essential to any significant discussion of sexual politics between individuals and among groups. The move towards coalition or queer politics within the lesbian and gay movement is indicative of this change. If queer politics—and my grandmother, with hindsight—were to rephrase the queer poem I used to open this discussion, it might read like this:

> All the world is queer,
>   Including thee and me.
> And no-one is really queerer
>   Than thee and me.

PART III

Contesting Male Power

FOURTEEN

Unequal Partners: Women, Power and the Trade Union Movement

Carmel Shute

In the 1990s, the Australian union movement presents contradictory possibilities for women. It is a movement facing a 'legitimation crisis'. Its role as the historic mediator in the relationship between capital and labour is under threat by global economic trends, the election of several hostile state governments, and its own dwindling membership base. Unions need women if they are to survive into the twenty-first century. Conversely, despite the challenges under which they now labour, unions continue to play a crucial role in determining the entry of women into the workforce, their wages and conditions, and their social and economic power more generally. The anti-union legislation of the Kennett Liberal government, elected in Victoria in 1992, posed the choices for women workers in a particularly stark fashion—women's rights in the workforce can disappear overnight without the protection of awards and unions. Never has the slogan of the 1970s—'women need unions need women'—been more pertinent.

Historically, of course, the Australian union movement has been a men's movement which has excluded women. It has been notoriously slow and conservative in responding to social change. Since the 1970s, feminists have made it a major site of struggle. The massive increase of women in the workforce and the ideological impetus of feminism have compelled the union movement, however reluctantly and hesitantly, to address the demands for equity, justice and power. In the 1990s the union movement now belatedly sees women as the salvation of its future. For women, this represents an unparalleled opportunity to seize power for themselves, both as workers and as social beings.

The union movement in Australia has historically been one of the most powerful and millitant in the world. It pioneered the eight-hour working day (for building workers) in 1856. By the end of the nineteenth century, it had created its own political party—the Australian Labor Party—to represent its interests, and had established what was purportedly a 'workingman's paradise'.[1] Of course, Australia has never been a 'working-woman's paradise'. Capital was obviously seminal in establishing the inferior position of working women, and trade unions, the main organ of the labour movement which rose in opposition to capital, also helped reproduce the conditions of women's subordination. Women's power in relation to unions must thus be seen in the broader context of the historical construction of masculinity and femininity. The Australian union movement had its origins in the nineteenth-century British movement which arose out of a crisis of masculinity. As historian Marilyn Lake has argued, unions restored men's self-esteem by establishing 'a self-respecting accommodation with capitalism',[2] and by attempting to exclude women (and non-whites) from the ranks of labour. Union action reinforced the gender segregation of the Australian workforce which, today, remains the most intense within the OECD. David Atkin observes in his history of masculinity, unionism and meatworkers in the 1950s that the

> study of the Australian trade unions shows that as a cultural and political force the movement has been largely male, representing male interests and commitments for masculine dominance. The union movement was a product of a distinctive culture of male solidarity and men invoked the collective strength of unions as a buffer against the degradations of capitalism. Trade union culture and industrial strategy were crucially linked to masculine subjectivities.[3]

Forty years later this masculinist heritage continues to manifest itself, both in overt ways such as the predominance of men in union leadership positions, and through a multitude of subtle cultural signs—structures, language, behaviour, imagery—which are exclusive to men and exclusive of women. Thus, even now, it is not surprising that female subjectivity does not respond to the imperatives of unionism in the same way.[4] Unless the union movement comes seriously to grips with this difference in subjectivity, it is bound to fail in its mission to represent more women and thereby save itself from the dustbin of history.

For women activists in the Australian union movement, it is a bitter irony that it has taken a crisis of the movement as a whole to draw real attention to the specificity of women and their needs. Many see it as a triumph of expediency over egalitarianism. Union membership in Australia plummeted between 1986 and 1988—the biggest fall since the Great Depression and indicative of the worst membership crisis for sixty years, perhaps ever.[5] By 1992, the membership decline had slowed, but only 40 per cent of wage- and salary-earners still belonged a union. This predicament can be partly explained by the decline of areas which have traditionally had high union membership: full-time, blue-collar, male, manual and trades workers in primary and secondary industries. The more significant reason for it is the union movement's failure to recruit in the areas of dynamic growth: retail, finance, recreation and community services, where the new jobs are largely going to young, part-time, women workers. The number of women joining the workforce increased by 34 per cent from 1976 to 1992, but the increase in women union members was only 20 per cent. As Table 14.1 reveals, unionisation rates of the female workforce declined from 43 per cent in 1976 to stabilise at 35 per cent in 1988. Ironically, women make up the majority of new recruits to the union movement, but this is because male membership rates have fallen so dramatically.[6] Debate about the crisis, and women's role in it, dominated the 1989 congress of the Australian Council of Trade Unions (ACTU), the peak council covering 95 per cent of the union movement. 'ACTU sends SOS to women', thundered the headlines.[7] ACTU secretary, Bill Kelty, took the pre-eminent role in the debate, saying,

> It is simply not good enough for us year after year, congress after congress, resolution after resolution to talk about it. It's about time we started to do it. That is, we have to ensure that women are seen and involved in unions as equal partners. Anything less is a failure.[8]

Irrespective of the crisis in the Australian movement, the level of unionisation of women is important in itself, not least because of the higher average wages and lower rates of unemployment of unionists. In 1992, for instance, the average weekly earnings of women unionists

Table 14.1 How women aren't joining unions ('000s)

	1976	*1982*	*1986*	*1988*	*1990*	*1992*
Total Workforce						
All workers	5,052	5,188	5,683	6,102	6,567	6,335
Union members	2,513	2,568	2,594	2,536	2,660	2,509
% Unionisation	51	49	46	42	41	40
% Women members	31	34	35	35	37	39
Female Workforce						
All women workers	1,848	1,993	2,322	2,558	2,823	2,798
Union members	772	861	909	896	976	973
% Unionisation	43	43	39	35	35	35

Source: Australian Bureau of Statistics, Catalogue No. 6325.0.

working full-time were $43 higher than for non-unionists, and $48 higher in the case of part-timers.[9] Australia's unique award system[10] and the associated conciliation and arbitration system also benefit women, who are less likely to be able to negotiate individual contracts successfully. An ANOP survey commissioned by the ACTU before the 1993 federal elections revealed that significantly more women than men supported the retention of the award system and penalty payments, both of which were targeted by federal Liberal policy.[11] However, if women workers are so much in favour of the award system, why aren't more of them joining unions? The 1992 figures told a complex story. Women who worked full-time in permanent jobs in the public sector were more likely to be unionised, as were women from non-English-speaking backgrounds. What was alarmingly clear was that unionisation was lowest in the new and expanding areas of female employment, such as service industries.

The challenge for the union movement is to start organising in new industries which typically employ women on a part-time or casual basis, often in hard-to-organise small establishments. This will require a major redeployment of union resources into organising and service provision. These resources are increasingly being freed as the ACTU's plan to reduce the number of unions in Australia from 300-odd to twenty better-financed, industry-based unions by the end of 1993 proceeds apace. Having the resources to put organisers in the field is 'a key to growth'.[12] But it is not simply a question of enough organisers. Crucial, too, is the ability to meet the specific needs of women in the 'new' industries: permanent part-time work, flexible working hours, childcare, portable superannuation and leave entitlements. Once a union base, however limited, is established in smaller enterprises, it makes further recruitment much easier, since management antagonism is often a barrier to unionism. According to Beryl Ashe of the New South Wales Labor Council, 'In non-unionised industries it is not uncommon for women to meet trade union officials in the carpark or the club because they're afraid of getting the sack'.[13]

If the campaign by the ACTU and individual unions to boost women's static unionisation rates is to succeed, the union movement must radically transform its practices, structures and image. A 1988 ACTU survey revealed that Australian women's attitudes towards the union movement were significantly more negative then men's. Women associated unions with 'intimidation, thuggery and irresponsible strike action'.[14] The spate of newspaper interviews with women which were published in the wake of the 1989 ACTU congress supported this conclusion. One woman complained, 'the union movement has failed the woman with kids entirely. I know women who work and they are spending three-quarters of their wages each week on child care'. She added that the union movement had done little to 'soften' its masculine image.[15] This perception is not surprising, since unions rely on an emotional dynamic which requires men to assert their strength. Militancy and masculinity become conflated. As Cynthia Cockburn has observed, 'Trade union procedures and customs, their language and ideology were cultural and political expressions of manhood as much as labourism'.[16] The very language of unionism ('in unity is strength') is one not traditionally employed by women. Women make good (sometimes the best) militants, but they do not necessarily respond to appeals for action cast in terms of 'brothers manning the barricades'. The union movement needs to develop and promote the 'nurturing' side of its activities. In any case, this often occupies a far greater proportion of union work-time than disputes and strikes: for instance, individual grievance handling, health and safety, workers' compensation, career paths, equal opportunity, affirmative action programs, and union–management consultative forums. Symbolically and politically critical is the representation of women in union leadership positions. Rows of grey-suited or grey-cardiganed men at ACTU congresses tell women that the union movement is a male show. On the job, this is practically confirmed when there is a preponderance of male organisers, shop stewards and delegates. Anecdotal evidence suggests that women workers relate better to women organisers, finding them more approachable and less convinced that they always know what is best for that particular workplace.[17] An Argentinian woman worker, interviewed in a New South Wales study, summed up the style of organising which she thought worked:

> I would get a cup of tea for everyone. I would treat them with respect and nicely. Everyone would get to say what they think. Everyone would listen to each other then.[18]

As always, the greatest incentive for women to join a union or to become activists comes when unions strenuously pursue issues of specific relevance to them. The majority of rank-and-file women unionists in Victoria interviewed by Alison O'Keefe in 1990 could not identify a course of action that unions had taken that was of relevance to them.[19] Many of the blue-collar women in the New South Wales study had 'the impression of their bosses and their union being in cahoots'.[20] These negative perceptions can be changed—if unions summon the will to do it. The Professional Officers' Association (now a division of the Public Sector Union), for instance, won a number of difficult pay equity cases for its women members in the 1980s and increased its female membership in the affected areas by 106 per cent.[21] The historic 1986 fifty-day nurses' strike in Victoria over wages resulted in a net increase of about 1500 members, despite many resignations from nurses opposed to the strike action. Some unions—though not enough—are developing programs and campaigns addressing the specific needs of women members, and also employing women's officers. Others aim publications at particular groups of women members. Even the conservative Shop Distributive and Allied Employees' Association, which pursues a policy of 'moderate feminism', in 1978 launched a 'Norma—Equality Be In It' campaign which was designed to alter company attitudes and practices and encourage women to assert themselves in their public and private lives. The campaign, which still continues, includes talks, films, an annual award and a ten-point plan encouraging women to learn to drive, to seek promotion at work, to share domestic tasks within the family, to participate actively in the union and to take time out for personal enjoyment.[22]

These developments are still far from the norm. A 1991 survey of Victorian unions found that only 10 per cent were concertedly implementing ACTU and Victorian Trades Hall Council policies and strategies to increase women's membership and participation in unions.[23] Union strategies aimed at women need to take account of women's subjectivity in other ways: for instance, in taking industrial action. Bev Thiele's study of industrial relations in Western Australia argues that because women are primarily located in industries which serve people rather than commodities, unions must contend with the ideology of service. It is one thing to stop a concrete pour—another to walk out of intensive care.[24] This does not mean that women workers in hospitals and other service industries will never take industrial action. What it does mean is that women have a more cautious attitude than men to industrial action. Many of the nurses who joined the 1986 Victorian nurses' strike burst into tears as they walked out to join the picket-line; nevertheless, they stayed out for fifty days.

Women's power within unions is, of course, not simply a matter of numbers, though reaching 'critical mass' is obviously important, particularly in male-dominated unions. It is imperative for women to become active members if their interests are to be promoted. However, as in all other social institutions, significant barriers stand in the way of their empowerment: 'family responsibilities; lack of knowledge about union organisation/issues; lack of knowledge about meeting procedures; negative attitudes of male members; and attitudes of other family members, especially husbands'.[25] Alison O'Keefe argues that the biggest problem is

> that unions continue to concentrate on a workplace unrestructured to accommodate those with family responsibilities. From the point of view of the women unionists themselves, union activities require domestic arrangements most women are unable or unwilling to make. The sexual division of labour remains intact and women's participation in unions continues to be limited.[26]

In a survey of the Municipal Officers Association, a white-collar union (now part of the Australian Services Union), some 41.2 per cent of women with dependent children (compared to 5.5 per cent of men) viewed the lack of childcare facilities as a major impediment to their participation in union activities.[27] This is particularly the case for part-time women workers, since lack of childcare is often the impetus for their employment status in the first place. A number of unions have tried to address this by scheduling daytime meetings in the workplace, or by providing childcare at evening meetings; but at the top level, little has changed.

Language is an enormous barrier for women from non-English-speaking backgrounds, who constitute over half the female workforce and about one-quarter of all women unionists.[28] Despite their numbers, immigrant women remain under-represented in all levels of union structures. Union services to meet their special needs are limited. A study of immigrant workers and trade unions in Victoria reveals that, if unions consciously change their approach, there can be a dramatic increase in the participation of immigrant women at all levels of union structures.[29] The Clothing and Allied Trades Union of Australia (CATU) is a case in point. The union has always had a predominantly female membership—90 per cent in 1991.[30] However, like many unions with a large female membership, its leadership was dominated by Anglo-Saxon men until the 1980s. Then there was a surge in women's participation, largely, it appears, as the result of deliberate policies by certain union leaders. Once the union started to employ immigrant women, there was a snowball effect. A CATU immigrant official recalled that she worked for twenty-three years in the industry and had never seen a woman organiser. 'Now I know how members feel when they see me, when they first saw me they were so happy.'[31] Two of the most significant findings of the Victorian study were that when immigrant women did get involved in union affairs 'they were very competent and often militant and outspoken'; and that immigrant workers as a whole were much more inclined to become involved with their union.[32] In an era of declining union membership, this has tremendous implications for the directions in which unions ought to be heading.

Training programs—especially women-only courses—by the government-funded Trade Union Training Authority (TUTA) and individual unions now play an important part in educating women in meeting procedure and the role and functions of unions. Formal courses, however, do not address the issue of the 'informal acquisition of knowledge'. Much of the knowledge acquisition—and power-broking—occurs over a beer in pubs, whose public bars officially excluded women until the early 1970s. The 'pub culture', in conjunction with the 'secret language of unions' ('the terms, acronyms, the intricacies of parliamentary procedure baffle'),[33] can be a powerful deterrent. Women unionists have attempted to counter this by a number of means: joining 'the boys' at the pub, joining 'the girls' at the pub, women's networks and women's dinners. Women's power within unions also depends on the extent to which unions are themselves democratic. Monthly or quarterly night-time general meetings, a common feature, are an inherently undemocratic form of organisation. Besides usually excluding workers with family responsibilities, they can be easily dominated by one workplace, occupational grouping or faction. Unions must adopt representative structures, based on workplaces, if women are to participate on an equal basis. The New South Wales Public Service Association, for instance, adopted a workplace organisational structure, initially because of technological change, but found it also had the effect of increasing the participation of women.[34] Women's committees, caucuses and conferences, now a common feature of a number of unions, can ameliorate some of the structural deficiencies. The New South Wales Teachers' Federation, for example, has set up Women's Action Committees throughout its membership. Meetings often combine a few drinks, a bite to eat, a speaker and debate; in many country towns they attract a better attendance than the general monthly meetings.[35] Besides their gender-specific nature, one factor in the better attendance may be the combination of pleasure with business. Most unions operate on a pleasure-denying basis—long, formal meetings with hardly a tea break, let alone the opportunity to chat or eat.

Until the early 1990s, no reliable figures existed for the numbers of women in positions of power in Australian unions. Fortunately, two major studies undertaken by peak union councils in Victoria and South Australia in 1991 and 1992 respectively have provided accurate figures and analysis.[36] As Table 14.2 reveals, women made remarkable gains in the 1980s but there is still a gender gap at the top levels. The better representation of women at the lower levels may be attributed to the nature of the shop steward or delegate role: 'perhaps the lowest status, and often the most stressful in the union movement, requiring hard work, considerable personal skills and a commitment to the welfare of fellow workers'.[37] It is also, of course, unpaid! The case of a 'young union', the Victorian Colleges Staff Association (now part of the Australian Colleges and Universities Staff Association), shows that unions can behave differently.

> As a union with a majority of female members and a majority of first-time unionists, the Association did not place the usual barriers in the way of active female participation. It was a union in which women were prominent from the formative times and retained that prominence.

The union was assisted by the equal opportunity movement; it gained a lot of support for its campaigns over repetition strain injury, a major occupational health and safety issue for women in the colleges.[38]

Table 14.2 Proportion of Women Union Officials, South Australia (1992) and Victoria (1991)

	Percentage of women	
Position	*South Australia*	*Victoria*
Secretary & Secretary/Treasurer	6.9	17
President	14.5	17
Vice-President	19.1	30
Assistant Secretary	20.0	15
Treasurer	30.0	19
Industrial Officer	41.3	28
Organiser	28.9	25
Combined Industrial Officer/ Organiser	22.6	32
Other type of officer	44.8	47
Women's Officer	100.0	100.0
All officers	25.0	31.2

Source: Barbara Pocock, *Women Count: Women in South Australian Trade Unions*, Centre for Labour Studies and the United Trades and Labor Council of South Australia, Adelaide, 1992, p. 23.

While it now appears that women's climb up the union power structures has accelerated, with some even reaching the top, there are a number of obstacles still in the way. Women from non-English-speaking backgrounds remain grossly unrepresented; the situation for Aboriginal women is even more desperate, since so few are in the workforce in the first place. Many of the positions which women hold in unions are appointed or, in the case of some specialist positions, funded by the government. Elected officers can participate in the decision-making processes of the union, whereas appointed staff 'occupy a much more ambiguous position'.[39] There is also a sizeable minority of unions which appear to remain untouched by union policies and efforts to increase the representation of women.[40] Almost half of the South Australian unions have no women officials at all. In many cases, women's hold over official union positions is still quite tenuous. The spate of (voluntary) redundancies in Victorian unions in 1993 following the Kennett government's abolition of payroll deductions for state public sector unions resulted in a number of reversals for women. In the Health Services Union of Australia (HSUA) No. 1 (Victorian Branch), for instance, 52 per cent of the female industrial and related staff lost their positions, compared to 21 per cent of the males.[41] Had the Liberal Party won the 1993 federal elections, a similar situation would probably have developed within federal public sector unions as a direct result of the abolition of payroll deductions and, more generally, amongst federally registered unions from the devastating impact of deregulation and anti-union legislation. The unexpected election outcome was an enormous reprieve for women unionists.

On the peak bodies of the union movement, such as the ACTU and state labour councils, the gender gap is even wider. The first woman on the ACTU executive, Jennie George of the NSW Teachers' Federation, was elected only in 1983. She became the only woman vice-president in the history of the ACTU; even more remarkably, she was a rank-and-file member at the time. In 1991, George was elected ACTU assistant secretary, another first. Although the ACTU and most state labour councils embraced 'affirmative action' positions in the 1980s, major structural barriers remain. The ACTU in 1992, for instance, included eight women, three of whom occupy 'affirmative action' seats, on its executive of thirty-eight. The ACTU's stated aim is for women to occupy half the positions by the turn of the century;[42] this can be achieved only by a major revolution in its structure, which currently favours male-dominated unions. Fortunately, this task, which once seemed almost impossible because of the gender segregation of both the workforce and unions, has been made a lot easier by the process of union amalgamation. Additionally, the 1993 ACTU congress adopted a proposal which means that half the executive will be women by 1999, via a series of staged increases.

One of the most positive initiatives taken to encourage women into official union positions is the Anna Stewart Memorial Project, which operates in Victoria and, more recently, South Australia. Set up by an ad hoc group of women activists in 1984, it is an on-the-job training program for rank-and-file women, who spend two weeks working as union organisers. A survey of participants in 1989 revealed that 38 per cent of respondents now hold official union positions.[43] The scheme has now been extended to a special program for women from non-English-speaking backgrounds. Union women are also formally caucusing—at least on the left. Again, these efforts to demolish the barriers to women achieving leadership positions are often stymied by women's family responsibilities. As one official put it, 'the whole structure of unions is about the culture of work to the exclusion of home. To move through the ranks you have to make a whole-hearted commitment which eats into your personal time.'[44] Many unions still do not provide paid maternity leave for their staff, and they are often notoriously bad employers. The hours involved in being a union official are punishing—often sixty hours a week, including night and weekend meetings. For those union officials with children, juggling union and family commitment can require more organisational ability than the job itself. Some union women are now questioning the worth of such demanding jobs. Union work differs from other taxing professional jobs in that it is bound up with conflict. Given that subjectively women are likely to want to work co-operatively, it does present somewhat of a disjuncture. It is also a job which is never done. 'It's a highly frenzied existence, so highly pressurized, so highly stressed,' according to Brenda Fortbath who has been an organiser for nearly twenty years.

> Being a union secretary, an organiser or industrial officer eats you up; it consumes you. Men can cope better with that, they have support at home. Women don't have the same supports in their domestic lives. Women don't get the same buzz out of the power—for them it's much more the stress of the commitment.[45]

In 1989, George resigned from the ACTU Executive (temporarily as it turned out), citing burn-out as the reason. 'It would be nice if one could balance the personal and political but often it's difficult,' she said at the time.[46] Men, of course, rarely face the problem of maintaining balance: they maintain a strict division between the personal and the political, between home and work.

The other key element in the ACTU's strategy for ensuring the survival of the Australian union movement into the twenty-first century is union amalgamation. This is another problematic development for women. While the ACTU has a women's checklist for amalgamating unions, it seems that it is more often ignored than used. Of the forty-five South Australian unions engaged in amalgamation in 1992, only eleven were taking special measures to improve women's representation in the new union. Only four were identifying positions specifically for women, and only two were adopting affirmative action programs as part of the process.[47] No study has yet been done of existing amalgamations, but the best guess is that the results for women have been mixed. Again, if unions consciously aim to use the amalgamation process as a mechanism for addressing women's inequities, the prospects are excellent. The Australian Services Union, during amalgamation in 1993, had an impressive affirmative program as part of the amalgamation deal. Larger unions will have the resources to provide better services, such as training, to women members, but there is also a danger that they will become more bureaucraticised and remote from the concerns of rank-and-file workers.

The future for women and the union movement in Australia in the 1990s is ambiguous. Unions are changing their policies and practices towards women, but in an uneven and sometimes contradictory manner. Since 1992, the attacks on working women's rights in states with deregulatory Liberal governments show how fragile the grasp still is. It also illustrates the degree to which the reforms and advances of the union movement in the 1980s in respect of women were interlocked with Labor governments in power nationally and in most states. Unlike other comparable OECD countries, such as the United States and Britain, the state in Australia has afforded a considerable space to feminist politics and this, in turn, has benefited women in the union movement. Following on from the Whitlam government's support for the ACTU equal pay case in 1972, federal and state governments from both sides of politics enacted a range of legislation in equal employment opportunity, affirmative action and sexual discrimination. This gave effect to some of the aims of the ACTU's Working Women's Charter which was adopted at the 1977 congress. The charter included

> a comprehensive and coherent set of policies promoting the interests of working women through trade union action . . . including: leave for working parents, comprehensive child care, equal remuneration for work of equal value, equal employment opportunity and affirmative action, and increased involvement in unions.[48]

During the 1980s, the Prices and Income Accord between the ACTU and the federal Labor government, in conjunction with the centralised conciliation and arbitration system, allowed considerable gains for women in the area of maternity and parental leave, hours, childcare and wages. The trend towards deregulation places some of these gains—especially pay equity—under threat. In its 1991 national wage decision, the Australian Industrial Relations Commission (AIRC) endorsed enterprise bargaining between employers and a single bargaining unit of unions representing employees. The decision did not address the position of women or other industrially weak workers, though it did establish a safety net which ensured that any agreements registered with the AIRC could not involve a reduction in ordinary-time earnings or departures in terms of the standard hours of work, annual leave with pay, or long-service leave with pay. Given that centralised wage decisions in the 1980s narrowed the gender gap in wages upfront, the decision has disturbed many women unionists. Some of the enterprise agreements trumpeted by the ACTU have addressed women's needs in terms of childcare and flexible hours and leave arrangements; but enterprise bargaining as a whole is likely to be dominated by the concerns of full-time workers, leaving women in part-time time or casual positions out in the cold. The emphasis on productivity bargaining again favours male workers, since many women are clustered in service areas where productivity is hard to gauge.[49] The ACTU has promulgated guidelines to assist unions in addressing the needs of members with family responsibilities, but again the adherence is likely to be very patchy. In 1992, the retiring Sex Discrimination Commissioner, Quentin Bryce, claimed that 'enterprise bargaining posed grave risks for pay equity and would exacerbate discriminatory treatment in over-award payments'.[50]

As Australia heads towards the new millennium, the fate of its traditionally strong union movement rests in women's hands. If it is not to become an historical anachronism, the movement must transcend its origins in the crisis of masculinity in the nineteenth century. It must radically reorder its priorities. It must change its organisational forms and structures, its language, its culture and its symbolism. It must attract women. It must promote them and their particular needs. As the capitalist imperative towards deregulation and restructuring continues to intensify, women also need unions to protect them and their hard-won gains. They need to seize the space created for them by the union movement's crisis of legitimacy and the reprieve granted in the 1993 federal elections. They can use this space, this interregnum, to remake unions in their own image and to continue the fight for equity, justice and power within both the union movement and the broader political arena. It is not an easy struggle, but it can be won if both the union movement and women workers grasp the historical moment.

FIFTEEN

Women, Paid Work and Social Policy

Lois Bryson

The last two decades or so have seen significant changes in the position of Australian women in relation to both the economy and social policy. Women's increasing participation in the workforce is widely acknowledged, but there is less recognition that the changes are far more comprehensive. As well as changes in women's employment patterns, we have a major shift in the way women are responded to by the state, which impacts directly on what is traditionally seen as the private sphere of social life. Taken together, the changes amount to a fundamental restructuring of women's position in the society: women are being directly absorbed into the class structure, rather than this relationship being essentially mediated by male kin.

This chapter is concerned with these changes in their historical perspective. It focuses on women's position in the public world of work, and the definition of women within social policy. The connections between the changes in these areas are teased out and the implications discussed for our understanding of that ubiquitous feminist question 'is gender equality increasing?'.

Women's Work in Historical Perspective

Despite steadily increasing participation in paid employment, women still clearly occupy an inferior position in the workforce. To understand the gendered patterns of the world of paid work today it is necessary to seek clues from history, or rather, herstory. These clues make clear that it has not been cultural inertia which has kept women in the domestic sphere and their involvement in the labour market at a low level: systematic political forces have operated. The historical evidence shows that women were actively excluded from the workforce[1] and their independent economic activity within households was redefined as non-economic. During the nineteenth century domestic labour was classified in official statistics as economic activity; at the beginning of the twentieth century, it was redefined as non-economic and expunged from the national accounts.[2]

From the time of colonisation to the beginning of the twentieth century and beyond, the poverty of most families ensured that virtually all members had to be economically active.[3] Aboriginal women were also often involved in work, besides the significant economic activity they undertook in their traditional societies where they were responsible for the collection of about 80 per cent of the food.[4] After colonisation many Aboriginal women were forced into domestic (including sexual) labour or work on properties, usually without financial remuneration.

Women contributed to family finances through waged work outside the home which Edna Ryan has termed their 'visible bread-winning'.[5] In 1891 this involved about 37 per cent of women in Melbourne; in the Sydney region, where there was less manufacturing, the figure was about 30 per cent.[6] The census of 1891, however, classified only 17 per cent of women from New South Wales and 21 per cent from Victoria as 'bread-winners'.[7]

A second strand of women's economic activity is identified by Ryan as 'invisible bread-winning'. The 'visible and the invisible earners overlapped but the invisible women were more likely to be married and of mature age'.[8] The invisible economic activities consisted of women earning money wherever they could.

> Besides taking in lodgers or boarders, women worked to earn money by laundering, or sewing at home, going out to do sewing, domestic work or child minding; teaching cultural accomplishments (such as elocution, music, dancing, painting); poultry keeping; vegetable gardening; cooking saleable edibles such as cakes and scones.[9]

From around the turn of the century, women's visible and invisible labour came to be progressively written out of economic history, as male unionists fought for and won a family wage for men. These unionists apparently believed that if they acknowledged the income earned by their wives, the case for higher wages would be undermined because the Arbitration Commission judges would take these earnings into account.[10] Women's wages were lower, and their work was intermittent; so it was, as Anne Curthoys has pointed out, important for working-class women, as well as men, to secure the male wage from cheap competition.[11] The unions might have taken the course of advocating equal pay to eliminate this possibility, but they did not choose to fight for this option.

Gradually, through persistently denying their wives' economic activity, 'union members were made to feel ashamed if they condoned it'.[12] Thus disapproval of women's employment and denial became 'a tradition, a myth distorting the true role of the history of women in Australia'.[13] A complementary facet of this process shows up in the construction of work in official statistics. Statisticians of the various states colluded with unionists by dividing the workforce into just two categories, breadwinners and dependants. Desley Deacon suggests that this was partly done 'in the interests of working-class men'.[14]

At the same time as married women's invisible employment was discouraged by male workers and denied by state statisticians, women's visible employment was being systematically restricted. Male unionists were intent on the exclusion of possible competition; they managed to achieve a raft of restrictions to women's employment opportunities[15] at the same time as they successfully excluded immigrant competition by means of the White Australia Policy. Arbitration Reports of the time show, during the period 1909 to 1912, women in New South Wales alone were prohibited from taking apprenticeships in more than twenty trades, including those of baker, butcher, pastrycook, and bootmaker. Some bans were industry-wide, for example, in the iron trade. Even where women were allowed to enter, it was on far less favourable terms than their male counterparts.[16]

From the 1970s on, with the establishment of formal equal pay and the gradual introduction of anti-discrimination legislation, the extensive restrictions on women's employment have been progressively dismantled, clearing the way for women to participate in the workforce on a more equal gender basis.

Recent Changes in Broad Outline

Recent developments can be understood only in terms of the earlier patterns. What has been happening is a gradual undoing of past exclusions and the systematic absorption of women directly into the class structure as paid workers.[17] Previously, at least from the turn of the twentieth century, the relationship of the majority of women to the economic system, and hence the class system, was mediated by male kin through *their* role as workers or, in a minority of cases, owners. Women are now moving into a more direct relationship to the class system as they take on the role of worker. While the process of change has been supported and indeed, promoted by the women's movement, it has been driven by economic imperatives, particularly the increasing demand for labour and, more recently, attempts to restructure and make more 'flexible' the conditions of work in many industries. It can readily be suggested that the logic of capital is best served by a large workforce of people who consequentially have greater spending power, and who are prepared to work under conditions that suit employers' interests.[18]

The changes have advantages for women insofar as they provide a degree of economic independence and place women squarely within the main structures of the society. They have disadvantages because women still occupy the least powerful positions in the employment structures, at the same time as they maintain major responsibility for the domestic sphere. Advantages and disadvantages notwithstanding, women's lives are being modernised. To be largely confined to the domestic sphere today, in contrast to peasant societies where the home is also the site of production, means exclusion from the socially powerful economic sphere.

Changes are not confined to the labour market. Many consequential strands of social policy can be pointed to as well. Social security provisions, for example, are moving away from defining women as mothers and wives, and moving towards defining them as workers. Policies in such areas as wages, education and training, childcare, equal employment opportunity and affirmative action have contributed to and accelerated the general trend. Women are thus gaining a place, albeit a secondary place, in the public domain, rather than largely being confined to the family sphere.

The gradual convergence of men's and women's involvement in the labourforce and the manner in which they are defined by public policy can be encapsulated as a move for women away from private dependency, and from a marginal to a more central role in the economy. The process is by no means complete, but it is readily discernible in virtually all countries. The movement of women into paid employment has led to an increase in their general well-being. This is particularly evident in Third World countries where, broadly, the higher the rate of women's employment outside the home and the higher their education levels, the longer their life-expectancy.[19]

It should be noted that in Western societies, since the beginning of the process of industrialisation, poor single and married women have usually not had much option but to stay in the labourforce despite bad working conditions, restricted work opportunities and low rates of pay. Nonetheless, social policy treated women as if they were financial dependants. This is nowhere more evident than in women's award wages in Australia during the first half of the century. Women's wages were set at just over 50 per cent of the male rate, regardless of their responsibilities. All adult men received the full rate of the male 'family' wage, whether or not they had a family. Single men were the major beneficiaries of this; single women, especially those with dependants, were the great losers. The family wage component of award wages was abolished only in 1974.[20]

Despite increasing female employment, there remains substantial financial dependence among partnered women. In the early 1980s the proportion of women in ten OECD countries who were totally financially dependent on their partners ranged from a low of 11.2 per cent in Sweden to a high of 68.2 per cent in the Netherlands. The Australian figure was 46 per cent in 1981, but dropped to 39.6 in 1985. Given that the proportion of women in employment has risen since then, this figure would no doubt be lower today. Only a minute proportion of women have achieved complete economic equality with their partners. This ranges from a high of 11.6 per cent in Sweden to a low of 2.6 per cent in Switzerland. Australia occupies one of the higher rankings, despite the fact that a modest 7 per cent of women are in positions of economic parity with their partners.[21]

Women certainly are being drawn into the labour market. But they are entering a secondary rather than a primary labour market, with poorly paid, often part-time, jobs; a narrow range of occupations; and, for mothers in particular, fragmented working lives. Both inside and outside the workforce, women are still subject to many impediments to equal power and equal resources. The restricted involvement of partnered women in the economy and their economic dependence is a major impediment to equality. As well, it remains a fundamental factor in the construction of family relationships. Decisions within families, particularly about who does the parenting, have been shown to be significantly influenced by the superior earning capacity of the male partner.[22]

Labourforce Participation

When we turn to the major characteristics of women's participation in the labourforce, we find that men's and women's participation rates have been gradually moving closer together. This trend has been fed from two directions. There has been a gradual reduction in male participation rates at the same time as there has been an increase in the participation rate of women (see Figure 15.1). Between 1981 and 1991 the overall rate of employment for men dropped from 77 per cent to 74 per cent; it maintained a high level, well over 90 per cent, for those men in the age bracket where the rate of child dependency is highest.[23] During the period between 1970 and 1986, while the labourforce rate for all men fell by 10 per cent, the rate for married women rose by 12 per cent—from 35.2 per cent to 47.1 per cent.[24] These trends have continued since.

Figure 15.1 Trends in the rate of participation in the workforce, 1983–92.

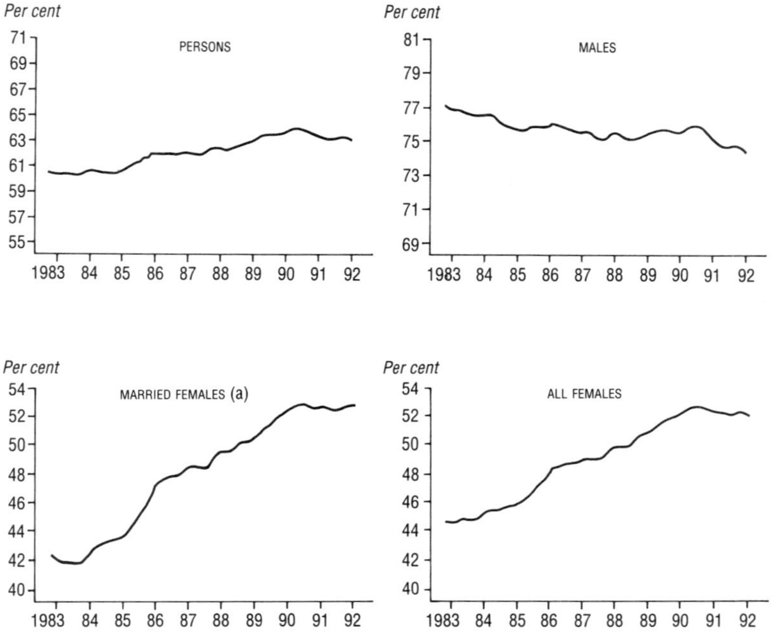

Source: Australian Bureau of Statistics, Catalogue No. 6203 (April 1992).

Although the overall labourforce participation rates for married and single women are at about the same levels today, with the married women's rate actually slightly higher, the age profile for married women shows a singular pattern and is clearly linked to family responsibilities. For males, the employment rate rises to age thirty-four then plateaus to age fifty-four. After this it decreases steadily, though with increasing speed in the older age groups. For married women there is an M-shaped pattern: that is, there are two peaks. Effectively the first is before the childbearing stage and the second is after the period of greatest child dependency, from thirty-five to forty-four years, when the peak is even higher. The rate then drops sharply, as it does at this age for men (see Figure 15.2).

In 1901 women made up 20 per cent of the officially recognised Australian workforce.[25] By 1961 this had reached 30 per cent[26] and by 1991 the figure was 41.8 per cent,[27] an increase of about 40 per cent in

Figure 15.2 Ratios of employment to population, by age, August 1991.

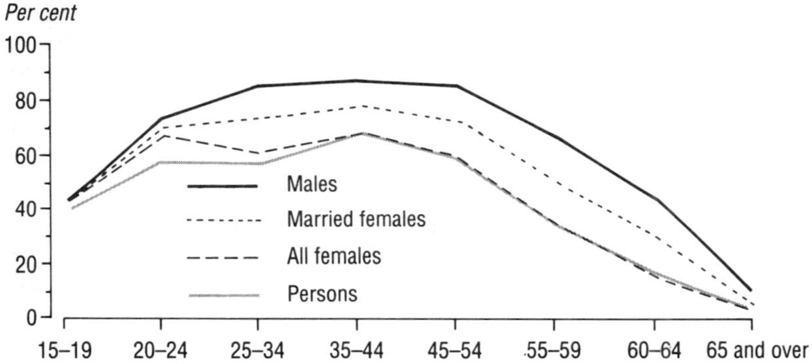

Source: Australian Bureau of Statistics, Social Indicatiors Australia 1992, Catalogue NO410L0, p. 172.

thirty years. The increase in women's rate of workforce participation has been entirely made up by married women. In the early 1950s the participation rate of married women was only about 12 per cent.[28] By 1970 it had reached 35 per cent[29] and today it is over 52 per cent (see Figure 15.1).

It seems almost certain that the increase in female employment would have been even greater had jobs always been easy to come by. This is indicated by the fact that, as research in Australia and other countries shows, women make up the majority of discouraged job-seekers. As well, many who have part-time work would prefer to work longer hours.[30]

When we consider the international picture, we find that Sweden has the highest proportion of women in employment of all the OECD countries. In 1987, 82 per cent of women were employed, making up 48 per cent of the workforce. The male rate, at 90 per cent in the workforce, is also higher than for Australian men.[31] Rates for women in the USA and Canada fall below those of Sweden but above those of the UK, Australia and Japan, which are all around similar levels and rising.

Increasing levels of education provide a key indicator of women's more equal workforce participation, as well as indicating the direction of social policy. During the 1970s low school retention rates for girls were targeted by governments around Australia. By 1976 these retention rates had reached the same levels as for boys, and they have continued to increase.[32] To an extent, these figures are misleading since apprentices are not included in the retention rates and apprentices are much more likely to be male (88 per cent in 1991).[33] However, this does not alter the marked trend for an increase in the education level for girls.

Female students now outnumber male students in tertiary education, accounting for 56 per cent of completions of higher education awards in 1990, a rise of over 6 per cent since 1981. The increase in female enrolments is continuing.[34] Also the pattern across fields is becoming less gender-distinctive, though the effects of traditional expectations are still evident. Whereas in 1979, arts and education enrolments made up 72 per cent of all female enrolments, this had dropped to 50 per cent by 1990. Apart from engineering, where the proportion of female students is rising very slowly (10 per cent in 1990), female students make up one-third or more in all fields of study.[35] Women are still under-represented in postgraduate enrolments; nonetheless, even here there has been a gradual improvement. In 1981, only 19.1 per cent of those completing a postgraduate degree were females; by 1990 this figure was up to 23.3 per cent. The projected figure for completions in 1992 is 26 per cent.

The data on education confirm a narrowing of the gender gap. The characteristics relating to women's employment profiles generally show that they are still disadvantaged, and are different in important ways from men's, as we have seen; but there is a trend of convergence, a trend which is not only a local phenomenon but an international one.

Rates of Pay

Women's earnings in Australia, as in other countries, are lower than men's, despite legislation on equal pay. For the decade from 1981, women's average earnings for full-time, ordinary hours of work were between 81 and 83 per cent of men's and they remained around 83 per cent from the late 1980s. This figure dropped to about 78 per cent when all hours of work were taken into consideration, because women work less over-time than men. Because of women's high rate of part-time work, all women's earnings as a proportion of men's dropped even further, to 65 per cent (August quarter 1990).[36]

For a period there were some signs that the wages gap was narrowing, evidence of a convergence of male and female patterns. The August 1991 figure showed a rise of women's average ordinary-time earnings to an all-time high of 84.5 per cent of men's; total earnings were up to 81.2 per cent of men's, and the rate for women employees was 66.8 per cent.[37]

Two factors largely accounted for the change: a number of flat-rate, rather than earnings-related, wage increases had been paid; and the Industrial Relations Commission was implementing a policy of 'minimum rates adjustment'. This policy involves pay increases 'determined by comparing the relative skill and responsibilities for classifications in an award, with key benchmark classifications in the metals and building industries'.[38] These adjustments brought some low rates up. Between January 1990 and November 1991, women's award rates increased by 7.6 per cent, while men's increased by only 6.9 per cent.[39] However, at the end of 1991, the effects of economic deregulation started to bite as enterprise bargains (that is, contracts between workers and management in individual organisations) were put in place. The trend was reversed, and the gap between men's and women's wages started to widen for the first time in some years.[40]

Despite the continuing unequal pattern, the earning rate of Australian women still ranks high in world terms. Figure 15.3 shows that the Australian rate compares favourably with those of six other OECD countries,[41] with New Zealand coming closest to the Australian rate. In fact, if we consider all the advanced capitalist societies, we find that the proportion of women's to men's rates of pay in Australia ranks close to Sweden, the top-ranking country, where women's hourly rate is 90 per cent of that of men.[42]

Figure 15.3 Women's earnings as a percentage of men's in selected countries, 1969–87.

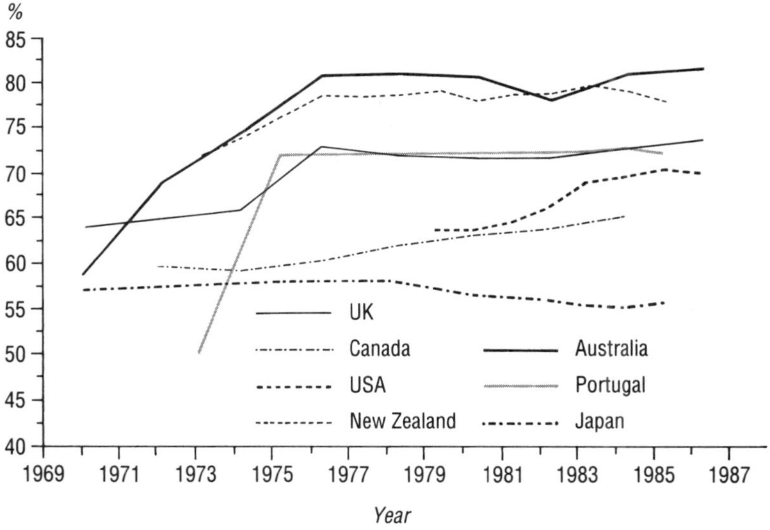

Source: Women's Bureau, Department of Employment, Education and Training, *Pay Equity: A Survey of Seven OECD Countries*, AGPS, Canberra, 1987, p. 66.

To find out what accounts for Australia's relatively favourable pattern internationally, we must locate the reason within the centralised form of wage-setting which each of the high-ranking countries has exhibited. Once women officially gained equal pay in Australia, consequential awards followed, across industries, at least for work in the formal economy. In 1983, 90 per cent of Australian female employees were in jobs covered by awards, determinations or collective agreements;[43] this was a higher rate than for males, reflecting the narrower range of occupations in which women are employed.

In those countries which have decentralised systems of bargaining, such as the USA, women in strongly unionised areas or with highly valued skills do very well. Other women do badly: women of colour are over-represented here. Women workers generally tend to be less well-qualified, and less unionised or in weaker unions. In Australia women's education and training have been going ahead by leaps and bounds over recent years, but they remain employed mostly in areas with poor conditions and least industrial muscle. There are therefore particular dangers for women in the recent moves away from a centralised wages system to enterprise bargaining. As industrial conditions are increasingly deregulated and decentralised, there will be decreasing protection. Women and other low-status workers are most vulnerable. This was confirmed by the reversal of the trend to close the gender gap in wage levels which occurred at the end of 1991.

In April 1991 the Industrial Relations Commission itself recognised that 'enterprise bargaining—especially for over-award payments—places at a relative disadvantage those sections of the labour force where women predominate'.[44] This danger was recognised by feminist organisations such as the Women's Electoral Lobby and the National Foundation for Australian Women, and the implications were explored in a submission to the Industrial Relations Commission.[45] This move shows that women's organisations are becoming involved in what has traditionally been male class activity.

Characteristics of Women's Work Today

Overall, the proportion of married and non-married women in employment is quite similar. But married women's working patterns, particularly where there are dependent children, vary in significant respects from those of both single women, and men. Women's paid work, regardless of whether the worker is partnered or single, still falls within the shadow of women's traditional domestic role. It is significant that it is very young women, those under twenty-one years, whose earnings come closest to parity with their male age peers.

The details about the nature of 'women's employment' are well enough known. The work that a majority of women do is still in the service sector, 'cleaning, cooking, nursing, typing'. These jobs are 'treated as natural extensions of their domestic roles and consequently devalued'.[46] Male definitions of skill prevail, with their emphasis on technology and hierarchically structured management.[47] Through recent downturns in the economy, while women's employment has continued to rise at a rate faster than men's, the conditions of that work have deteriorated. Much is part-time, intermittent, or performed on a contract basis. The high rate of women's part-time employment is usually taken to stem from the desire of mothers to combine childcare and paid employment.

While this explanation tells an important part of the story, it is too simplistic. For a start, the fact that there is a lack of adequate childcare impedes many mothers' working aspirations. Moreover, reduction of working conditions has applied more and more to jobs for men as well as women, as the recent increase of both men and women in part-time work suggests. This general process has been tellingly named as a 'feminisation of work',[48] and is another way in which the profiles of men's and women's work are converging. The continuing increase in the employment of married women must be seen as partly based on their greater readiness to accept the poorer working conditions which are increasingly offered. This readiness is largely a result of their family responsibilities, more modest expectations and weaker bargaining power. Certainly women, particularly married women, still occupy a majority of part-time jobs. However, the hours that women work have been consistently increasing, while men's hours have been decreasing. Overall women's weekly paid working hours in Australia in 1986 averaged 29.5 compared with 39.8 for men.[49]

Women's shorter hours of paid work are mainly accounted for by women's high rate of part-time employment. In 1990, 90.8 per cent of employed men were in full-time employment, but only 59.3 per cent of women were.[50] In 1990, 83.7 per cent of all part-time employment was undertaken by women; by September 1991, however, the figure had dropped to 76.1 per cent.[51] While it is possible that this trend will not survive the downturn in the economy, it is consistent with the general pattern of convergence. It is also in line with international trends for employers to seek greater flexibility of the workforce[52] and therefore seems likely to prove a long-term trend.

Part-time work in Australia can now be undertaken, at least in the public sector, with occupational benefits and conditions proportionate to those for full-time work. Job-sharing is available in some areas. Maternity and paternity leave are now covered in wage awards but, with the exception of public-service occupations such as teaching, maternity leave is rarely paid. This no doubt explains why few women take up the right to maternity leave.[53] In Sweden such leave attracts insurance benefits similar to those provided for sickness and unemployment.

Table 15.1 Full-time and part-time workers as a percentage of employed persons

	Males				*Females*			
	Married		*Total*		*Married*		*Total*	
	Full-time	*Part-time*	*Full-time*	*Part-time*	*Full-time*	*Part-time*	*Full-time*	*Part-time*
1981	40.9	1.5	60.0	3.5	11.7	9.9	23.5	13.0
1982	40.9	1.6	59.3	3.8	11.8	9.9	23.6	13.3
1983	40.8	1.7	58.7	3.8	12.1	10.1	23.8	13.6
1984	40.1	1.6	58.3	3.8	12.2	10.2	23.9	13.9
1985	39.3	1.5	57.8	3.8	12.1	10.5	24.1	14.3
1986	38.5	1.6	56.7	4.1	12.8	11.2	24.4	14.9
1987	37.9	1.7	55.8	4.5	12.8	11.4	24.1	15.6
1988	37.5	1.6	55.4	4.2	13.0	11.7	24.5	16.0
1989	36.5	1.7	54.6	4.6	13.2	11.7	24.5	16.4
1990	37.0	1.7	54.0	4.6	13.5	11.8	24.8	16.6
1991	36.2	2.2	52.6	5.3	13.9	12.0	24.9	17.2

Source: Australian Bureau of Statistics, *Social Indicators* Australia 1992, Catalogue NO4101.0, p. 172.

Married women not only undertake much more part-time work, their work histories are likely to be broken by childrearing. Taking all these factors together, women who raise two children are estimated to suffer a financial loss over a lifetime of about $384,000 at 1988 monetary values, with no allowance for interest on the money.[54] If we add to this the lifetime loss that all women, married and single, suffer through unequal wages, women's financial exploitation takes on massive proportions.

Trends in Welfare Policy

Some areas of social policy show changes which are complementary to those in the employment field. Trends in welfare policy, for example, are linked to those occurring in the workforce, with men's and women's situations drawing closer together. The pressures towards change here have also been exerted by macroeconomic forces, including pressures on governments to reduce welfare spending.

Until the late 1980s women were eligible for support from the state if they could be defined as wives, widows or mothers, that is, in various states of 'legitimate dependency'.[55] If they had been partnered but were currently without a man to support them, the state was prepared to step into the role and provide support. The widow's pension is an entitlement for which there has never been a male equivalent, because social welfare legislation has always constructed men in the economically independent capacity of worker and breadwinner. Unemployment and sickness benefit, invalid pensions and worker's compensation are state provisions originally established for working men; they have always included provision for dependent children and wives (not, as now, gender-neutral spouses). In 1978 the Supporting Mother's Benefit, instituted by the Whitlam government in 1973, was changed to the Supporting Parent Benefit. It thus became available to fathers. While not widely recognised as such, this was a potentially revolutionary change: it was the first time social security policy explicitly recognised the parenting role of fathers in other than economic terms (through, for example the family wage, or through the allowances for dependants attached to social security benefits).

Gendered welfare policy has deep historical roots, yet from the mid-1980s a fundamental change became evident. A variety of systematic efforts were made to direct recipients of social security benefits into the labourforce. An important change was the development of labour-market programs targeted at sole female parents; these indicate that women are gradually being reconstructed within social policy, as workers as well as mothers. First, the widow's pension was restricted to mothers with dependent children (Class A widows' pension). Formerly, older widows could receive a pension whether or not they had dependent children; these Class B widows' pensions can no longer be claimed and are only available to fulfil the entitlements of earlier recipients. As well, the age to which offspring in full-time education count as dependent was reduced from twenty-four to sixteen years.

The 1988 federal budget announced a new employment training scheme for sole parents, the JET scheme (Jobs, Education and Training). The move by the state to translate women's dependent domestic status into independent worker status was made quite explicit. The Minister for Employment, Education and Training said in a press release about the JET scheme:

> JET will offer concerted, practical support and direction to improve sole parents' job skills and help them into the labour market . . . JET will build on previous Government moves to encourage sole parents out of dependence on the social security system and into economic independence.[56]

The following year, Class A widows' pensions and the Supporting Parent Benefit were both abolished and were replaced by one provision, the Sole Parent Pension. This is gender-neutral and eligibility remains dependent on having responsibility for a child under sixteen years. The Class C pension became the Widowed Person's Allowance, equally available to men. This provides for a period of rehabilitation after the death of a partner for a period of twelve weeks (formerly six months).[57]

Social security policy has thus, in the space of just over a decade, redefined both women and men. Men and women now have equal entitlement to supporting parental benefits. Women no longer are defined as entitled to 'legitimate dependent' status. Unless they warrant support from the state on the basis of childcare, they like men, are treated as workers.

Childcare represents another policy area inextricably linked to the current trend to absorb women into the class structure as workers. This issue clearly shows up differences that remain between men's and women's work patterns. For example, childcare is still routinely referred to as a service for mothers rather than for working parents and has, until recently, been generally provided with reluctance. An important change in official attitudes in 1988 was triggered, predictably, by economic forces. The government's official commitment to the provision of childcare increased, almost overnight in fact, when it was demonstrated that direct costs of providing childcare are more than repaid immediately by increased revenue. This repayment is not a matter of that vague index, increased productivity. It is an increase in revenue resulting from the taxation paid by the women released into the workforce, and from direct savings on the dependent spouse rebate and social security outlays.[58] In 1988 the childcare funded by government was sufficient to cater for only 9.5 per cent of preschool children.[59] By 1991 there had been an increase from about 70,000 places when the Labor government came to office in 1983 to about 250,000 places.[60] The intention is to meet 66 per cent of the demand by 1996.[61] This would place Australia on a level with the leading Western countries in relation to childcare provisions.

Conclusion

Over recent decades we have been witnessing a revolution in terms of women's position in the society. This has brought about greater parity with men, and moved women squarely into the class structures of society as independent workers, rather than their connection being mediated by male kin. This transformation has the advantages of offering fuller citizenship to women and providing a measure of financial independence, a fundamental ingredient of equality. Disadvantages remain in the subordinate position women occupy within class structures, which seems certain to be exacerbated by a deregulated labour market. In enterprise bargaining, most women workers will not be bargaining from a position of strength.

The changes that have occurred have been fought for by women, but the greatest gains have been made where these are consonant with the demands of the economic system or where they serve state purposes. There has been far less evidence of change in evaluations of the worth of women's traditional activities; there is little change where male power is directly challenged; and there is little change where women have been seeking cultural change, for instance in attitudes relating to violence, and in the achievement of more cooperative, less hierarchical forms of group interaction and management.

As women move into the class structure they move into another societal arena, though this too is dominated by men. Feminist writers have suggested that such a change can readily be understood as a move from private patriarchy to public patriarchy.[62] This conceptualisation has validity, though it must not be taken to imply too much. Private patriarchy clearly remains a powerful cultural force, as the incidence of violence against women attests. Even at the economic level, without genuine equal pay and equal opportunity, partnered women remain partially dependent, and non-partnered women live in the shadow of this dependency. Nonetheless, it is important that women are represented, in their own right, in class structures; for this, financial independence is fundamental. Equality in both public and private spheres is intimately related; thus the convergence of women's and men's patterns of work, partial though it is, is highly significant to the question of gender equality.

SIXTEEN

'She' Will Mean 'A Complaining Customer': Women as Shoppers, c.1945–1970

Beverley Kingston

In an address in 1962 to a group of retailers on 'The handling of adjustments and complaints', Mr A. L. Carthew, managing director of Sydney Snow Ptd Ltd, asserted that since about 99 per cent of complaints were from women or involved women in some way, 'all future reference in this talk to complaining customers will be in the feminine. "She" will mean "a complaining customer".' At the head of his list of 'classes of people who complain', however, he placed women staff complaining about each other and about the rudeness of women customers. They also complained about their jobs, the lack of amenities, and the way they were treated by senior executives. Most of these complaints, Mr Carthew thought, could be traced to emotional stress outside the business, usually frustration or trouble at home. Similarly, the complaining woman customer, he thought, was often making a nuisance of herself for the sake of hearing her own voice.[1]

Misogny of this kind was common among retailers, especially during the 1950s and 1960s. It flourished in the distance between men and women; men were concentrated among owners, managers and executives, while women increasingly constituted the customers and the sales staff. The distance between men and women in retailing had been growing slowly since at least a decade before World War II, as the department store which had been dominant since the middle of the nineteenth century was challenged by the newer chain store. This transformed shopping from a bourgeois pleasure into something more egalitarian—the coming of the mass market.

It had once been assumed that the woman entering a department store, or any other self-respecting shop, was a lady. Service was considered the cornerstone of a store's image and reputation, and sales staff worked hard to win and maintain customer loyalty. The department stores were essentially middle-class institutions, and treated their customers as guests who were to receive every consideration from the staff. The chain stores were introduced to bridge the gap between the market stall and the fashionable end of town. They sold a wider range of non-essential consumer goods—clothing, cosmetics, household equipment and ornaments—on a more regular and reliable basis than the market stall and more cheaply than the little general store. They relied on bulk purchasing, quick turnover and mass marketing to keep their prices low. They also expected customers to look after themselves in a more egalitarian way. And they exploited new approaches to packaging, advertising and selling, at the same time developing a new attitude to women as shoppers. In the chain store, if there was to be any customer loyalty it came from a perception of value and accessibility.

Women who felt intimidated by the sales staff in the big stores, ill at ease with their deferential behaviour, or embarrassed in asking to be shown the cheapest goods, found the self-help style of the chain store a godsend. Prices were clearly marked, so there was no need for anxiety about what you could afford, nor any suggestion of disapproval when the choice was made. Self-selection also required more informative packaging and prior advertising, so that the customer could be better informed and more confident in her judgement without help from the sales staff. For many women, this was the beginning of their self-education as consumers. Formerly they had been reliant on understanding and remembering what the sales assistant told them about the goods as part of the sales pitch. Often they felt confused by what they were told, or were too intimidated to ask. Being able to read and re-read the label gave the purchaser a much better chance of making an informed decision, provided, of course, that the label was truthful and helpful. The deference of management towards customers in the department stores, which concealed a superior sense of style and a patronising attitude, in the chain stores came closer to equality.

Chain-store selling methods were resisted by retailers, who put their faith in bigger mark-ups and more affluent customers. World War II hastened acceptance by destroying both the practice of salesmanship and the quality of service. During war-time shortages and subsequent rationing, roles were reversed. It was the shopper who was keen to buy, even though, often, the storekeeper had little to sell. Customers became dependent on the goodwill of storekeepers in deciding how to distribute what supplies did come their way. And storekeepers discovered to what lengths women were willing to go to get the things they really needed. After the war, retailers began, largely as a way of cutting costs and becoming more competitive, to reassess the kind of service they provided for their customers. Self-selection became a virtue in most department stores, and self-service was quickly introduced to grocery shopping. Though much was made of the convenience of self-service to the housewife, in fact retailers were quick to place new charges on old services such as orders, deliveries, and credit facilities to discourage their use.

Retail expansion into the suburbs, which had been halted by the war, was resumed with enthusiasm. Much of the inspiration for the chain stores, before the war, had come from the US experience. After the war, developers turned once more to America for the latest in retail design and cost-saving ideas. This meant planned shopping centres on a large scale; dramatic extension of the existing chains; and new kinds of management to cope with the scale of operation.

As the emphasis shifted from selling to buying, retailers relinquished some of their power over their customers and became dependent on the activities of advertisers and the initiatives of shoppers. Women lost whatever status they had had previously as valued customers; they became, in retailing jargon, mere 'purchasing agents' for their 'spending units'. Moreover, they were considered tabula rasa for every sexual, fashion and beauty aid known to packaging. Shopping became quite impersonal. The retailer began to rely on market surveys to discover what his customers wanted, and consumers could express their opinions only by refusing to buy. The increasingly high-powered and largely masculine retailing industry needed, more than ever, to woo, cajole, trick or bludgeon consumers—obviously, mostly women—into parting with their money. The methods of persuasion, however, had become mechanical. There was some resentment that the profits in retailing should be so dependent on the illogical minds and whimsical behaviour of women. Popular psychology was heavily applied through advertising and in daily encounters, as manufacturers and retailers saw themselves at the mercy of the irrational and the inexplicable. Thus, because they really did exercise a kind of collective power through their purses and shopping trolleys, women individually were resented, ridiculed, treated as children, and otherwise put in their place. Jokes about women, especially their irrationality, became a standard feature of the popular illustrated magazines, and even filled every spare corner of the otherwise earnest monthly journal of the NSW Retail Traders Association. Eventually this insensitive treatment of women became counter-productive; the re-emergence of feminism was welcomed by intelligent retailers and advertisers, albeit cautiously, for the creative tension it brought back into their industry.

Postwar retailing was also affected by the renewed move to the suburbs. Initially this suited both retailers and the women they served as customers. As the cities grew, shopping became increasingly difficult, especially for women with children, even with public transport and extensive order and delivery services. Existing suburban shopping centres thrived on these difficulties and expanded where feasible. During the 1950s and 1960s new regional shopping centres were built, following the spread of suburban housing. Much of this expansion was predicated on rising car ownership. Indeed, in new shopping centres, the needs of cars effectively replaced those of the customers. American experience had already discovered that it was desirable to separate the customers from the cars; hence the creation of pedestrian shopping malls within huge car parks. The customer, it seemed, was the only statistic not able to be planned, regulated or predicted. Obviously the most desirable shoppers were those who came in cars: not only because ownership of a car indicated a higher level of disposable income, but also because shoppers with cars were more likely to carry away their own purchases, both small and large. Unfortunately, however, car ownership was still a male prerogative in Australia.

As far as retailers were concerned, these new shopping centres were the best way to take their services to the customers in the most economically efficient way. Suburban land was cheaper than land in the central business district, and there was plenty of space for parking. The buildings were designed to incorporate the latest technology for the highest possible turnover at the least possible cost. To the suburban housewife, the regional shopping centre represented convenience. So long as transport was available, she could shop easily and casually with her children for everything she needed, from food and groceries to hardware or clothing. The crowds, the discomforts, and the difficulties of a day in the city were a thing of the past. She did not have to dress up or feel intimidated by the smart salesgirls in the city stores. Retailers quickly found that they were wasting their time in trying to sell high fashion or expensive decorator items in their suburban stores. The suburbs were more concerned with comfort, affordability, convenience and necessity. The gulf between the aspirations of the retailers to educate their customers to more of the expensive high fashion items, and the commonsense and cost-consciousness of suburban women soon developed into a stereotype of the dowdiness of the suburban housewife.

It had been thought that after the uniformity and self-denial of the war years, an emphasis on fashion was the obvious way to stimulate retailing.

> We must endeavour to again build up and cultivate the fashion sense of women folk, the existence and indulgence of which does so much to raise their living standards and bring to them such pleasure and satisfaction.[2]

Sir Sidney Snow was also of the opinion that an interest in fashion made women

> better citizens—a women without a fashion sense and to whom the more beautiful things in life do not appeal, generally remains on the lower rungs of the human ladder.[3]

It was assumed that 'Every woman loves to shop in a fashionable store. There is glamour, prestige—and most of all—the authority of fashion.'[4] Indeed through the late 1940s and early 1950s, an immense amount of effort was applied to selling the postwar Paris 'New Look' to women who read the daily press and the *Women's Weekly*. Great numbers of words were expended on the exact length of the hemline, the complete silhouette, the perfect waistline and bust measurement, seeming to confirm that women were only too willing to accept the 'authority of fashion'. But in all this there was an element of make-believe or wishful thinking. An American fashion expert visiting in 1960 thought Australian women as a whole looked too dull and matronly. She put the blame on retailers and manufacturers who did not have the courage or imagination to offer them anything better.[5] An advertising illustration proclaiming the 'authority of fashion' shows an elegant woman in a tight skirt making a grand entrance—down an escalator! She has no audience except her own image reflected in a mirror, and the skirt is far from practical for anything but mincing along in high-heeled shoes.[6] The reality was the thousands of women in sensible coats and shoes with shopping bags, who were regularly shown jamming the footpaths as they waited for the opening of a new store in the hope of buying some of the cut-price opening specials. Escalators, in fact were now specially built to accommodate a woman and child side by side, since it had been observed that women shopping were usually accompanied by a child. Narrow cleats and combs were installed at top and bottom of escalators, however, as a precaution 'in these days of stilt heels'.[7]

The architects and designers who were responsible for building new shopping centres travelled to America, and came back with the latest American ideas about what women wanted to make them buy more. Bright feminine colours would make a hardware store attractive to women. A polished silver-ash counter padded and studded in mushroom-pink vynex and char black was said to constitute 'feminine appeal' in a fashion store.[8] The homewares department was a woman's world where she should find the 'pretty things' she wanted for the kitchen. Furthermore, the homewares could be linked to fashion displays throughout the store—oven gloves to match her new spring dress, maybe.

> She may come in to buy a utilitarian carrot peeler. But her eyes will wander to that decorative cookware or fancy chopping board. Fashion in homewares offers unlimited display possibilities in windows and various departments. In this age of modern living, it's important to a woman to save time, career as well as non-career women. She wants easy ways to

> prepare meals, to serve and to clean up. But she still wants to be the master over the machine that does all the work! She needs to be shown what wonderful things she can do with it, as well as what it can do for her.
>
> Cooking demonstrations are a good way to get this across; or advertisements showing the finished meal with a "you can do this" appeal.[9]

It was said that women didn't like to bend too far to get things out of the freezer cabinets—34 inches (860 cm) was decreed 'the exact height at which a woman bends to reach into the case'.[10]

Peter Yeomans, a consultant on the design of supermarkets, advised his clients to give special thought to the design of the parking lot:

> most of the drivers will be women and you will have to make parking easy for them. You should allow lanes right through so that there is a minimum of backing necessary, preferably one-way driving lanes to reduce the accident risk . . . I have seen women shy away from a parking area because of the entrance crossing from the main road. [Some councils require a deep gutter.] When a woman drives over that gutter and the car bounces she becomes nervous. Next time she may try to park somewhere else.[11]

While owning and driving a car remained the husband's prerogative, drive-in shopping centres would not prosper. It became necessary for women to learn to drive and have access to the family car for shopping. The number of drivers' licences issued to women rose steeply, it was noted, during the 1960s and 1970s.[12]

Women were now decreed to be clever enough to shop on their own:

> The housewife of the 19th century had a limited education and needed the help of a specialist salesperson. National and mass marketing nowadays makes a more informed consumer who can be expected to choose intelligently from the open stock presentation.[13]

Yet advertising became less helpful, thanks to smart young men imposing their own fantasies about women on the kind of advertising copy they wrote and sold. Newspapers and radio competed for women's attention, the papers with social news and cooking features, the radio stations by employing male announcers whom they thought authoritative and irresistible. Prospective advertisers were reminded that women couldn't argue with the radio, or that they were easily addicted to radio serials.[14] Most advertising derived from America, though there the position of women was rather different. Before the 1960s, unlike their American sisters, not many Australian women had a college education or a chance to enter one of the professions. Australian men were still protective and conservative about their womenfolk. Even in retailing, though a great many women worked behind the counter of a family shop or even large store, very few women were well paid—if they were paid at all—or in senior positions. In fact one of the more obvious reasons for the tendency of Australian retailers to misunderstand the needs of their women customers was that they had little or no communication with women, probably not even their wives. Visiting American marketing experts took a dim view of the condescending attitudes of their Australian counterparts towards women shoppers. Retail executives were advised to get out among their customers to try to find out what they were really thinking.

An accident of demography in the 1950s and 1960s tended to emphasise the image of the Australian woman as wife and mother. Birthrates fell during the depression of the 1930s and the early years of World War II. This meant that the number of young adults with money to spend while courting and then working at building a home and establishing a family was at its lowest in the mid-1950s. Unlike the teenagers of the baby boom in the 1970s, for whom another new style of retailing was created, there were hardly enough young people in the 1950s generation to constitute a worthwhile market. So the tendency was to treat them as undifferentiated adults as soon as they ceased to be children; indeed, young marriages were quite the thing, so that they quickly also became young parents and the girls, young mothers. Bridal registries like those devised in the USA in the 1930s, established in some stores in the late 1950s, were probably the nearest approach to the recognition of a special market. Anthony Hordern's encouraged groups of girlfriends to join their 'Glory Box Register' so they could enjoy the friendly rivalry of collecting their china, cutlery and glassware with the aid of the 'Stock Pattern Plan', with a 'Colour Quest' for their household linen. They could also buy a 'new style contemporary glory box with swinging doors and pull out trays in highly polished Queensland maple' to house the collection.[15] This was undoubtedly an earnest generation, determined that its children would not suffer insecurities and disruptions such as the depression and the war had brought for them. It was a generation bent on security in employment, in housing, in belief. It was also, because of its circumstances, fortunately a generation which experienced full employment and high average wages, so that home ownership, family comfort and good educational opportunities for the children were all within reach. Yet these were the women who were being wooed on the one hand with the very sophisticated (and at the same time surprisingly ageing) fashions of the 1950s, and sold on the other, the shoddy equipment and furnishings designed for quick production and a mass market. Needless to say they rejected expensive Paris-inspired fashion in preference for clothes which adapted to babies and pregnancy, and washed well. A sewing machine was a popular present for an engagement, twenty-first birthday, or wedding in the 1950s, and deemed a good investment. By making their own and their family's clothes, these women were opting for better quality as well as saving for more important household equipment.

When decimal currency was introduced on 14 February 1966, the *Sydney Morning Herald* published prices of 'an extensive range of grocery and other items from a typical shopping list . . . as a guide to housewives', with instructions to 'cut out the list and take it shopping'. The culture assumed the shopper was a she. As might be expected, the culture was harsh on men who might need or wish to shop. The almost universal 9-to-5 working hours of the 1950s meant that 'non-working' wives perforce did all the shopping, even though they might have preferred to share it with their husbands. A man who worked from nine o'clock to five on weekdays and also on Saturday mornings had no time to shop apart from his lunch hour, or occasional days off. If he worked in the city, his wife had to meet him there if they wished to shop together for furniture or clothes. Some couples overcame this difficulty by window shopping at night or at weekends, with the wife going later to make the agreed purchase on her own; this was difficult if both signatures were required on a hire-purchase agreement. Evening home demonstrations and sales became popular as a way of involving the husband. The conventional wisdom was that he was often willing to spend more than his wife dared if shopping on her own, and that a man would demand better quality with less concern for value for money.

It was known that something like 40 per cent of men had all their shopping done for them by their wives, and that perhaps 80 per cent of menswear was sold to women. Again, this was partly a result of the limited and strictly enforced shopping hours. It was also believed that men preferred to shop in places where they were not bothered by women. To make the menswear departments attractive to both groups without alienating either was a real challenge to store designers. A common compromise was to have different entrances, one of which was clearly for men, perhaps through the smokers' section. Still, women were generally held responsible for the lack of fashion-consciousness among men.

Retailers were eventually forced to acknowledge the difficulties imposed on the increasing number of women returning to the workforce, if only because so many were in retailing. These women had to do all their shopping, for themselves and their families, in the lunch break. Stores were reorganised to entice the working woman in a hurry; they ensured quick service and easy access to stockings, cosmetics, blouses, and costume jewellery on the ground floor, assuming her to be a career woman spending money on herself. Women who worked as sales assistants could sometimes get shopping time during slack periods. Other women workers were not so well off, especially if their work was not handy to the shops. It made little sense that even those women who did have money to spend had no time in which to do serious shopping.

The rising proportion of women in the workforce, especially in retailing, and the slow but inexorable move towards equal pay did nothing to endear their female workers to the dominant males of the retail trade. The retailers had supported, even welcomed the changes which allowed women into selling areas previously reserved for men, in the belief that their wages bill would fall. For example, groceries and cooked provisions had been reserved for men, though women could sell cakes and pastry if they were on a separate counter. Only men had been allowed to sell household hardware, crockery, glassware, and electrical appliances, though women were allowed to sell small devotional and ecclesiastical items. After a long battle with the union, women were permitted to drive lifts, provided no qualified male was available.[16] Equal pay, retailers warned, would be a bad thing for women, since it would lower male wages and thus bring hardship to housewives and their children.[17]

By the late 1960s, women were beginning to resist the sales pitch and the patronising treatment. They were growing tired of promises that were not fulfilled and things that did not work, and were ready to join consumer organisations like the Australian Consumers' Association, formed in 1959. The image of the wife and mother was increasingly in conflict with the much more interesting sexy image of 'woman' produced by Hollywood and the advertising agencies. So the unmarried woman, hitherto of little use in Australia as a consumer because she had so little to spend on herself, became more interesting. The consumer culture needed young women with disposable incomes and frivolous ideas. It also needed kids to put more pressure on mum to spend less sensibly. And the housewife herself needed liberating from her own image as responsible for every aspect of her family's life, if she was to be persuaded to buy more expensive prepared foods and ready-made clothes. Hence for example the 1960s revolution, which made fashion exciting for both manufacturers and wearers. The simple shift and the miniskirt transformed underwear and shoe fashions, but they were too easy to run up at home and used too little fabric. By moving women into trouser suits and jeans as well, manufacturers were able to reclaim a large part of the ready-made clothing market.

The return of feminism may have been as necessary for the health of consumerism as it was for the sanity of the female population. By permitting an alternate set of images of women to those which had become increasingly stereotyped since the 1930s, feminism virtually doubled selling opportunities for retailers and advertisers. They could now target both markets, the housewife buying for her family and the working woman spending her larger-than-ever pay packet on herself. While women attacked the stereotype of 'the housewife' as consumer,[18] the advertisers themselves were quick to respond.[19] Significantly, the long-term best-selling *Women's Weekly* was joined on the newstands by the new, sexy *Cosmopolitan*. In many ways the liberated Australian woman of the 1970s was merely an updated version of the 'new woman' as created by American advertisers in the 1920s, and increasingly, because consumerism was a worldwide necessity for modern capitalism, she had much in common with her fellow consumers all round the world. But the underlying toughness of the modern women's movement in Australia may also be related to all those years as a customer with a complaint which no-one would take seriously.

SEVENTEEN

Ladies to Women: Women and the Professions

Rosemary Pringle

For feminists of the late nineteenth century, women's entry to the professions was a major issue. The struggles to gain access to medicine and law evoked similar passions and intensities to the current struggles for ordination. Women were admitted to architecture degrees in 1880, but it was 1897 before the first woman was admitted to medicine and 1903 to law (in Victoria). New South Wales did not follow until 1918, one year earlier than England, and Western Australia was the last of the states in 1923. Access to education was only the beginning. In all three professions women had difficulty in getting practical training, experience and employment. Three other major sites of masculine professional privilege, the church, the armed forces and engineering, had to wait for the period of Second Wave feminism to receive a similar challenge.

Women were not expected to be present in equal numbers to men, or even on equal terms. The professions were to be available to those with unusual ability and commitment and a genuine sense of vocation. Most would be unmarried women who devoted themselves to their careers, that is, a secular version of the nuns. The professional use of maiden names prefaced by 'Miss' has diverted attention from the number who were actually married with children, and has helped to reinforce the 'honorary man' image of these early female professionals. Given the intensity of the early struggles, the numbers who entered the professions remained small. Instead, careers opened up for women in the 'semi-professions' as nurses, teachers and secretaries. These occupations were seen almost as women's 'equivalent' of the professions, but they were less demanding and did not require heavy financial backing.

Since the early 1970s there has been a great influx of women students into law, medicine and architecture throughout the Western capitalist world. This is associated with the rapid increase in professionals generally. The number of lawyers in Australia, for example, rose only modestly between 1911 and 1947, but there was a 600 per cent increase between 1947 and 1986.[1] The absence of women from maths, science and engineering was challenged; the movement for the ordination of women gathered steam; and women's right to join the armed forces, become officers and engage in combat was asserted and debated. Expectations about equality of opportunity implied that women should take an equal place in professional life, regardless of marital status and whether or not they had children.

There is now debate as to whether this movement of women into the professions represents a gain or merely creates new forms of discrimination. Feminist writers have generally been pessimistic, tracing a shift from outright exclusion to segregation within occupations. A common theme in the literature is 'continuity in change'.[2] It is argued that women are channelled into the less desirable sectors of the professions, in jobs that are regarded as 'appropriate' to their gender, as general practitioners, paediatricians, family lawyers or domestic architects. There is continued resistance to them as surgeons, barristers, and designers of large public works. Their presence is explained by the sheer growth in the overall numbers of professionals and the emergence of 'secondary' job markets within professions. Attention has been given to the 'glass ceilings' which stand between women and the top jobs, and the primary responsibility that women continually take for children and the smooth running of the domestic sphere. Women's absence from the top positions is now regularly monitored and publicly discussed. The television programme *Four Corners*, for example, reported that women constitute less than 3 per cent of the upper echelons of business, government and the professions.[3] Margaret Beazeley QC, interviewed the week before the football Grand Final in Melbourne, observed that corporate seats at such events do not get 'wasted' on women, and that as a result they lose out on valuable business and professional contacts. The Law Society established a taskforce to examine discrimination, and women lawyers have been outspoken in the pages of its journal and in the major newspapers.[4] Women gynaecologists quickly went public with their anger when no female registrars were appointed to George V Hospital in Sydney in 1992, forcing the hospital administration onto the defensive.[5]

Ironically, the more women have entered male-dominated professions, the more the literature has focused on gender disadvantage: whether it can be explained by the difficulties of reconciling a career with family or is the result of occupational closure.[6] While it is easy to rehearse the facts of discrimination, it is also important to acknowledge the shift involved in staking a claim for equal representation. Women have broken much more successfully into the professions than they have into the trades. The number of female apprentice electricians, plumbers, car mechanics or butchers is still minuscule. For a woman to enter one of these trades is to put her gender on the line to a much greater extent than in most of the professions. Apart from the obvious class differences operating here, it is clear that different forms of masculinity are implicated. Professions are perceived to be about 'people', whereas trades are about 'things'. The professions are already, to some extent, 'feminised'. This makes it possible for 'equality versus difference' debates to take place, posing the question, will women by their special qualities change law, medicine or architecture or are patriarchal values so imbued that there is little scope for women to make a difference?[7] It is more difficult to imagine these questions being pursued in the trades. That they are, nevertheless, taking place in the professions is indicative of a profound change since the mid-1970s.

How are we to characterise this change? Does it mark a significant shift in gender relations, with women laying claim to professional authority? Or is it more pertinent to see it in class terms? Bottero suggests that the complaints about ongoing discrimination mask something deeper, namely a strengthening of class divisions. As professional opportunities decline in the 1990s, the women who are coming in are predominantly upper middle class, and displace men from the working and lower middle classes.[8] There is something in this argument but some points of caution are in order. We must be careful not to assume that it applies in quite the same way to Australia, whose education system is arguably more open than the English one. While women lawyers in Australia are drawn, even more than the men, from professional and managerial families,[9] this is less true of medical students, who include a higher proportion of 'idealists'. It is also dangerous to assume that 'class' has precisely the same meaning for women as it does for men, or that the presence of more 'upper-middle-class' women necessarily amounts to class closure and does not, in its own way, threaten the existing class system. While class analysis is important, it will be argued here that women's presence has done more than reinforce class relations. It has thrown down an important challenge to masculine authority.

The symbolic significance is easiest to recognise in relation to the ministry, probably because of its relatively humble status. Few would enter the church in search of worldly riches or upward social mobility. For most women who seek it, it is likely to be a matter of downward mobility, a life of relative poverty compared with the other available professional options. The significance of this issue is not in its employment dimensions, but in its symbolic ones. The church retains enormous moral authority and Christian doctrine evokes patriarchy at its most fundamental levels. Women priests challenge the whole way the ministry operates, as well as the masculinity of God. This is recognised by opponents of ordination who, in circumstances where the number of men coming forward is dwindling rapidly, might well have been relieved to have this new pool of enthusiastic workers from which to draw. The wider implications are present in the intensity of interest with which the general public follow these matters. A vote of the Anglican synod is headline news; it is not relegated to the religious columns.

Feminists of the 1960s and 1970s experienced ambivalence about the movement of women into the professions. The claims of the professions to self-sacrificing idealism were criticised and their strategies of power identified by radical political movements of the time. The sociological tradition of Durkheim and Talcott Parsons, which had celebrated the professions as a means of regulation and integration, and as a counter to too much bureaucracy, was rejected.[10] Freidson, Johnson and Willis, among others, documented the ways in which professional dominance was achieved by strategies that subordinate, limit or exclude other occupations from practice in the field.[11] Some saw the professions as part of a new middle class whose privileges rested on state patronage and the support of strategic elites.[12] Ivan lllich criticised the whole notion of professionalism.[13] Michel Foucault demonstrated the power of legal and medical discourse to construct 'normality' and bring our everyday lives under routine surveillance.[14]

For socialist and radical feminists in the 1970s and 1980s, equal opportunity was only part of the issue. Becoming a professional could only be justified as part of a strategy of *de*-professionalising. The professions had to be demystified, the gap between professionals and the community reduced, and skills shared. At women's health centres doctors were frequently excluded from collective decision-making, treated as 'technicians' who should share their skills, do their share of shitwork, and take equal wages with other health workers. That women who took these positions had placed themselves at the bottom of the medical hierarchy was overlooked. In the legal context feminists have often made a show of not needing professionals, defending themselves and refusing to be bound by the conventions of the legal system. Groups like Constructive Women in Sydney and E1027 in Melbourne challenged the division between architects and builders.[15] While professionals have made important contributions to feminist projects, they are often the recipients of envy, jealousy, anger and frustration from other women and can easily be represented as part of the privileged classes who exercise power.

Radical politics of the 1970s directed itself to the overthrow of the existing political system through 'class struggle'. While the presence of 'contradictory locations' was recognised, it was necessary to line up on one side or the other. It was thus easier to support nurses than to sympathise with the often heavily medicalised or conservative attitudes of women doctors; to identify with victimised client groups than to worry about glass ceilings. The struggles of factory workers for jobs at BHP or the nurses for better pay and conditions seemed more heroic than the struggles of women doctors or lawyers. Professional women could be allies only insofar as their conditions of work showed signs of declining, or where there was clear evidence of discrimination, harassment or child-care problems. The literature that developed used the language of 'proletarianisation', discrimination and exploitation, and shied off assessing the larger implications of the movement of women into the professions.

The advent of post-structuralism has enabled some of these questions to be opened up. For a start, we are less likely to see power in sovereign terms, as something that must be overthrown by a coalition of opposing forces, and more aware of the operations of power in all human relations, as a productive force as well as a negative one. Power and knowledge are integrally linked and mutually dependent. This is not the power of state and class, but politics at a more 'micro' level. Subjects are discursively constructed, and in turn have access to a range of discursive strategies.[16] Questioning the older sense of political struggle against a readily identifiable adversary created tensions between 'theorists' and 'activists'. The women's movement itself became professionalised, its idea of itself reshaped as its knowledge became influenced by the culture of academia. As 'oppression' became translated into sophisticated social theory, the gap grew larger between 'professional' feminists and community-based groups seeking to identify a common enemy. Yeatman argues, I think rightly, that the professionalism of modern university-based knowledge is necessary for critical feminist theorising.[17] The 'safeguard' is that feminist professionals can be criticised too. That power and knowledge are inseparable is an argument, not for rejecting scholarly expertise, but for continuing dialogue.

The professions associate themselves with notions of individual creative genius which attaches to men but not to women.[18] The doctor or lawyer is characterised by brilliance in saving patients or clients from threatening situations; the architect or engineer takes on the heroism of creating buildings and public spaces. Architectural theory has invariably used the 'great monuments of great men' approach in naming what is deemed 'memorable' architecture. Elizabeth Partridge has argued that, 'Despite its neuter pretensions, the creation of architecture is apparently only possible through adapting a masculine subjectivity.' Le Corbusier's famous definition of architecture as 'the masterly play of forms in light' is characteristic of this.[19]

Anne Witz notes that the 'spectre of semi-profession' has haunted the discussion of gender and professions, marking a distinction between women's occupations, like nursing, teaching and librarianship, and 'real' professions.[20] Central here has been the idea that a profession is a full-time commitment in the sense that one is prepared to give oneself to it body and soul, placing it before all else, implicitly prioritising it at all times. It presumes either that people are single and childless (the original monk or priest), or that they are serviced by others in such a way as to enable them to devote themselves unstintingly to their careers. Heather Carmody of the Business Council of Australia comments that at executive management level not 100 but 150 per cent is required.[21]

Given the (different kinds of) masculine ethos attached to all the recognised professions, it is hardly surprising that women have experienced discrimination. Three related questions are taken up here. What strategies have women used in the face of this discrimination, and what are the long-term implications of these strategies? What new opportunities are opening up in the context of current restructuring and at what compromise? Is there a point at which an influx of women forces change, regardless of the worldviews of the women concerned?

New Zealander Michael Belgrave notes that the barriers preventing women from entering medical school were more easily overcome than the subtle obstructions that frustrated them from competing in the medical economy. Medicine was compatible with stereotypes of woman's role as long as it was contained within the stereotype of 'lady doctor', which implied that women doctors continued to fulfil roles consistent with late-nineteenth-century norms of behaviour acceptable for middle-class women. In contrast, 'medical men' were free to set themselves up as aggressive entrepreneurs. By emphasising respectability, the early women doctors created difficulties for those who came later. While it became perfectly acceptable for women to study medicine, they had difficulty in buying or selling practices and were obliged to take salaried positions or practise within the confines of the stereotype 'lady doctor'. Although status was defined by hospital or university appointments, all this was meaningless without a successful private practice. As long as the choice hospital positions remained honorary, there was little opportunity for women to compete without proof of entrepreneurial success.[22] Similarly in law, architecture or engineering, the constraints of ladylike behaviour meant restricting their competition, concentrating on areas that were regarded as appropriate to their gender, and subordinating their careers to family responsibilities.

Those who *have* made it to the top often present themselves as ultra-feminine. This may be interpreted as strategy of masquerade designed to disguise the inroads into men's power.[23] I have interviewed consultants prominent in sub-specialities where the women can be counted in single digits. They have made sacrifices to get where they are, and quite deliberate decisions not to have children. But they make light of their talents, career struggles, or personal sacrifices. Says one:

> I don't think it ever occurred to me that it was a silly career for a woman . . . I mean, it *is* a silly career, because of the years when you're climbing the tree, every six months or every year you're changing jobs, working

> every other night on call, every other weekend, long hours, irregular life. Unlike men, who can usually get women to wait for them, I don't think most women can get men to wait for them . . .

Describing her work she says laughingly:

> It's a power phenomenon isn't it? I'm the one with the knife. You submit to my power, I with my skill will make you better . . . You come to me a cripple. I do the operation. You walk out of the hospital carrying your bed or whatever it is . . .

She says her older sister, a barrister, was regarded as the intelligent one, and attributes her own success to the fact that she does not feel good about herself and work makes her feel better. She recalls her mother saying, 'We never expected *you* to be a consultant. We thought you'd just be a GP!' It would be hard to imagine a male counterpart talking in this way. Yet she has given herself to entirely to her work. At forty, she is clear that she could not have combined it with children, and she is aware of the sacrifice. She compensates with a close relationship with her sister and nephews. She describes her affairs, and her recent marriage, at thirty-eight, to the man upstairs. She had little time, she said, to look further afield, and at least he had ample opportunity to become acquainted with her work routine. Opposition within surgery is laughed off: 'There's often people that say to me 'Why don't you do hand surgery or something, that's delicate. Well, I mean, it's just not my particular interest.' Her style is light and breezy and feminine. It does not correspond at all to the 'honorary male' stereotype. But she remains in control of the conversation and one senses her authority.

While similar strategies are used in other professions, they are probably most effective in medicine. For example, 'patient-centred' medicine is perceived as feminine, and its incorporation into medical practice has undoubtedly facilitated the public acceptance of women doctors. By contrast, 'feminine' legal discourse has been slower to develop. Whereas women doctors are now preferred by a high proportion of the population, women lawyers are not. Of female medical graduates, 90 per cent are in active practice compared with only 78 per cent of law graduates.[24] Part of the explanation here is the greater availability of part-time employment in medicine, at least in general practice, and strong public demand at this level. The stereotype of the woman GP has shifted from the spinster devoting her life to medicine, to the 'family woman' who is a good doctor precisely because she has children of her own. The media have replaced Dr Kildare images with the women in *E Street* and *GP* who muddle along. Like any other women in the soaps, what is notable about them is their ordinariness. Marriage and motherhood have become virtually compulsory for women doctors. Yet the pressures of working even 'half-time' with children are enormous. (In medical parlance, half-time is upwards of twenty hours a week of consulting, plus paperwork and home visits.) Perhaps the men do not feel unduly threatened by competition from women with children. There is no overt resistance to women in the lower ranks of medicine. Women registrars have a reputation for working harder, being more reliable and flexible, and talking to patients. Only at consultant level, it would seem, do men become fearful that they will steal the phallus.

Specialist training courses are now typically five years in duration. On top of six undergraduate years and one or two years as an intern, this places women in their mid-thirties before they can achieve consultant status. Not surprisingly, their movement into the specialities has been slower and is closely linked with notions of gender-appropriateness and flexible working arrangements. An AMA survey of the colleges found the highest percentage of women in dermatology (25) and psychiatry (21), followed by anaesthetics (16.6), radiology (10.7) obstetrics and gynaecology (10.5) physicians (9.3) ophthalmology, (5.7) and surgery, 2.2.[25]

Part-time training is available in most of the colleges but is token outside the College of Psychiatrists which has forty-seven people (7 per cent) registered. It is not necessarily an attractive option, since training experiences have to be exactly comparable with full-time. The colleges will not be seen to compromise standards and have no intention of offering cheaper, easier 'inferior' qualifications for women. Hospitals and health services are reluctant to offer part-time training positions because of the added administrative costs. Interrupted training is more widely accepted, but it has less to do with maternity leave than the discrepancy between the available advanced training posts and the number of trainees qualified to enter them. It has also been designed to facilitate recognition of overseas experience. Women have undoubtedly taken up the interrupted training option for maternity reasons, but no figures were available from any college.

Despite the difficulties, the colleges report a doubling in the number of women who are training. The percentages of women students are: dermatology 45.5, psychiatry 38.9, obstetrics and gynaecology 33.5, physicians 29.4, paediatrics 45, rheumatology 43.5, infectious diseases 38, anaesthetics 25, radiology 21, surgery 10.9 and ophthalmology 9.[26] A NSW survey of the career aspirations of first-year medical students carried out 1987–91 confirmed these changes.[27] Nearly 30 per cent of the women who wanted to specialise nominated paediatrics and 21 per cent obstetrics and gynaecology (compared with 10 per cent and 3.9 per cent for the men). On these figures we can predict a substantial increase of women, not only in general practice but in most of the specialties. Surgery, particularly orthopaedics, will remain the most resistant to change. There will be a striking increase in the proportion of women in obstetrics and gynaecology, facilitated by the development of group practices to alleviate the pressure of night and on-call work. Given the tendencies towards sub-specialisation, men may retain the most prestigious positions, but women will have a strong presence at the more generalist end of the specialities.

In law the changes are slower. The past president of the Women Lawyers Association, Jenny Mattila, feels that the hope of ensuring equality for women 'by force of numbers seems to be coming to nought'.[28] The percentage of women doing law rose to 30 by the mid-1970s, 50 by the mid-1980s, and in 1991 it had reached 65 in the first year of some law schools. Yet less than 8 per cent of 2600 barristers in Australia are women, and less than 5 per cent of judges.[29] Of the 11,000 solicitors in New South Wales in January 1991, nearly 2500 were women; but only 10 per cent were partners compared with 41 per cent of the men. Ten years may be an insufficient lead time; more likely, they are facing direct discrimination for which 'glass ceiling' is an overly polite term. Women are concentrated in family law and probate; they are strongly under-represented in commercial law, company law and criminal law and somewhat under-represented in taxation and estate planning, personal injury and litigation. Their median income is just over half that of the men.[30] Criminal lawyers (like abortionists) are perceived as 'tainted' by their work and associations. It is not fit work for 'ladies'.

A national survey of recent law graduates found that 35 per cent of the women reported that their gender was a disadvantage in finding work, and 33 per cent said being a woman was a disadvantage in day-to-day legal work.[31] Women speak of the climate of condescension, indifference and hostility. They report feelings of social isolation, and difficulties in finding 'professional mentors' who can provide guidance. The refusal to offer them partnerships is the crux of it. Men are thought to make better 'rainmakers', that is, better able to attract new clients; yet one's ability to attract clients is not considered until the eve of admission to partnership.[32] Increasing numbers of women solicitors are choosing to practise as government or corporate lawyers, including many who were in the top 10 per cent of graduates and had been successful employed senior solicitors. As Adele Horin comments, 'in the face of the glacier-like pace of reform, many deliberately choose paths more conducive to family life'.[33] Legal Aid solicitors work a 35-hour week and have the benefit of flexitime and maternity leave.

Where medicine projects a 'caring' image, law presents an adversarial one. When lawyers talk about their work they commonly liken it to a game, a contest with rules, winners and losers. Research on children's play confirms that girls and boys interact differently.[34] Girls choose smaller play groups whose interactions are based on shared confidences. Boys, by contrast have larger groups and centre on some competitive, goal-directed activity with clear rules and with winners and losers. They learn to 'depersonalise' the attack, to enter adversary relations with friends, and to cooperate with people they dislike. In short, girls play and boys game. For boys, pre-law training begins almost at birth. That women may place personal relationships above success threatens the old paradigm.

If women are uncomfortable with the win-or-lose nature of litigation, how well can they defend their clients' interests? Client bias is claimed by law firms, but the women say this is a projection. Judge Jane Mathews commented that 'a lot of solicitors have reservations in instructing female barristers because they perceive if the case goes badly, it might somehow be blamed on their unorthodox decision in briefing a woman'.[35] Forms of argument and legal authority are so fundamentally gendered that women must face obstacles unless they can switch entirely into the masculine mode. You have to be 'one of the chaps' to succeed. This means not that you dress like a man but that you behave like one, and dress immaculately in the female equivalent of the uniform. The bar is extraordinarily demanding. You are constantly on public display, with every error recorded in the court transcripts and available for dissection. Not even surgeons are in quite this position. It may get harder for women barristers as less work is available. Solicitors, having lost valuable conveyancing work, are taking on the local court work that was once the province of barristers. Legal work is harder than medical work to pass on to another practitioner. Few senior legal positions are available on a part-time basis and those that are tend to be poorly paid and not highly respected. There is also pressure to be in the office between 5 and 7 p.m., an impossible time for those with children.

Despite these difficulties, the current restructuring of the profession creates some prospects for change. The bifurcation of solicitors into consumer-oriented, high-volume legal clinics for routine representation of individuals and large firms offering customised, specialised services for corporations and wealthy individuals will overshadow any remaining division between barristers and solicitors. This will create the momentum towards a more unitary, though highly stratified, profession. Legal practices are amalgamating into large national and international firms, relegating more lawyers to the role of employed solicitor, with limited scope to be part of management. The large corporate law firms have steadily shed the sort of small-scale private work that can be handled by smaller firms, such as family law, criminal law and conveyancing, in favour of large-scale work from corporations and governments. By the late 1980s there were four Australian law firms with more than 375 solicitors each.[36] Within these firms there will be more specialisation and more team work, in which women are deemed to excel, and a change in the nature of the work from direct client service to background research. If lawyers are no longer required to be at the office to transact business efficiently, part-time work ought to become more available.

The loss of income from conveyancing, probate and personal injury threatens the continued viability of sole practitioners and small firms, particularly in the suburbs and the country. The Law Council of

Australia has calculated that the profitability of solicitors' practices in Victoria has declined 15 per cent a year in recent years.[37] Between 1956 and 1986 the real incomes of Australian lawyers declined more against average male earnings than any of the other professions. Only law and engineering declined; medicine kept pace, and architecture, accounting and dentistry increased substantially against the mean.[38] Such a situation could easily usher in a higher proportion of women, with licensed conveyancers emerging as a kind of 'subclass' of solicitors; or solicitors may be accredited to practise only within certain defined areas.[39]

Women have moved into the professions at an impressive rate since the 1970s, though their impact remains varied. The Institute of Engineers reported in 1986 that it had a mere 289 female members out of 36,000.[40] Even here there have been changes, and it is currently part of the national women's strategy to ensure that 15 per cent of engineering students are female by 1995.[41]

Despite continuing discrimination, the claim for equality in the professions as an important democratic goal has made considerable headway. This has major structural and symbolic implications. In one future scenario the structure of work will be more flexible and the care of children and households equally shared between men and women. In another, women will conform to current, masculine patterns of work and employ full-time nannies and housekeepers. The first foreshadows a breaking down of the gaps between professional and other work, with a plurality of working arrangements, while the second implies a shoring up of the class structure. Both tendencies are likely to co-exist.

The issue of combining work and family is not restricted to professional women. The entry of women, and especially mothers, to the paid workforce has increased dramatically in the past two decades, and not many can afford nannies! Examples can easily be found of individuals who have managed to negotiate suitable work and family arrangements, but as yet they have had little structural assistance in the form of easily available childcare for the right hours, or flexible working arrangements. While the existence of a supportive husband appears to be a crucial ingredient of women's professional success, we are a long way from a culture in which that can be expected. All too often the debate assumes a stark choice between celibacy and motherhood. The strength and companionship that women draw from their relationships with each other, including lesbian relationships, are seldom mentioned but constitute an important base for many a professional life. Whatever their class background, the impact of women on the professions in the next two decades will be significant. This cannot be read off from propositions about the ways in which women as a category are 'different' from men. Rather it will be worked out in a myriad of ways in a variety of rapidly changing contexts.

EIGHTEEN

The Seductive Allure of EEO

Margaret Thornton

The Concept

There is a Pythagorean symmetry associated with an idealised notion of equality. Perhaps it is because of this that EEO (equal employment opportunity) continues to carry with it the faint hope that the workplace might one day be restructured on fair and equitable terms without pejorative inferences being drawn from crucial dimensions of one's identity, including sex, race and sexuality. For feminist scholars, envisioning the way society might be has always been an important endeavour, while bringing us back to earth is the inevitable visceral response of liberal legalism. With particular reference to sex, but recognising the intertwined nature of the strands which construct identity, about which law is normally obtuse, I propose to appraise briefly the legal initiatives which fall within the rubric of EEO.[1]

Equal opportunity in respect of what? is the inevitable threshold question. Within liberal legalism, EEO has been construed narrowly to mean opportunity in respect of *access*; it does not refer to an equal distribution of substantive benefits, such as jobs themselves. This focus on the facilitation of access reveals why EEO is a less contentious concept than AA (affirmative action) which is not so restricted, at least in theory, although the terms are frequently used interchangeably.

The distinction between formal and substantive equality pervades the notion of legality. Formal equality entails treating everyone the same without regard to differences emanating from sex and other characteristics, thereby ignoring the potentially devastating effect of equal treatment on those who are not similarly situated to the benchmark. This benchmark is invariably an Anglo-Celtic, heterosexual, able-bodied male. The androcentrism of allegedly universal norms has been unmasked within law, as elsewhere, by feminist scholars.[2] Legal discourse has nevertheless remained largely immune to this critique; the benchmark male continues to be a powerful normative force within law, whose eminent reasonableness is used to disqualify the disorderly voices of women. This is the case with EEO, no less than with rape, wife-battering, provocation, pornography or with any of the manifold social harms to which women are subjected.

Sex Discrimination Legislation

Initially, the liberal view was that EEO would be effected through the cumulative resolution of individual complaints of sex discrimination. The principle of formal equality permitted atomised acts of discrimination to be conveniently characterised as the isolated and aberrant acts of abnormal individuals, thereby denying the systemic nature of discrimination. It was believed that occasional deviant employers would learn from their transgressions; moreover, the resolution of individual complaints would magically deter the occurrence of discriminatory employment practices generally. That is, it was assumed that a reactive mechanism would exercise a proactive effect. The fact that Australian legislation mandates the resolution of discrimination complaints within the confidential and privatised setting of conciliation in the first instance was not acknowledged as a logical flaw in the educative aim. More cynically, one might opine that the confidentiality prescript was a deliberate ploy to occlude the nature and extent of discriminatory harms perpetrated by benchmark males themselves, a class whose voices echo resoundingly throughout the legislative texts.

The *Sex Discrimination Act 1984* (Cth.) was enacted in order to comply with Australia's obligations under the United Nations *Convention on the Elimination of all Forms of Discrimination against Women*. Although the convention is expressly sex-specific, the Australian Parliament made the Act sex-neutral, thereby permitting men to lodge complaints alleging sex discrimination.[3] The concept of gender neutrality, found within all Australian sex discrimination legislation,[4] is attributable to the heritage of formal equality within liberal discourse. 'Neutrality' serves as an effective device to occlude the reality of women's subordination, for it seeks to delude us into thinking that an act of discrimination against a woman is simply a replication of an act of discrimination against a man. The attempt by liberal legalism to impose its characteristic cloak of neutrality over a range of asymmetrical dualisms, which include male/female, Anglo-Australian/Aboriginal, heterosexual/lesbian and able-bodied/otherwise-abled, sanitises discriminatory harms at the legislative threshold.

The paradigmatic manifestation of sex discrimination involves an instance of 'direct discrimination' in which a woman complains of less favourable treatment than a similarly situated man. However, the 'otherness' of woman is such that she is rarely similarly situated to the benchmark male, so that it is impossible for her to meet the requisite burden. The sexual division of labour, different career patterns, as well as the masculinist construction of merit, skill and work itself drain all meaning from the comparability provision for most women. Even a woman ostensibly better qualified than a successful male appointee is likely to encounter difficulty in meeting the burden of proof because the individual instance is but one manifestation of a societal phenomenon. Ms Teed, for example, was not appointed as a pharmacist because the members of the hospital selection panel preferred a man with whom they 'had more in common and felt more comfortable'.[5] The selection panel had adjusted the selection criteria specified in the advertisement to support their preference for a man in a position of authority rather than the self-assured complainant. The Victorian Equal Opportunity Board took the view that if the panel chose to accord greater weight to administrative and interpersonal skills, it was not for the board to substitute its judgment for that of the panel. No cognisance was taken of the blatant manifestation of 'homosocial reproduction', the phenomenon which causes decision-makers to appoint only those people most like themselves.[6] Accordingly, sex discrimination was found not to have occurred.

Direct discrimination complaints are the least efficacious way of achieving EEO. The doctrine 'lets in' a few women who appear to be most like benchmark males (but less assertive!) in accordance with the assimilationist ideal, thereby ensuring that the prevailing organisational structure, including its masculinist managerial style, is not threatened.

The *Sex Discrimination Act* does recognise the need for 'special measures' in some circumstances to ensure that 'persons of a particular sex . . . have equal opportunities' (section 33). It is nevertheless virtually impossible to read coherently the two competing principles of non-discrimination and special measures (that is, neutrality and partiality) within the one legislative instrument, given that the norm of maleness which pervades judicial and administrative decision-making operates to privilege the assumed neutrality of the non-discrimination principle. This form of gender blindness entails always treating men and women in the same way, regardless of the differences in their lives. The assumption of neutrality has encouraged men to challenge measures initiated in recognition of women's different situatedness, that is, different from *them*. A notorious example, albeit not in the workplace, was the challenge by several men to the ACT and Canberra Women's Health Services.[7] The complainants unsuccessfully argued that the establishment of such centres constituted discrimination against men because women live longer than men and men also suffer from sex-specific diseases.[8] The problem of treating equality as neutrality 'assumes that equality is an end in itself, rather than a mechanism for correcting disadvantage'.[9]

Indirect discrimination was introduced in the belief that it would address the more covert and insidious forms of sex discrimination not tractable to direct discrimination doctrine. However, it is a mistake to think that indirect discrimination could deal effectively with systemic discrimination. A major legal impediment to dealing with systemic discrimination arises from the basic requirement of any legal action that there must be an identifiable wrongdoer who can be held responsible for a harm which is legally cognisable. That is, unless the complainant can connect her harm to a particular employer, there can be no liability and no remedy. Since systemic discrimination, by its very nature, is diffused throughout the entire psycho-social fabric of society, either to personify or to individualise its perpetration is necessarily an artifice. 'Indirect discrimination' does suggest an ability to venture beneath the surface of the neutrality carapace, but the limited legislative definition ascribed to the phrase serves to remind us that systemic harms against women are not legally cognisable.

Indirect discrimination applies to a particular workplace practice which appears to be gender-neutral, such as the 'last-on first-off' rule, but which exerts a disproportionate effect on women. As a deterrent to complainants, proof of indirect discrimination involves a complicated four-part test. It should therefore not be a surprise to learn that few complaints of indirect discrimination have proceeded to a hearing. The establishment of liability involves more than a choice between the attribution of *fault* and the *effects* of the discriminatory conduct.[10] A complainant must show that there was a particular requirement or condition with which the aggrieved person was unable to comply, that there was a disproportionality between complying men and women, and that the requirement was not reasonable.

The *Australian Iron and Steel Case* involved the struggle by women to be admitted to 'men's jobs', in this case, blue-collar jobs in heavy industry. While one group of complainants did succeed before the High Court,[11] the proceedings spanned more than a decade because of various challenges and appeals initiated by the respondent. The cost of legal representation posed a particular problem for a group of unemployed women, most of whom were from non-English-speaking backgrounds. While representation is not formally required in the hearing of discrimination complaints, to take on a subsidiary of Australia's largest corporation and expect to win within the aggressive adversarialism of a formal hearing would be tantamount to committing legal hara-kiri. Indeed, one of Australia's largest legal firms was reputed to have devoted half a floor to preparation of the case, and leading barristers were engaged as counsel. EEO complainants have not normally been seen as the appropriate recipients of legal aid, so this case was a breakthrough in two areas: the Legal Services Commission agreed that the Public Advocacy Centre should take the case; and the New South Wales Women's Advisory Council persuaded the Premier to authorise a special one-off grant.

Despite vindication of the women complainants before the Equal Opportunity Tribunal, the Supreme Court of New South Wales and the High Court, Australian Iron and Steel has nevertheless continued to resist settlement of further complaints filed by large numbers of women. Men, who dominate the world of work and who have organised it to their own satisfaction, are not going to surrender well-paid jobs to women without a struggle. Indeed, to accept the entry of women into the steelworks would constitute a direct challenge to the sexual division of labour, a significant structural device for maintaining the subordination of women. The entry of women into non-traditional jobs is therefore likely to be an indefinite site of contest, exacerbated by the reality of a deteriorating job market.

Complaint-based mechanisms represent no more than a halting and ephemeral step in the direction of EEO. The lodgment of a complaint of discrimination requires both perspicacity and fortitude: perspicacity on the part of complainants to recognise that an act of discrimination has occurred against them (after all, what has happened could just be normal life!), and fortitude to persevere in an adversarial relationship with a respondent who could be their boss. Complainants are always vulnerable in the face of corporate power. The tactics which operate to maintain women in subordinate positions include the socialisation of women not to complain. Far from entering into adversarial relations, we are supposed to defuse conflict; this expectation underscores the difficulty men have in taking discriminatory harms against women seriously. One has only to take a cursory glance at defamation actions to appreciate the difference. Such actions are overwhelmingly instituted by men; they are generally public figures,[12] and they may receive comparatively large damages awards for comparatively trivial name-calling.

Affirmative Action

AA measures were designed to obviate the need for the heroic complainant. Instead of waiting until the discriminatory harm had occurred, it was envisaged that institutional action would prevent individual harms occurring. It was also hoped that AA would be able to confront the systemic nature of sex discrimination.

A range of conduct can be subsumed within the rubric of AA. At the minimalist level, an example would be the couching of advertisements in sex-neutral rather than sex-specific language. The most extreme manifestation of AA is the use of quotas, engendering a fear that hordes of women, conceptualised as 'unqualified', could take away jobs from deserving men. The idea of AA as a 'swallowing up' of men in the workplace contains echoes of the myth of the vagina dentata; it conveniently serves to revive the misogyny that AA purported to discourage. In reality, AA is firmly in the hands of men, as managers of and superordinates within the Australian workforce.

The *Affirmative Action (Equal Opportunity for Women) Act 1986* (Cth.) requires all employers with 100 or more employees to prepare an AA plan and to report annually to the AA Agency. Having been created by benchmark males, the legislation is more concerned with the reporting function than with ameliorating gendered workplace practices. Hence, as with complaint-based mechanisms, the focus is again on form rather than substance. The Act confers no rights on individuals, and the only sanction for failure to report is to name the transgressor in parliament. The Act is a classic piece of edentate, or toothless, legislation, in which the state has unsuccessfully sought to mediate the diametrically opposed interests of subordinated women workers and management. The dilemma was that anything stronger would have led to the withdrawal of support by the business community, represented by its peak body, the Business Council of Australia.

The support of management for AA has had to be maintained by constant assurances that 'it is good for business' to utilise the talents of 50 per cent of the population which have hitherto lain dormant; that discriminatory practices are dysfunctional in the workplace; and that greater efficiency will result from changed practices. This is apparent in the literature, in respect of which I shall refer to one example.

The Council for Equal Opportunity in Employment, a body set up by the Business Council of Australia, has prepared a set of ten booklets to help employers comply with the *Affirmative Action Act*.[13] A linguistic shift occurs: the less threatening *EEO* is preferred to *AA*. We learn that EEO is about excellence and about the realisation of individual and organisational potential. As well as providing guidance as to appropriate 'action steps', the booklets also provide examples of EEO strategies undertaken by a number of major companies. (One cannot help but observe that some of these companies, such as BHP and Qantas, have become habitual respondents in discrimination cases!) The main focus of EEO, as revealed by the case studies, is directed towards incorporating women into non-traditional jobs. For example, EEO 'successes' include Mobil Oil's appointment of women as operators, storemen (who are 'to be renamed terminal operators') and drivers.[14] Other initiatives recorded include Comalco's audio-visual kits prepared for schools and its scholarship programme for women undergraduates in engineering, metallurgy, physics, chemistry and maths.[15] These initiatives do not transcend the characterisation of EEO as a modest 'letting in' of women. Access is geared towards technically-oriented jobs, in keeping with the official exhortation that Australia become the 'clever country.' In accordance with the 'reserve army' thesis of women's labour, women are welcome in the public world of paid work only when there is a demonstrated national need. EEO can therefore be usefully harnessed in a way which does not threaten the status quo. Hence, equal opportunity is largely confined to base-level entry; it does not apply to the more powerful upper echelons of management.

In the final booklet, entitled *Women, Work and the Future*, the need is acknowledged for changes to work design to accommodate the family and childcare commitments of women. However, regular work-based childcare initiatives do not appear to have extended beyond the well-known examples of Esso/Lend Lease and IBM, although some other companies are 'investigating options,' and the National Mutual Life Association has conducted a 'pilot' holiday childcare programme. None of the initiatives appear to be devoted to improving the conditions of 'women's work' in which approximately 82 per cent of women in the paid workforce are involved;[16] nor do they appear to be attempting to deal with the oppressive culture of masculinity which pervades most workplaces.[17] The failure to effect any alteration to these phenomena, in other than a tokenistic manner, can be justified as not economically rational.

The publication of the Council for Equal Opportunity in Employment clearly reveals the managerial orientation of AA/EEO initiatives. The legislation has placed responsibility on management to prepare AA plans and to alter its workplace profile, and it is in managerial interests to foreclose the possibility of discrimination complaints being lodged with an external agency. Not only are unconciliated actions expensive to defend, but the adverse publicity is not good for the corporate image. Although the *Affirmative Action Act* does set out a series of steps to be taken in the development of an AA plan, including consultation with women employees, the genuineness of that consultation and the realisation of initiatives lie entirely within the prerogative of management. It is therefore inevitable that AA has been deployed to serve managerial ends. If management is magnanimous and women are sufficiently deferential, a few will be admitted to the organisation *as it is*. Although the hegemony of masculinity is challenged by the admission of women, management will do its best to ensure that those few women who are admitted are as much like the incumbents as possible, so that the homogeneity of the workplace is disturbed as little as possible. The occasional dissident who slips through the net as a statistical adornment to the corporate image can be 'taken care of' by a strategically-placed man or male-identified women.

The initiation of EEO measures in the public sector has been contingent on the good graces of the government of the day. For example, in New South Wales, pro-feminist policies were fostered under the labor government from the late 1970s,[18] but were instantaneously contracted when the Liberal government assumed power in 1988. More recently, public sector restructuring has led to a devolution of EEO to department managers.[19] Economic rationalism has therefore provided a timely justification for diluting commitment to EEO. Universities are a case in point.

Public higher education institutions are, rather surprisingly, included with private sector companies under the *Affirmative Action Act*. Despite this initiative, the recent restructuring of universities has rendered them even more oppressively masculinist than has traditionally been the case.[20] The flurry of amalgamations in the higher education sector has created mega-institutions, and the imperialistic designs of some vice-chancellors have included the development of off-shore markets for the export of educational services. On campus, amalgamations between faculties have created mega-faculties, presided over by mega-deans. The concentration of power in these new-style managers has necessarily led to a contraction in collegial life. Thus, mega-deans are appointed, not elected, to 'manage' faculties. This powerful masculinist style of governance offers little scope for the possibility of (some) women presenting alternative models of leadership in which feminist scholarship is valued. Furthermore, as Jill Blackmore shows, the spread of the new corporatism to universities has allowed EEO to be mainstreamed.[21] The trend towards devolution means that EO units can be disbanded in the interests of cost-cutting and efficiency.[22] The transfer of EO functions to line management can be effected by evoking echoes of the softer rhetoric of the past that has been co-opted and given a new lease of life by the asseveration that 'equity [is] . . . everyone's concern'.[23]

EEO can therefore be deployed to facilitate the retention of hegemonic masculinity in the academy, as elsewhere. Its essential malleability, designed to permit workplaces to fashion practices to suit particular cultural norms, has not worked in the interests of women. Minimalist legislative prescripts have resulted in regimes of veritable self-regulation. Given the masculinist and managerialist orientation of corporate authority, we would be deluding ourselves if we were to think that EEO could function as a feminist instrument. While I accept the Foucaultian proposition that power is located in the capillaries as well as in the central organs of the state, power is not evenly distributed. If women struggle collectively and heroic complainants are prepared to martyr themselves through individual actions, minor changes do occur. However, the ebb and flow of political and economic life enable managerialism to regain the high ground. The 'public good', that is, the good of the market, then acts as a convenient cloak under which the status quo can be insidiously restored. The economic recession of the 1990s highlights the vulnerability of EEO and the parlousness of women's status in paid work.

Workplace restructuring was signalled by the emergence of the New Right in the mid-1980s. Pressure was generated to do away with

Australia's unique centralised wage-fixing system in favour of enterprise bargaining, supposedly in the interests of flexibility and efficiency. While it is the case that the trade union movement is a masculinist organisation which has quite often been obtuse as to the needs of its women members, it is also undeniable that Australian women have been better off in respect of both wages and conditions than women in Canada, the United Kingdom and the United States.[24] The dismantling of the centralised wage-fixing system is likely to be disastrous for women in paid work; they are expected to be grateful to have a job, regardless of the decline in pay and the erosion of conditions. The Kennett Liberal government in Victoria passed its highly contentious *Employee Relations Act 1992* only one month after coming into office. Following the decentralised model, state awards were abolished in favour of 'employment agreements'; other 'benefits', including maternity leave, were reduced to a minimal level or abolished altogether in the interests of revitalising the economy. Those who are most vulnerable have been subordinated to the 'common good', meaning free enterprise; this has been apparent even to those who have felt sanguine about the future of working women. In contemporary economic reality, managerial imperatives favour measures which clearly run counter to the interests of most women workers. A dilemma emanates from reliance on that same management for the development of gynocentric EEO practices. Nevertheless, this is a familiar paradox for feminists that is inherent in all state initiatives.

Conclusion

The public/private dichotomy is the linchpin of liberal legalism. Legality pertains only to the public sphere. Thus, the assignation of women to the private sphere has proved problematic for laws purporting to effect EEO.[25] The sterility of formulaic incantations of equality is starkly revealed when it is acknowledged that women's essential role as reproducer and nurturer is irrelevant in an employment context, despite the fact that this role is an undeniable and inescapable dimension of what it means to be a woman in our society. That is, seeds of invidiousness attach to a woman in the paid workforce who is over thirty-five and has no children, no less than to the woman with children. The reality of a particular woman's familial life must be functionally severed from the workplace in order to conform with the autonomous, unconnected ideal of the employee who is free to serve [his] boss most productively; but woman cannot shed her identity as a real woman. Her sex renders her subordinate. It is only if individual women comport as closely as possible with the male model in the public sphere that they will be 'let in' and possibly even rewarded for being 'good'. Women's indelible association with corporeality continues to prevent the acceptance of women within the world of work as equals. The good woman worker acknowledges her subordination and is deferential to men and masculine values. The example of this paragon, when rewarded (bribed?) with a modest promotion, is touted as tangible evidence of the attainment of 'equality' for women generally.

Conversely, the concept of EEO is incomprehensible in the private sphere. Equality has no meaning amongst those who are inherently unequal. Equality is realisable only amongst those who belong to the 'society of equals' within the public sphere. Traditionally, only benchmark males qualified as equals. Although women have now been 'let in' to citizenship, it is only as fringe-dwellers with subordinate status.[26] Men claim a monopoly on rationality and neutrality, exemplified by liberal legalism, as I have already pointed out. The idea of woman as a sexually embodied and disorderly force in the public sphere continues to prevail because it is lodged deep within the societal psyche and given credence by influential theorists, like Aristotle, Rousseau and Freud. It is reiterated through legal discourse, as well as by numerous lesser theorists and popular pundits, and it is indubitably believed by many. While the disorder of women may be an ideological device designed to maintain our subordination, it effectively nurtures the seeds of doubt accompanying the appointment of any women to a non-traditional job, exercising autonomy and authority. Women in the academy, the boardroom, or the workshop cannot expect to be taken seriously when regarded as incarnations of disorder. However, we should not ignore the psychological desire of benchmark males to subordinate 'others', a factor which represents a major gap in economic models of discrimination, as Becker points out.[27]

EEO undoubtedly holds an allure for women in light of the subordinated reality of most women's working lives. In recognition of the fact that legislative reform provides a public forum for the discussion of harms to women that had never before been publicly debated (such as sexual harassment), many feminist law reformers have supported a legislative route.[28] Many are now disillusioned. But their expectations were unrealistic. In my brief overview of legislative initiatives, I have drawn attention to the structural limits of liberal legalism and the inexorable pull towards inequality in employment exerted by the hegemonic dualism of masculinity and managerialism.

NINETEEN

Provoking Comment: The Question of Gender Bias in the Provocation Defence—A Victorian Case Study

Adrian Howe

Over the past decade, feminist research has exposed the masculinist form and bias of various aspects of Western criminal justice systems. These systems, it is now clear, function in deeply gendered ways. For example, feminist research in Australia, the United Kingdom and North America has demonstrated that 'provocation' is interpreted by courts in gender-specific ways in homicide cases. In particular, it is now notorious that courts frequently claim or infer that women who were killed by men they knew—their husbands, ex-husbands, lovers or former lovers—provoked their own deaths. In sharp contrast to this newly-emerging understanding of the operation of 'justice' in homicide cases in the West, the Law Reform Commission of Victoria, in a recent review of the law of homicide, concluded that the defence of provocation is not gender-biased. Are Victorian courts, as the commission seems to be suggesting, an exception in this regard? Or did the commission rely on a narrow, positivistic conception of gender which precluded a proper understanding of the unquestionably gendered operation of the defence of provocation in this state, as elsewhere?

The question of gender bias in the interpretation of 'provocation' takes on added significance in the context of recent research, including research undertaken by the commission, on so-called domestic killings in Australia. In Victoria, as in other Australian states, domestic homicide—defined as including all killings where the victim and offender were living in or intimately connected with the same household—constitutes approximately 40 per cent of all homicides. As we will see, the most striking finding within this 'domestic' category is that 75 per cent of spouse killings in Victoria are committed by men. While the commissioners noted that men were overwhelmingly responsible for homicide, including domestic homicide, this 'discovery' did not impact as directly and emphatically on their recommendations as one might have hoped. Certainly, the significance of highly gendered domestic killing patterns appear to have passed them by when they came to consider the law of provocation.

Perhaps paradoxically, the publication in 1991 of the commission's report on homicide, which included its recommendation that the law of provocation be reformed rather than abolished, has been overtaken by events—notably, the election of a new government which has decided to abolish the commission. Whether the commission's recommendations will be implemented remains to be seen. My concern here is to ensure that, although the state's law reform body lost an opportunity to expose the deeply gendered operation of the defence of provocation in homicide cases, the feminist critique of gender bias in the operation of the criminal law continues. Nowhere is this bias more apparent than in those so-called domestic homicides in which men kill women. Nowhere, except perhaps in rape cases, is the gendered—or, more accurately, 'sexed'—nature of law more apparent.[1]

In 1988 the Law Reform Commission of Victoria was given a reference to formulate proposals which would provide 'a more just law of homicide' for this state.[2] As part of that reference, it canvassed arguments for and against the abolition of the provocation defence. From a feminist perspective, it is noteworthy that one of the four arguments put for abolishing the defence was that provocation is gender-biased in two significant ways. First, it was claimed that the defence 'operates in practice predominantly as an excuse for men who kill women'.[3] Second, it was suggested that the suddenness requirement of the defence—the requirement that the response to the allegedly provocative act be immediate—is gender-biased in that it is more consistent with 'patterns of male response to mental trauma' than to female reaction patterns. Thus, the provocation defence could be seen to operate 'in an uneven way to excuse aggressive male behaviour'.[4] Against this, it was argued that 'the claim that provocation is gender-biased requires evidence to support it'.[5] Accordingly, the commissioners announced that their study of Victorian homicide cases would be especially concerned 'to see whether there is empirical evidence to support' the claim of gender bias. Significantly, they foreshadowed that this empirical study would analyse 'the frequency of the provocation defence and the circumstances in which it is used'.[6]

The commission's *Prosecutions Study* was to provide the empirical evidence thought to be required to resolve this question of gender bias.

On the basis of this long-awaited study of all homicides prosecuted in Victoria between 1981 and 1987, the commission determined that:

> Although juries may sometimes too readily accept provocation defences from men who kill women, this data did not support the conclusion that the provocation defence generally operates in a gender-biased way.[7]

For this and other reasons, the commission recommended that the provocation defence be retained as a partial defence to murder. However, three of the nine members of the commission's homicide reference dissented from this majority recommendation. Significantly, one of the reasons offered by the dissenters for abolishing the defence of provocation was that the rules usually operated 'in favour of male defendants and against female victims'.[8] Thus, notwithstanding the 'empirical evidence' provided in the *Prosecutions Study*, the dissenters still insisted that the defence is gender-biased.

While the dissenters did not provide data to support this contention, a critical consideration of the data provided by the *Prosecutions Study* raises serious problems for the majority view that the provocation defence is not gender-biased. Indeed, the first criticism to be made of that view is that the empirical data actually supports the dissenting position relating to gender bias. Provocation was recorded as an issue in 75 of the 319 cases studied (see Table 19.1). In relation to the principal consideration here, namely gender bias, we are told that women raised provocation in 10 instances (21 per cent of the 47 cases involving a female accused), whereas men raised it in 65 cases (24 per cent of the 272 male accused). We are also told that 9 of the 10 cases where women raised provocation involved a male victim; that two-thirds of the victims of men who raised provocation were men; and that 5 (11.6 per cent) of the male accused who argued provocation were convicted of murder where the victim was male, compared to 8 (36.4 per cent) where the victim was female. While 5 (50 per cent) of the women accused who raised

Table 19.1 Homicide cases and the provocation defence, by sex of accused, Victoria, 1981–7

	Male defendant		*Female defendant*		*Total*	
	n	%	*n*	%	*n*	%
Accused	272	85.2	47	14.7	319	100
Raised provocation defence	65	24	10	21	75	24
Provocation defence as a proportion of all homicides	65	20	10	3	319	23

provocation were convicted of manslaughter, none was convicted of murder.[9]

It is clear from the way in which the study presents this information that the commission believes that the data does not indicate gender bias in the operation of the provocation defence. The study notes that male defendants pleaded provocation twice as frequently in respect of a male victim (43/65) compared with a female victim (22/65), and that a higher proportion of these male defendants was convicted of murder when the victim was female than male. On the other hand, it makes a point of mentioning that no female defendant raising provocation was convicted of murder.[10] From this the commission concluded that the provocation defence is not used more frequently and more successfully by male defendants. Importantly, it was conceded that more research was necessary to decide the matter conclusively. Such research would involve examining the individual cases and evaluating the influence of other defences and arguments which operated in each case. The commission conceded too that, as we have seen, more male defendants used the provocation defence than female defendants, both 'in absolute terms and as a proportion of all accused charged with murder'. But this was seen to be offset by the success rate of female defendants raising the defence.[11] Further, the commission regarded it as especially significant that, as noted above, the provocation defence was more likely to be rejected if a male defendant killed a female victim than if a male defendant killed a male victim.[12] It also noted that males convicted of manslaughter where provocation was an issue 'received significantly heavier sentences than women in these cases'.[13]

The thrust of the commission's argument is clear: the provocation defence is not gender-biased because, on the one hand, men claiming provocation are getting away with killing males rather than females. Thus, if anything, the provocation defence operates in Victoria as a licence to kill men, not women. On the other hand, the defence does not appear to discriminate against female defendants. They use it more successfully than male defendants and, in addition, women who raise provocation are punished less harshly than men. It followed for the majority that the defence should be retained, albeit with a reformed objective test. While the commission's proposals for reforming the test need not detain us, the majority's interpretation of the prosecution data is crucial to the resolution of the question of gender bias.

Subjecting that interpretation to critical analysis reveals that it rests on doubtful foundations. First, the commission's data indicate clearly that men use the defence far more frequently than women. It could be argued that the discrepancy between the numbers of men and women charged with homicide is so great as to suggest that comparisons may be misleading; but it is surely important to note that overall, men raised provocation in 20 per cent of the homicide cases, whereas women did so in only 3 per cent of the cases. Second, we need to know the circumstances of each case and, in particular, what counts as provocation for men compared to women, in order to ascertain whether the defence operates in a gender-biased way. The study does not provide this information. Third and related, in domestic killings—which constituted the largest category (31.3 per cent) of prosecuted cases[14]—men were presented for murder or manslaughter in 64 cases compared to only 26 women. Inasmuch as domestic killings and in particular spouse killings are precisely the cases which have concerned feminists and attracted critical comment,[15] it is most unfortunate that we are not informed about the victims in the 30 domestic cases (47 per cent of the 64 cases involving a male defendant) in which men raised provocation. All we are told is that 7 of these cases resulted in a murder conviction, and 20 resulted in a manslaughter conviction.[16] But who are their domestic victims when provocation is raised? While this is not specified, the commission notes in its final report that the provocation defence is used more frequently by men who kill women (22 cases) than women who kill men (9 cases).[17] Yet this discrepancy is not regarded as significant. Nor is the fact that self-defence rather than provocation was the main argument in several cases. Futhermore, no gender analysis is provided for the cases in which self-defence, rather than provocation, was the major argument.[18] Was the defendant in these cases more likely to be man or a woman? This is surely an extraordinary omission in view of the fact that the issue of self-defence is central to feminist analyses of battered women who kill.[19]

From a feminist perspective then, the commission's analysis of its empirical evidence pertaining to the operation of the provocation defence leaves a lot to be desired. Certainly, the now defunct law reform body did make a commendable effort to highlight the predominance of killings occurring in a 'domestic context' in Victoria. It reported that four out of ten homicides can be classified as 'domestic'—that is, where the victim

Table 19.2 Homicide cases and the provocation defence, by sex of accused and sex of victim, Victoria, 1981–7

	Male defendant $n = 65$		*Female defendant* $n = 10$	
	Male victim	*Female victim*	*Male victim*	*Female victim*
Number accused	43	22	9	1
Percentage convicted of murder	12	36	–	–

and offender were living in or intimately connected with the same household, including separated spouses. This definition allowed for a more realistic assessment of the magnitude of the problem of domestic killings in this state than earlier assessments—a problem which is of comparable size to that revealed for New South Wales in the late 1980s.[20] Furthermore, the commission noted the gendered nature of these killings. We are informed that most accused were male; that 'men were overwhelmingly responsible for the homicides' included in the prosecution study; and that far more men (42) than women (14) killed their spouse, sexual partner or former sexual partner. Indeed, the 34 cases in which a male killed his spouse represented 76 per cent of the spouse killings.[21] Yet the commission failed to see the crucial significance of this clearly gendered pattern when it came to assess the use made of the provocation defence. Furthermore, it is precisely the circumstances of men's and women's homicidal acts, especially those occurring in a domestic context, which determine whether the provocation defence operates in a gender-biased way. The commission's failure to provide this information is surely the most unsatisfactory aspect of the empirical analysis.

This critical examination of the empirical evidence reveals that, even within the terms of the commission's positivistic framework, in which 'gender' means a gender-bias which can be quantified according to male and female usage of the defence, its conclusions cannot be supported. Even within that framework, the data indicate that many more men than women resort to a provocation defence. The argument against gender-bias that more male defendants raise provocation simply because men kill more frequently than women is of no consequence to feminist analysts: we still want to know about the victims in those 30 domestic cases in which provocation was raised by male defendants. How many of them were women who were presented at trial as having 'provoked their own demise'? Beyond these questions, however, there are some further considerations which are also fatal to the commission's view that gender is immaterial in provocation.

From a feminist perspective, the law of provocation can be shown to be deeply gendered in ways which fall outside the commissioners' comprehension, whether they were for or against the abolition of the provocation defence. Indeed, the commission's findings represent a masculinist and therefore unsatisfactory appropriation of long-standing feminist concerns, not simply about 'gender-bias' in the law, but also about the inherently sexed nature of law.[22] As such, those findings are symptomatic of the problems which can arise when gender is not discussed within a feminist analytical framework. Space does not allow for an elaboration of all the concerns which have been raised by feminists about the law of provocation, or even of their two primary concerns—namely, the problems attendant on raising provocation in cases of battered women who kill and the way in which the defence operates as a licence to kill women.[23] However, I would like to indicate some of the feminist issues which were ignored by the commission but which must be addressed in order to understand the deeply sexed operation of provocation.

For several years now, feminist researchers have noted the vastly different circumstances in which men and women kill. What eludes masculinist writers is what is most apparent to feminists: that a woman is expected to tolerate a far greater degree of provocation on the part of the male, from adultery through to severe abuse, than the man whose female partner is alleged to be sexually 'promiscuous'. Non-feminist analysts do not question the fact that allegations of promiscuity on the part of the dead woman feature strongly in men's provocation defences. Indeed, this is by far the most common ground given when a male defendant claims he was provoked to kill a woman. Nor do they appear to have reflected on the significance of the fact that while an adulterous woman is seen to have 'provoked her own demise', a husband's adultery 'has never been mentioned as sufficient to provoke a wife in similar circumstances'.[24]

Certainly, there is much case law to support the view that provocation 'is considered great' in cases of adultery by the wife, such that her adultery 'nearly always amounts to a provocation defence'.[25] A very long list of homicide cases in which men raise the provocation defence clearly demonstrates that it operates in an insidious but demonstrably gender-biased way in adultery cases, or more broadly, in cases where men kill because of sexual possessiveness. Indeed, many of the reported cases, including several of the leading provocation cases, involve men killing women or sometimes other men because of sexual jealousy, proprietary interest in the body of a former sexual partner, or some felt sense of sexual slight or sexual inadequacy.[26] Consider for example these old cases: *R v Maddy*[27] supported the principle that a finding in adultery (understood, of course, as meaning a woman's adultery) was sufficient to support a defence of provocation; in *R v Mawgridge*[28] the court said that 'jealousy is the rage of man, and adultery is the highest invasion of property'; in *R v Pearson*[29] the defendant killed his wife in the drunken belief that she had previously committed adultery; in *R v Kelly*[30] the defendant shot his female partner when he saw her in the presence of another man, and the judge told the jury that killing a wife found in adultery was manslaughter; in *R v Rothwell*[31] the defendant killed his wife when she admitted to having an affair with another man.

A non-feminist commentator can note all these cases and yet fail to see the deeply gendered presumptions which underly the rules pertaining to a finding in adultery or confessions of adultery in provocation cases.[32] Courts may in many instances have operated on Blackstone's masculinist presumption that there can be no greater provocation than a finding in adultery,[33] but feminists who are cognisant of the vastly different reasons why women get provoked to kill would respectfully disagree. Once again the case law supports the view that women experience 'extremes in degradation, violence and humiliation' before they kill brutal male partners; and that even in these cases, their self-defensive or retaliatory actions are likely to be perceived by the courts as warranting convictions for murder, not manslaughter.[34] Admittedly, there has been some relaxation of both the requirement of suddenness and the narrow view of the relevant context in cases where women raise provocation defences. *Queen v R*[35]—the famous South Australian axe murder case in which a woman killed her husband after learning that he had sexually abused their daughters for years—is usually cited to demonstrate these modifications of the provocation defence in favour of female defendants. It is also cited to support the argument against abolishing the defence when it is becoming more available to 'women with genuine claims'.[36] However, feminist analysts have been critical of what Bebe Loff described as 'the most timid of judgements' in favour of the defendant in that case.[37] It is also noteworthy that the 'genuineness' of men's claims to have been provoked to kill a woman rarely attracts the attention of masculinist commentators.

This point raises the problematic issue of unsworn statements in provocation cases involving male defendants. From a feminist perspective it is ironic that it was in *Duffy*, a case where a woman killed a violent husband in his sleep, and not in one of the many cases in which a man kills a woman for some sexual slight, that a judge observed that the victim 'has not been heard in this court. He cannot now ever be heard. He has no defender here to argue for him.'[38] No such concern for the silenced female victims of men's 'provoked' killings seems to trouble masculinist judges. However, it does not escape this feminist commentator that allegations about the female victim's sexual 'taunts' and similarly 'provoking' behaviour were made by the defendant in unsworn statements in, for example, *Moffa*, *R v Dutton*, *R v Romano* and *R v Gardner*.[39] Masculinist commentators may be outraged by *R v Dincer*, where a Muslim man was provoked by what they see as his daughter's 'entirely normal and trivial sexual rebellion',[40] but they cannot see the outrage of a man making an unsworn statement and getting away with murder of a woman who will not be held by a marriage or relationship to him.

Consider for example the case of *Gardner*, a reported case heard in the Victorian Court of Criminal Appeal in 1989. Inasmuch as *Gardner* involved the killing of a man as well as a woman, the case has the added 'attraction' of clarifying a point which masculinist commentators like the Victorian law reformers seem to miss: that men sometimes kill men in sexual jealousy cases does not negate the argument that provocation operates as a deeply sexed excuse. On the contrary, such cases strengthen this argument immensely. *Gardner* is a case in point.

In January 1988 Brian Gardner killed Sylvana Marino—a woman with whom he had once had what the court called 'a torrid sexual relationship'—and a man, Golly Shears, sleeping in another room in her house. Gardner was charged on two counts of murder. He was acquitted of murdering the woman but found guilty on an alternative charge of manslaughter. Convicted of murdering the man, he appealed against his murder conviction. The legal import of the case is that the appeal court held that provocation was a good defence in relation to both killings—that is, that there was 'a sufficient nexus' between the woman's 'provocative words' and the killing of Shears by his 'proximity' in a bed nearby.[41] *Gardner* thus further extended the ambit of the provocation defence by relaxing the requirement of presence—the requirement that the provocative act take place in the presence of the accused. Our interest in the case however, lies in the way it demonstrates what counts as 'provocation' in the view of the courts. More specifically, it demonstrates just how damning—that is, exculpatory of male killers—the 'provocative' behaviour of a woman can be.

The information provided by the appeal court in *Gardner* typifies what could be called the provocation defence genre in which the court permits the male defendant's unsworn statement to construct his woman victim as sexually blameworthy. We learn from the appeal judgment that Sylvana Marino, homicide statistic, provoked her own demise by terminating her 'torrid' relationship with the violent Gardner, resuming it a year later, buying a house with him and then inciting him to attack her with a knife at a party. She also incited Gardner to threaten to burn the house down before he stormed out, taking some of her possessions with him. She then exacerbated a delicate situation by going to the police to express concern that Gardner might return to the house and injure her and then getting her ex-husband to secure the doors with bolts for protection. Furthermore, within a week of the knife incident, she invited another man (Shears) to live at her home, again with a view to providing her with protection. That same night, she let Shears take abusive phone calls from Gardner, thereby annoying Gardner to the point that he told his new 'female companion' that he intended to kill Sylvana. Then, when Gardner broke into her house at about 4 a.m.—apparently to collect some tools—she taunted him when he walked into her bedroom, using language indicating that she and Shears, who was asleep in another room in the house, had had sexual intercourse frequently during the night. Of course (as women in these situations tend to do, according to male defendant's unsworn statements) she also denigrated Gardner's sexual capacity. No wonder then, that he lost his self-control, struck her, went to the other bedroom to strike Shears and then returned to Sylvana's bedroom to strike her again. And no wonder too, that he could not recall anything else, not even where he disposed of her body.

In circumstances such as these, men get away with murder. No matter that this particular man had on several occasions told people that he intended to kill Sylvana, discussed several methods of doing so, produced a knife at a party and threatened to cut her throat, told his new partner that he intended to kill her within a few hours of doing so, broke into her house in the early hours of the morning, and found himself so 'out of control' that he killed her and a man in another room. It is noteworthy, and typical of the provocation defence genre, that the killer informed the court of the woman's provocative behaviour in an unsworn statement, thereby avoiding cross-examination. We have only his unsworn, uncorroborated evidence that her behaviour on the fatal night conformed to the stereotype of the provocative woman who taunts her former male partner by deriding his sexual potency and boasting of the sexual prowess of his new rival. The only witnesses are both dead, the woman having provoked their demise, and Gardner stands convicted of manslaughter on both counts, having successfully got away with murdering Shears on appeal.

One final related point about the provocation defence: much has been made of the new emphasis since *Queen v R* on considering the whole context of the provoked killing.[42] However, it is illuminating to contrast the circumstances in that case with those in *Moffa*, one of the cases cited in *Queen v R* as authority to allow the jury to view the total provoking situation.[43] In *Moffa* the victim's sexual taunts and the conceded 'small matters'—that she allegedly threatened physical violence, threw a telephone book and showed him nude photographs of herself—formed 'the whole situation'. The court determined that:

> in the total situation described by the applicant, an ordinary man might so far lose his self-control as to form at least an intent to do his wife grievous bodily injury.[44]

Contrast this kind of 'total situation' to that in *Queen v R*, where the 'whole context' hinged on a man's sexual violation of his daughters, behaviour which even in the view of the dissenting judge was 'about as repulsive as it is possible to imagine.'[45] From a feminist perspective, these vastly different 'provoking' contexts are simply incommensurable. In the case of the male killer, the provocation is readily apparent to masculinist judges; whereas in the case of the woman who kills a man with a long and continuing history of violence, judges struggle to perceive provocation, let alone the necessity of self-defence.

To conclude: the recommendations to reform the law of provocation made by the late Law Reform Commission suffered from its singular failure to address the key issues raised by feminist analysts, as well as from a faulty empirical study. It is perhaps beyond the capacity of law reformers to see these key issues when, here as in other Western jurisdictions, as Hilary Allen has noted:

> The fact of sexual division is taken as a fundamental *a priori* of legal reasoning; it structures the legal argument from within, not simply at the level of particular cases, but at the deeper level of the legal logic itself.[46]

Moreover, as Allen has convincingly argued, the law's betrayal of its notion of a neutral legal person and, by extension, its notion of a gender-neutral provocation defence, occurs at a still deeper level than that of legal argument. It appears that the law cannot even allow itself to 'think' or conceive of gender-neutral provocation. On the evidence of the case law and the recommendations of the Victorian law reformers, gender-neutral provocation is simply 'unthinkable'.[47] Fortunately, however, feminist analysts will continue to think and to transgress masculinist modes of understanding gender relations long after the demise of the Victorian Law Reform Commission.

TWENTY

Women and the Secret Garden of Politics: Preselection, Political Parties and Political Science

Marian Simms

Women, Gender and Political Science

In Australia the study of government and political institutions (including parties, unions and other pressure groups) has largely been the study of men. Men have dominated the formal political stage in Australia. Women did not make their presence felt until the late 1970s. Before then their role was largely confined to women's auxiliaries, community organisations and feminist groups, or informal political activity.

If we define the political broadly, then clearly those earlier roles of women were political.[1] From a methodological point of view, much of the debate about Australian politics has focused upon the clash of material interests; traditionally these have not included women's issues. In political terms, the political party system has also been the channel for the articulation of material interests and issues. Women and women's issues have been 'defined out' of the political arena: 'the political' has not been defined in ways which emphasise women's interests.

The emergence of the so-called Second Wave of organised feminism from the late 1960s had a major impact upon women and 'the political'. More recently, particularly since the mid-1980s, the impact of the Second Wave encountered a degree of reassessment which will be discussed below. The changes wrought by the impact of the women's movement from the 1960s were significant and were felt in two directions, the theoretical and the practical.

At the theoretical level, feminist activists and scholars challenged many of the conventional understandings of 'the political'. McClure has summarised this process of redefinition as follows:

> The critical power of feminism, in this view, lies in its politicization of activities traditionally excluded from 'the political', and more specifically in its erasure of distinctions between public and private life, between political and domestic economy. Its 'new definition of politics' is thus represented as analogous to nineteenth-century politicizations of the realm of production and exchange . . . In effect, just as Marxist theory and practice politicized what was taken to be the factual terrain of previous political economy by recasting it in a fundamentally different way, so does feminist theory and practice politicize what has been taken as the factual terrain of the private or domestic realm by re-constituting it in fundamentally different terms.[2]

It is widely agreed that the work *Feminist Frameworks: Alternative Theoretical Accounts of the Relations between Women and Men*, co-edited by A. Jagger and P. Rothenberg in 1984, provides an excellent summary of the key attempts by feminists to redefine 'the political' and to claim domestic and private spaces as political arenas.[3] This collection includes *inter alia* descriptions of the main varieties of feminism, namely, liberal, socialist (or Marxist) and radical. If pushed to make a choice, feminists of all types would have agreed that 'the personal is political' but the radical feminists might have claimed (with some justification) to have been the primary inventors.

At the practical level the Second Wave of feminism brought with it a substantial increase in the numbers of women active in the formal political arena. In Australia much of this activity was on the Labor side of politics.[4] This was particularly true until the mid-1980s when there were increases in the ranks of Liberal Party women. These developments meant that women were able to come under the gaze of orthodox political science. As Silverberg says:

> With the appearance of a feminist social movement, the organization of feminist interest groups, the enactment of new public policies for women, and the growing number of women running for public office, women's political behaviour increasingly took the forms for which the categories of the discipline had been crafted. As a result, feminist scholars' research questions moved easily into channels carved out by many previous decades of research on men.[5]

As a discipline, political science has also been criticised by some feminist political scientists for viewing women simply as a new topic of enquiry. In contrast, within other disciplines gender has been viewed as a category of analysis. In other words political scientists have tended to work with a particularly narrow and old-fashioned concept of gender as concerning 'sex roles'. Within political science, for example, the political psychology and political sociology sub-disciplines have at times examined political socialisation and regularly taken sex roles as a '*theoretical point of departure*, employing them to explain a range of political behaviours such as political learning, voting choice or likelihood of holding public office'.[6] Silverberg has argued, for example, that several leading American feminist scholars have used this approach to examine the nature of women's entry into formal political life.[7] This point about the dominant interpretation of gender as 'sex roles' should not be taken to mean that political scientists have been preoccupied with the role of women! It is both important and illustrative to note that one of the classic studies of political behaviour of the 1950s and 1960s was called *Political Man*![8]

What have these developments meant for feminist scholars concerned with 'the political'? On the one hand, it would seem that the entry of women into the formal political arena could probably minimise methodological and epistemological problems. To put it simply, one could describe, explain and analyse these new developments. On the other hand, some feminists might be left with unease about reconciling a focus on the formal political arena with the recognition that the 'personal is political'.

In this chapter I wish to outline one case study (the secret garden of politics) which demonstrates one scholar's attempts to deal with this process of reconciliation. Yet at the same time as I was attempting to undertake research which brought together analyses of the public and the private political worlds, certain other feminist scholars and critics were seriously questioning such enterprises—in the name of feminism. These critics mostly see themselves as postmodern:

> Feminists indebted to darker, less optimistic, European traditions of scepticism about the beneficial effects of the agendas of the Enlightenment and modernity are beginning to add the feminist science and epistemology projects to their mainstream targets of criticism. They ask whether it is realistic to imagine that the scientific traditions can be harnessed in ways that will advance women's situations.[9]

S. Harding, the author of this quotation, has developed a threefold interpretation of feminist approaches towards epistemologies, namely, feminist empiricism, feminist standpoint theories, and feminist postmodernism. Harding defends the usefulness of the three perspectives precisely *because* they are all flawed and this contributes to their value. She argues, for example, that feminism itself 'stands on Enlightenment ground' but that '*feminist postmodernism* has important contributions to make to feminist theory and politics'[10] At the same time 'feminist science thinkers . . . stand with one foot in modernity and the other in the lands beyond'.[11]

There is a growing literature which focuses on the problem of the connections between the feminist and the postmodernist enterprises. One of the most powerful critics of the postmodernist tendency is Nancy Hartsock:

> Why is it that just at the moment when so many of us who have been silenced begin to name ourselves, to act as subjects rather than objects of history, just then the concept of subjecthood becomes problematic? Just when we are forming our own theories about the world, uncertainty emerges about whether the world can be theorized.[12]

Postmodernist approaches are likely to be hostile to both standpoint theories and empiricist methodologies. This hostility is clear in the following quotation from the very influential work of Julia Kristeva: 'If women have a role to play . . . it is only in assuming a negative function: reject everything finite, definite, structural, loaded with meaning in the existing state of society.'[13] Feminist and other standpoint theories are extensively discussed in Nancy Hirschmann's excellent study of feminist theory and political theory, *Rethinking Obligation: A Feminist Method for Political Theory*.[14] The chapter entitled 'Implications for a Feminist Epistemology' is mandatory reading for students of feminist theory. Hirschmann points out that

> Feminist standpoint epistemology rejects the idea that epistemology is objective or universal; it holds that epistemology is itself a product of particular social relations. Not just knowledge, or what we know, is shaped by particular experience and the relations we have to others, but *how* we know and how we conceive of knowledge one also similarly shaped.[15]

In other words, feminist standpoint epistemologies, according to Hirschmann, are less 'pure' than the more traditional Kantian or Cartesian varieties. There is still room for debate about the degree of purity and/or rigidity of feminist standpoints. Joan Smith's exposition of the materialist framework, approach or 'standpoint' provides a good example of the 'firm end' of the standpoint category. According to Smith, the feminist enterprise through the materialist prism is part of a sustained process of understanding 'what structures, processes or forces have created, sustained and reshaped inequalities? Inequalities between men and women are but one kind of inequity.'[16] This approach is a first cousin of the Marxist feminist framework mentioned above. There is now a well-rehearsed feminist literature which criticises the view of feminist theory as being divided into the Marxist, liberal and radical streams and also criticises the first two as simply being 'add-ons' to existing traditions.[17] Hartsock is one scholar who has rejected the impulse to 'go postmodern', but who at the same time has called upon feminist scholars to reflect carefully upon the categories of analysis which they use. Perhaps an awareness of the need to be reflective is one useful legacy of postmodernism! (Sceptics might like to note at this stage that anarchists have been subverting the dominant paradigm for several generations now at least). Hartsock, too can be used to sanctify methodological eclecticism.

It is in this spirit that it seems to me useful to draw upon three of the great inheritances of modern feminism namely, the liberal, Marxist and radical streams. None of these projects has been completed. There are outstanding questions from each. Liberal feminism has given us the impetus to expand the participation of women in the public world of work and politics. Even if we question the whole ethic of achievement, it remains important to ask why women have not achieved parity with men in these public worlds. We are still debating too whether parity means 'sameness' or 'difference'. Materialist feminism asks interesting questions about the connections between the formal political arena (i.e. the state) and the broader material forces which create and reproduce gender and other kinds of inequities. Recent debates here have focused upon whether feminism should bother with a theory of the state.[18] Within the materialist feminist tradition the state remains essentially a black box; this leaves little room for the analysis of institutions and/or processes *per se*. There is, however, some potential for picking up the loose ends of both strands of feminism. This can occur if we take the ideal of broad-based gender equality as a goal and examine the processes by which the current crop of male-dominated political elites have been created and continue to be reproduced. This begs the normative question of the role of political elites in society, but that can be left to other scholars and other days.

The Secret Garden of Politics: A Note on Women and Party Preselection

It is no accident that the recent revival of interest by political science in 'preselection' has been sparked at least partly by women researchers asking questions inspired by feminism. Different views (to be discussed below) about the reasons for women's low participation rates in the formal political arenas were often based on stereotypes and rarely based on empirical research. Clearly the process whereby parliamentary candidates are selected is literally crucial to the gatekeeping process.

Preselection, consequently, is important for scholars interested in *how* political processes work. It is also significant for those concerned with *who* participates in the process. One of the issues which is raised in this chapter is how the pre-selection process determines who is included and who is excluded from political decision-making. We are looking for biases within the system. A bias is not the same as conscious prejudice, and is related to the structural dynamics of a system. In other words if women (or any other self-defined group) constitute 10 per cent of people who seek to become parliamentary candidates, then we would expect them to become 10 per cent of candidates.

In the absence of reliable information, commentators have been divided between supply and demand models for the under-representation of women in legislatures.[19] Supply-siders have argued that there is no supply of women, because women do not come forward (for an Australian example see the Australian Institute of Political Science's seminar on women and parties, 1977). Demand-siders have maintained that there is little demand for women on the part of the political elite. There is a considerable amount of anecdotal and illustrative information supporting the demand-side model. There is some overlap between the demand and supply approaches. Women's perceptions that barriers do exist may deter them from being contenders. In other words,

> if women believe that discrimination will operate against their selection, then they are likely to weigh up possible humiliation and failure against the potential rewards which they perceive accrue to electoral office.[20]

The 'iron law of andrarchy' has become a widely used catchphrase for the range of factors which have restricted women's participation in parliamentary politics. Responsibility for families, limited political resources, and socialisation have all been listed as factors responsible for the under-representation of women. These all resonate with a supply-side explanation. The view that parties discriminate against women is a demand-side explanation. The argument that women have to work harder to prove themselves is also a demand-side explanation. According to this view women need more extended political apprenticeship than men, and hence only exceptional women are 'chosen'.

There are different ways of finding out about the process of candidate selection. It is interesting that the processes themselves are part of the 'private' face of political parties as opposed to their more 'public' role of running election campaigns and nominating candidates for public office. Candidate selection (in Australia at least) is not regulated by public laws, except insofar as it is sensible for the parties to select as candidates people who meet the requirements for candidates as set out in legislation. The parties themselves publish their own constitutions and rules. The selection process itself is mostly conducted behind closed doors. Exceptions include those states which have ballots by the rank and file (known as plebiscites). In most cases the formal selection itself is made by a committee of party activists (chosen on different bases—to be discussed below). Clearly the values and orientations of these people are crucial. In the Australian case this is one layer which remains subterranean. There are several important questions to be asked (perhaps in the next research project?). In the first instance, who are these selectors? Secondly, what kinds of people are they seeking? Thirdly, how real is their role? (We know that for the Labor Party the factions—which are not mentioned in the formal rules—often have a major role in the selection process. This can override the actions of selectors, whose role can become formal and nominal.) The second question is particularly important when considering gender politics. Are the criteria of selectors related to characteristics which have more applicability to men or women?

We now know more about the candidates themselves and some of their perceptions of the selection process. The Candidates Studies (1987 and 1990) and the State Secretaries Studies (1988) have enabled us to make informed comments about the operation of the 'iron law of andrarchy' in Australia.[21] We now have some information about the pool of candidates who have sought party endorsement. We are also in a position to make systematic comparisons between male and female candidates. Information about candidates is but the 'tip of the iceberg'. Interviews based on a structured set of questions were undertaken with the senior party officials in order to locate the lower seven-eighths of the iceberg. In most cases the party's state director or secretary has little *formal* role in the preselection process. The actual process is in the hands of a range of different categories of person. Some of these processes are described in an earlier paper which I co-authored with colleagues from Britain and Canada. (The group included four women and one man.) There are enormous logistical difficulties in interviewing members of the selectorate, particularly if we are examining plebiscites. Consequently the state officials can be viewed as 'surrogates', at least in the sense of indicating the values and orientations of the state branch. State officials, too, provided information about the processes of preselection.

In both the ALP and the Liberal Party, the general trend since World War II has been towards greater centralised control—at least at the level of the main constituent body, the state branch or division. The ALP (except in New South Wales and the ACT) has moved away from plebiscites. The Liberal Party has moved towards a system of selection committees with a mixture of representation, both local (i.e. branch delegates from the electorate) and central (i.e. members of the executive of state council etc.). It retains the traditional system of local branch-based selection in Victoria, Queensland and Tasmania.

The state secretary (or equivalent) of one of the conservative parties in three states made the point that the ALP has a better chance of picking good candidates. In the words of one such secretary: 'The ALP can draw candidates from where the salary is roughly the same [as an MP].' The ALP was also envied for its capacity to place high-profile people. Clearly the system of factional deals enables the ALP to accomplish this. One conservative state secretary made the following two points in respect of the ALP:

> The ALP has organised not a bad system to stop 'brawls' under its promotion and voting system. [In the Liberal Party] you can ask people to apply but they may not get up.

The conservative party secretaries were keen to accomplish this, but they recognised that it was a circular process and that good candidates were not attracted to losing parties.

The main non-Labor parties (except in New South Wales) were all undergoing difficulties of one kind or another. There was a consequent tendency to see good-quality candidates as a panacea. The general comments about candidates were made in response to the following question: 'In your view, what constitutes a good candidate?' In the majority of interviews, with one or two startling exceptions, the quality candidates were seen as having characteristics which conventionally belong to males. It is difficult, for example, for a woman to have had a career as a footballer, to be judged as a good 'family man', or to be 'tall, dark and handsome'.

With only two exceptions, all state secretaries constantly used the male pronoun. One secretary listed the qualities of his ideal candidate in the following terms: 'a former state footballer who goes to confession'. Ever-mindful of what is known as the marginal seat strategy, this secretary's 'classic marginal candidate' was described as the 'principal of the local school, who goes to church and reads the bible, a former state football player who does sports commentary in his spare time'. Ties with the community were also seen as important. Local government experience was one indicator of this. For one ALP state secretary, a record of business and trade union work was another. For women, trade union and business links are not common. Both areas are still heavily male-dominated.

Labor and non-Labor officials alike emphasised two further features, namely the traditional 'horses for courses' approach and the importance of media appeal. Some talked about having a mix of candidates. Different kinds of candidates were required for the different kinds of seats. Four kinds of seats were identified by the Liberal and the Labor officials: safe, marginal, country and 'flagwavers'. The safe seat could be saved for the 'potential premier', or the 'quality' person who lacked electioneering skills. Discussion about marginal seats focused upon the electioneering skills of the candidate. It was here that the question of television appeal became important.

In two states, in response to my comment that their initial responses had ignored women, the state secretaries made reference to the attractiveness of women with high media profiles: 'a newsreader or weather reader would be worth looking at', commented one state secretary. Echoing this idea, one of the two state officials who had mentioned women candidates without prompting said, 'In these days of electronic media it is important to have someone who can sell himself (or herself).' Most party officials did not have a conscious model for marketing women candidates in terms of a 'gender gap' strategy. In fact in 1988 the prototype was clearly still male.

This was the case in 1987 even though the ALP and the Liberals had both increased the number and percentage of women candidates. There was, however, a decline in the overall percentage of women candidates, from approximately 25 per cent (1984) to about 20 per cent (1987). For the major parties, women constituted a greater proportion of Senate candidates than of House candidates. The ALP's story for 1987 was similar to its 1984 story: the number and percentage of women candidates grew but the number of women MPs remained the same. The Liberal Party increased its number of women MPs, with two additional female Senators. The Australian Democrats also gained two female Senators, as did the Greens. Women continue to fare better in the Senate than in the House, with the exception of ALP women. The poor representation of women in the House is partly a reflection of the low percentage of women candidates running for the two major parties.

As in comparable countries, part of the problem is the clustering of women into marginal and hopeless constituencies. Women are over-represented among those candidates with no chance of election. We will call such candidates 'flagwavers'. In 1987 among ALP candidates, for example, women constituted about 50 per cent of the flagwavers, but just over 12 per cent of the House of Representatives candidates.[22] For the Liberal Party the picture was broadly similar, if not as dramatic: women were just over 20 per cent of the Liberal flagwavers and about 11 per cent of House of Representatives candidates. In other words the situation was biased against women, because in a fair situation if women were x per cent of all candidates they would be x per cent of candidates in both good and bad seats.

Candidates at the other end of the spectrum from the flagwavers are the gladiators, who contest the marginal seats. These candidates have become increasingly important for two main reasons. In the first instance, incumbents are reselected almost automatically; they are re-elected at a high rate; and they retire only occasionally. For an aspiring politician, contesting a marginal seat held by the other party provides a potentially good start to political career. Secondly, increasingly during the tight contests of the 1980s the ALP in particular has placed great store upon its so-called marginal seat strategy. Selected marginal seats were targeted for additional resources and media treatment, apparently to good political effect. The big shift in Australian politics has been the increasing presence of women in the gladiator class, most dramatically on the Liberal side of politics. There were no gladiators in 1987, but in 1990 women were one-quarter of the party's gladiator class.

The Liberal party had a *de facto* gender gap strategy for the 1990 election. This resulted in a record number of three Liberal women MHRs serving concurrently, namely, Kathy Sullivan (Moncrieff, Qld), Christine Gallus (Hawker, South Australia) and Fran Bailey (McEwen, Vic). The 1990 Liberal women candidates were an interesting group. They were likely to have had links with business, whereas in the past the lack of such experience was seen as a handicap by many Liberal women.

There was other evidence that women candidates were similar to men candidates. At least for the 1987 and 1990 federal elections there was little suggestion that women candidates had to jump through more hoops than their male counterparts. (See Tables 20.1 and 20.2.) On important factors such as length of party membership, age, number of children and community involvement, the picture looked very similar for male and female candidates of the Labor and Liberal parties, respectively. One intriguing difference, however, was for ALP women; for 1990, at least, they were more likely to have worked in an MP's office prior to becoming a candidate.

When we turn to attitudes towards gender politics, there were some interesting differences. In general, irrespective of political party, women candidates were more likely than their male counterparts to believe that women do have a special role in Parliament and that more women should enter politics. Within the ALP and the Australian Democrats women were more likely to believe in gender equality and to support abortion rights. In contrast, the women from the coalition parties were *not* more progressive than the men and the picture was more complicated.

Conclusions

The conclusions fall into two categories: the findings of the research projects themselves and the meaning of the projects for broader debates about the methodology of research. As with any research, new sets of questions emerged and old stereotypes bit the dust. We can see that the political apprenticeships of male and female candidates for the two major parties have not differed significantly, at least not for the 1987 and 1990 election snapshots. The findings (which were not presented in depth or detail here) also indicated that Liberal women were less successful than Liberal men in the preselection stakes. (In other words, if you were a women nominating for preselection in the Liberal Party, you were less likely to be successful than your male counterpart.) The situation was different for the ALP, where women's chances were as good as or better than men's. This does not take into account the kinds of seats which candidates gained selection for. Women are still more likely to be in unwinnable seats—but for the 1990 election at least there were indications that women were increasingly seen as good bets for marginal seats. In general, however, the findings point to the need for more research on the politics of the selectors themselves.

The research drew from the agendas of different strands of feminist theory. It is drawn from liberal feminism to the extent that it focused on the formal political arena; from materialist feminism because of its focus on elites; and from radical feminism on account of its concern with the linkages between private and public spaces.

Table 20.1 Characteristics of Labor and Liberal federal parliamentary candidates, by sex, 1987

	ALP *(n = 147: Males 113; Females 33)*		*Liberal Party* *(n = 125; Males 114; Females 11)*	
Characteristic	*Female*	*Male*	*Female*	*Male*
Age of first interest in politics	20	18	19	21
Year joined current party	1973	1970	1976	1975
Year of first federal contest	1980 (n = 9)	1978 (n = 67)	1980 (n = 2)	1979 (n = 45)
Year of last federal contest	1984 (n = 9)	1983 (n = 67)	1980 (n = 2)	1984 (n = 45)
No. of times federal candidate	3 (n = 6)	3 (n = 67)	1 (n = 2)	3 (n = 45)
Year of first local government contest	1978 (n = 6)	1975 (n = 32)	1978 (n = 2)	1977 (n = 27)
Year of last local government contest	1980 (n = 6)	1977 (n = 32)	1982 (n = 2)	1982 (n = 27)
Current age	44	44	42	42
No. of children	2.2 (n = 30)	2.5 (n = 102)	2.9 (n = 8)	2.5 (n = 97)
No. of service or voluntary organisations	3.3	2.8	3.2	2.9

Table 20.2 Characteristics of Labor and Liberal federal parliamentary candidates, by sex, 1990

	ALP		*Liberal Party*	
Characteristic	*Female*	*Male*	*Female*	*Male*
Years of membership current party member of 5 years or less	2 (n = 15) 13.3%	13 (n = 95) 13.3%	4 (n = 10) 40%	24 (n = 80) 30%
Ever elected to local government	1 (n = 16) 6.3%	19 (n = 97) 19.6%	0 (n = 10) 0%	16 (n = 83) 19.3%
Ever elected to state government	1 (n = 15) 6.7%	5 (n = 96) 5.2%	0 (n = 10) 0%	1 (n = 82) 1.2%
Ever employed in MP's office	6 (n = 16) 37.5%	17 (n = 96) 17.7%	0 (n = 10) 0%	7 (n = 84) 8.3%
Ever employed as party official	0 (n = 15) 0%	9 (n = 94) 9.6%	0 (n = 10) 0%	6 (n = 82) 7.3%
Delegate to party conference	11 (n = 14) 78.6%	68 (n = 96) 70.8%	6 (n = 10) 60%	49 (n = 79) 62%
Held state or territory position	9 (n = 14) 64.3%	32 (n = 91) 35.2%	1 (n = 9) 11.1%	25 (n = 79) 31.6%
Held federal or national position	2 (n = 14) 14.3%	16 (n = 91) 17.6%	2 (n = 9) 22.2%	8 (n = 76) 10.5%

(cont'd next page)

Table 20.2 cont'd

	ALP		*Liberal Party*	
Characteristic	*Female*	*Male*	*Female*	*Male*
Actively involved in community service organisation	9 (n = 15) 60%	41 (n = 93) 44.1%	7 (n = 10) 70%	52 (n = 79) 65.8%
Actively involved in business organisations	1 (n = 14) 7.1%	18 (n = 92) 19.6%	6 (n = 9) 66.7%	44 (n = 78) 56.4%

TWENTY-ONE

Boys' Own Stories: Reading Gender in the Teen Movie

Stephanie Bunbury

James Dean, so the story goes, invented the teenager. Right there on screen in 1955, his rebel mumble defined a newly distinct class, that was to be regarded over the succeeding decades as, variously, a bizarrely hedonistic bunch of scatterbrains, the steamy breeding ground of disruptive social ills, and the hope of the Aquarian future. His blueprint for the Deanager was shambling yet glamorous, renegade yet vulnerable. He was winsomely inarticulate in the midst of a welter of neon inscriptions, his sensitive mind practically imploding with the pressure of American dreams. The screen teenager was rampantly mobile in his hotted-up car, yet had nowhere to go. The teenager was a rock'n'roll animal. Most notably, the teenager was a boy.

Almost forty years later, teen movies are such hot news that one of the biggest films of 1992, *Wayne's World* (Penelope Spheeris), was not simply of the genre, but a parody of it that amounted to *hommage*. Teen movies' popularity is scarcely surprising, given that teenagers are the cinema's best customers; while parents may be relieved that video cassette recorders allow them to be entertained in the comfort of home, the movies provide an opportunity for their growing children to escape from the nest, if only for a few hours. Teen movies mirror this physical separation between teenagers and their parents in the theme that defines the genre: the delineation of an adolescent world.

In all these films, the narratives turn on teenage isolation, and their authorial voices appear to speak from within this constructed space; adolescent life, as depicted within these fictions, is taken on its own terms. Nothing is viewed through the dark glass of nostalgic adult memory, nor is there any sense that puppy love and pimples add up to a rite of passage to a richer world beyond. There is no richer world beyond the teen movie. There is only now, and the agony of now.

On the face of it, this attempt to get inside teenage attitudes reflects a straightforward commercial decision by the Hollywood moguls selling these films to a lucrative youth market. 'Youth', however, is a hold-all category that implicitly smooths over many fissures, most notably that of gender difference, which would reasonably be expected to be of paramount concern among teenagers.

It is a film distributors' truism that women decide the box-office fate of most categories of film: popular movies prosper through dating, and girls or women usually choose which film to see. The kind of teen movies that were particular to the 1980s—the 'teen bonding' films, as Thomas Leitch described them in *Film Literature Quarterly*,[1] that reached their apotheosis in John Hughes' work—are defiantly ordinary. James Dean was the leader of his little pack, but Molly Ringwald inherits the beaded mantle of the girl who met him in the candy store. You get the picture? Yes, breathes the audience of fellow teens, we see. It is the stuff of soap operas, the minutiae of emotion that has been regarded as the soft centre of much women's fiction—the little world of little things, the private sphere of familial crisis and sexual promise, of uncertainty and fears of inadequacy—that is foregrounded in the teen movie.

And yet these are not 'women's films'. Indeed, it is through teenage boyishness, the life of the merry prankster, that this morass of adolescence can be transcended (*Tex*, Tim Hunter, 1982; *Rumble Fish*, Francis Ford Coppola, 1983; greaser films such as *The Wanderers*, Philip Kaufman, 1979): the power of flight is marked as masculine. And the fact that girls and boys inhabit the same fictional space and are dominated by sexual desire does not mean that the dividing line between them is not clear.

Boys and girls are seen to negotiate the rocky horrors of heterosexuality from different bases that are boldly stereotyped. The girls' sphere is silly, vain and cruel, ruled by the most venomous of its vixens; the paradigm is taken to a very funny extreme in *Heathers* (Michael Lehmann, 1989). Incidentally, it is almost indispensible to the plots of teen horrors, where girls are pursued by marauders and must pull themselves out of the morass of femininity to defeat them.

The boys' sphere, by contrast, is confused but comradely, goofy but decent. Above all, boys have more fun. It is the same cultural split that underlies boys' own adventures, swashbuckling yarns and the beat generation's ranging of America's roads, where women are an interruption: what is powerful and enviable about masculinity is the sheer fun of being a boy. After all, what is the abrasive Valley Girl[2] but a monstrous burlesque of an adult woman, absorbed by nonsense and constantly conniving at getting her own way? And in the teen movie, adulthood is another country where the customs are repellent.

Mapping Wayne's Little World

The teen movie inhabits its own Never-Never land, an over-determined physical space where the characters may frolic away from adult eyes. A series of motifs are repeated in one teen-bonding movie after another; they are like checkpoints at the borders of its universe, which is thus rendered manageably miniature. The co-educational high school is, unsurprisingly, a dominant setting, depicted as only nominally under adult control. Home scarcely features—apart from the cave of the teen bedroom, where posters of rock bands economically codify the character's social positioning (a nerd, a bohemian of sorts, a member of a tribal subculture). Home belongs to Them.

The town centre—these days, usually a mall—is another primary setting for the teen film, not unlike school as a social space. Then there is the town itself, squeezed into the frame of a car's front window: a customary teen-movie setpiece is a drive around town at night. After dark, when the adults have gone home to their videos after another numbing day of mercenary respectability, Jimmy Dean's descendants invade the neon world. The town is Denver, Chicago, or a smaller town in the American midwest, signifying a monochrome culture where Burger Kings outnumber books. This town has become Luna Park. The streets are cleared of other generations, the lights are flashing, the stereos are on; it is a cathartic moment of joy for the (usually male) characters on screen and for the audience. For the teenage audience, this is the movies' liberating message: that their identity lies in their very youth.

Questions of Identity

Two of the most distinctive examples of the sub-genre described by Leitch as 'teen-angst', which wears its beat heart on its leather sleeve, are Francis Ford Coppola's *The Outsiders* (1983) and *Rumble Fish*. Both are based on novels by S. E. (Susie) Hinton (who also wrote *Tex*). Hinton is a childless middle-aged woman who lives in the kind of town usually found in teen movies and has told any number of film magazines how much she liked teenage boys in general and Matt Dillon, the star of both these films, in particular. 'When I was a teenager I didn't understand what girls were talking about,' she said during the making of *The Outsiders*.

> They were always waiting for something to happen; they got to stand in the john, rat their hair and outline their eyes in black. Even now, when I go to baby showers, I still feel like I'm an anthropologist at some weird rite.

Even for women themselves, the imagery and social relationships defined as feminine are problematic, if not ludicrous.

It is worth noting that the teen movie has hit its stride in the wake of the buddy movie, *Butch Cassidy and the Sundance Kid* being the seminal example of that genre; both reflect the crisis in representation of women that has accompanied the successive social upheavals of the sexual revolution and the Second Wave of feminism. The films based on Hinton's work follow the buddy movie's example and resolve their problem with girls through the somewhat clumsy strategy of portraying only one gender.

The teen-bonding films, on the other hand, avoid the feminine enigma through a strategy that is superficially a contradictory one: while girls are portrayed and, indeed, are frequently central characters, they are grounded so heavily in stereotype that they frequently have no actual 'characteristics' at all.

The opening scene in *Sixteen Candles* (John Hughes, 1984), for example, establishes Molly Ringwald as nothing more nor less than a representative teenage girl through three stock observations: she is on the telephone as soon as she wakes up, she feels unattractive, and she habitually misses breakfast. These features, which have defined the category 'American teenage girl' since Patty saw the sights from Brooklyn Heights,[3] remain her chief distinguishing features. Her utter blankness makes her a perfect vehicle for shared teen experience; for the viewer, it is the world, not the individual, that is important.

Film theory has long accommodated the idea that women will identify 'up' to adopt the male point of view because this is the view taken by the camera itself. Women are seen by the camera as the 'other', both the objects of desire and, according to a psychoanalytic reading that interprets woman symbolically as a castrated man, the bearers of the uncomfortable knowledge of loss and, hence, powerlessness. The cinematic discourse was thus one of the many stories told by patriarchy about itself to its own. Women watching could be assumed, on the one hand, to assimilate the ideology of their own oppression by seeing the world through patriarchal eyes and, on the other hand, to internalise and repress a sense of inferiority. The ideology of patriarchy was thus a seamless one, enveloping both men and women.

The missing person here, of course, is the woman as subject. While this enervating view of women's acceptance of themselves as objects on screen may describe a dominant discourse and, perhaps, a specific moment of history, it shrinks from the vexed question of what women want—and what they have, apparently, repeatedly got. Even operating from within ideology, the female subject has her own wishes, wants and needs and evidently recognises them within the films she enjoys.

Recent work on genre fiction, notably romance, suggests that women and girls may read these ludicrously stereotyped texts tactically. They find distracting satisfactions in them that are not available in their own lives, or use their mythical ideals to question the contradictions between the ideology of romance and the lived experience that falls short of its giddy heights. Similarly, the teen movie, replete with cliché and reassuring sexist certainties though it is, has its own satisfactions for girls buried, like hidden jewels, in the clapboard stereotypes.

You Can't Tell if They're Boys or Girls

In her study of horror narratives *Men Women and Chainsaws*,[4] Carol Clover asserts that the codes of horror demand that the victims be women, but that the genders here serve the needs of archetype. The horror genre is repeatedly self-referential and its cast of characters are fixed in a series of readily understood oppositions (pursuer and pursued, rural redneck and city interloper, etc.). As a result, she argues, the instant a character appears on screen it is clear to all initiates what niche that character is supposed to occupy in the story and what emotions he or she can be expected to bear on the viewer's behalf, much as a Greek tragedian's mask instantaneously signifies his place in the scheme of the drama. The majority of the horror audience is made up of boys in their teens. A more 'realistic' reflection of the terrors of the everyday lives of young men might be disquieting, even 'emasculating'. Packaged in this concentrated, fantastical form and embodied by girls—whom one expects to be weak, who are allowed to be afraid—fear becomes not only palatable, but cathartic. Paradoxically, it is the fixity of the genre's conventional stereotypes that facilitates identification by boys with these threatened girls.

This reading of horror also illuminates the workings of genre formulas: how it is that viewers will reproduce numerous similar texts to their own satisfaction with relish and, frequently, against their ostensible grain.

Teen movies focus squarely on a phase in life (as currently constructed) when the rituals, rigours and rewards of heterosexual courting circumscribe social interaction, and fill every cranny of the hormonally charged teenager's emotional being: true or not, necessarily so or not, this is the shifting sand on which the teen movie is built. The real counterparts of these characters are presumed to be engaged in attempting to renegotiate their places in the world as sexual subjects and the objects of sexual admiration. It is a venture into a threatening territory littered with obstacles, where conventional stereotypes offer some clear guide on how to behave and, it appears, the surest, shortest and safest path to social success. Small wonder that it is the institutions that cater to youth culture that retain a severity of sexual distinction that is discredited, at least nominally, elsewhere: girls may grow up to be prime ministers, but they still don't surf.

Attempts at girls' teen-bonding films that adhere to the narrative thrust of male 'buddy' movies have been less than successful. *Mystic*

Pizza (Donald Petrie, 1988), for example, purports to centre on the friendship between three girls who work in a pizza shop but actually hedges its bets by concentrating on three parallel narratives of the respective girls' romantic liaisons. The 'buddy' sequences are the weakest moments. The woman at the centre of the problem-page plot, fixed as the conduit for (hetero)sexuality, has no claim to this kind of strength.

Sixteen Candles reeks of the problem page. It works, however, by introducing a secondary male character, a proto-Ferris Bueller (as in *Ferris Bueller's Day Off*, John Hughes, 1986), who is a puckish foil to Molly Ringwald's fairy queen and gives raucous voice to the sexual fears and hungers she represents. As described above, she is so blank as to be a nonentity, a sad teenager whose desire to be valued is conflated with her enervating longing to lose her virginity (to the right boy, of course—but he, a clean-cut jock in a higher form, is even more colourless than she). Her scrubbed face becomes a vehicle through which the audience can contemplate—rather than identify with—a state of mind endemic to the real and fictional teen world, backed up by the fraternity of jollity represented by her cheeky younger suitor.

Thus, the girls bear the brunt of the emotional burden: heroines in the Molly Ringwald mould are tossed about by events, alternately full of joy and distress, driven by emotional needs, worried and worn by their little failures. The boys, on the other hand, drive cars. But girls are the teen movies' chief consumers and it is to them that their fantasies of freedom surely offer the most potent promise of escape. It is the formula itself that provides their imaginative points of entry into this fantasy, not only through identification with the emotional concerns typed as feminine, but through identification with the mobile males.

A confusion of identity is already inscribed in the teen movie; in fact, it is inscribed in the distinguishing trait of the genre itself, that sense of adolescents as a caste trapped in someone else's society. Within the films' imaginative corrals, everyone is united against an Other that has no specific gender—the adult. Heterosexual desire may be the screen teens' chief torment, but their mating manoeuvres are conducted in the shadow of an over-arching unity. This affords to the construction of identity a kind of freedom. It is the teens' very groupishness, their sense of a limited, shared universe peopled by characters who are frequently ciphers, that allows identification to wobble across gender lines. In part, it is the same possibility proffered by horror according to Carol Clover's formulation: the opportunity to slip between characters and genders as if donning different costumes. But there is a further twist to this tale.

Any genre acquires coherence, not only by the distinct and unifying motifs that make it recognisable, but because it is read by its fans as a body of work. The teen movie audience—an audience, remember, of unusually frequent film-goers—also sees them unroll as a generic serial, a related series of episodes in the teen movie pantheon—even a series of episodes in life itself. Given the fact that the males and females in the entire body of work are built to such predictable design, the ascription of inappropriate attributes to any particular character, attributes that contradict the expectations resting on him or her, represents a kind of calculated rupture. Where girls and boys appear to have the 'wrong' characteristics, this suggests a gender ambivalence that does not simply facilitate cross-identification, but encourages it.

John Cusack's endearingly vulnerable young swain in *Say Anything* (Cameron Crowe, 1989), who rejects an unwanted career to accompany his academically gifted girlfriend to Cambridge 'because being with her is what I'm good at', conflates gender identities quite explicitly. For girls, his absorption in his beloved is a point of identification: as any quick skim over girls' magazines will reveal, to be swept away in perfect love is a perennial ideal. But it also makes him an ideal boy. He is the perfect romantic at the same time as being a rebel who refuses to conform to his elders' demands and get a proper job. He does not need the male group and indeed spurns it, pointing out to the push outside the local all-night store that their much-touted knowledge of girls doesn't seem to be bringing them much luck on a Saturday night. His own friends are girls. But he also carries the light of the misunderstood bad boy in him; he is of the male sphere, even as he deals with female troubles. Intriguingly, the combination gives his character a vigorous erotic charge.

The satirical bent of *Wayne's World*, a hugely successful film ostensibly about boyish togetherness, makes the workings of this kind of gentle gender bending clear. The most important woman in the film is Cassandra, played by Tia Carrere, a heavy metal singer whom Wayne meets when she is performing in his local headbangers' dance club.

Cassandra is a heroine, a luminous Valkyrie, with something of the style of the vamp—the phallic woman who is powerful, but whose power rests in an identity constructed by the desire of others. But she also represents a more modern version of the distant object of desire: a rock'n'roll singer. Thus, while the way in which her body is consumed by the camera has a recognisable screen history that stretches back to the bad girls of silent movies, it has a real-life referent that is much more immediate to most viewers. Cassandra has the sexual presence, intensified by a gender ambivalence inherent in a woman singing aggressive, noisy rock'n'roll, conferred by her position as a performer on stage with a bass guitar in her hand. Both Cassandra and her audience find their pleasure in her person, but she recalls Mick Jagger more immediately than she does Marlene Dietrich.

Cassandra is a 'role model' of some representational appeal—the female viewer may well entertain some fantasies of becoming a heavy metal queen herself—but it is unlikely that any girl could identify with her as a sister in teenhood. The plot hinges on our sharing Wayne's point of view, positioned as female by Cassandra's ambivalence, which includes a worshipful distance from the axe-grinding queen of his heart.

As a structuring of desire, it is by no means unfamiliar. The female as erotic is a cinematic staple, a repetitive equivalence of meaning as rigidly conventional as the woman-as-subject-of-terror. It is part of patriarchy's pantheon, certainly. But this does not mean that the pleasure gained by women and girls from this imagery is merely the lowly false consciousness of the unwitting collaborator in oppression. How much more probable is it that the phallic woman holds as much erotic appeal for women as it does for men—that the female subject may identify with the jaunty, carefree, autonomous male while coveting the allure and erotic potency of the phallicised woman?[5]

It is the same kind of potency, indeed, that was so beguiling in James Dean, and that sustains him as an icon today. Held forever in a cherubic youth by his premature death, Dean retains the glamour of beauty nipped in the bud, but the persuasive appeal of that beauty lay, at least in part, in its sexual ambivalence. The subjective meaning of this image of youth for women evidently cannot lie in a straightforward identification along gender lines; nor does it follow the prescriptive I-camera determinacy of the male gaze. Rather, it is the crises and crossings of gender in a teen world predicated on isolation and opposition to the dominant culture that provides a point of identification—no matter how petty that opposition may seem, or how far the imperatives of the teen world, such as material greed, may seem to ape, even exaggerate, those of their elders.

Many of the crop of teen movies that echoed, confronted and elided the smooth certainties of the 1980s were ham-fisted, feeble or retrograde. As a genre, however, the teen movie has an effervescent vitality, a daffy lack of resolution, that subverts its own conventions. For girls, there is an escapist energy here that is ripe for the plucking. Like the original teenager, that bundle of androgynous gentleness still ready for a rumble, like Wayne and Garth, they can cock a snook at an inadequate world and party on regardless.

TWENTY-TWO

Can a Boy be a Girlfriend?[1] The Legacy of Gender Segregation in Childhood Play

Norma Grieve

The initial impetus for this essay was when I learned of some unusual doubts that had been expressed about a woman who was on the short list for a senior position. A man on the selection committee was concerned that the candidate might be unable to confine spirited differences exchanged in committees to the meeting room. He appeared to have doubts about her ability to 'play the game'. To understand the reasons for his misplaced wariness seemed important. Then, a London club voted not to accept women as members, an event that in itself was not remarkable. What was of interest was the justification given for their refusal. Women, it was said, were not 'clubbable', in the sense that they might feel hurt in the atmosphere of conversational jousting and the 'rough and tumble exchanges' which men understand and enjoy.[2]

The selection of persons on the basis of social similarity ('homosocial reproduction') has long been recognised as the basis for a form of 'soft' discrimination against women. Women are at risk of being placed in the category of 'incomprehensible and unpredictable'.[3] In recent evaluations of affirmative action programmes, there are, at all occupational levels, reports from women that men feel more comfortable with, and prefer to work with, other men, and that women feel excluded.[4]

Recently, in the domain of developmental psychology, a new and promising approach to gender differences has emerged, which suggests a link between these forms of what have become known as 'boys' games' and features of childhood play. There is now a body of psychological research, summarised and analysed by the developmental psychologist Eleanor Maccoby,[5] which examines the differences in *social* behaviour of boys and girls as they play in same-sex and mixed-sex groups. From the preschool years through to puberty, children show an increasing preference for play groups of the same sex whenever they have a choice of playmates near their own age. School is one of the contexts where this choice is available, and a number of Australian studies[6] have described robust sex-segregated groupings in the primary school and the early years of secondary school, notwithstanding that the playgrounds are no longer segregated as they were in the 1960s.

This means that all Australian children attending schools large enough to provide companions of the same age and sex engage in and contribute to the practices and the implicit and explicit rules of behaviour of their same-sex peer group. Maccoby suggests that in this experience girls and boys acquire different skills, adapted to interacting with their own sex. These skills or practices can be carried over into adolescent and adult life, with important implications for social interactions in mixed-sex groupings.

The observational, experimental and discursive data discussed here are from 'captive samples' in kindergarten or school, and the question can fairly be raised whether the preference for same-sex play occurs only in this context. There is no direct answer to this question, but Maccoby says that these patterns of play are not limited to technologically advanced societies or to middle-class children.[7] When children have the opportunity, they tend to congregate with same-sex playmates in communities which are very different from her source of studies, the USA. If children, in or out of schools, are in isolated settings with few playmates of either sex, or if they are required to be caretakers of younger children, then this preference will not be apparent. Maccoby cites the psychological anthropologists Edwards and Whiting, whose studies ranged from tribal villages in Africa, Mexico, and India to industrialised New England, USA, and who concluded 'that the emergence of same-sex preferences in childhood is a cross-culturally universal and robust phenomenon'.[8]

To understand the significance of this research into children's play, we need to place it within the broader context of research into gender difference. Firstly we discuss the relative failure of existing psychological and neuropsychological evidence to speak to feminist concerns, notwithstanding the popular interest in these issues. The second section describes the different styles of play and the different modes of social influence that girls and boys develop in their same-sex groupings, and the consequences for the social interactions between the sexes. This section draws on relevant Australian studies[9] as well as Maccoby's impressive review of North American evidence.[10] Possible reasons for the development of gender-segregated groupings are discussed. The third section explores the relevance of this apparently modest difference in social behaviour to some questions currently being raised in relation to co-education.

Sex Differences and Gender Differences

The field of gender differences as it has developed in psychology is something of a paradox. An immense amount of academic labour has been spent by scholars, mostly women, and usually feminists, yet the results have contributed relatively little to feminist thought. On the other hand, the topic frequently turns up in the popular media.[11] What appears to arouse most interest is when gender differences relating to cognitive and motor abilities are linked to biology, particularly to the functioning of the brain. Then it is claimed that we are discussing 'real differences in the way males and females perceive the world, and respond to it'.[12] Why are the discourses of biological essentialism so appealing? Before trying to answer that question, we need briefly to consider substantive aspects of gender difference research.

Twenty years ago the field was known as 'sex' differences, a title still retained by neuropsychologists to signify that they, unlike contemporary psychologists, are primarily concerned with differences which they believe have a biological basis in the brain. The evidence from some twenty years of gender difference research indicates that, in addition to the well-established difference in aggression, differences are still evident in some highly specialised cognitive and motor skills, which include some aspects of spatial reasoning.[13] For those abilities and skills which have been identified as showing 'quite substantial sex differences',[14] the overlap between men and women varies from approximately 50 per cent to 75 per cent, and even in the case of neuropsychological findings there is no consensus on the biological basis. In any case from a feminist perspective, these differences—even if a biological basis for them could be unequivocally established, and irrespective of how 'substantial' they are—fall into the same category as the greater incidence of baldness in males. That is to say, they are coincidental to, and co-exist with, the dominance/subordination relations of patriarchy. The subordination of women is not built on male aggression or some males' superior performance in map reading.

What then of the differences in social behaviour which are the subject of this essay? The position taken here is that these differences are ultimately an expression of patriarchal relations, and that if biological factors have any role, it is neither necessary nor sufficient. Initially, children's play preferences may depend, in part, on styles of play. Rough-and-tumble play has an acknowledged biological basis, mediated through the degree of exposure in the womb to the predominantly 'male' hormone, testosterone; thus it is predictably more characteristic of the play of males, but not exclusively so. Children who engage in this type of energetic play are likely to prefer each other's company; those who do not are likely to avoid such boisterous companions. However, the move from a not-always-consistent preference for companions, boisterous or otherwise, to the rigidly enforced gender segregation observed by five or six years of age is, we would argue, a cultural matter. It relates to the gender categories, boys and girls, and not to differences in qualities such as engaging in 'rough-house' play, or aggressiveness, qualities which are distributed differently between the sexes, and can operate as signifiers of 'masculinity' or 'femininity' in particular cultures. The gender-segregated experience of boys and girls is relevant not only to questions of gender separatism in education, whether in co-education or single-sex education. It is also relevant to the understanding of the ways in which precursors of 'soft' forms of discrimination in social interactions between men and women are actively produced and maintained in the peer groups of childhood.

Individual Differences and Social Differences

Maccoby recalls that in the 1970s she and her co-researcher, Carol Jacklin, considered that the yield from their summary analysis of gender differences was thin, but that this fitted in with the prevailing discourses of that time, when males and females were represented as basically alike.[15] Twenty years on, the findings are basically unchanged, but they are less relevant to the ideas of the 1990s. Feminists are still attending to the workings of masculinist power, but they are concerned with social differences as well as similarities. There is also the possibility that the discourses of equality are merely giving women the option of being like men.

Maccoby makes another important point, of particular relevance to psychologists. She believes that the lack of findings of differences between men and women is partly illusory, in that 'they are an artifact of our historical reliance on an individual differences perspective'.[16] The research strategies used have underestimated the social/personality differences between the sexes because

> social behaviour, as many have pointed out, is never a function of the individual alone. It is a function of the interaction between two or more persons. Individuals behave differently with different partners. There are certain important ways in which gender is implicated in social behaviour—ways that may be obscured or missed altogether when behaviour is summed across all categories of social partners.'[17]

Amongst preschool children, qualities such as lack of assertiveness, the tendency to stay close to the teacher, or to retreat or stand and watch rather than engage in play with another child, are indeed displayed in greater degree by girls. But the social circumstances in which these behaviours occur *and do not occur* (in this latter case, when boys are absent) are critical to understanding the dynamics of gender interactions.[18]

The Popularity of the 'Biological' Discourse

This seems an appropriate point to return to the problem of why 'biological' discourses are so popular. Frequently the discussion of cognitive and personality gender differences is embedded in speculative sociobiological arguments concerning sexual practices, of the sort, 'men are naturally more promiscuous than women'. All gender differences are explained as the automatic playing out of genetic and hormonal programmes which have remained relatively unchanged since our progenitors were hunting and gathering. Such 'innocent' and reductive biological arguments simplify and offer closure on a debate which is complex and sometimes threatening. Feminism frequently casts familiar, customary, time-honoured, and 'natural' gender practices as problematic.

More importantly, the focus on individual differences 'produces understandings of gender that deflect attention from the social relations through which the meanings of gender are continually being constructed'.[19] It is not surprising that one of the features of popular discussions of biological differences is the ease with which they move into the justification of gender inequity. For example, in a recent best-selling publication, *Brain-Sex: The Real Difference between Men and Women*, which was the basis for an international (American) television series, we read that females, by virtue of 'a lack of testosterone . . . may not want to move [to equality in society]'.[20]

The implications drawn by those who are actively engaged in research into sex differences and the brain, and who subscribe to the genetic/hormonal/evolutionary argument are, in the event, not far-reaching. For example, Doreen Kimura, a neuropsychologist, concludes that

> the finding of consistent and, in some cases, quite substantial sex differences suggests that men and women may have different occupational interests and capabilities, *independent of societal influences* [my emphasis]. I would not expect, for example, that men and women would necessarily be equally represented in activities or professions that emphasize spatial and math skills, such as engineering or physics. But I might expect more women in medical diagnostic fields where perceptual skills are important.[21]

It is doubtful whether even this modest proposition could be tested, since the sorts of 'societal influences' implicated here are unlikely to be able to be isolated and measured.

If, as Maccoby suggests, research strategies have underestimated the personality and behavioural differences between the sexes in social contexts, this may offer another possible reason for the popularity and robustness of the 'biological' discourse. To many readers of this 'research', it 'comes at first as a revelation, a confirmation of that faint, unfocussed sense one has of playing the game by the wrong rules'.[22] The interpretative appeal of this popular discourse, which frequently and incorrectly implies that these behaviours, specific brain processes, and the binary variable, sex, are all perfectly correlated, is that it appears to explain a long-standing 'mystery' of the different gender styles.

The argument of this essay is that greater understanding is more likely to emerge from investigations of the gendered social practices produced and maintained in childhood peer groups, and their carry-over into adult practices, than from theories of the evolution of brain organisation. That is the question to which we will now return.

Girls' Games and Boys' Games

There is evidence that even before the age of three years, children's social behaviour is attenuated when they are paired with a child of the opposite sex compared with their own sex. The behaviour of boys and girls is affected in different ways. Girls tend to retreat and stand and watch the boy play with toys, although this is not characteristic of their behaviour when paired with another girl. A boy is likely to ignore the verbal prohibitions of a girl, even though he responds to the same prohibition from a male partner.[23]

By four-and-a-half years of age, children are showing a preference for same-sex playmates, and this is well established by the age of six years. Up to the age of at least eleven years, children continue to show this preference, if that option is available and if they are free to choose. Within the school playground, sanctions against mixed-sex play are strongly enforced by the children themselves. In one systematic attempt by preschool teachers to encourage cross-sex interactions in free play, it was found that these interactions only continued as long as they were explicitly rewarded.[24]

The ways in which boys and girls differ in group interactions can be reported briefly. (One important omission in this corpus is the different ways that girls and boys engage in sport, and in particular the significance of sport as an arena for the apprenticeship for masculinity.) Maccoby's summary indicates that the play of boys and girls differs in at least two aspects, styles of play and modes of social influence.[25]

Styles of Play

Girls tend to play in smaller groups than boys; boys' play is rougher, takes up more of the space in schools, and more frequently takes place in public spaces, such as roads. Girls' close friendships with a few girls are marked by shared confidences, whereas boys are friends on the basis of shared activities. This distinction is echoed in findings on adult friendships.[26] Broken friendships occasion more distress for girls. As to style of play, it is not the level of activity which distinguishes girls and boys but the boisterousness of their interactions. If, for instance, girls are observed on a trampoline, their style of play is just as active as that of the boys, but they do not show the rough-and-tumble quality noted in boys' play, the wrestling and mock fighting, the throwing of bodies on one another in a rough body-contact play which, nevertheless, does not usually involve hostility. Observations of verbal behaviour indicate that boys compete and try to establish dominance by insults, threats, teasing, capping others' stories, all of which are expected to be taken in good part. In contrast, girls in their smaller groups tend to be less competitive and to facilitate other girls' participation more. Turn-taking is more characteristic of all-girl groups, and they are more likely to express agreement with other speakers and pause to give others a chance to speak. Boys frequently interrupt each other and with age are increasingly less willing to comply with other boys' commands.[27]

This is not to say that the style of interaction in girls' groups is one of unproblematic sisterhood. Girls' groups have their own tyrannies. Unlike the experience of boys, boasting, bragging and displays of superiority, or even achievements, are reacted to as a 'violation of girls' egalitarian ethic'.[28] Girls who engage in this behaviour are not 'likeable', they are immodest and self-promoting; yet discussing with one's trusted friends *the problems* associated with one's 'success' can be seen as an appropriate act of disclosure. Connection and similarity are stressed in the group, but not in simple ways, since innovation can be one of the ways girls achieve dominance in a group.[29] Questions of what is considered 'false' and 'authentic' modesty or assertion are clearly complex issues for girls. The life of primary-school girls who violate the often implicit rules of their group can be a misery, with no-one speaking to them except to deliver epithets such as 'Brace Ace', 'Ugly', 'You're a pain' and the like.[30]

Modes of Social Influence

One interesting experimental situation involves small groups of, say, four preschool children, where two helpers are needed so that one child can view a movie.[31] In same-sex groups, both boys and girls are equally co-operative, and one child emerges as dominant and gets more than a fair share of viewing time. But the boys and girls achieve dominance by different methods. The boys are openly competitive; they tend to shoulder and push others out of the way, all apparently in a spirit of fun, whilst the girls use verbal reasoning to persuade. In another study, same-sex groups of three children aged four-and-a-half years were brought into a free play room with a range of toys. The girls organised their play by making rules, a pattern not shown by the boys. When a girl took more than her allotted share, the other girls argued with her, appealing to the rules, but not engaging in physical constraints practised in playful ways by the boys.[32]

During the preschool years, boys' verbal attempts to influence others increasingly take the form of direct demands, whereas girls' attempts increasingly move in the direction of making suggestions. One socio-linguistic study concludes 'that when girls talk they seem to have a double agenda: to be "nice" and sustain social relationships, while at the same time working to achieve their own individual ends'.[33] Amongst themselves, girls are *not* unassertive, but they tone down blatant domination. Boys on the other hand are more confrontational, competitive, and power-assertive in same-sex groups; this seems to be understood as not personally directed, as it does not impede co-operation.[34] These different styles give abundant opportunities for misunderstanding and incompatibility between boys and girls. However, the behaviour in mixed groups, at least at school, rarely emerges as differences that require negotiation. By primary school, the lines have been firmly drawn.

Girls and Boys in Mixed-sex Groups

It is in mixed-sex groups that gender relations become problematic for girls. Earlier, it was noted that when 2½-year-old girls were paired with a boy they showed less activity and watched more.[35] In preschool, when boys are present, girls show less assertion and place themselves close to the teacher; these behaviours are *not* observed when boys as a group are absent. In the viewing experiment, boys managed to secure more time in the viewing position while girls spent more time as handmaidens.[36] Techniques adopted by girls to gain dominance or control resources in all-girl groups are less effective with boys, and increasingly so during the preschool years. These interactions are repeated in the school classroom. Boys respond almost exclusively to other boys' requests, and boys are more influential over group decisions than are girls. Girls' methods of influencing others are more acceptable to other girls and, at least in the early years of primary school, to teachers, but become increasingly ineffective with boys. Many studies have shown that at school boys engage more of the teacher's time, not only with direct requests, but by behaviour which requires disciplinary actions.[37] The conclusion can be drawn that the practices in mixed-sex groups can be, at least, uncongenial and uncomfortable for girls, and 'strengthen their (mainly negative) stereotypes about boys'.[38] However, when adults set the children absorbing, well-structured joint projects, then boys and girls can work together co-operatively.[39] Co-operative play between boys and girls also occurs in non-public settings. The question of the effect of the 'audience', particularly on boys' behaviour, will be discussed later, when possible explanations for these peer-group developments are canvassed.

Ways of Maintaining Gender Segregation

For children in primary school, it becomes increasingly difficult for cross-sex play to occur in public, even though children may prefer to play with the other sex for reasons of liking, familiarity, or style or type of activities. By the age of seven years, long-standing cross-sex friendships have gone underground, at least at school. Maccoby reports that intense teasing is observed when a child reveals an interest in a child of the other sex. This is frequently expressed in sexual or romantic terms: 'he's your boyfriend', 'you love him, you're going with him'. The so-called 'border work' of teasing is supplemented by taunts about contamination, and other behaviours such as chasing, accompanied by threats to kiss.[40] These examples of North American children seem benign when compared with two recent Australian accounts of the highly antagonistic playground relations between primary and secondary-school boys and girls, largely initiated and maintained by the boys. 'Border work' has in many cases become sexual harassment. Margaret Clark observes that teachers often do not understand the force of the boys' behaviour in excluding girls from playing space, and their mockery and disdain for girls' games and girls' physical ability. Merely to give girls the message that 'they can do anything' misses the point. The oval is clearly marked as a male arena. Clark provides the following extreme example from a parent: 'My daughter, who is in Year One, wanted to play on the oval. A boy in her class flashed himself at her and told her to keep away, "girls don't come here".'[41]

The difference is, in part, explained by Maccoby's reliance, to a large degree, on preschool observations, although, as will emerge later, there are basic differences in theory and methodology. The North American material comprises, in the main, observations of interactive behaviour, while the Australian studies employ open-ended interviews specifically directed to gender practices.

Maccoby concludes that children who might enjoy playing with the opposite sex are, by the social controls enforced by the children, confined to the same-sex peer group, at least at kindergarten and school. Girls who are particularly active, the so-called tomboys, do not play with boys.[42] Boys who do not like boisterous games, or dislike sport, or who early show a great aptitude for schoolwork and are popular with teachers, can be isolates. There is no question of publicly crossing the boundary. Often boys who do not care for sport eventually position themselves at the margins of the male peer group in literary, musical or other artistic sub-groups.

One of the important aspects of same-sex groupings is that initially children are segregating themselves on the basis of the binary gender category, girls and boys, and not on the basis of other similarities such as types of games (children segregate on both sex-typed and gender-neutral games) nor on dimensional qualities such as the degree of sex-typing of the child in terms of so-called 'masculinity' and 'femininity'. The evidence strongly suggests that we are dealing with a social group phenomenon, boys and girls, and not one that is related to the personal qualities of individuals.

Why This Gender Segregation of Play?

A number of reasons for gender segregation have been suggested, and all have some plausibility. The simplest proposition is that the children's behaviour is an outcome of what they see in the family, on television, and in the wider society, as well as an expression of the differential socialisation of boys and girls. Maccoby argues that this is only partly so, and that the characteristics of the same-sex peer group are only partly derivative. She has long held a cognitive-developmental position that proposes that 'children contribute to their own social encounters', and it has long been known from the work of the cognitive constructivist, Jean Piaget, that children construct and inherit games, independent of adults.[43] Forms of sexual harassment in schools, such as boys stealing sanitary pads from schoolbags and throwing them around the classroom, or pulling down girls' knickers, are clearly elaborated in the male peer group, rather than informed by observational learning.[44] Maccoby argues for a culture of childhood that is influenced by the surrounding culture, but 'is a sexist culture in its own right'.[45] Paul Willis observes from his study of Birmingham working-class boys that ideology does not always proceed from the top down, but can be constructed from the bottom up. 'The male counter-school culture promotes its own sexism—even celebrates it as part of its overall confidence.'[46] He observed that the 'lads' constructed a hyper-masculinity, well beyond what seemed to be required of them in their labouring futures.

The two Australian analyses also work with the notion of an inherently sexist culture of childhood.[47] They see the problematic cross-sex interactions of primary-school children as the outcome of discursive practices arising from the child's location, by virtue of anatomy, within the essentially binary *opposites* of male and female. They do not address questions of gender preference, the elaboration of same-sex play, or the effect of context on boys' and girls' behaviour *per se*, presumably because these issues would be considered epiphenomena of discursive practice.

Bronwyn Davies writes that the opposition of male and female is 'not an opposition of equals, but one in which part of the definition of one is its dominance over the other'. Later she argues: 'Taking oneself up as unequivocally male or female, and taking that to mean opposite to the other, then requires maintenance of the forms of discourse which sustain that oppositional difference.'[48] Margaret Clark's interviews provide many transparent examples of boys enacting their developing masculine practices, in ways that sustain and accentuate their difference from, and dominance over, girls.[49] Girls are denigrated: they are boring, dumb, weak in the sense that they cry when teased, they are not strong enough to run fast enough to play with boys. These are all reasons for boys to believe that they are engaging in male activities beyond the girls' capabilities. 'Sometimes the contrast between what was said and the actual physical size of some of the little boys verged on the absurd.' In one school where the boys described girls as weak things, there was a girl who was the under-eight world BMX champion.[50] By Year 6 of primary school the girls have got the message that the boys are signalling their (fragile) masculinity. 'They have to be mean to us because otherwise they will turn into girls or something—I don't know.' 'They can't bear to think that any girl is smarter than them.' 'I think sometimes they like really dumb girls . . .' Even a Grade 4 girl understands that 'they can't cope with the embarrassment of not being superior'.[51]

In the company of a male audience, boys appear to engage in a degree of hyperbole as they enact and receive recognition for what they take (or hope) to be masculine behaviour. Even being civil to ('weak') girls can be seen as 'weakness', with the resulting contagion leading to loss of status in the dominance hierarchy. The girls observe that the boys are 'really nice' at home, but when with their boyfriends they get 'really mean'. One boy says, to the mocking laughter of his friends, 'It takes courage to treat girls nicely. You have to be really brave to do that.'[52]

But what of the girls? Surprisingly, the post-structuralist accounts of Davies and Clark provide a more vivid account of masculinity than of femininity. Girls emerge as socially perceptive about what is going on, but frequently feeling powerless and reactive, and sometimes envious of boys. They appear to be preoccupied with two R's, relationships and romance. What seems missing is how these interests and discourses relate to the now well-established educational achievements of many girls.

In contrast to the post-structural position with its emphasis on the inherent inequality of power in gender categorisation, Maccoby's account of gender segregation is more descriptive. In Davies' terminology, Maccoby considers the binary boy/girl category, at least initially, as an opposition of equals, who are somewhat incompatible. She suggests that the biologically based rough-and-tumble play of boys, combined with 'an assertive-dominant interaction style' and their puzzling early unresponsiveness to girls' demands are the initial impetus to the development of gender preference and segregation. Rough-and-tumble play, she asserts, 'has a clear developmental curve and falls off rapidly before adolescence'.[53] A 10-year-old boy in Clark's study puts it simply: 'Girls won't play with us, cos we're too rough.'[54] Maccoby does acknowledge that there is no clear answer why the boys' and girls' groups function in the way they do.

How then does Maccoby account for the move from this early incompatibility to the primary-school boys' attempts to publicly dominate and denigrate girls? She acknowledges that the gender-segregated male peer group is a site where 'attitudes toward members of the opposite sex are strongly forged . . . in which members sustain one another's exploitative attitudes toward women as sex objects.'[55] Yet in the end her explanation is too general, asserting that with increasing cognitive development the child will selectively attend to and internalise the gender-appropriate stereotypes of the culture.

A more promising account of how the sexism of the male peer group (and its extreme form, sexual harassment) is generated develops from the analysis of discursive practices. In this interpretation, the derogation and domination of girls is not based on 'exploitative attitudes' *per se*, or indeed stereotypes, but is part of the boys' exaggerated and group enactment of some of the tenets of masculinity. In relation to females, this means exercising more power, possessing superior physical capacities and emotional control to females, being the ones who do the sexual categorising, who do the accepting and rejecting, and who have control of outcomes. Their power is demonstrated 'whenever a girl is made to feel embarrassed, frightened, hurt or uncomfortable because of a comment or an action which [is] in some way related to being female.'[56] On the other hand the tenets of femininity do not appear to give girls access to strategies which would lead them to harass boys.

Nevertheless, I, as a psychologist, feel some unease in accepting that all gender developmental phenomena—including gender preference for same-sex play, the different styles elaborated in boys' groups and girls' groups, the effect of context, particularly on boys' behaviour ('the pack mentality')—can be all be subsumed within, or reduced to the workings of 'the constitutive force of spoken and written language, and, the metaphysical nature of the male/female dualism' as Davies contends.[57] There is also the question of how literally the actions and verbalisations of young boys should be taken as an index of their misogyny, without knowing more about the cognitive limitations of children's concepts of masculinity and femininity. This reservation does not imply that the behaviour should be condoned. There is some slight but suggestive evidence that children between the ages of six and eleven years have *periods* of extreme conformity and rigidity in their gender concepts, interspersed with more liberal periods.[58]

There are, of course, other explanations of masculinity, femininity, and misogyny, notably psychoanalytic oriented theories which focus on the mother–infant relationship. Nancy Chodorow, for instance, observes that the boy, in the context of relatively limited paternal contact, 'often comes to define masculinity largely in negative terms, as that which is not feminine or involved with women.'[59] These ideas may be relevant to early primary education, where 'at the overt level it appears that classrooms are female dominated spaces'.[60] Boys in Year 1 say of little girls that 'they walk around like a teacher, they think they're smart, and they look at everybody's work'.[61]

Co-education: Some Issues

A decade ago there was concern about the impact of co-education on girls' learning and self-concepts. The sexism recognised then predominantly concerned the curriculum and the dynamics of the classroom; social relations outside the classroom were barely considered.[62] In a recently released report *Listening to Girls*, commissioned as part of the review of the National Policy for the Education of Girls, Sandra Milligan and Karen Thomson suggest that sex-based harassment is 'endemic' in many co-educational schools.[63] Some forms of classroom and curriculum sexism may have disappeared, but this report and Clark's study suggest that boys' classroom practices are still disadvantaging many girls. In addition, they both identify the extreme form of sexism, sexual harassment of girls, in at least some schools. The issue of single sex education is now being canvassed, with the advantages of co-education for girls being reassessed.[64]

Milligan and Thomson report the now familiar complaints that boys take over space, equipment, attention and 'airtime', and embarrass girls when they make errors.[65] There are suggestions from some mathematics teachers that the difference goes further: that girls have a more exploratory style of learning compared with the boys' 'solution-oriented' approach. These observations echo other findings emerging from analyses of the conversations of boys and girls while they solved mathematical problems in same-sex groups.[66] Where schools have instituted single-sex classes for some subjects, it seems that girls have benefited, although in some cases the teaching of boys then became more difficult.[67]

One of the outcomes of present forms of the sex-segregated peer culture is that even in co-educational primary schools, 'boys and girls barely know each other',[68] and many boys and girls say that they do not even like the other sex very much.[69] Yet within this context, the practice of 'going with' a boy or girl is something 'you do in Year Five' at some schools. 'Girls take the whole business a lot more seriously . . . [and] both boys and girls recognize that girls were more vulnerable to being hurt.'[70] Given this context, it is not surprising that in secondary schools, the girls' 'intimacy through disclosure' style of interacting is expressed at this stage in a preoccupation with the vicissitudes of relationships. They discuss who it is they like and hate, with boys as a favourite topic, in a seeming prototype of the 'societies of consolation' identified by Carolyn Heilbrun as an historical basis for women's friendships.[71] Boys, when asked what they talk about with their friends, are 'more inclined to say they didn't talk about anything, they just played'.[72] Again this is a prototype of men's friendships which are commonly based on joint projects rather than disclosure. Individually many girls complain about the exclusion of other topics, yet where schools have allotted staff for counselling on relationships, girls are almost the sole consumers.[73]

The extreme forms of sexual harassment in some schools, reported in *Listening to Girls* suggest that the problem is not just that boys like to 'be one of the boys' and direct to girls the 'normal' practices of teasing, insulting, mocking, and threatening that they have playfully learnt to direct to each other and to accept in good part. What emerges in many co-educational schools is harassment as part of everyday experience for many girls and some non-conforming boys; it is sometimes as brutal as the 'bastardisation' practices of young adult male communities. Complaints from the girls in some schools mention frankly physical sexual harassment, but the harassment is more commonly an aggressively sexual 'showing off'. At one high school, the junior boys engaged in 'dakking' (pulling down girls' pants). Other girls complain of teasing about 'your period, your breasts', and public insults of 'slut' and 'dog'. In some schools, the girls begin by saying that the boys and girls are friends, and teachers 'treat us the same', yet one of the girls adds in relation to the teasing: 'It's OK if you can look out for yourself' and tells of one girl who could not handle it, and left the school.[74] At least between some groups of boys and girls in co-education there has developed a mutual incomprehension. On the girls' part, there is sometimes a distaste and even fear of boys in groups, not primarily for what could happen to them physically but because of the humiliation, ignominy and dominating behaviour that many girls have experienced.

This essay does not presume to enter the co-education debate, but rather to provide a psychological perspective by drawing attention to the developmental history of peer-group relations. These observations at least suggest that there may be benign precursors to present outcomes, and that the move from a preference for same-sex playmates to gender segregation, through to the male-initiated sexist interactions between girls and boys, which shade into overt sexual harassment, needs to be a focus of continuing research and action. The developmental perspective would also caution against immediately accepting the boys' outrageous sexual harassment when in the company of other boys as a literal expression of their degree of male misogyny.

Educationalists have long recognised that sexism is a problem which the school is uniquely placed to contest. But what has not been sufficiently emphasised is the significance of the peer group, and the active part that teachers and 'girls and boys play in the production of and maintenance of particular forms of femininity and masculinity'.[75] Programmes encouraging individual assertiveness or self-esteem in girls or individual sensitivity in boys, or even policies of gender neutrality, need to be evaluated for their effectiveness in the playground as well as the classroom. Programmes seeking to develop awareness of how gendered behaviour is enacted in the interactions between girls, boys, and teachers appear closer to the concerns of this essay.[76] Margaret Clark concludes: 'No attempt to break down gendered practices and attitudes will work if the active and significant role that girls and boys play . . . is ignored.'[77]

Conclusions

To return to the not entirely serious initial question in the title of this essay, it would seem that a boy can never be a 'girlfriend'. Nor, and more importantly, can a girl be 'one of the boys'. They do not have the necessary knowledge of either the agenda or the procedural rules. There are children in our society whose lives outside school have situated them in mixed or opposite-sex groups, where they acquire the possibility of being an 'honorary boyfriend/girlfriend'. There are other childhoods that are different. In some small-scale traditional cultures, preference for same-sex companions and exclusion of the opposite sex occurs without the overt sexism and sexual harassment reported in local studies.[78] In some societies, boys can expect from their male peers not only companionship contingent on shared activities, or 'mateship' developed through shared hardships, dangers, and adrenalin, but friendships which embody disclosure (for instance, the Nigerian example of a 'secrets man').[79] Most heterosexual Australian males achieve this only, if at all, with their spouse or 'girlfriend'. On the other hand, increasingly in our society, females are complementing the customary 'intimacy through disclosure' basis of female friendship with the so-called 'male' pattern of friendship based on joint projects.

What girls and boys, and women and men in Australian society need is a richer, better-articulated and more conscious understanding of their own practices and those of the opposite sex—a gender ethnography, if you will, of their interactions in the various contexts of social life. Practices, like discourses, can be unthinkingly or consciously employed, modified, and/or contested, and new practices can be developed. Although many women now believe they have cobbled together their own styles which have served them in what has been a journey without maps, there is good reason to believe that many of the interaction patterns of childhood, already identified, will be mirrored in the interactions of adult groupings. (See chapters by Rosemary Pringle and Ailsa Burns in this volume.) Amanda Sinclair, writing on 'Sex and the MBA' (Master of Business Administration), provides another example. She observes that

> Syndicate work is a powerful norm among MBAs, governed by all sorts of, I would argue, mistaken beliefs about the benefits of teamwork . . . . For some women 'teamwork' is a sustained exposure to systematic discrimination—their ideas are dismissed, their comments overruled, their contributions relegated to clerical or secretarial tasks.[80]

For many readers, other examples will readily come to mind, reminding them that when men and women interact in groups, male practices usually prevail and women still make most of the adjustments.[81]

TWENTY-THREE

Why Do Women Put Up With the Double Load?

Ailsa Burns

The 1970s feminist critique typically depicted women's position in the family and the paid workforce in industrialised societies in chicken and egg terms. The chicken—the family—loads women down with the tasks of reproduction, servicing men, and childcare. The demands of these tasks, all of them unpaid, keep women too busy to get very far in the paid workforce. The egg—the labourforce—constructs this situation as demonstrating women's lack of ability and/or commitment to the workforce, and arranges itself so as to restrict these unsatisfactory workers to the lowest-status and lowest-income (though not the easiest) jobs. Women consequently have little opportunity to escape economic dependence on men, and are vulnerable to all the other subordinations that economic dependence entails.

In order to crack the labourforce egg, feminist activists pushed government to introduce a range of equal opportunity and affirmative action programmes. These have met with some success.[1] However, many saw the chicken—the family and its demands—as the more important source of women's subordination, and doubted that real equality could ever be achieved within marriage. They warned women against it, and proposed singlehood, cohabitation or lesbianism as better recipes for equal rights.[2]

Twenty years on, what has happened? Due to economic restructuring and other factors, women's employment has massively increased, while that of men has decreased.[3] Has this been compensated for by greater equality in the family and greater male involvement in family work?

The answer is no. A large body of evidence attests that women continue to do most of the work in the modern home, even when they are in full-time employment.[4] In Australia, the most extensive information comes from Bittman's 1987 survey.[5] Bittman found that statistically the most powerful predictor of the amount of paid work (employment) and unpaid work (housework) done by women was marriage. When a woman married, she increased her housework time by almost eleven hours per week if she had previously lived alone; by almost fourteen hours a week if she had shared a household with others; or by over twenty-one hours per week if she had left her parents' household in order to marry. Most of this time went on cooking, cleaning and laundry. Compared with the effects of marriage in increasing women's housework, other influences, for example the hours of paid work, were quite minor. By contrast, men on marriage mildly decreased an already low level of indoor housework.

The birth of a first child increased the new mother's housework time by 91 per cent, and concomitantly lowered her labourforce participation. New fathers (on average) did not increase housework time 'by a single minute' but they did more paid work. When mothers returned to the workforce, the amount of time devoted by their husbands to housework did not increase with the wife's hours of employment. Nor did older children contribute much of their time to the household enterprise. Later still in the life cycle, married women who retired picked up a heavy load of domestic work, while retired men and women living alone spent only average (and equal) amounts of time on domestic tasks.

The fact that men make more domestic work than they do is neatly summarised by the fact that single mothers spent less time on housework than did partnered mothers (even when doing the same amount of paid work), and had more time for leisure pursuits and socialising. Bittman concludes that husbands are a net drain on family resources of unpaid labour time.

Why this gross inequity? One explanation is the continuing gender-segregation of domestic tasks. Bittman found that men's main contributions continue to be in home maintenance. Since 1974, men have increased their time spent on shopping, cooking, and laundry, but these increases have been slight. In addition, shopping time has itself increased, meaning that wives have only kept even in this respect.

To attribute these outcomes to 'continuing gender-segregation' is not of course a very profound explanation. Why does gender-segregation continue? In discussing this question, a number of authors note the fact that wives often defend their husbands' non-contribution.[6] Husbands are excused domestic work on account of 'not being any good at it', 'not seeming to notice it needed doing', and because 'he would do it if it was really necessary'. Bittman and Lovejoy offer an explanation in terms of 'non-decision making',[7] whereby a couple never discuss the allocation of household work, and wives sooner or later pick up most of the tasks by default. This may occur in the context of frequent (often fruitless) arguments, or the wife may avoid airing her dissatisfaction for fear of disturbing marital harmony.

In Bittman and Lovejoy's sample most of the men expressed egalitarian attitudes, but these did not match their behaviour. These authors suggest this discrepancy puts the men in a position of cognitive dissonance. They deal with this by categorising the wife as especially competent at or fond of domestic work, or as having different standards; or by themselves treating the tasks involved as too trivial for serious consideration ('I don't know who does the bathroom, she must do it, 'cause I don't').[8]

American and British researchers have explored the same phenomenon. Komter[9] found that although the American women whom she interviewed did not seem to like domestic work any more than men, they accepted it rather than face a conflict that might disturb the relationship. Furthermore, they did not just give in at the threat of anger and conflict, but often pre-empted the issue by second-guessing what the husband might want, and acceding to his unspoken wishes. They also adopted strategies of denial and resignation that had the effect of suppressing (partly) their own sense of grievance. Ferree[10] notes that wives often failed to demand equal rights, and/or persecuted themselves with unrealistically high standards because of their investment in family care as a measure of themselves as good wives and mothers.

Ferree, Komter and others ascribe these behaviours to the 'hidden power of gender ideology', inculcated from the earliest years, which leads many women to believe that they should be running the perfect, conflict-free household. Their data suggests that this hidden power commands an alarmingly high level of appeasement from wives, accompanied by a large and inequitable input of 'emotion work'—keeping relations smooth, foreseeing and preventing potentially disruptive events, maintaining an attractive household, listening, supporting, soothing and the like.[11] Added to the paid job that has become typical of women in the 1990s, all this makes for a substantial workload.

Why do modern women put up with this situation? When we ask this question, a hundred answers crowd to mind. In what follows, some of the most commonly advanced are briefly discussed; and the outcomes for marriage are then considered.

They may not have much choice: patriarchy is still alive and well

'I'll be a postfeminist when society is postpatriarchal' reads a T-shirt marketed by a US feminist group. The evidence is that this may involve quite a wait. As other chapters in this book show, masculinist attitudes remain firmly entrenched in Australian society. These can be defined as aspects of the belief that what men do is important and constitutes the focus of life; what women do is subsidiary and supportive. While such attitudes have weakened over the last twenty years, they remain robust. Surveys regularly show they are strongest in rural areas; among older people, those of lower education and socio-economic status, and the non-English-speaking born; and, of course, among men rather than women.[12] An interesting example of the first-mentioned factor is Dempsey's account of 'Smalltown', a community in rural Victoria.[13] Smalltown in the 1990s is still 'a man's town' in the old tradition. A high proportion of the men are self-employed, as farmers or small businessmen, and plan to take sons into the business, leaving daughters to move away, or take low-status jobs, or wait for a husband. As wives, they are likely to do a good deal of unpaid work for the business, as well as all or most of the domestic work. Drinking and sports are the men's major leisure pursuits ('more beer consumed per head than in any other centre in the state'),[14] rendering the men frequently unavailable for family activities, and conscripting the wives and girlfriends into money-raising and other unpaid labours in 'ladies' auxiliaries'. Marital roles are well practised before marriage

> A common practice was for young women to drink quietly in the lounge while their boyfriends drank and talked in the nearby bar as long as they chose to. When the young men had finished drinking they departed via the lounge where the young women were waiting. As the men passed they motioned to the women to follow.[15]

In Smalltown, female subordination is buttressed by the fact that outside employment for married women is hard to find, and generally frowned upon as deleterious to the family; although an exception is made where their wages are needed to pay the farm bills and keep the farm viable. Conformity is enforced by gossip and community criticism of the offender, which itself draws on an entrenched belief (by women and men) that women are at fault more than men. One wife (a nurse) told how

> In this community if a kid is in trouble or just has untidy clothes the mother is always blamed. 'It's her fault'. That's my husband's attitude too. He won't take responsibility for Bill [their 18-month-old child]. After a lot of effort I've got his father doing things like taking Bill for a walk . . . but it is not sustained. He sees Bill as my responsibility. He's got most of the town's backing on that.[16]

Of course, you don't have to leave the cities to find patriarchy. While the last twenty years have seen great increases in women's education and employment, men remain overwhelmingly dominant in business, finance, the professions, politics, agriculture and the trades—and their wives fit in with this. A complication here is the frequent discrepancy between attitudes and behaviour. Well-educated urban men tend to have liberal attitudes on social issues, including gender issues. However, as Bittman and Lovejoy found, this does not necessarily mean they are going to be home very much, or translate their attitudes into action when they are. Similarly, blue-collar men with relatively conservative attitudes may in practice engage in a lot of childcare while wives do shift work. Hence surveys of gender attitudes may be quite misleading.[17]

The fact that high achievement in women does not necessarily free them from patriarchal constraints is highlighted by Dennerstein's[18] comparison of 1744 male and female Melbourne medical graduates. She found that the men were more likely than the women to hold specialist postgraduate qualifications, to be in high-status, high-profile jobs, to have published research papers, and to be married. The women were more likely to be single, divorced or separated, to be childless, and to be in lower-status jobs. Those who were married were likely to have married male doctors, to work part-time, and to name 'compatibility with husband's career preferences' as a reason for their own career paths.

The men's involvement in home activities and childcare was low, at all ages. They were clear that being male had been a major career advantage; and those who did not see themselves as having a commitment to the family were the most successful of all. The least career success was reported by married women for whom compatibility with the husband's career was an important consideration.

Similar outcomes have been described for other occupational groups.[19] Dennerstein concludes that gender ideologies have up till now resulted in massive career underachievement by highly trained women; but she notes fewer differences between younger doctors, implying a generational change. Rosemary Pringle (in this volume) also suggests generational differences in other occupations that may reduce the effect of gender ideologies in the future. Nevertheless, it is clear that for the moment patriarchy is alive and well, and that women often accede to it through the mechanisms described by Bittman and Lovejoy, Komter and Ferree.

It may not seem important: women value men for reasons other than equality

This line of argument holds that women do not mind, or even enjoy, taking over major domestic responsibility, because it is for other qualities that they value their men. The importance of a man being a good breadwinner may have declined somewhat, but many inegalitarian couples seem happy together. So there must be other qualities of men that are more important than willingness to share household work. What are these other qualities? A substantial literature has described the characteristics that attract men to women, usually with a strong emphasis on physical attributes. Rather less has been said about the male characteristics that engage women. They appear to be more varied: life and literature present many examples that are not obviously paralleled by male-to-female attachments. For example: despite their many differences,

Woody Allen and J. F. Kennedy are both reputed to have been outstandingly attractive to women; Simone de Beauvoir devoted herself to Jean-Paul Sartre, who, despite the fact he was 'undersized, wall-eyed and shabbily dressed, had no more difficulty finding women to sleep with than Cary Grant', in the words of de Beauvoir's disgruntled American lover.[20] Playwright John Osborne managed to attract and marry four more women after he had pilloried his first wife in the smash hit *Room at the Top*.[21] Even Hitler was loved by Eva Braun.

Just this short list suggests that qualities other than egalitarianism—power, good looks, fame, intellectual dynamism come to mind—are powerful attractors that can more than compensate (at least for a time) for lack of balance within a relationship. The inequality may itself be an attraction, especially if the partner is perceived as devoted to higher pursuits—artistic, political, scientific or other. De Beauvoir, for example, so admired Sartre that she was prepared to vet all his writings, cosset him, tolerate his infidelities, and even procure younger women for him when his fancy turned in that direction (which it often did).[22]

Two qualifications need to be borne in mind. Firstly, the qualities that attract women to men may not be the same as the qualities that maintain attraction. All but the last of Osborne's wives eventually gave up on him, and even de Beauvoir finally cooled somewhat towards Sartre. Secondly, men of power and authority have generally been considered attractive to women, because the women have had little ability to acquire these qualities themselves, and can only experience them vicariously, through a man. The last twenty years' opening up of achievement opportunities should therefore have lessened the attraction of dominant men. There appears to be no evidence either way regarding this proposition.

They put up with it because they believe that men have different interests from women

Many people believe that men and women have by nature different interests. One major strand of feminist thinking also holds that over and above the power of gender ideologies in shaping us, there is an essential difference between the psychology of men and women.[23] The basic difference seen is that men are more interested in activities, achievement and dominance, and women in relationships, caring and other engagements associated with their biological heritage as potential mothers. In pursuing these ends, they play by different rules.[24] From this point of view, most women are unwise to model their careers and lives on those of men. After all, a job is only a job and, if demanding, can force the abandonment of all sorts of activities (including motherhood) that women find rewarding; playing by the boys' rules is inherently frustrating; and in particular, having and raising children is still one of the most rewarding and growth-promoting experiences in life, and requires much time and energy. Constructing one's life in order to make the time and energy available is a serious matter, and given the options currently available, a semi-traditional role combining work and family (as chosen by many of Dennerstein's women doctors) may for the present be the most rational choice.

Theorising the positive aspects of motherhood has not been a strong strand in feminist thinking. In practice, feminists have campaigned energetically for improved children's services, but at the theoretical level they have been more concerned with women's rights to be treated as individuals with interests other than serving the family.[25] This makes a problem for explaining the behaviour of women who both wish to have a child, and do so. This is still the great majority, even though birth rates around the Western world have fallen.[26] Having had a child, most women find it more than they bargained for, but most also voice feelings of strong attachment, fulfilment, personal growth and commitment.[27] As Bittman notes, they also find themselves increasing their hours of household labour by 91 per cent, while their partners stay longer at work. One recent US survey found that many women reported that parenthood had worsened their marriages and felt discouraged and frustrated with their husbands' lack of involvement in parenting and family.[28] Given this constellation of reactions, it is not hard to see some wives concluding that men think in different ways to women, and resigning themselves to a heavy domestic workload in consequence.

Not all women do put up with it: men and women sharing

Some couples have already accepted the principle of sharing, and worked out an egalitarian division of family work. An interesting example is Goodnow and Bowes' study of fifty Sydney couples who agreed to be interviewed jointly.[29] Although generally above-average in socio-economic status, the couples proved to be a mixed group. Some had come from gender-egalitarian backgrounds and had spontaneously recreated this arrangement in the new household. Others had terminated unsatisfactory first marriages and were determined to work out a better relationship second time around. Others, interestingly, had spent long periods in 'traditional' arrangements until some incident had brought about a radical change. One wife—a schoolteacher and mother of three—explained that, in her forties, she began to feel that her workload had become 'all too much'.

> WIFE: I think that I said to Frank that it had to stop. You feel like you are on a merry-go-round. And I thought 'how do I get off this?'. Because I really enjoy teaching and yet I felt it was just everyone getting at you. Apart from that we had added responsibilities . . .
> HUSBAND: You got really upset one day.
> WIFE: And so then we decided that we would do something about it.[30]

Goodnow and Bowes describe a number of characteristics of these families that seemed relevant to their ability to develop a sharing arrangement. Firstly, they were not very concerned about whether tasks were traditionally masculine or feminine, and did not feel threatened by taking on opposite-gender tasks. Secondly, they had the ability to communicate their dissatisfaction and to negotiate change—some more readily than others, but all to some extent. These two important features seem to distinguish these couples from those of Ferree and Bittman and Lovejoy, described earlier.

Some other characteristics also emerged as important. Especially important for wives was some personal experience and/or observation that had provided a standard of what was not tolerable in a relationship. Many of these experiences related to parents:

> When I was a child, the girls were expected to do girls' things. The boys did the boys' things. The girls usually did a lot of work, and had a lot of responsibility. My mother *always* cooked for the boys when they came home from work. The girls, it was assumed that you'd do it for yourself. Now my sisters and I are all capable, but the boys are lazy slobs. I'm consciously trying to change this difference between what boys do and girls do.[31]

In other cases a commitment to feminism, or a radicalising adult experience was central. One wife had once shared a house with three men, one of them her boyfriend.

> It was just me and the guys, and that was a rude awakening. They were incredible. They'd have bathtubs that were green with mould and that kind of stuff. And my partner let me do everything . . .[32]

Among men, a common concomitant of sharing was a conscious commitment to equality and justice. The husband might have taken a long time to perceive that his egalitarian principles had any application to gender, but when the point was made to him, he found it hard to refute. For example, one husband who had been a non-sharer for many years now felt that

> It is just not fair for me to come home and play the traditional male role and then wait for the weekend to do my bit out in the garden. So that is one of the reasons for the way we do things—fairness, equality. You know—what is the male role or the female role?[33]

Goodnow and Bowes are unable to estimate the frequency among Australian couples of the kind of negotiating and sharing that they describe. However, they note that two American studies, one conducted in the 1970s, the other in the 1980s, show a substantial increase over time. Possibly then, the widespread non-sharing displayed in Bittman's Australian study may be in process of change.

Not all women do put up with it: lesbian couples

Second Wave feminism from its inception has included an articulate group who have advocated lesbian relations. They have seen traditional marriage as invariably oppressive to women. In addition, since women do most of the emotion work, communication work and domestic work in close relationships, two women will naturally get on better than a woman and a man. This includes sexually, since there will be more understanding of, and willingness to meet, female sexual desires. This point of view has become more popular in Australia since the 1970s, but no figures regarding the proportion of women living in such relationships are available. Research in the area suffers from small volunteer samples, which may not be representative; it has generally found that partnerships are close and intimate, as one might expect from two relationship-oriented people.[34] One US study that compared lesbian and heterosexual women found that unequal power was less of an issue for the former,[35] and others have found the division of labour to be more equal, and sexual communication greater.[36]

Not all women do put up with it: the retreat from marriage

One way to avoid being oppressed by marriage is not to marry, or not to stay married. As we saw earlier, many 1970s feminists (and their predecessors) urged women not to marry. What has happened since?

Figure 23.1 shows that the marriage rate has indeed declined markedly since the late 1960s. Current Australian marriage rates are the lowest in our history, excluding the early settlement period.[37] A decline in the marriage rate can reflect either a delay or an abandonment of marriage by substantial numbers of younger adults, but a steep and continuing decline—as seen in Figure 23.1—is considered sure evidence of movement away from legal marriage. McDonald writes,

> There is absolutely no question that, in the near future, much higher proportions of men and women will not marry at all compared with the boom years of marriage from the 1940s to the mid-1970s.[38]

Figure 23.1 also shows that there is nothing unique about the Australian figures. These run in parallel with those of other Western nations, and somewhat behind, suggesting that a further decline is likely. In the northern and western European countries recent figures show that 40–50 per cent of younger adults may not marry at all.[39] The figures do not, of course, tell us whether it is the women or the men who are reluctant to marry, but the available data suggests that both are marriage-shy.[40]

Figure 23.1 Marriage rates in selected countries, 1960–80.

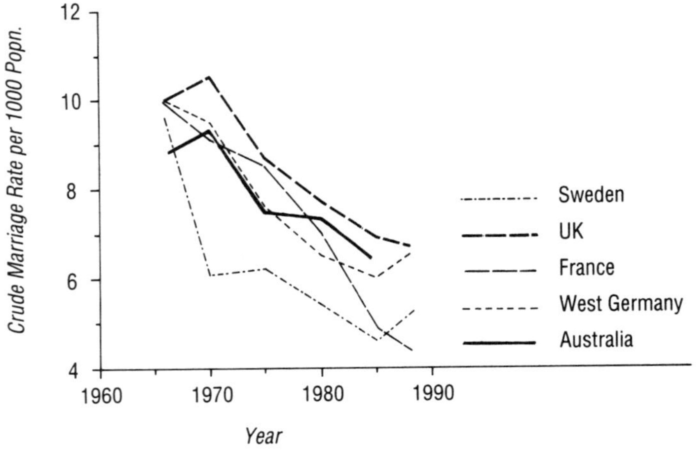

Source: *United Nations Demographic Yearbook*, New York, various edns.

Figure 23.2 Divorce rates in selected countries, 1948–88.

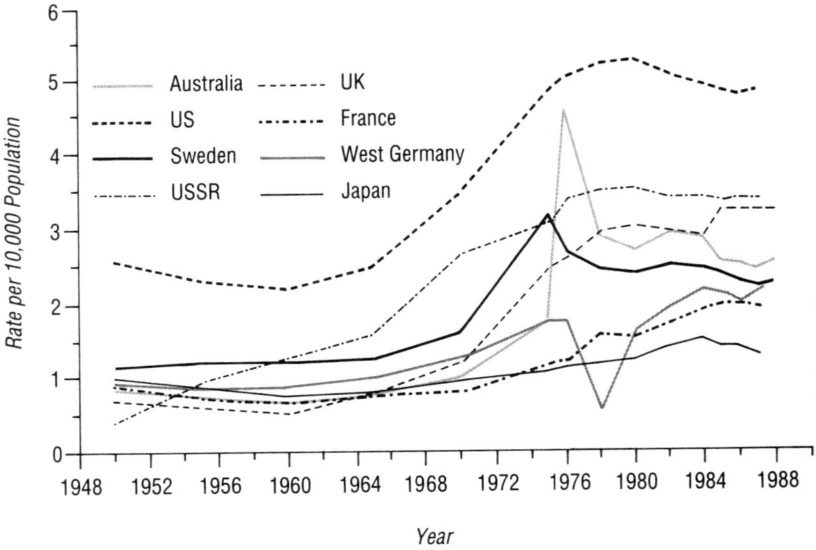

Source: *United Nations Demographic Yearbook*, New York, various ends.

Figure 23.2 show a similar move away from marriage among those who have already sampled it. Again we can see that the Australian divorce figures parallel those of other countries, showing a steady rise from the mid-1960s, escalation in the 1970s, and stabilisation at a high rate in the 1980s, by which time new marriages had declined, reducing the population 'at risk' of divorce. Again also, the Australian move away from marriage is modest so far, compared with that of some other countries. The evidence here is that it is women who are most likely to end a marriage. Husbands and wives agree that some 55–65 per cent of separations are initiated by wives, and a further 2–20 per cent are joint decisions.[41]

Despite the defection from marriage both by those who have experienced it and by those who have not, the majority of Australian women continue to marry (an estimated 75–80 per cent) and the majority of the married stay married (an estimated 60 per cent). Some very rough arithmetic gives a figure for recent cohorts of about one-quarter who never marry, a further quarter who marry and divorce, and one-half who marry and stay married. Twenty years ago the marriage rate for women was about 95 per cent, and the divorce rate very modest. Insofar as the retreat from marriage since the 1970s is initiated by women, it thus clearly represents a significant means of not putting up with marital oppression. (It does not necessarily involve a retreat from parenting: increasing numbers of births—currently between one-fifth and one-quarter in Australia—are ex-nuptial.)

What does it all mean for the future of marriage?

Two important points need to be made. Firstly, retreat from marriage does not mean retreat from living together. During the years that marriage has been declining, couples have been cohabiting in increasing numbers, and some of these units are indistinguishable in commitment and longevity from legal marriages. In general however, this is not the case. De facto units are much more likely to break up than legal marriages, even when children are involved. Glezer found that of unmarried women in Victoria who bore a child in 1984, 45 per cent did so while living with the father; eighteen months later, 20 per cent had split up, compared with only 2 per cent of the married.[42] Scandinavian figures indicate a breakup rate for unmarried parents two to three times higher than the married.[43] Thus, even when de facto living is as common as marriage, it is still a more transient status.

Secondly, the people who choose legal or de facto marriages vary with time and place. Etzler reports that while in older Swedish cohorts it was women of lower socio-economic status who were likely to cohabit (and to bear ex-nuptial children), today this pattern is typical of all social classes.[44] In Australia and the USA, however, cohabitors continue to differ somewhat from the married; typically they are either divorced or separated people, or younger couples with below-average income, job security and job status. They are also usually native-born, live in the cities, and lack religious affiliations.[45] Studies in Australia and the USA have found that, compared to married couples, the cohabiting couples have certain characteristics: they are less committed to their partners, have less contact with their parents, hold less traditional views on social issues, share domestic tasks more, and have more utilitarian attitudes to relationships; once married, they are more likely to divorce.[46] Taking these characteristics together, it appears that when unmarried cohabitation is a minority status it attracts those with lesser commitment both to the partner and to traditional roles. When it becomes a majority status it attracts people of all backgrounds, and commitment to less-than-satisfactory relationships is low overall. This outcome is best exemplified in the northern European countries, where a high rate of union formation and dissolution outside of marriage is accompanied by a high divorce rate among those who do marry.

One explanation of all this sees marriage, like other industries, as having become the subject of deregulation. Until the 1970s marriage was clearly the favoured marital status. Legal, economic, social and religious arrangements all placed the non-married at relative disadvantage. For women, to be unmarried suggested unattractiveness and pathos, or something worse. To be divorced meant shame and poverty. To be married meant social approval, housing subsidies and a built-in breadwinner, even at the cost of some subordination.

Then, quite suddenly, changes in the law, the job market, welfare policy and popular attitudes combined to erode marriage's favoured status. Previously stigmatised alternatives—unmarried cohabitation, serial partnerships, single parenthood, gay and lesbian households, non-residential partnerships and plain singlehood—offered new forms of freedom, and developed a new popularity. Compared with the alternatives, marriage of course retains the advantage of being traditional, respectable, a sign of commitment, and hopefully, a source of emotional security for both partners. However, it has the disadvantage of being seen as the arrangement most likely to push spouses into the old inegalitarian domestic roles.

Since all the evidence is that many women (and men) do not like these roles, it seems likely that in future marriage in Australia may have trouble in retaining even its present market share. Social changes may, of course, return marriage to its previous hegemonic status, but it seems more likely that current trends (e.g. towards more education for girls) will move us more toward the Scandinavian pattern. Any comeback by marriage therefore seems dependent on a widespread move to the sharing patterns described by Goodnow and Bowes.

TWENTY-FOUR

Women's Studies in Australia

Susan Magarey, Lyndall Ryan and Susan Sheridan

The year 1993 marks the twentieth anniversary of the establishment of the first course in Australia which was actually named 'Women's Studies'—at Flinders University in South Australia. This anniversary provides opportunity to consider the development of Women's Studies and its future prospects: the impetus propelling Women's Studies into Australian universities, the structure and organisation of Women's Studies programmes, questions raised by its definitions of itself, and the politics of knowledge in Women's Studies.

Impetus

Women's Studies began as a reflex of a social movement upon the world of learning and scholarship. The exuberant Women's Liberation Movement of the early 1970s, and the more broadly-defined and inclusive Women's Movement since then, has always been an educational movement. Meetings of Women's Liberation groups during the early 1970s in Australia were often engaged in what Italian feminists have, more recently, called the 'theoretical practice of *affidamento* (recognition of, and reliance upon, differences in competence between women)'—informal classrooms.[1] In the later 1970s, feminist discussion groups met to prepare collective research papers on such topics as the impact of technological change on women's work.[2] National conferences on such explicitly political topics as Feminism and Socialism or Women and Labour heard a substantial proportion of scholarly papers. The Women and Labour Conferences, for instance, produced three published collections of articles which remain among the best material available to Women's Studies students in the 1990s.[3] From the energy and the intellectual ferment of such activities developed the demand for Women's Studies within the institutions of higher learning—the universities, colleges of advanced education and institutes of technology.

Definitions

Definitions of Women's Studies are much harder to come by than descriptions. Publications as wide-ranging and comprehensive as Gloria Bowles' and Renate Klein's *Theories of Women's Studies* (1983), Catherine R. Stimpson's report to the Ford Foundation, *Women's Studies in the United States* (1986) and Sneja Gunew's *Feminist Knowledge: Critique and Construct* (1990)[4] all provide historical descriptions rather than definitions. This fact may well reflect both the newness of Women's Studies as a field of intellectual endeavour, and the variety of feminisms deployed and examined in Women's Studies units. It may also reflect, more pragmatically, the difficulties with which Women's Studies has had to grapple to gain even a toe-hold in the institutions of higher learning. These difficulties have meant that Women's Studies has developed a variety of self-definitions in accordance with—or against—the particular structures and cultures of those institutions. There is some common ground, though.

Such common ground is ringingly represented in the preamble to the constitution of the United States National Women's Studies Association, founded in 1977. This asserted that research and teaching in Women's Studies at all educational levels and in all academic and community settings would be not only *about* women, but also *for* women, guided by

> a vision of a world free not only from sexism, but also from racism, class-bias, ageism, heterosexual bias—from all the ideologies and institutions that have consciously or unconsciously oppressed and exploited some for the advantage of others.[5]

Australian feminists involved in Women's Studies might have less faith than those in North America in the power of education to bring about social change,[6] but the NWSA's vision can still be discerned in Australian claims for the political importance of feminists redefining knowledges and knowledge-institutions at the beginning of the 1990s.[7] Accordingly, we have taken that vision as our starting point. We have then gone on to define Women's Studies as a new field of research and teaching which is focused upon women in relation to the worlds that they inhabit and construct. The study of these relationships must include consideration of change over time within any one culture, and also attention to similarities and differences between cultures. This relationship also necessarily includes the critical consideration of the works of the fathers of knowledge and the divisions that they have erected within the academy.

Acceptance of such a definition of Women's Studies raises questions about how Women's Studies relate to other sections of such institutions which define their practice as that of a 'discipline', questions to which we will return. First, though, we offer a sketch of the structures that have developed in Women's Studies in Australian tertiary education.

Structure and Organisation

Contexts

The abolition of fees for university education by the Whitlam Labor government of 1972–5 brought into Australian universities a host of women looking for courses that spoke specifically to them about their place in the world. The conservative Fraser government of 1975–83 did not alter this public provision, but the Hawke Labor government of 1983–92 reintroduced a modified form of fee-paying for tertiary education. This move effectively excluded a significant number of the mature women students who had been flocking to the universities while tertiary education was free. But the same government also passed the *Sex Discrimination Act* of 1983 and the *Affirmative Action Act* of 1986, which compelled universities, for the first time, to look seriously to their appointment and promotion procedures. One result was a small increase in the appointment of women to teaching posts in universities, and in the promotion of women who had been teaching their hearts out for decades in the same institutions without any recognition of their capacities or achievements.

The Hawke government also abolished the binary division between the colleges of advanced education, institutes of technology and the universities, and created a unified national system of tertiary education which included amalgamation of many institutions from previously separate systems.

Such changes undoubtedly reduced the number of 'mature-age women' students, who were demanding Women's Studies courses during the 1970s and early 1980s. But they did also, marginally, increase the number of feminists on the academic staffs of universities, and bring into university cultures some remnants of more adventurous pedagogical approaches to Women's Studies, like those of the first model (see below), sustained in the former colleges of advanced education.

Models

Women's Studies units were first offered in three Australian universities in 1973 and 1974, usually after a series of institutional struggles between feminist faculty and students, on one hand, and curriculum committees, on the other. These units not only reflected the tensions within the Women's Movement about its relationship to the academy and the tensions within the academy about its accommodation to feminism. They also represented distinctive models of the approaches to Women's Studies for the next two decades.

The first model of Women's Studies emerged from the Philosophy Discipline at Flinders University in 1973, when two units named

Women's Studies were given the university's imprimatur. These units broke many of the rules associated with the credentialling of conventional university units. Firstly, they were conceived and planned by a female curriculum committee consisting not only of members of the faculty, but also students intending to enrol in the units, and women in the community who would otherwise have had no involvement with the university. Secondly, the units were offered to students who were not enrolled in the university, as well as those who were. Thirdly, the pedagogical practices within each unit stressed the radical goals of self-management in teaching and assessment; this meant that, in relation to assessment, students who were enrolled would be given the *grade* that they needed in relation to any further units that they needed to take at the university, regardless of the *assessment* of the value of their work. Assessment was carried out collectively by everyone participating in the unit. The coordinator of this programme of Women's Studies was the first academic appointment in the field to be named as such, even though she was both junior (a tutor) and temporary.[8]

From the outset, those involved in establishing these units never intended them to become part of the mainstream university curriculum, in case they lost their revolutionary potential and became disloyal to the Women's Movement. This model of Women's Studies still survives in the vestiges of 'self-management' left in courses that are otherwise dominated by those hierarchical structures that the Flinders units initially set out to challenge, and in the open access policies of the 'Opportunities for Women' courses that Technical and Further Education Colleges have offered throughout Australia since the early 1980s.

The second model was pioneered by Kay Daniels' honours history seminar at the University of Tasmania, 'Women in English Society, 1791–1928'.[9] Daniels offered this unit in a traditional discipline at advanced level, when students could be expected to have learned the traditional methodologies, and the conventional approaches to the study of history. Nevertheless, her unit offered students the opportunity to critique those traditions in the discipline, by drawing attention to the absence of women from mainstream historiography, and by inviting them to suggest ways in which this absence might be addressed.

This unit inspired a small number of feminist academics hiding in universities in other parts of Australia to follow her example. There were criticisms from outside the universities that the political approach represented by such units was inadequate, because they were located within traditional academic disciplines and accepted conventional teaching and assessment practices;[10] despite this, such units have often been the site of intense struggle between feminist and anti-feminist faculty. As became clear from the tussle that erupted from Sydney University into the public arena in 1973 over students' rights to determine the content of their courses, a struggle that had originated in the demand for a unit on Women and Philosophy,[11] such struggles depended crucially upon the support and active engagement of the students.

This model persists both in the traditional universities, and in the former colleges of advanced education and institutes of technology that became universities during the 1980s. Gretchen Poiner's *Report on Women's Studies at Macquarie University* in 1992, for instance, listed no fewer than fourteen units that were not called 'Women's Studies' units, but which could nevertheless have been co-ordinated into a major in Women's Studies.[12] Sometimes such units are denigrated as merely 'additive'; the criticism is that they 'add women to the conventional range of topics' to be considered, much as a cook might add a spice to a stew, but then fail to stir the pot. Such criticisms come from those who maintain that 'it is not possible simply to add women and stir': the minute one stirs, the stew becomes a very different brew. But some such units 'stir' extremely effectively, their students emerging with full-scale critiques of the political assumptions of the other units in the courses that they are taking.

A third model of Women's Studies was signalled with the establishment of an interdisciplinary unit, 'The Political Economy of Women', at Sydney University in 1974, organised and taught by feminist faculty-members from the Departments of Fine Arts, Economics, Economic History and Government.[13] This unit set out to develop feminist critiques of mainstream political economy, itself something of a challenge to mainstream economics; to raise new ways of addressing political economy from feminist perspectives; and to use 'open learning approaches'. This unit is still being taught in the early 1990s, and maintains its challenge to the mainstream disciplines of both economics and political economy. Like all of the earlier models outlined here, though, it relies heavily on the voluntary labour of committed feminist faculty. Units in the second model of Women's Studies have come and gone chiefly because they too depended upon the voluntary efforts of graduate students and junior faculty, who must, in order to win themselves livelihoods, eventually move on.

A fourth model of Women's Studies, which emerged in 1975 at the Australian National University, represented a breakthrough. This was achieved not so much in relation to the revolutionary goals of the initiators of Women's Studies units, but rather, in gaining a permanent place for Women's Studies, in the form of an independently located programme or course of study, in the institutions of higher learning. This model, first established by Ann Curthoys, was subsequently developed with local variations at Deakin, Murdoch, Flinders after 1987, and other places. ANU was also the first university to establish named and tenure-track lectureships in Women's Studies, and a programme of integrated, trans-disciplinary units, with an honours year. Despite a period of shrinking resources and morale during the late 1980s,[14] the ANU programme, like the interdisciplinary unit at Sydney University, and a multitude of other courses in Women's Studies across the country, seems to be on the campus and in the calendar to stay.

Achievements

Much has been achieved in the past two decades.[15] The single Women's Studies course established at Flinders University and taught by a tutor in the Philosophy Discipline twenty years ago is now an autonomous Women's Studies Unit employing two full-time and one half-time senior academics whose positions are *named* posts in Women's Studies. At Sydney University, the Political Economy of Women unit and units on Women and Philosophy which had their origins in the early 1970s are now complemented by a full Women's Studies programme co-ordinated by a Senior Lecturer specifically appointed to do so. Wherever there are feminists willing and able to offer them, 'women and . . .' courses are offered across the board.

There are now no fewer than twenty-four programmes of both undergraduate and postgraduate courses in Women's Studies in Australian universities, and a consortium of seven Women's Research Centres, all also based in universities.[16] The first Professor of Women's Studies was appointed at Griffith University in 1990. The first fully-fledged university department of Women's Studies was formed in 1992, at the University of Adelaide. A professional body, the Australian Women's Studies Association, was established in 1989 and has held annual conferences attracting more than 200 registrations in each year since.

Given such status, it has become important to provide answers to the questions that arise if Women's Studies is to establish itself as a fixture in the academic landscape.

Women's Studies—'field' or 'discipline'?

Women's Studies is variously characterised as 'inter-disciplinary', 'multi-disciplinary' and 'trans-disciplinary'. Such characterisations depend upon current and local definitions of an academic 'discipline', and they are a movable feast, as any historian of anthropology, biochemistry, electrical engineering or geomorphology—for instance—would testify. In some cases, a discipline is thought to be defined by its object of enquiry: physics is concerned with inanimate matter, biology with living organisms, psychology with the behaviours and psychic construction of human individuals (despite all the time it spends with rats). But such definitions do nothing to explain why physics and geology are distinct disciplines, or politics and sociology. Administrative assumptions that equate disciplines with university departments ignore the processes by which both disciplines and departments have been formed, historically, and blur the issue.

The Oxbridge pundits generally agree that a discipline can be defined as a body of knowledge, coupled with characteristic ways of extending knowledge, such characteristic methods including 'an isolable and self-defining repertory of procedures' or 'dependence on some particular kind of test against experience' as the hallmark of a discipline.[17] Such definitions make any inter-disciplinary, multi-disciplinary or trans-disciplinary enquiry a 'field', not a 'form' of knowledge, and suggest that the distinction between the three must be drawn according to differences in methodology, technique and procedure. Accordingly, an *inter-disciplinary* enterprise adopts specific repertories of procedures from the disciplines between which it is developing. A *multi-disciplinary* exercise must be one that draws upon the procedures of a multitude of different disciplines; it will face enormous difficulty in establishing criteria for doing so, and for deciding what to do with whatever results it arrives at. A *trans-disciplinary* enquiry, by contrast, endeavours to transcend a specific range of disciplines, by establishing criteria for assessing and selecting the techniques and procedures from those disciplines that illuminate the questions that participants in the enquiry wish to address, and suggesting ways of finding answers to them.

According to these definitions, Women's Studies is a *field*, not a *form*, of knowledge. Consequently it is not necessary to make claims about specifically feminist methodologies, claims which sometimes fail to distinguish them from several methodologies (such as interactionism or phenomenology) already clearly defined in anthropology and sociology before late-twentieth-century feminism appeared on the public scene.[18] Moreover, the very scope of the challenge that Women's Studies offers to the traditional disciplines requires it at least to aspire to trans-disciplinarity; and its politically critical stance calls into question the assumptions about approach and methodologies of *all* of the disciplines that it draws upon. But since the practice of trans-disciplinarity requires that its practitioners be polymaths, this aspiration has not yet been achieved in any one Women's Studies programme. Team-teaching might be one way of achieving such an intellectual range, but in practice the ideal of team-teaching—that each team-member attend all classes, and learn about the discipline-based assumptions of all of the other team-members—has proved impossible, if not inconceivable, amid the nail-paring economies being imposed on tertiary education institutions. This ideal has not, yet, been achieved.[19]

Apart from these intellectual dimensions of the claim of Women's Studies to autonomy as a trans-disciplinary field of knowledge, questions still remain about whether Women's Studies is becoming or should aspire to become a discipline in the administrative or structural sense of the word. By this we mean that, at a minimum, it would provide a distinctive training for its graduates and would form a professional association of practitioners. Such an association was formed in 1989. We also confront this issue when we argue for the inclusion of Women's Studies as a distinct category of scholarship by the Australian Research Council. Among the disadvantages of such a development into a 'discipline' would be the necessity of 'policing' the boundaries of the field and 'screening' applicants to join it. On the face of it, such activities contradict Women's Studies' vision of itself as anti-disciplinary—and 'discipline' has unfortunate associations to most feminist ears.

The Politics of Knowledge: Challenges for the 1990s

In 1990, Australian feminist historian Judith Allen identified several debates in feminist theory which will need to be pursued simultaneously with the policy and institutional changes that Women's Studies may be called upon to make in the 1990s. She stressed the interrelatedness of the two areas of theory and policy. In relation to theory, she named debates 'around the cluster of postmodernism, feminism, race and the problem of essentialism' as having important consequences for the teaching and research objectives of Women's Studies.[20] These debates have been with us for some time now. At a 1981 Women's Studies conference an anguished exchange followed the presentation of two papers, informed by poststructuralist theories of discourse, which questioned the long-held assumption that a unifying 'common language' was the *sine qua non* of feminism. And the last of the Women and Labour conferences (Brisbane 1984) indelibly marked the advent of Aboriginal women and women of non-English-speaking backgrounds as strong presences on the hitherto 'white' feminist scene. However, the questions raised on these occasions have far-reaching implications which have not yet been fully worked through in Women's Studies, nor indeed in many other areas of feminist endeavour in Australia.

Theoretical debates on postmodernism and feminism, and political struggles on the question of differences *among* women, historically coincided in the 1980s. It is useful to consider them together because they can illuminate one another. Both address centrally questions of difference and essentialism in the way we think and act as 'women'.[21] On the one hand, calling upon women to unite around our shared oppression under patriarchy inevitably involves a suppression of the specific histories and cultural formation of those who belong to the so-called 'minorities'—a suppression of differences of race, ethnicity, class, sexuality, age and so on. On the other hand, to speak of 'women' is to invoke a category constructed by patriarchal or phallocentric discourses which insist upon the mutually-exclusive and hierarchically-ordered dualism of men/women. The category 'women' is defined only by its difference from 'men' and consequently, cannot allow for heterogeneity or difference within it.

The theoretical debate on difference as it applies to the reconceptualising both of women's subjectivities[22] and of feminist politics[23] continues on an international level. Locally, this potent coincidence of theoretical and political rethinking is evident in the development of autonomous feminist groupings of women of non-English-speaking background, and of Aboriginal women (like the presenters of the 'Tiddas Manifesto').[24] While lesbians have always been a significant presence in the women's movement, there has been a recent resurgence of interest in theorising lesbian sexuality and identity, and new political alliances with gay liberation.[25]

Although Australian feminist scholars have always read widely in the work of European and North American feminists, there is a new awareness of the international scope of the Women's Movement, and the research and intellectual debate which accompanies it.[26] This new internationalism will undoubtedly also contribute to significant changes to the face of Women's Studies in Australia, as will the growing cultural diversity of the student population as it includes more visiting overseas students as well as those from the Aboriginal and the newer migrant communities.

In several other areas, the playing out of innovative moves made in feminist theory in the 1980s will become more evident in feminist practice in the 1990s. One example is the process of reconceptualising the sexed female body, which has preoccupied feminist philosophers like Elizabeth Grosz and Moira Gatens: this has important implications for research and policy-making on such issues as reproductive rights, women's health, sexual autonomy and strategies for combating violence against women. A second example is the deconstructive understanding of the way masculinist culture claims its authority through the suppression of its debt to the feminine, an analysis which has been developed through the work of French post-structuralist thinkers like Luce Irigaray. This deconstructive approach already informs much feminist research and writing on the arts, popular culture and cultural history. We might expect its further application to more broadly defined cultural issues such as workplace and union 'cultures', examining issues of sexual harassment and women's work needs, and rethinking such patriarchally defined terms as 'skill' and 'merit'.

Much of the theoretical work on which this new feminism draws is unfamiliar and difficult, but this is nothing new. There has always been a significant engagement with theoretical material in Women's Studies, starting with Marxism in the 1970s, then psychoanalysis, and now this terrain called variously postmodernism, post-structuralism or deconstruction. Many feminists who heaved a sigh of relief at the eventual breaking-off of the long romance between socialist feminists and Marxism must have recoiled in horror when it became clear that some of their sisters were at it ('theory') again. There is still much opposition to feminist engagements with postmodernism, not only because it is thought to be inaccessible but also because it is seen as 'male theory'[27]—despite the fact that some of its major thinkers are feminists.[28]

The place of theory in Women's Studies has always been a contested one, and there is cause for concern that within an increasingly competitive academic climate 'theory' gains a certain fashionably elite status.[29] However, it should also be noted that the role of theory is changing, as feminists develop dialogues among themselves as well as (and as a consequence of) engaging with patriarchal theories: Sue Himmelweit has pointed out that the British Open University Women's Studies programme that she was involved in has recently produced a theory unit that emphasises debates among feminists rather than direct challenges to patriarchal ideas.[30] It is this shift of emphasis which United States feminist theorist Teresa de Lauretis thinks we should see as a sign that feminist theory has come into its own as a critical and self-critical enterprise. This has happened, she maintains, through the interventions in particular of 'women of colour' which made it necessary for any feminist critiques of sociocultural formations to

> question its own relation to or possible complicity with those ideologies, its own heterogeneous body of writing and interpretation, their basic assumptions and terms, and the practices which they enable and from which they emerge.[31]

As one of those practices, Women's Studies has seen much of this necessary and often painful self-questioning. Yet it has also provided a vital space for the emergence of a richer and more constructive understanding of feminism's heterogeneity, its 'differences within itself'. This will be the intellectual challenge for Women's Studies in the 1990s.

Conclusion

The universities have not always been hospitable to Women's Studies. Its presence within the privileged environs of these patriarchal institutions has been conceded grudgingly and with daily rudeness and deskilling. In the Scrooge-like ethos of the recession-ridden 1990s the prospects for Women's Studies within the universities are uncertain. We will, undoubtedly, have to learn—very quickly—the skills that our sisters who have already taken to the market as consultants have learned, and we will encounter a more crowded market than they did. We will learn, of necessity, and again very quickly, to read the market for courses that may attract full-fee-paying overseas students. In the early 1990s, these seem to be postgraduate courses that couple the political vision of Women's Studies with consonant and sympathetic visions in relation to the politics of the environment and of gender and development.

Nevertheless, the student demand for Women's Studies at both undergraduate and postgraduate levels has steadily increased. The survival skills its practitioners have learned over the past twenty years in the academy will stand us in good stead, whatever the changes we face. And Women's Studies, in continuing to be a political undertaking as well as an educational and academic one, will continue to draw much of its strength from the Women's Movement, both locally and internationally.

Notes

1 Australian Feminism since 1970
Ann Curthoys

1 For a fuller discussion, see Ann Curthoys, 'Doing it for Themselves: The Women's Movement Since 1970', in Kay Saunders and Raymond Evans (eds), *Gender Relations in Australia: Domination and Negotiation*, Harcourt, Brace, Jovanovich, Sydney, 1992.

2 See Ann Curthoys, 'Mobilising Dissent: The Later Stages of Protest', in Greg Pemberton (ed.), *Vietnam Remembered*, Weldon, Sydney, 1990; and Ann Curthoys, *For and Against Feminism: A Personal Journey into Feminist Theory and History,* Allen and Unwin, Sydney, 1988. See also John Docker ' "Those Halcyon Days": The Movement of the New Left', in B. Head and J. Walter, *Intellectual Movements and Australian Society*, Oxford University Press, Melbourne, 1988.

3 Susan Eade, 'Now We Are Six: A Plea for Women's Liberation', *Refractory Girl*, 13–14, 1986, pp. 3–11; Sylvia Kinder, 'Adelaide Women's Liberation: The First Five Years, 1969–74', in Margaret Bevege *et al.* (eds), *Worth Her Salt: Women at Work in Australia*, Hale and Iremonger, Sydney, 1982, pp. 367–78; Jocelyn Clarke and Kate White, *Women in Australian Politics*, Fontana/Collins, Sydney, 1983.

4 H. Glezer and J. Mercer, 'Blueprint for a Lobby: the Birth of WEL as a Social Movement', in Henry Mayer (ed.), *Labor to Power: Australia's 1972 Election*, Angus and Robertson, Sydney, 1973.

5 See, for example, M. Smith, 'The Struggle for Women's Health Centres in NSW', *Refractory Girl*, 27, 1984, pp. 3–6.

6 J. McVey, 'The Right to Life Offensive Since 1969', *Hecate*, 9, 1/2, 1983, pp. 35–43; Irene Webley ' "Women Who Want to be Women" in Australian Politics in the 1980s', *ibid.*, pp. 7–24.

7 Susan Sheridan, 'Feminist Knowledge, Women's Liberation, and Women's Studies' in Sneja Gunew (ed.), *Feminist Knowledge: Critique and Construct*, Routledge, London, 1990.

8 'Afterthoughts on "Australianism" ', *Cultural Studies*, 6, 3, October 1992, p. 473.

9 *Ibid.*, p. 471.

10 Moira Gatens, *Feminism and Philosophy: Perspectives on Difference and Equality*, Polity Press, Cambridge, 1991; Elizabeth Grosz, *Sexual Subversions*, Oxford University Press, Melbourne, 1990; Sneja Gunew,

(ed.), *Feminist Knowledge: Critique and Construct*, Routledge, London, 1990; Pauline Johnson, 'Feminism and the Enlightenment', *Radical Philosophy* no. 63, 1993, pp. 3–12; Marilyn Lake, 'A Revolution in the Family: The Challenge and Contradictions of Maternal Citizenship in Australia', in Seth Koven and Sonya Michel (eds), *Mothers of a New World: Maternalist Politics and the Origins of Welfare States*, Routledge, New York, 1993, pp. 378–95; Genevieve Lloyd, *The Man of Reason: 'Male' and 'Female' in Western Philosophy*, University of Minnesota Press, Minneapolis, 1984; Meaghan Morris, *The Pirate's Fiancée*, Verso, London, 1988; Carole Pateman, *The Sexual Contract*, Polity Press, Cambridge, 1988; Sophie Watson (ed.), *Playing the State: Australian Feminist Interventions*, Verso, London, 1990.

11 Hartmann, 'The Unhappy Marriage of Marxism and Feminism: Towards a More Progressive Union', *Capital and Class*, 8, 1976, pp. 1–33.

12 'Marxism and the Man Question', in Judith Allen and Paul Patton (eds), *Beyond Marxism? Interventions After Marx*, Intervention Publications, Sydney, 1983; and *Sex and Secrets: Crimes Involving Australian Women Since 1880*, Oxford University Press, Melbourne, 1990.

13 *Sexual Subversions*, Oxford University Press, Melbourne, 1990; and *Lacan. A Feminist Introduction*, Oxford University Press, Melbourne, 1991.

14 In Allen and Patton, *Beyond Marxism*, p. 148.

15 'Towards a Feminist Philosophy of the Body', in Barbara Caine, Elizabeth Grosz and Marie de Lepervanche (eds), *Crossing Boundaries: Feminisms and the Critiques of Knowledges*, Allen and Unwin, Sydney, 1988, pp. 59–70.

16 'Inscriptions and Body Maps: Representations and the Corporeal', in Terry Threadgold and Anne Cranny-Francis (eds), *Feminine, Masculine, and Representation*, Allen and Unwin, Sydney, 1990, p. 64; see also Vicki Kirby, in this volume.

17 Genevieve Lloyd, *The Man of Reason: 'Male' and 'Female' in Western Philosophy*, University of Minnesota Press, Minneapolis, 1984.

18 'Feminism and the Enlightenment', *Radical Philosophy* 63, 1993, pp. 3–12.

19 *Ibid.*, p. 4.

20 I am indebted for this point to Marian Sawer, who made it during the discussion following my presentation of a paper at the 'Women and the State' symposium at the Australian Historical Association Conference, Canberra, 30 September 1992.

21 *Hecate*, 17,1, 1991, p. 33. See also Gillian Bottomley, in this volume.

22 See Jan Larbalestier, 'The 1980 Women and Labour Conference: Feminism as Myth: Aboriginal Women and the Feminist Encounter', *Refractory Girl*, 20–21, October 1980, pp. 31–9; Fay Gale (ed.), *We Are Bosses Ourselves: The Status and Role of Aboriginal Women Today*, Australian Institute of Aboriginal Studies, Canberra, 1983; Heather Goodall and Jackie Huggins 'Aboriginal Women are Everywhere: Contemporary Struggles', in Saunders and Evans, *Gender Relations in Australia*; Jackie Huggins, in this volume.

23 Bronwen Levy, 'Sisterhood in Trouble: The Fourth Women and Labour Conference, Brisbane, 1984', *Hecate*, 10, 2, 1984, pp. 105–9.

24 I discuss this issue at greater length in 'The Three Body Problem: Feminism and Chaos Theory', *Hecate*, 17, 1, 1991, pp. 14–21; 'Identity Crisis: Colonialism, Nation, and Gender in Australian history', *Gender and History*, 5, 2, 1993, pp. 165–76; and in 'Feminism, Citizenship and National Identity, *Feminist Review*, 44, 1993.

25 Marilyn Lake, 'The Politics of Respectability: Identifying the Masculinist Context', *Historical Studies*, 86, May 1986, pp. 116–31.

26 See John Docker, *The Nervous Nineties*; Bruce Scates, 'Socialism and Feminism, the Case of William Lane: A Reply to Marilyn Lake', *Labour History*, 59, November 1990, pp. 45–58; and Jill Roe, in this volume.

27 Gail Reekie, 'Contesting Australia', in Gillian Whitlock and David Carter (eds), *Images of Australia*, University of Queensland Press, St Lucia, 1992.

28 Kay Saunders, 'All the Women Were White? Some Thoughts on Analysing Race, Class and Gender in Australian History', *Hecate*, 17, 1, 1991, pp. 157–60; Sue Sheridan, ' "Wives and Mothers Like Ourselves, Poor Remnants of a Dying Race": Aborigines in Colonial Women's Writing', in Anna Rutherford (ed.), *Aboriginal Culture Today*, Dangaroo Press, Sydney, 1988, pp. 76–91; Marilyn Lake, Patricia Grimshaw and Andrew May, in this volume; Susan Magarey, Susan Sheridan and Sue Rowley (eds), *Debutante Nation: Feminism Contests the 1890s*, Allen and Unwin, Sydney, 1993.

2 *What Has Nationalism Offered Australian Women?*
Jill Roe

1 Stephen Alomes, *A Nation at Last? The Changing Character of Australian Nationalism, 1888–1988*, Angus and Robertson, Sydney, 1988; Bessie Rischbieth, *March of Australian Women: Fifty Years' Struggle for Equal Citizenship*, Paterson, Brokensha, Perth, 1964.

2 *Nationalism and Sexuality: Respectability and Abnormal Sexuality in Modern Europe*, Howard Fertig, New York, 1985, p. 64. A woman-centred view is Cynthia Enloe, *Bananas, Beaches and Bases: Making Feminist Sense of International Politics*, Pandora, 1989, ch. 3.

3 'Wildman, Alexina Maude', *Australian Dictionary of Biography* (hereafter *ADB*) vol. 12, Melbourne University Press, 1990 (my entry); *Oxford Companion to Australian Literature*, ed. William H. Wilde *et al.*, Oxford University Press, Sydney, 1985, p. 444.

4 Ian Turner (ed.), *The Australian Dream*, Sun Books, Melbourne, 1968, p. 131; W. Pember Reeves, *State Experiments in Australia and New Zealand*, 1902, Macmillan, Melbourne, 1969, ch. III.

5 Audrey Oldfield, *Woman Suffrage in Australia: A Gift or A Struggle?* Cambridge University Press, Melbourne, 1992, p. 212.

6 Arnold Whittick, *Woman into Citizen*, Athenaeum, London, 1979, p. 31; Ian Tyrrell, *Woman's World/Woman's Empire: The Woman's Christian Temperance Union in International Perspective, 1880–1930*, University of North Carolina Press, Chapel Hill and London, 1991, p. 275; Jill Roe,

'Social Policy in the Antipodes', *Australian Historical Studies*, 22, 88, April 1987, p. 395.

7 Miles Franklin to Isabella Goldstein, 13 October 1911, Vida Goldstein Papers, Fawcett Society Library, London.

8 Miles Franklin to Margaret Dreier Robins, nd [13 March 1924] Robins Papers, University of Florida Libraries, Gainesville, Fla.; Marian Sawer and Marian Simms, *A Woman's Place: Women and Politics in Australia*, Allen and Unwin, Sydney, 1984, tables 1.1, 1.2.

9 Helen Jones, 'Mary Lee', Susan Magarey, 'Catherine Spence', Jennifer Mulvaney, 'Vida Goldstein' in Heather Radi (ed.), *200 Australian Women*, Women's Redress Press, Broadway, NSW, 1988.

10 'Booth, Mary', *ADB* vol. 7, 1979 (my entry)

11 *Proposed Soldiers' Club, Sydney*, 22 March 1915, Mitchell Library Pamphlet File; *Camp and Gunroom*, 28 April 1915.

12 *Sydney Morning Herald*, 4, 10 June, 12, 13, 17 August 1915; Soldiers' Club Regulations and letter from Dr Booth 4 April 1917, Anzac Fellowship of Women Records (hereafter AFWR) NLA MS 2864, box 14.

13 *Camp and Gunroom*, 4 August 1915; Centre for Soldiers' Wives and Mothers, *Letter Book*, 1915–17, Mary Booth Papers, Mitchell Library MSS 329/3.

14 Margaret Kentley, 'Historical Notes re the Anzac Fellowship of Women, 1914–1970' 1979, Mitchell Library Doc. 3404; 'At the Gates of Remembrance', undated cutting, Booth Papers.

15 Kentley, 'Historical Notes', AFWR, boxes 11, 12, 19.

16 Letter from Dr Mary Booth, OBE, *To The Electors*, AFWR, box 12; *ADB* vol. 7.

17 Miles Franklin to Margaret Dreier Robins, 6 May 1929, Robins Papers.

18 'Hodge, Margaret', in H. J. Gibbney and Ann G. Smith (comps), *A Biographical Register, 1788–1939*, vol. 1, ANU, 1987; Franklin Papers, Mitchell Library MSS 364/6 (Byles correspondence).

19 Rischbieth, *March of Australian Women*, p. 127.

20 Quoted *ibid.*, p. 59; W. J. Hudson, *Australia and the League of Nations*, Sydney University Press, 1980.

21 Susan Magarey, *Unbridling the Tongues of Women: A Biography of Catherine Helen Spence*, Hale and Iremonger, Sydney, 1985, p. 159; Tyrrell, *Woman's World*, p. 45.

22 Jill Roe, *Beyond Belief: Theosophy in Australia, 1879–1939*, University of NSW Press, 1986, p. 296; *Oxford Companion to Australian Literature*, pp. 570, 597; Rischbieth, *March of Australian Women*, p. 127; Audrey Tate, 'Dale, Marguerite Ludovia', *ADB*, vol. 13, 1993.

23 Nancy Lutton, 'Rischbeith, Bessie Mabel', Marie Munne, 'Nicholls, Elizabeth Webb', *ADB*, vol. 11, 1988; Kate White, 'Bessie Rischbieth, Jessie Street and the End of First-wave Feminism in Australia' in Margaret Bevege *et al.* (eds), *Worth Her Salt: Women at Work in Australia,* Hale and Iremonger, Sydney, 1982, p. 321; 'Bennett, Emily', *ADB*, vol. 13 1993 (my entry); Rischbieth, *March of Australian Women*, pp. 60, 133–5. The Rome delegation consisted of Mrs G. F. Giblin (Tas.), Dr Eleanor Allan (SA), Dr Renfrey Morris, Mrs Emily Bennett, Miss George,

Mrs Jamieson Williams JP (NSW), Mrs Elizabeth Clapham, Mrs Joyner JP and Mrs B. M. Rischbieth (WA).

24 Hudson, *Australia*, p. 196; 'Citizenship', *Australian Encyclopedia*, 3rd rev. edn, 1979, vol. 2; Jessie Street, *Documents and Essays*, ed. Heather Radi, Women's Redress Press, Broadway, NSW, 1990, pp. 122, 208.

3 Women in Europe and Australia
Gisela Kaplan

I wish gratefully to acknowledge the research assistance on this chapter by Dr Gail Reekie, now ARC Research Fellow, Research School of Social Sciences, Australian National University, Canberra.

1 Judith Allen, 'Contextualising Late Nineteenth-Century Feminism: Problems and Comparisons', *Journal of the Canadian Historical Association*, 1, 1990, pp. 17–36.

2 Donald Denoon, 'The Isolation of Australia History', *Historical Studies*, 22, 87, 1986, p. 253.

3 Dennis Altman, 'The Personal is Political: Social Movements and Cultural Change', in Brian Head and James Walter (eds), *Intellectual Movements and Australian Society*, Oxford University Press, Melbourne, 1988.

4 Allen, 'Contextualising Feminism', p. 17.

5 Gisela Kaplan, *Contemporary Western European Feminism*, Allen and Unwin, Sydney, University College of London Press, London, New York University Press, 1992.

6 *Ibid.*

7 'A Short History of Feminism, 1970–1984', in *For and Against Feminism: A Personal Journey into Feminist Theory and History*, Allen and Unwin, Sydney, 1988, pp. 79–94. 'Equal Pay, a Family Wage or Both: Women Workers, Feminists and Unionists in Australia since 1945' in Barbara Caine, E. A. Grosz and Marie de Lepervanche (eds), *Crossing Boundaries: Feminisms and the Critique of Knowledges*, Allen and Unwin, Sydney, 1988.

8 'Gender, Class and the Women's Movements in Australia 1890–1980', in N. Grieve and A. Burns (eds), *Australian Women: New Feminist Perspectives*, Oxford University Press, Melbourne, 1980, p. 23; and cf. M. Dixson, *The Real Matilda: Woman and Identity in Australia, 1788 to the Present*, Penguin, Harmondsworth, 1984, pp. 221–43.

9 Hester Eisenstein, *Gender Shock: Practising Feminism on Two Continents*, Allen and Unwin, Sydney, 1991.

10 Ann Curthoys, 'Equal Pay, a Family Wage or Both: Women Workers, Feminists and Unionists in Australia since 1945' in Caine, Grosz and de Lepervanche, *Crossing Boundaries*; and Patricia Grimshaw, 'Only the Chains Have Changed', in Verity Burgmann and Jenny Lee (eds), *Staining the Wattle: A People's History of Australia*, McPhee Gribble, Melbourne, 1988.

11 Margaret Gardner, 'The "Fateful Meridian": Trade Union Strategies and Women Workers', in *Managing Labour? Essays in the Political Economy of Australian Industrial Relations*, McGraw-Hill, Roseville, NSW, 1986. Cf. also Meredith Burgmann, 'Revolution and Machismo: Women in the

New South Wales Builders Labourers Federation, 1961–75' in E. Windschuttle (ed.), *Women, Class and History: Feminist Perspectives on Australia, 1788–1978*, Fontana/Collins, Melbourne, 1980; Anna Booth and Linda Rubinstein, 'Women in Trade Unions in Australia', in S. Watson (ed.), *Playing the State. Australian Feminist Interventions*, Allen and Unwin, Sydney, 1990.

12 John Logue, 'Social Welfare, Equality, and the Labour Movement in Denmark and Sweden', *Comparative Social Research*, 6, 1983, p. 245.

13 Kaplan, *Contemporary Feminism*, pp. 41–2, 142–3.

14 Sheila Shaver, 'Focusing on Women: From Difference to Equality in the Australian Social Security System', paper presented at the Academy of Social Sciences in Australia, Annual Symposium, ANU, Canberra, 4 November 1992.

15 Venetia Nelson, *A Decade of Change: Women in New South Wales, 1976–1986*, NSW Women's Advisory Council, Sydney, p. 31.

16 Shaver, 'Focusing on women', p. 2.

17 Sar A. Levitan, *Programs in Aid of the Poor*, Johns Hopkins University Press, Baltimore, 1988.

18 Michael Bittman, *Juggling Time: How Australian Families Use Time*, Office of the Status of Women, Department of the Prime Minister and Cabinet, ACT, 1991; Jacqueline J. Goodnow, and Jennifer M. Bowes, *Men, Women and Household Work: New Views, New Ways*, Macquarie University, Sydney, 1992. European studies include *Kvinnor och Män i Norden: Fakta on jämställndheten*, Nordic Council of Ministers, Stockholm, 1988; *Women and Men in Sweden: Equality of the Sexes*, Stockholm Statistics Sweden, 1990.

19 McNeill cit. Betty Olle; Kate McNeill, Sue Jackson, and Pat Morrigan, 'A New Phase for Equal Pay. "Comparable Worth" Signals a New Approach to a Long Campaign', *Australian Society*, January 1986, p. 26.

20 Linda Haas, 'Fathers' Participation in Parental Leave', *Social Change in Sweden*, Swedish Information Service, New York, 1987; Sheila B. Kamerman and Alfred J. Kahn (eds), *Childcare, Parental Leave and the Under 3s: Policy Innovation in Europe*, Greenwood, Westport, 1991; cf. also Carol Bacchi *et al.*, *Shifting Ground: The Dialectics of Work/Care*, Report of an International Colloquium held at the ANU, 6–8 July 1992.

21 K. Törnudd, *Finland and the International Norms of Human Rights*, Martinus Nijhoff, Dordrecht, Boston, Lancaster, 1986, p. 114.

22 Cf. Carolyn T. Adams and Katherine T. Winston, *Mothers at Work: Public Policies in the United States, Sweden and China*, Longman, New York and London, 1980, p. 20; Birgitta Wistrand, *Swedish Women On The Move*, ed. and trans. J. Rosen, Swedish Institute, Stockholm, 1981, p. 33.

23 *Kvinnor och Män*, p. 101.

24 *Women and Men of Europe*, Commission of European Communities, Brussels, 1983.

25 Marian Sawer, 'Women in Australian Parliaments, June 1992' (Table) in *Broadside*, February 1993, no. 12, p. 2.

26 Helen Glezer and Jan Mercer, 'Blueprint for a Lobby: the Birth of WEL as a Social Movement' in H. Mayer (ed.), *Labor to Power: Australia's 1972*

Election, Angus and Robertson, Sydney, 1973; *Broadside*, 12, February 1993.

27 Marian Simms, in this volume.

28 Kaplan, *Contemporary Feminism*, p. 88.

29 Sara Dowse, 'The Women's Movement's Fandango with the State: The Movement's Role in Public Policy since 1972' in C. V. Baldock and B. Cass (eds), *Women, Social Welfare and the State in Australia*, Allen and Unwin, Sydney, 1983; Lesley Lynch, 'Bureaucratic Feminisms: Bossism and Beige Suits' *Refractory Girl*, May 1984, pp. 38–44; Suzanne Franzway, 'With Problems of Their Own: Femocrats and the Welfare State', *Australian Feminist Studies*, 3, Summer 1986; Marian Sawer, *Sisters in Suits: Women and Public Policy in Australia*, Allen and Unwin, Sydney, 1990; Hester Eisenstein, 'Femocrats, Official Feminism and the Uses of Power' [EEO legislation], and Lyndall Ryan, 'Feminism and the Federal Bureaucracy, 1972–1983' both in Sophie Watson (ed.), *Playing the State. Australian Feminist Interventions*, Allen and Unwin, Sydney, 1990. A sceptical account is Anne Summers, 'Mandarins or Missionaries: Women in the Federal Bureaucracy' in Norma Grieve and Ailsa Burns (eds), *Australian Women: New Feminist Perspectives*, Oxford University Press, Melbourne, 1986.

30 Kaplan, *Contemporary Feminism*, p. 227.

31 Drude Dahlerup, (ed.), *The New Women's Movement: Feminism and Political Power in Europe and the USA*, Sage Publications, London, Beverley Hills and Newbury Park, New Delhi, 1986, pp. 225.

32 Jan Pettman, *Living in the Margins: Racism, Sexism and Feminism in Australia*, Allen and Unwin, Sydney, 1992.

33 Interview with German feminist Alice Schwarzer, published in Alice Schwarzer, *Simone de Beauvoir*, Rowohlt Verlag, Reinbeck/Hamburg, 1983.

4 Feminism on Two Continents
Anne Summers

This chapter is adapted from the revised edition of *Damned Whores and God's Police*, Penguin, Ringwood, 1994.

1 Following the 1992 Congressional elections, which accompanied the Presidential elections which saw Bill Clinton elected, and which occurred in what was widely dubbed 'the year of the woman', the numbers increased to 52 (5 Senators and 47 members of the House of Representatives) but US women are still a far smaller proportion of elected federal representatives than is the case in Australia, where women are 12.5 per cent of the federal parliament.

2 See 'Special Report: How Women Will Elect the Next President', *Ms.*, April 1988, pp. 75–9.

3 'The Borking of Bill', *New Republic*, 17 May 1993, p. 7.

4 See Marcia Cohen, *The Sisterhood: The Inside Story of the Women's Movement and the Leaders Who Made It Happen*, Fawcett Columbine, New York, 1989, pp. 310–11.

5 *Ibid.*, pp. 336–7.
6 See, for instance, the anthologies edited by Robin Morgan: *Sisterhood is Powerful*, Vintage, New York, 1970, and *Sisterhood is Global*, Anchor Books, New York, 1984.
7 'On the Road', *Ms.*, May–June 1993, p. 1.
8 In 1991, during a Senate Judiciary Committee confirmation hearing to review the suitability of Clarence Thomas to be appointed to the US Supreme Court, allegations were brought forth that he had, many years before, sexually harassed Anita Hill, another lawyer and a colleague at the Equal Opportunity Commission where they both worked at the time. Professor Hill's and Mr Thomas's testimony to the committee—where she outlined the allegations and he staunchly denied them—were televised live in the United States and gave the issue of sexual harassment an instant national profile.

5 Living across Difference
Gill Bottomley

1 For a more comprehensive overview, see M. de Lepervanche, 'Holding It All Together: Multiculturalism, Nationalism, Women and the State in Australia', *International Review of Sociology*, 2, 1991, pp 73–96; J. Pettman, *Living in the Margins*, Allen and Unwin, Sydney, 1992.
2 J. I. Martin, *Refugee Settlers*, ANU Press Canberra, 1965; E. Cox, *et al.*, *We Cannot Talk Our Rights*, NSW Council of Social Services Sydney, 1975; R. Huber, *From Pasta to Pavlova* University of Queensland Press, St Lucia, 1977; G. Bottomley, *After the Odyssey*, University of Queensland Press, St Lucia, 1979.
3 G. Bottomley, 'Some Greek Sex Roles: Ideals, Expectations and Action in Australia and Greece', *Australia and New Zealand Journal of Sociology* 10, 1, 1974, pp. 8–16; G. Bottomley, 'Migrant Women', in J. Mercer (ed.), *The Other Half*, Penguin, Harmondsworth, 1975.
4 D. Storer (ed.), *But I Wouldn't Want My Wife to Work Here*, Centre for Urban Research and Action, Melbourne, 1975; S. Nord, *Migrant Women Workers: These Are Your Rights*, South Coast Labour Council, Wollongong, 1984.
5 C. Alcorso, *Newly Arrived Immigrant Women in the Workforce,* Centre for Multicultural Studies, Wollongong, 1989; Centre for Working Women, *Women Outworkers*, Footscray, Vic., 1986.
6 M. de Lepervanche, 'Racism and Sexism in Australian National Life' in M. de Lepervanche and G. Bottomley (eds), *The Cultural Construction of Race*, Sydney Studies in Society and Culture, 1988.
7 J. Zubrzycki 'Immigration and the Family in a Multicultural Australia', Meredith Memorial Lecture, La Trobe University, 1978.
8 G. Bottomley and M. de Lepervanche (eds) *Ethnicity, Class and Gender in Australia*, Allen and Unwin, Sydney, 1984.
9 Jeannie Martin, 'Non-English Speaking Women: Production and Social Reproduction' in Bottomley and de Lepervanche, *Ethnicity, Class and Gender.*

10 G. Bottomley, 'Women on the Move: Migration and Feminism' in *ibid.*
11 G. Bottomley, M. de Lepervanche and J. Martin (eds), *Intersexions: Gender/Class/Culture/Ethnicity*, Allen and Unwin, Sydney, 1991.
12 Cambridge University Press, 1988, p. 106.
13 K. Herne, J. Travaglia and E. Weiss (eds), *Who Do You Think You Are?*, Women's Redress Press, Sydney, 1992.
14 Verso, London.
15 E. Erikson, *Identity: Youth and Crisis*, Faber and Faber, London, 1968.
16 *Etrangers á nous-mêmes*, Fayard, Paris, 1988; and in S. Clarke and K. Hulley, 'An Interview with Julia Kristeva', *Discourse*, 13, 1, 1990–1, pp. 149–80.
17 Gish Jen, *Typical American*, Houghton Mifflin, Boston, 1991.
18 P. Bourdieu, (tr. Richard Nice) *The Logic of Practice*, Polity Press, Cambridge, 1990.
19 'Appropriating Bourdieu', *New Literary History* 22, 4, Autumn 1991, pp. 1017–49.
20 D. Robbins, *The Work of Pierre Bourdieu*, Open University Press, Buckingham, 1991 p. 112.
21 J. Lechte and G. Bottomley, 'Difference, Postmodernity and Imagery in Multicultural Australia' in G. Clarke, and D. Forbes (eds), *Image, Difference: Multiculturalism, Postmodernism*, Longman, Melbourne, 1993.
22 G. Bottomley, *From Another Place: Migration and the Politics of Culture*, Cambridge University Press, Melbourne, 1992; and 'Culture, Ethnicity and the Politics/Poetics of Representation', *Australia and New Zealand Journal of Sociology* 28, 2, 1992, pp. 208–23.
23 G. Greer, *The Change: Women, Ageing and the Menopause*, Hamish Hamilton, London, 1991; U. Le Guin, 'The space crone', 1976, republished in *Dancing at the Edge of the World*, Paladin, London, 1992.
24 S. Arber and J. Ginn, *Gender and Later Life*, Sage, London, 1991; B. Macdonald and C. Rich, *Look Me in the Eye: Old Women, Ageing and Ageism*, Spinsters Ink, San Francisco, 1983.
25 M. Gatens, 'Corporeal Representation in/and the Body Politic', in R. Diprose and R. Farrell (eds), *Cartographies: Poststructuralism and the Mapping of Bodies and Spaces*, Allen and Unwin, Sydney, 1991.
26 B. Cass, 'The Feminization of Poverty' in B. Caine, E. Grosz and M. de Lepervanche (eds), *Crossing Boundaries: Feminisms and the Critique of Knowledges*, Allen and Unwin, Sydney, 1988.
27 K. Blakemore, 'Does Age Really Matter?' in Blytheway *et al.* (eds), *Becoming and Being Old*, Sage, London, 1989.
28 K. Markides and C. Mindel, *Ageing and Ethnicity*, Sage, London, 1987.

6 Aboriginal Women's Relationship to the White Women's Movement
Jackie Huggins

This article was originally published by Deakin University in 1992, and a segment was also included in my chapter in K. Saunders and K. Evans,

Gender Relations in Australia, Harcourt Brace Jovanovich, Sydney, 1992. Permission to reproduce it here is gratefully acknowledged.

1 B. Sykes, 'Black Women in Australia: A History' in J. Mercer (ed.), *The Other Half: Women in Australian Society*, Penguin, Ringwood, Vic., 1975; L. Watson, 'Black is the Colour of My Soul', and P. Eatock, 'There's a Snake in My Caravan', in J. Scutt (ed.), *Different Lives: Reflections on the Women's Movement and Visions of Its Future*, Penguin, Ringwood, Vic., 1987.

2 M. Burgmann, 'Black Sisterhood: The Situation of Urban Aboriginal Women and their Relationship to the White Women's Movement', *Politics*, 17, 1982, pp. 22–37.

3 E. Williams, 'Aboriginal First, Woman Second'; Watson, 'Black is the Colour'; and Eatock, 'There's a Snake'; all in Scutt, *Different Lives*.

4 J. Huggins, 'Black Women and Women's Liberation', *Hecate*, 13, 1, 1987, pp. 77–82; B. Flick, 'Colonisation and Decolonisation: An Aboriginal Experience' in S. Watson (ed.), *Playing the State: Australian Feminist Interventions*, Allen and Unwin, Sydney, 1990.

5 See Huggins, 'Black Women'.

6 Magabala Books, Broome, WA, 1987.

7 K. Willetts, 'In Search of the Authentic Voice', *Hecate*, 16, 1–2, 1990, p. 167.

8 'Sisterhood?' *Aboriginal History*, 14, 1988, pp. 34–5.

7 Between Old World 'Barbarism' and Stone Age 'Primitivism' *Marilyn Lake*

1 See, amongst others, Pat O'Shane, 'Is There Any Relevance in the Women's Movement for Aboriginal Women?', *Refractory Girl*, 12 September 1976; Cherie Moraga and Gloria Anzaldua (eds), *This Bridge Called My Back: Writings by Radical Women of Color*, New York, 1983; bell hooks, *Ain't I a Woman*, Boston, 1981; Chandra Talpade Mohanty, Ann Russo, and Lourdes Torres (eds), *Third World Women and the Politics of Feminism*, Bloomington, 1991.

2 Aida Hurtado, quoted in Mohanty, Russo and Torres, *Third World Women*, p. 9.

3 See, for example, Bobbi Sykes in R. Rowland, *Women Who Do and Women Who Don't Join the Women's Movement*, London, 1984, pp. 64–5.

4 Rey Chow, 'Violence in the Other Country: Crime as Crisis, Spectacle and Woman' in Mohanty, Russo and Torres, *Third World Women*, p. 83; see also Patricia Borero, 'The Double Burden; A Woman and a Wog' in Jocelynne A. Scutt, *Different Lives*, Ringwood, Vic. 1987, p. 59.

5 Barbara Smith and Beverly Smith, 'Across the Kitchen Table: A Sister to Sister Dialogue' in Moraga and Anzaldua, *This Bridge Called My Back*, p. 122.

6 Vron Ware, *Beyond the Pale: White Woman, Racism and History*, London, 1992, p. 119.

7 'The White Woman's Burden: British Feminists and "The Indian

Woman'', 1865–1915' in Nupur Chaudhuri and M. Strobel (eds), *Western Women and Imperialism: Complicity and Resistance*, Bloomington, 1992, p. 137.

8 Ada A. Holman, 'Primitive Woman', *Lone Hand*, 1 June 1915.

9 'An Open Letter to Mary Daly' in Moraga and Anzaldua, *This Bridge Called My Back*, p. 94.

10 'Under Western Eyes: Feminist Scholarship and Colonial Discourses' in Mohanty, Russo and Torres, *Third World Women*, p. 74.

11 *Gender at the Crossroads of Knowledge: Feminist Anthropology in the Postmodern Era*, Berkeley, 1991, p. 24.

12 'Asian Pacific American Women and Feminism' in Moraga and Anzaldua, *This Bridge Called My Back*, p. 73.

13 'Sister, Black is the Colour of My Soul' in Scutt, *Different Lives*, p. 52.

14 'Introduction' in Mohanty, Russo and Torres, *Third World Women*, p. 10.

15 April 1932, Rischbieth Papers, National Library of Australia, 2004/12.

16 *Ibid.*

17 Heather Radi (ed.) *200 Australian Women*, Women's Redress Press, Sydney, 1989, pp. 128–9, 99–100.

18 Marilyn Lake, 'The Independence of Women and the Brotherhood of Man', *Labour History*, 63, 1992.

19 On primitivist discourse see Marianna Torgovnick, *Gone Primitive: Savage Intellects, Modern Lives*, Chicago University Press, 1990, pp. 8–9; on investigating the constitutive character of whiteness see Catherine Hall, *White, Male and Middle-Class: Explorations in Feminism and History*, Polity, Cambridge, 1992, pp. 20–2.

20 See Burton, 'The White Woman's Burden' for a discussion of British feminists' construction of the 'Indian woman' as a foil against which to gauge their own progress; also Ware, *Beyond the Pale*, especially Part Three.

21 Annual Report, 15 June 1933, Rischbieth Papers, NLA, 2004/12/215.

22 *Ibid.*, 2004/12/327.

23 Eden, Remington and Co., London, 1892, p. 86.

24 See for example Vida Goldstein's report from Colombo (Sri Lanka): 'At this stage of our civilisation the black and white cannot dwell together without both deteriorating', *Woman Voter*, April 1911.

25 Quoted in preface to Angela Booth, *The Payment of Women's Work*, Melbourne, 1919.

26 *Woman Voter*, 26 August 1913.

27 Rischbieth Papers, 2004/4/371.

28 *Labor Call*, 26 June 1919.

29 *Woman Voter*, 13 January 1914.

30 *Ibid.*, 20 March 1914.

31 Mary Bennett to Bessie Rischbieth, 16 November 1934, Rischbieth Papers, 2004/12/-.

32 Mary Bennett, 'The Aboriginal Mother in Western Australia', 1933, Rischbieth Papers, 2004/12/218.

33 Women's Service Guilds, letter to newspaper, Rischbieth Papers 2004/12/56.

34 On her courage see Kay Daniels and Mary Murnane (eds), *Uphill All the Way*, University of Queensland Press, St Lucia, 1980. The Department of Native Affairs attempted to discredit Mary Bennett's activism by referring to her 'ill health' and her 'obsession' with the 'wrongs of the natives'.
35 Mary Bennett, 'The Aboriginal Mother'.
36 Mary Bennett to Bessie Rischbieth, April 1932, Rischbieth Papers, 2004/12.
37 Rischbieth Papers, 2004/12/314.
38 Torgovnick, *Gone Primitive*, p. 102.
39 David Stead to Professor A. P. Elkin, 20 January 1934, Rischbieth Papers, 2004/12/71.
40 *Ibid.*
41 'A Native Policy for Australia', *ibid.*, 2004/12/217.
42 A. O. Neville to Women's Service Guilds, 15 June 1933, Rischbieth Papers, 2004/12/41. The 1905 Western Australian *Aborigines Act* made it a criminal offence for a white man to have sexual relations with an Aboriginal woman. See also Patricia Jacobs, 'Science and Veiled Assumptions: Miscegenation in WA, 1930–37', *Australia Aboriginal Studies*, 2, 1986.
43 'A Native Policy for Australia', Rischbieth Papers, 2004/12/217.
44 Mary Bennett to Bessie Rischbieth, April 1932, Rischbieth Papers, 2004/12.
45 Rischbieth Papers, 2004/12/197; 2004/12/319.
46 Petition for the Half-Castes of Broome, Rischbieth Papers, 2004/12/234.
47 Mary Bennett to Bessie Rischbieth, April 1932, Rischbieth Papers, 2004/12.
48 16 November 1934, *ibid.*

8 'Inducements to the Strong to Be Cruel to the Weak'
Patricia Grimshaw and Andrew May

Jackie Huggins, Vera Mackie, Stuart Macintye, Maila Stivens, Patrick Wolfe, Jo Kijas, Julie Evans, Deb Hull, Adele Murdolo and Katharine Grimshaw read and made comments on this chapter, and we are grateful for their help. The work of Andrew May was in part supported by a grant from the Australian Research Council.

1 Public Record Office of Victoria (PROV), Victorian Public Record Series (VPRS) 4410, Unit 2, Item 52. Edward Parker, Assistant Protector, Northwest District, Periodical Report, 11 April 1840. We have used the word 'Koori' to denote Aborigines in Victoria throughout, except in quotations, and 'Aborigine' for inclusive references.
2 E. S. Parker, *The Aborigines of Australia, A Lecture Delivered at the Mechanics Hall, Melbourne, before the John Knox Young Men's Association on Wednesday, May 10th, 1854*, Melbourne, 1854, p. 15. For a discussion of nineteenth-century racial ideas, see S. J. Gould, *The Mismeasure of Man*, London, 1981, and for a fuller discussion of white Australian ideology, see H. Reynolds, *Frontier: Aborigines, Settlers and Land*, Sydney, 1987, especially chs 4 and 5.

3 *The Aborigines of Victoria: With Notes Relating to the Habits of the Natives of Other Parts of Australia and Tasmania*, 1876: Melbourne, 1972 [1876], vol. 1, p. 95.
4 J. Bonwick, *The Lost Tasmanian Race*, London, 1884.
5 'Multiple Mediations: Feminist Scholarship in the Age of Multinational Reception', *Feminist Review*, 35, pp. 24–41. See also C. T. Mohanty, 'Under Western Eyes: Feminist Scholarship and Colonial Discourses', in C. T. Mohanty, A. Russo, and L. Torres (eds), *Third World Women and the Politics of Feminism*, Bloomington and Indianapolis, 1991, pp. 51–80; G. G. Spivak, *In Other Worlds: Essays in Cultural Politics*, New York, 1987; P. Chatterjee, 'Colonialism, Nationalism and Colonized Women: the Contest in India', *American Ethnologist*, 16, 4, 1989, pp. 622–33; S. Perera, *Reaches of Empire*, New York, 1991. For a discussion of European women's intercultural encounters with indigenous women in colonial situations see: N. Chaudhuri and M. Strobel (eds), *Western Women and Imperialism: Complicity and Resistance*, Bloomington and Indianapolis, 1992; V. Ware, *Beyond the Pale: White Women, Racism and History*, London, 1992.
6 See E. Said, *Orientalism: Western Conceptions of the Orient*, London, 1978.
7 For discussion of Europeans' interaction with Kooris in nineteenth-century Victoria, see: J Critchett, *A Distant Field of Murder: Western District Frontiers, 1834–1848*, Melbourne, 1990; B. Attwood, *The Making of the Aborigines*, Sydney, 1989; M. F. Christie, *Aborigines in Colonial Victoria, 1835–86*, Sydney, 1979. For discussion of gender and the colonial frontier in the Australian colonies see A. McGrath, 'The White Man's Looking Glass: Aboriginal–Colonial Gender Relations at Port Jackson', *Australian Historical Studies*, 21, 95, pp. 189–206; M. A. Jebb and A. Haebich, 'Across the Great Divide: Gender Relations on Australian Frontiers', in K. Saunders and R. Evans (eds), *Gender Relations in Australia: Domination and Negotiation*, Sydney, 1992, pp. 20–41; and J. Huggins and T. Blake, 'Protection or Persecution? Gender Relations in the Era of Racial Segregation', in *ibid.*, pp. 42–58; D. Barwick, 'Coranderrk and Cumeroogunga: Pioneers and Policy', in T. Epstein and D. Penny (eds), *Opportunity and Response: Case Studies in Economic Development*, London, 1972; M. Tonkinson, 'Sisterhood or Aboriginal Servitude? Black Women and White Women on the Australian Frontier', *Aboriginal History*, 12, 1, pp. 27–40.
8 E. M. Curr, *Recollections of Squatting in Victoria*, 1883: Melbourne, 1965; C. J. Griffith, *The Present State and Prospects of the Port Phillip District of New South Wales*, Dublin, 1845; G. H. Haydon, *Five Years' Experience in Australia Felix*, Exeter and London, 1846.
9 R. B. Smyth, *The Aborigines of Victoria*, 2 vols, Melbourne and London, 1878; L. Fison and A. W. Howitt, *Kamilaroi and Kurnai*, London, 1880; E. M. Curr, *The Australian Race*, 4 vols, Melbourne, 1886–7. See P. Carter, *The Road to Botany Bay*, London, 1987.
10 G. Presland (ed.), 'Journals of G. A. Robinson, May to August 1841', *Records of the Victorian Archaeological Survey*, no. 11, 1980, Department of Conservation, Melbourne, p. 103.
11 *Ibid.*, p. 51.

12 *Ibid.*, p. 19.
13 *Ibid.*
14 *Ibid.*, p. 27.
15 *Ibid.*, p. 51.
16 *Ibid.*, p. 43.
17 *Ibid.*, p. 129.
18 *Ibid.*, p. 36.
19 *Ibid.*, p. 77.
20 *Ibid.*, p. 75.
21 PROV, VPRS 4410, Unit 2, Item 52, Edward Parker, Assistant Protector, Northwest District, Periodical Report, 11 April 1840.
22 PROV, VPRS 4410, Unit 2, Item 61, Edward Parker, Quarterly Journal, 1 March–31 May 1842.
23 PROV, VPRS 4410, Unit 2, Item 47, James Dredge, Assistant Protector Northeast District, Report for the period 1 July 1839–29 February 1840.
24 PROV, VPRS 4410, Unit 3, Item 67, William Thomas, Report, 7 November 1840.
25 PROV, VPRS 12, Unit 3, Item 10, W. B. Wilmot, 17 August 1842.
26 PROV, VPRS 4410, Unit 2, Item 62, Edward Parker.
27 *Ibid.*
28 PROV, VPRS 4410, Unit 3, Item 67, William Thomas, Report, 7 November 1840.
29 PROV, VPRS 4410, Unit 2, Item 47, James Dredge.
30 *Recollections of Squatting in Victoria*, pp. 52–3. See also C. Twomey, 'Understanding the Aboriginal: The Language of Control in Early Victoria', B. A. Hons Thesis, History Department, University of Melbourne, 1989.
31 For overviews see: F. Merlan, 'Gender in Aboriginal Society: A Review', in R. M. Berndt and R. Tonkinson (eds), *Social Anthropology and Australian Aboriginal Studies*, Canberra, 1988, pp. 15–76; N. M. Williams and L. Jolly, 'From Time Immemorial? Gender Relations in Aboriginal Societies Before "White Contact" ', in Saunders and Evans, *Gender Relations in Australia*, pp. 9–19. For a discussion of earlier twentieth-century anthropologists see R. Rohrlich-Leavitt *et al.*, 'Aboriginal Woman: Male and Female Anthropological Perspectives', in R. Reiter (ed.), *Toward an Anthropology of Women*, New York and London, 1975, pp. 110–26. See also F. Gale (ed.), *Woman's Role in Aboriginal Society*, Canberra, 1970.
32 W. Thomas, 'Brief Remarks on the Aborigines of Victoria, 1838–9', La Trobe Library, Victoria, MS 7838, p. 10.
33 *Report of the Select Committee of the Legislative Council on the Aborigines, together with the Proceedings of Committee, Minutes of Evidence and Appendices, Victorian Parliamentary Papers*, 1858–9, p. 236.
34 J. C. Symons, *Life of the Rev. Daniel James Draper*, Melbourne, 1870, p. 356.
35 *The Aborigines of Victoria*, p. 46.
36 *Ibid.*, p. 76.
37 *Five Years' Experience in Australia Felix*, vol. 2, p. 43.

38 PROV, VPRS 4410, Unit 4, Item 96, William Thomas, Quarterly Report, 1 March 1847.
39 *The Aborigines of Australia*, p. 22.
40 *Ibid.*, p. 23.
41 Haydon, *Five Years' Experience in Australia Felix*, p. 43.
42 PROV, VPRS 4410, Unit 2, Item 60, Edward Parker, Quarterly Journal, 1 December 1841–28 February 1842, entry for 19 February.
43 H. E. A. Meyer, *Manners and Customs of the Aborigines of the Encounter Bay Tribe, South Australia*, in Smyth, *The Aborigines of Victoria*, p. 85 note.
44 T. L. Mitchell, *Three Expeditions into the Interior of Eastern Australia*, 1838, *ibid.*
45 PROV, VPRS 4410, Unit 2, Item 47, James Dredge.
46 *Five Years' Experience in Australia Felix*, p. 43.
47 *Ibid.*, p. 41.
48 *The Aborigines of Victoria*, p. xxi.
49 Parker, *The Aborigines of Australia*, p. 23.
50 Smyth, *The Aborigines of Victoria*, p. 98.
51 *Five Years' Experience in Australia Felix*, p. 42.
52 See A. S. Wohl, 'Social Explorations Among the London Poor: Theatre or Laboratory?', *Revue Française de Civilisation Britannique*, 6, 2, 1991, pp. 76–97.
53 C. Griffith, *The Present State and Prospects of the Port Phillip District . . .*, p. 148.
54 *The Aborigines of Australia*, p. 8.
55 *Five Years' Experience of Australia Felix*, p. 27.
56 *Brief Remarks . . .*, pp. 43–4.
57 Fison and Howitt, *Kamilaroi and Kurnai*, p. 212.
58 C. Paclt, *Wide World Travels of Cenek Paclt: Incidents and Experiences, on his Travels in America, Australia, New Zealand and South Africa*, trans. Olga B. M. Riha, John Oxley Library, Brisbane, [first published 1888], La Trobe Library of Victoria, MS 10249, p. 17.
59 Smyth, *The Aborigines of Victoria*, p. 138.
60 PROV, VPRS 2896, Unit 3, B1859/2707, William Thomas, 25 May 1859.
61 PROV, VPRS 2210, Unit 3, Item 67, William Thomas, 7 November 1840.
62 Presland, 'Journals of G. A. Robinson, May to August 1841', p. 103.
63 PROV, VPRS 4410, Unit 3, Item 78, William Thomas, 1 December 1843.
64 *Passim* in PROV, VPRS 10, Unit 3, Registered inward correspondence to the Superintendent Port Phillip District relating to Aboriginal Affairs, and VPRS 11, Unit 7, Unregistered inward correspondence to the Chief Protector of Aborgines; VPRS 2896, Unit 1, Registered inward correspondence to the Superintendent Port Phillip District from W. Thomas and E. S. Parker.

9 A Narrative on the Limits of Theory
Philipa Rothfield

I would like to thank Rose Rothfield, Norma Grieve and Ekaterine Zarbos for their comments on an earlier draft, and Liz Grosz for her comments on the paper whose ashes formed the basis for this chapter.

1 The first piece is published as 'Alternative Epistemologies, Politics and Feminism', *Social Analysis*, 30, December 1991, pp. 54–67. The second piece was to form the basis of this chapter.

2 For a critique of the universalist practices of feminist theory and a discussion of what is at stake in their abandonment see N. Fraser and L. Nicholson, 'Social Criticism without Philosophy: An Encounter between Feminism and Postmodernism', in L. Nicholson (ed.), *Feminism/Postmodernism*, Routledge, London and New York, 1990, pp. 19–38.

3 To explain, a totalising theory is one which *exclusively* covers an entire field. It leaves no space for any alternatives. For further discussion of the way in which totalisation can be a problem for feminism, see P. Rothfield, 'Alternative Epistemologies', and for a discussion of the will to totalise in relation to social and political discourse, see P. Patton, 'Marxism and Beyond: Strategies of Reterritorialisation', in C. Nelson and L. Grossberg (eds), *Marxism and the Interpretation of Culture*, University of Illinois Press, Urbana and Chicago, 1988, pp. 123–39.

4 'Situated Knowledges: The Science Question in Feminism and the Privilege of Partial Perspective', *Feminist Studies*, 14, 3, 1988, pp. 575–99.

5 Haraway's response to the ubiquity of 'the God's-eye view' is to propose that knowledge is always *situated*. She argues that in virtue of being situated, the subject of knowledge is never able to claim 360-degree vision, nor is able to exempt him/herself from any complicity in relation to that field of knowledge.

6 There is a real struggle involved for a group to find the symbolic, discursive and political means to represent itself. In 'Can the Subaltern Speak?', in Nelson and Grossberg, *Marxism and the Interpretation of Culture*, pp. 271–313, Spivak asks whether it is possible for an Indian subproletarian woman to make herself heard. Somewhat more optimistically, but in a parallel fashion, Melucci details the ways in which social movements are able to develop the symbolic means to represent themselves, and indeed, have to in order to articulate their politics: A. Melucci, 'Social Movements and the Democratisation of Everyday Life', in J. Keane (ed.), *Civil Society and the State*, Verso, London, 1988, pp. 245–60. By way of example, Second Wave feminism was clearly involved in a struggle to give meaning to some of the concerns that Betty Freidan in the 1950s could only call 'The Problem with no Name': B. Freidan, *The Feminine Mystique*, Dell Books, New York, 1963.

7 The asymmetry exists because one lot does the speaking whilst another lot are spoken for. Trinh makes the more subtle point that to speak for oneself requires the words (the theoretical means) to say it, and that a dominant form of discourse may not provide such a means: Trinh T. Minh-ha, *Woman, Native, Other, Writing, Postcoloniality, and Feminism*, Indiana University Press, Bloomington and Indianapolis, 1989, p. 80. After all, feminism has had to develop its own terms of analysis. This requirement applies to each step towards self-representation. Complications also arise in relation to the kind of language within which

representation occurs: is there an onus upon the dominated to make themselves understood in the 'language of the oppressor'?

8 Jean-François Lyotard, *The Postmodern Condition: A Report on Knowledge*, trans. G. Bennington and B. Massumi, University of Minnesota Press, Minneapolis, 1984.

9 See Nicholson, *Feminism/Postmodernism*.

10 See A. Yeatman, 'The Epistemological Politics of Postmodern Feminist Theorising', *Social Semiotics*, 1, 1990, pp. 30–49, and J. Flax, 'Postmodernism and Gender Relations in Feminist Theory', *Signs*, 12, 4, 1987, pp. 621–43, for two positive views on the possibilities of an alliance between feminism and postmodernism; and see Di Stephano, 'Dilemmas of Difference: Feminism, Modernity, and Postmodernism' in Nicholson, *Feminism/Postmodernism*, pp. 63–82, for a more cautious appraisal. See M. Morris, *The Pirate's Fiancée: Feminism, Reading, Postmodernism*, Verso, London, 1988, for a discussion of feminism and postmodernism that refuses to put the two fields in separate camps. Morris puts questions of postmodernism *within* certain feminist works as a means to resist the assumption that postmodern theory originates as an exclusively male domain with feminism as its other. Also see N. Richard's 'Postmodernism and the Periphery', *Third Text: Third World Perspectives on Contemporary Art and Culture*, 2, pp. 5–12, whose discussion on postmodernism and difference is framed from 'the perspective of cultures marginalised by the hegemonic structures of international discourse', p. 5. See also S. Gunew, 'PMT (Post Modernist Tensions): Reading for (Multi)Cultural Difference', in S. Gunew and K. O. Longley (eds), *Striking Chords*, Allen and Unwin, Sydney, 1992, pp. 36–46, for a valuable discussion of the tensions within postmodernism for postcolonial and multicultural notions of representation, identity and culture.

11 Thanks to Dipesh Chakrabarty for the turn of phrase, forced universal.

12 'On the Logic of Pluralist Feminism', in C. Card (ed.), *Feminist Ethics*, University Press of Kansas, 1991, p. 41.

13 Shambala Publications, Berkeley, 1973.

14 Monty Python's *The Life of Brian* provides a nice illustration of this point where Judith rushes in to tell a meeting of the revolutionary Peoples' Front of Judea that Brian is being crucified. The response from their leader, Reg (John Cleese), was to table the remark, move a motion 'that there be immediate action', and then do nothing.

15 I find it interesting to think about the ways in which harm can be addressed within academic writing. The tendency of theory is towards abstraction, rendering the concrete important only as a basis upon which to build theory, and from which to generalise. Harm can thereby feature within academic work, and be ignored at the same time. In more empirically oriented studies, the documentation of underprivilege can be used in the context of a broader political struggle, especially where suffering has hitherto been 'invisible'. But here also, the need to develop statistical data, ideal types and generalised scenarios can also leave the domain of the specific. There is no answer to this inertial pull towards generality, for the specific has both importance and limitations.

16 This relates to the point made earlier regarding the distinction between a

theoretical acknowledgement of responsibility, and a more concrete acknowledgement.

17 Trinh writes of the shared responsibility to develop an understanding of difference, Trinh, *Woman, Native, Other*, p. 85.

18 For example, Yeatman, 'Epistemological Politics'.

19 J. Gallop, *Reading Lacan*, Cornell University Press, Ithaca and New York, 1985, p. 20.

20 Nor do white feminists necessarily have the right to speak on behalf of all other white feminists. This depends upon how a particular category is constituted, who is able to speak for whom, and about what. For a discussion of category politics, that is, of the social and political movements which organise around questions of identity (e.g. gay, lesbian) see J. Pettman and H. Meekosha, 'Beyond Category Politics', *Hecate*, 17, 2, 1991, pp. 75–92.

21 It is not necessarily easy to determine whether one does have the support to speak on behalf of a group or even to represent its concerns. Conversely, there are times when one has an obligation to 'speak out' on questions of social and political justice. By drawing a distinction between individualistic and communitarian notions of authority, I do not assume that in practice one can easily determine the source, nature or extent of one's authority. This is sometimes argued in terms of whether a person is 'really' representative of a particular community. It is an open question who is to say whether an individual is so authorised. It is also an issue what constitutes a community in any given context.

22 Perhaps I should distinguish between speaking and writing here. Speaking is more immediate. It has an audience who can respond at the time of delivery. Any response to writing will always involve a degree of deferral. It is hoped that the discussion (below) of the relation between theory and practice as a relay can inform the ways in which deferral operates around the event of writing and its accountability.

23 In 'Intellectuals and Power', a conversation between Deleuze and Foucault, in M. Foucault, *Language, Counter-Memory: Practice, Selected Interviews and Other Writings*, Cornell University Press, Ithaca, 1977, p. 206.

24 'Black Women and Women's Liberation', in S. Gunew (ed.), *A Reader in Feminist Knowledge*, Routledge, London and New York, 1991, pp. 6–12.

25 *Ibid.*, pp. 7–8. Huggins' work underlines the role which class analysis continues to have in relation to race/domination. Class analysis, whilst not a total perspective, reminds us that the division of labour, material conditions, relations of production and the organisation of work are critical when it comes to racist oppression.

26 *Ibid.*, p. 11.

27 'Multiculturalism and Feminism', in G. Bottomley, M. de Lepervanche and J. Martin (eds), *Intersexions: Gender/Class/Culture/Ethnicity*, Allen and Unwin, Sydney, 1991, p. 126.

28 'Cultural Identity and Cinematic Representation', *Framework*, 36, 1989, p. 72.

29 Thanks to Chris Healy for this point.

30 Penguin, Harmondsworth, 1978.

31 Since my identity consists of many more elements than my being an Australian Jew, this can only be one aspect of my speaking position. This is also to ignore the ways in which elements of subjectivity may well exist in tension with each other; in other words, subjectivity's more problematic, incomplete aspects. In a sense, identity is a provisional matter. It is the coherent face of something far less whole which could be called subjectivity. I refer to identity to explore questions of privilege and domination not to assert its coherence nor necessarily the commensurability of its constituent parts. (See following discussion of de Lauretis.)
32 *The Facts: A Novelist's Autobiography*, Penguin, Harmondsworth, 1988.
33 'Imagined community' is a term developed in B. Anderson, *Imagined Communities: Reflections on the Origin and Spread of Nationalism*, Verso, London, 1983.
34 'The New Historicism: Political Commitment and the Postmodern Critic', in S. Harasym (ed.), *The Post-Colonial Critic: Gayatri Chakravorty Spivak*, Routledge, London and New York, 1990, p. 157.
35 Perhaps I ought not assume that other ethnic groups are necessarily coherent. This would depend upon historical factors such as migration, the qualities which constitute a particular form of ethnicity, and its varieties of forms of membership.
36 See M. Gilbert, *Atlas of Jewish History*, Steimatzky, Jerusalem, Tel Aviv and Haifa, 1976.
37 The Jewish Secular Humanist Society writes on these matters, and holds workshops on intermarriage, and secular Bar and Bat Mitzvahs.
38 The Gilgul Theatre put on two productions of *The Dybbuk*, one in late 1991, and one in early 1992. The production gained the 1991 Green Room Award.
39 'Cultural Identity', p. 72.
40 T. de Lauretis, 'Displacing Hegemonic Discourses: Reflections on Feminist Theory in the 1980's', *Inscriptions*, 3/4, 1988, pp. 127–44.
41 *Ibid.*, p. 136, original emphasis.
42 *Ibid.* See also T. de Lauretis, 'Feminist Studies/Critical Studies: Issues, Terms, and Contexts', in T. de Lauretis (ed.), *Feminist Studies/Critical Studies*, Macmillan, London, 1986, pp. 1–19.
43 G. Spivak refers to these two senses in relation to the notion of representation, in 'Can the Subaltern Speak?'
44 *Woman, Native, Other*, p. 80.

10 Viral Identities: Feminisms and Postmodernisms
Vicki Kirby

1 For shorthand convenience, I am collapsing the differences between post-structuralism and postmodernism. For a helpful introduction to some of these debates, see A. Huyssen, 'Mapping the Postmodern' in *After the Great Divide: Modernism, Mass Culture, Postmodernism*, Indiana, 1986; J. Rajchman, 'Postmodernism in a Nominalist Frame: The Emergence and Diffusion of a Cultural Category', *Flash Art*, 137, 1987, pp. 49–51;

K. Silverman, *The Subject of Semiotics*, Oxford, 1983; H. Foster (ed.), *The Anti-Aesthetic: Essays on Postmodern Culture*, Bay Press, 1986; B. Wallis (ed.), *Art after Modernism: Rethinking Representation*, New Museum of Contemporary Art, 1984; H. Klotz, *The History of Postmodern Architecture*, MIT, 1988; M. Benedikt (ed.), *Cyberspace: First Steps*, MIT, 1992.

2 On the historical specificity of sex/sexuality, see especially M. Foucault, *The History of Sexuality*, vol. 1: *An Introduction*, Vintage, 1980; and T. Lacqueur, *Making Sex: Body and Gender from the Greeks to Freud*, Harvard, 1990.

3 For examples of this type of thinking, see F. Jameson, 'Postmodernism or the Cultural Logic of Capitalism', *New Left Review*, 146, 1984, pp. 53–92; J. Habermas, 'Modernity—An Incomplete Project' in Foster *The Anti-Aesthetic*; B. Christian, 'The Race for Theory', *Feminist Studies*, 14, 1, 1988, pp. 67–79; F. E. Mascia-Lees, P. Sharpe, and C. Ballerino Cohen, 'The Postmodernist Turn in Anthropology: Cautions from a Feminist Perspective', *Signs*, 15, 1, 1989, pp. 7–33; P. Johnson, 'From Virginia Woolf to the Post-Moderns: Developments in a Feminist Aesthetic', *Radical Philosophy*, 45, 1987, pp. 23–30.

4 See, for example, G. Lloyd, 'Concluding Remarks', especially p. 105, in *The Man of Reason: 'Male' and 'Female' in Western Philosophy*, Minnesota, 1984.

5 See, for example, S. Faludi, *Backlash: The Undeclared War against American Women*, Crown, 1991.

6 See, for example, A. Game and R. Pringle, *Gender at Work*, Allen and Unwin, 1983; and V. Schultz, 'Women "Before" the Law: Judicial Stories about Women, Work and Sex Segregation on the Job' in J. Butler and J. W. Scott (eds), *Feminists Theorize the Political,* Routledge, 1992.

7 See N. Jay, 'Gender and Dichotomy', *Feminist Studies*, 7, 1, 1981, pp. 38–56; and E. Gross, 'Derrida, Irigaray and Deconstruction', *Leftwright/Intervention*, 20, 1989, pp. 70–81.

8 The perceptual flip/flop that turns figure into ground and then back again is not, of course, possible when translated into man/woman. The ground, or absence of the figure, is mutable but *always* feminised. This unfair exchange illustrates why equity politics, which is organised around undeclared exclusions and debts that favour maleness, must inevitably fail to deliver its promise to women.

9 For a sophisticated analysis of identity through a discussion of the ambiguities of the frame, see J. Derrida, 'The Parergon' in *The Truth in Painting*, Chicago, 1987.

10 There is not space here to offer an extended commentary on the relationship between feminism and psychoanalysis, except to acknowledge the important pioneering work of such women as Juliet Mitchell, Jacqueline Rose, Jane Gallop, Laura Mulvey and Mary Kelly, among others. The significance of these feminist interventions lies in their ability to discover the pertinence of psychoanalysis as a theory which can offer some explanatory insights into how the political asymmetries of sexual difference are produced. They were able to argue that the description of this process need not be read prescriptively. More recent postmodern

accounts would include L. Irigaray, *Speculum of the Other Woman*, especially 'The Blind Spot of an Old Dream of Symmetry', Cornell, 1985; S. Kofman, *The Enigma of Woman: Woman in Freud's Writings*, Cornell, 1985; E. Grosz, *Jacques Lacan: A Feminist Introduction*, Allen and Unwin, 1990. Also intertwined with these contributions is a recognition of the political usefulness of psychoanalysis to an understanding of the construction of cultural difference.

11 See for example, E. Said, 'Representing the Colonized: Anthropology's Interlocutors', *Critical Inquiry*, 15, 2, 1989, pp. 205–25; J. Fabian, *Time and the Other: How Anthropology Makes its Object*, Columbia, 1983; S. Price, *Primitive Art in Civilised Places*, Chicago, 1989.

12 See for example, V. Kirby, 'On the Cutting Edge: Feminism and Anthropology', *Australian Feminist Studies*, 8, 1989, pp. 1–24; 'Corporeographies', *Inscriptions: Journal for the Critique of Colonial Discourse*, 5, 1989, pp. 103–19; C. Talpade Mohanty, 'Under Western Eyes: Feminist Scholarship and Colonial Discourses', *Boundary 2*, 2/3, 1984, pp. 333–58; L. Mani, 'The Construction of Women as Tradition in Early Nineteenth-Century Bengal', *Cultural Critique*, 7, 1987, pp. 119–56; G. C. Spivak, *In Other Worlds: Essays in Cultural Politics*, Methuen 1987.

13 See P. Foss, 'Theatrum Nondum Cognitorum', in P. Botsman, C. Burns and P. Hutchings (eds), *The Foreign Bodies Papers*, Local Consumption Papers, 1981, pp. 15–38.

14 There is a rapidly expanding body of work that addresses these issues. For a good introduction, see J. Clifford and G. Marcus (eds), *Writing Culture: The Poetics and Politics of Ethnography*, California, 1986; and R. Ferguson, *et al.* (eds), *Out There: Marginalization and Contemporary Cultures*, MIT, 1990.

15 The discussion that follows attempts to problematise the desire for pluralism, where the claim is made that universalising knowledges can be called to account by a battery of local, situated knowledges. For an example of this claim, see D. Haraway, 'Situated Knowledges: The Science Question in Feminism and the Privilege of Partial Perspective' in *Simians, Cyborgs, and Women: The Reinvention of Nature*, Routledge, 1991.

16 The beginnings of this history are interestingly discussed in 'Relations of Theory: Meaghan Morris Talks with Stephen Muecke' in D. Carter (ed.), *Outside the Book: Contemporary Essays on Literary Periodicals*, Local Consumption Papers, 1991. Two other important publications from this period are P. Foss and M. Morris (eds), *Language, Sexuality and Subversion*, Feral Publications, 1978; and M. Morris and P. Patton (eds), *Michel Foucault: Power, Truth, Strategy*, Feral Publications, 1979.

17 A. Freadman, cited in M. Morris, *The Pirate's Fiancée: Feminism, Reading, Postmodernism*, Verso, 1988, p. 3.

11 The Gendering of Knowledge
Maila Stivens

This is a revised version of a chapter, 'The Gendering of Anthropological Knowledge: More Thoughts on the Awkward Relationship between Feminism and Anthropology', which was published in *Studies in Gender: Essays in Honour of Norma Grieve*, Committee for Gender Studies, University of Melbourne, Parkville, 1992.

1 See M. Strathern, 'Dislodging a World View: Challenge and Counter Challenge in the Relationship Between Feminism and Anthropology', *Australian Feminist Studies*, 1, 1, 1985, pp. 1–25; and 'An Awkward Relationship: The Case of Feminism and Anthropology', *Signs*, 12, 2, 1987, pp. 276–92; H. Moore, *Feminism and Anthropology*, Basil Blackwell, Oxford, 1988; Micaela di Leonardo (ed.), *Gender at the Crossroads of Knowledge*, University of California Press, Berkeley, 1991; and L. Abu-Lughod, 'Writing Against Culture', in R. Fox (ed.), *Recapturing Anthropology*, School of American Research Press, Santa Fe, 1991.

2 Cf. Abu-Lughod, 'Writing Against Culture'.

3 There is no satisfactory alternative term for the problematic 'Third World' that does not privilege the West as the 'centre'; the 'West' continues to act as a central reference point.

4 L. Nencel and P. Pels (eds), *Constructing Knowledge*, Sage, London, 1991, p. 8.

5 For example, the editorial board of the journal *Critique of Anthropology*, of which I was a member, saw some tension in the 1970s over the mainly masculinist cast of the French structural Marxist thought heavily represented in the journal at that point.

6 Nencel and Pels, *Constructing Knowledge*.

7 Variously and loosely labelled the New Ethnography, the postmodernist and/or literary turns in anthropology, a number of approaches have developed, marked by increasing reflexivity (with debates about the ethnography as merely one text among texts, its hegemonic authority to describe the 'truth' denied), and a privileging of the 'cultural' in explaining social phenomena. What the 'culture' being invoked actually refers to is highly contested, however, and many critics are worried by the reification and essentialisation of the concept in much of this work. See G. Smith, 'Writing for the Real', *Critique of Anthropology*, 11, 3, 1991, pp. 213–32; F. E. Mascia-Lees *et al.*, 'The Post-modern Turn in Anthropology', *Signs*, 15, 1, 1989; R. Keesing, 'Asian Cultures?', *Asian Studies Review*, 15, 2, 1991, pp. 43–50; and J. Friedman, 'Further Notes on the Adventures of Phallus in Blunderland', in Nencel and Pels, *Constructing Knowledge*, pp. 95–113.

8 E.g. the writings of Homi Bhabha and Gayatri Spivak, among others.

9 Nencel and Pels, *Constructing Knowledge*, argue that within much of the New Ethnography anthropological authority is contested, 'simultaneously reaffirmed and denied by a process of inscribing oneself and writing off others' (p. 17). They are suggesting, therefore, that the apparent 'post-modern' turn in anthropology in fact appears to be little more than a way of dressing up the long-term practices of ethnography, in particular (positivist) claims to describe a 'real' and 'true' 'other' culture, in new clothes.

10 See *ibid.*

11 *Ibid.*

12 See Moore, *Feminism and Anthropology*.
13 E.g. M. Torgovnick, *Gone Primitive: Savage Intellects, Modern Lives*, Chicago University Press, 1990.
14 Bell hooks, *Yearning*, Turnaround Books, Boston, 1991.
15 See Edward Said, 'Intellectuals in the Post-colonial World', *Salmagundi*, 70–71, 1986, for a discussion of the essentialisation of the West in the debates about the post-colonial world.
16 G. E. Marcus and M. J. Fischer, *Anthropology as Cultural Critique*, University of Chicago Press, 1986, p. 135.
17 J. Clifford and G. Marcus, *Writing Culture: The Poetics and Politics of Ethnography*, University of California Press, Berkeley, 1986.
18 See Moore, *Feminism and Anthropology*.
19 *Ibid.*
20 D. Schneider, *A Critique of the Study of Kinship*, University of Michigan, Ann Arbor, 1984.
21 'Social Criticism Without Philosophy', in A. Ross, (ed.), *Universal Abandon? The Politics of Postmodernism*, Edinburgh University Press, 1988.
22 'Postmodernists seek *inter alia* to develop conceptions of social criticism which do not rely on traditional philosophical underpinnings . . . Writers like Richard Rorty and Jean-François Lyotard begin by arguing that Philosophy with a capital P is no longer a viable or credible enterprise. From here, they go on to claim that philosophy and, by extension, theory more generally, can no longer function to *ground* political and social criticism. With [this] demise of *foundationalism* [my emphasis] comes the demise of the [modern] view that casts philosophy in the role of *founding* discourse vis-à-vis social criticism': *ibid*., p. 85.
23 'What is Feminism?' in J. Mitchell and A. Oakley (eds), *What is Feminism?*, Basil Blackwell, Oxford, 1987, p. 28.
24 S. Bordo, 'Feminism, Postmodernism and Gender-Scepticism', in L. Nicholson, (ed.), *Feminism/Postmodernism*, Routledge, New York, 1990, pp. 133–56.
25 Moore, *Feminism and Anthropology*.
26 C. Ramazanoglu, *Feminism and the Contradictions of Oppression*, Routledge, London, 1988; b. hooks, *Feminist Theory: From Margin to Center*, South End Press, Boston, 1984; M. Lazreg, 'Feminism and Difference: The Perils of Writing as a Woman on Algeria', *Feminist Studies*, 14, 1, 1988, pp. 81–107; C. A. Mohanty, 'Under Western Eyes: Feminist Scholarship and Colonial Discourses', *Feminist Review*, 30, 1988; K. Ram, ' "First" and "Third World" Feminisms: A New Perspective?', *Asian Studies Review*, 15, 1, 1991, pp. 91–6; G. C. Spivak, *In Other Worlds*, Methuen, New York, 1987; C. A. Mohanty, L. Russo and L. Torres (eds), *Third World Women and the Politics of Feminism*, Indiana University Press, Bloomington, 1991; di Leonardo, *Gender at the Crossroads*.
27 For example, M. Barrett and A. Phillips, *Destabilizing Theory: Contemporary Feminist Debates*, Polity, London, 1992.
28 'Feminism and Difference', p. 95.

29 'Intellectuals'.
30 Hooks, *Yearning*; Lazreg, 'Feminism and Difference'; Mohanty, 'Under Western Eyes'; Ram,' "First" and "Third World" Feminisms'; Spivak, *In Other Worlds*; M. Stivens, 'Perspectives on Gender: Problems in Writing about Women in Malaysia', in J. Kahn and F. Loh (eds), *Fragmented Vision: Culture and Politics in Malaysia*, Allen and Unwin, Sydney, 1992.
31 The term 'subalternist' refers to the group of scholars associated with the originally Indian-based journal *Subaltern Studies* (drawing on Gramsci's use of the term 'subaltern'), centred on Ranajit Guha. Their project has generally been seen as aiming to restore the suppressed histories of the dispossessed of the periphery, especially of South Asia.
32 L. Mani, 'Multiple Mediations: Feminist Scholarship in the Age of Multinational Reception', *Feminist Review*, 35, 1990, p. 37.
33 ' "First" and "Third World" Feminisms'.
34 J. Flax, 'Post-modernism and Gender Relations in Feminist Theory', *Signs*, 12, 4, 1987. See also Nicholson, *Feminism/Postmodernism*.
35 See M. Wolf, *A Thrice-Told Tale: Feminism, Postmodernism and Ethnographic Responsibility*, Stanford University Press, 1992.
36 Mascia-Lees *et al.*, 'The Post-modern Turn'.
37 E. Fox-Genovese, 'The Claims of a Common Culture: Gender, Race and the Canon', *Salmagundi* 72, 1986, p. 134; N. Hartsock, 'Foucault on Power: A Theory for Women?' in Nicholson, *Feminism/Postmodernism*.
38 Cf. hooks, *Yearning*; Trinh T. Minh-ha, *Woman, Native, Other*, Indiana University Press, Bloomington, 1989; G. Yudice, 'Marginality and the Ethics of Survival', in A. Ross (ed.), *Universal Abandon? The Politics of Postmodernism*, Edinburgh University Press, 1988.
39 'Feminism and Difference', p. 101.

12 Neo-classical Economics: A Feminist Perspective
Gillian Hewitson

I would like to thank Linda Barclay, Susan Donath, Pauline Kennedy, John King, Marilyn Lake and Gregory Moore for their discussion and comments.
1 The hegemony of NCE includes, but is not limited to, the English-speaking world. Apparent challenges to this hegemony, such as the 'new growth economics', are largely conducted within the neo-classical framework.
2 Gary Becker, the 1992 Nobel Prize winner in economics, has described the breakdown in the boundaries between social sciences as the long-awaited, single 'unified framework for understanding behavior'. See his *The Economic Approach to Human Behavior*, University of Chicago Press, 1976, p. 14.
3 However, there is evidence that a growing number of feminist economists are challenging the discipline. See, for example, Nancy Folbre and Heidi Hartmann, 'The Rhetoric of Self-Interest: Ideology of Gender in Economic Theory', in A. Klamer, D. McCloskey and R. Solow (eds), *The Consequences of Economic Rhetoric*, Cambridge University Press, Cambridge, 1988; Michelle Pujol, *Feminism and Anti-Feminism in Early*

Economic Thought, Edward Elgar, Hants, 1991; and Julie Nelson, 'Gender, Metaphor, and the Definition of Economics', *Economics and Philosophy*, 8, 1992.

4 The NHE applies the 'economic method' to such 'markets' as those for marriage, divorce, and children, and to the division of labour within the household. This essay limits its examination of NHE to Becker's contributions (see his *A Treatise on the Family*, Harvard University Press, Cambridge, Mass, and London, 1981).

5 See Moira Gatens, 'A Critique of the Sex/Gender Distinction', in J. Allen and P. Patton (eds), *Beyond Marxism? Interventions After Marx*, Intervention, Leichhardt, NSW, 1983.

6 A binary opposition consists of one term, A, which is defined in opposition to, and privileged at the expense of another, not-A. Since neither the privileged nor the subordinated term can exist independently, these binary oppositions are an illegitimate splitting of wholes. The construction of these categories is important because of the complex linkages which exist between the privileged terms and masculinity, and the subordinate terms and femininity. See M. Gatens, *Feminism and Philosophy*, Polity, Cambridge, 1991.

7 'Introduction: the Theoretical Subversiveness of Feminism', in C. Pateman and E. Gross (eds), *Feminist Challenges*, Allen and Unwin, Sydney, 1986, p. 7.

8 Gatens, *Feminism*, p. 118.

9 The Austrian school will not be addressed in this essay.

10 Chris Weedon, *Feminist Practice and Poststructuralist Theory*, Basil Blackwell, Oxford and Cambridge, Mass, 1987, p. 21. Strictly, REM need not be literally conscious of his maximising behaviour. Rather, his behaviour is never inconsistent with his consciously-defined needs and wants; he behaves *as if* every action is decided at the conscious level.

11 Clem Tisdell, *Microeconomics*, Wiley, Sydney, 1972, p. 1.

12 Competitive markets are those with many buyers and sellers, none of whom can unilaterally affect market prices. It is the ideal market structure because it maximises the gains from exchange by equating the benefit and cost of a commodity at the margin. It also offers anonymity to market participants, in the sense that profit and utility (happiness) maximising ensures that an individual's personal characteristics are irrelevant.

13 Lionel Robbins, *An Essay on the Nature and Significance of Economic Science*, 2nd edn, Macmillan, London, 1948, p. 16.

14 Market equilibrium is the equality of the quantities demanded and supplied of a good or service. This equality determines the market price. Stable preferences are required for the claim that NCE is a science. If preferences were allowed to vary, hypotheses could not be falsified. In the *Economic Approach*, Becker directs readers interested in 'how preferences have become what they are, and their perhaps slow evolution over time', to the sociobiology literature (p. 14).

15 Mary Hawkesworth, 'The Affirmative Action Debate and Conflicting Conceptions of Individuality', in A. Al-Hibri and M. Simons (eds), *Hypatia Reborn*, Indiana University Press, Bloomingdale and Indianapolis, p. 138. The new institutional economics explains the

institutions themselves as resulting from voluntary interactions of individuals. This interesting development is outside the scope of this essay.

16 Altruism cannot be defined in any other way in NCE since self-interest is assumed to be applicable to all behaviour: individuals never voluntarily reduce their utility. A different conception of the subject is required to make sense of altruism as something other than self-interest. Radically separate individuals define their desires only in terms of their separate selves; others can only be instruments, or means, to serve those self-defined ends.

17 *Economica*, 48, 1981.

18 The fact that these particular historically and socially positioned needs may find an outlet in the commodification of women's bodies is a question which is discussed further below.

19 The paradigmatic REM is the neo-classical version of Robinson Crusoe, who is used as a teaching device in undergraduate courses (see for example Hal Varian, *Intermediate Microeconomics*, 2nd edn, Norton, New York and London, 1990). A feminist discussion of the retentions and departures of the neo-classical version of Robinson Crusoe with respect to the Daniel Defoe novel can be found in the author's 'Deconstructing Robinson Crusoe', unpublished paper, Economics Dept, La Trobe University.

20 Ross Poole, 'Modernity, Rationality and "the Masculine" ', in T. Threadgold and A. Cranny-Francis (eds), *Feminine/Masculine and Representation*, Allen and Unwin, Sydney, 1990, p. 54.

21 *Ibid.*

22 Nancy Hartsock, *Money, Sex and Power*, Northeastern University Press, Boston, 1983, p. 39.

23 'Gender, Metaphor and . . . Economics', p. 116.

24 *Money, Sex and Power*, p. 50.

25 *Feminist Practice*, p. 84.

26 Power relationships of the productive type are also ruled out by the assumptions of NCE. For a discussion of power as productive see Michel Foucault, *Power/Knowledge*, ed. C. Gordon, Pantheon, New York, 1980, and his other works.

27 Becker, *Treatise*, p. 173. We can only assume that, should this marriage break up while the children are young, an *ad hoc* change in the preferences of the previously self-interested 'w' ensures that they survive.

28 In the *Treatise*, Becker argues that women's biological role is not limited to the 'production and feeding of children', since 'they also are biologically committed to the care of children in other, more subtle ways'. His readers are again referred to the sociobiological literature for more information (pp. 21–2).

29 *Ibid.*, pp. 14, 21–3.

30 As Folbre and Hartmann discuss, the relationship between the distribution of power and market incomes within families is eliminated in NHE by the assumption that those who hold power are altruistic.

31 The marginal productivity theory of distribution claims that each productive input is rewarded according to the productivity of the last unit of that input used (the marginal product of that input).

32 *Feminism and Anti-Feminism*, p. 115.
33 'The Just Price, the Free Market, and the Value of Women', *Feminist Studies*, 14, 2, 1988.
34 Barbara Bergmann, 'Does the Market for Women's Labor Need Fixing?', *Journal of Economic Perspectives*, 3, 1, 1989, pp. 44–5.
35 'The Affirmative Action Debate'.
36 Carole Pateman, *The Sexual Contract*, Polity, Cambridge, 1988, p. 131.
37 See for example Anne Phillips and Barbara Taylor,' Sex and Skill', in Feminist Review (ed.), *Waged Work: A Reader*, Virago, London, 1986.
38 Cited in Pujol, *Feminism and Anti-Feminism*, p. 56.
39 *Economic Science*, p. 28.
40 The prostitute is by construction feminine, and the buyer of the prostitute's 'services' is by construction masculine, buying in this case being 'part of the construction of what it means to be a man, part of the contemporary expression of masculine sexuality'. While some men do sell their 'sexual services' (to men), Pateman has noted that 'the sale of men's bodies for homosexual use does not have the same meaning'. See Pateman, *Contract*, p. 199.
41 *Ibid.*, p. 203.
42 *Ibid.*, p. 207.
43 'Sexuality and Power: A Review of Current Work in the History of Sexuality', *Feminist Studies*, 8, 1, 1982, p. 136.
44 Pateman, *Contract*, p. 208.

13 Queer Theory and Its Discontents
Barbara Creed

1 Allan Bérube and Jeffrey Escoffier, 'Queer Nation', *Outlook: National Lesbian and Gay Quarterly*, 11, 1991, p. 12.
2 Historically, 'queer' has been used to apply to male homosexuals. See Bruce Rogers, *The Queen's Vernacular: A Gay Lexicon*, Straight Arrow Books, California, 1972.
3 'Sisters and Queers: The Decentering of Lesbian Feminism', *Socialist Review*, 22, 1, 1992, pp. 33–55.
4 The papers from the conference were published in a volume with the same title, edited by Bad Object-Choice, Bay Press, Seattle, 1991.
5 *Ibid.*, p. 11.
6 *Homosexual Conference Papers: Supplement*, Melbourne, August 1975, pp. 3–4.
7 Angus and Robertson, Melbourne, 1972, p. 101.
8 Pantheon, New York, 1978.
9 See Elizabeth Grosz, *Jacques Lacan: A Feminist Introduction*, Allen and Unwin, Sydney, 1990; Juliet Mitchell, *Psychoanalysis and Feminism*, Penguin, Ringwood, Vic., 1975; Jacques Lacan and the École Freudienne, *Feminine Sexuality*, ed. Juliet Mitchell, and Jacqueline Rose, Macmillan, London, 1982.
10 Laura Mulvey, 'Visual Pleasure and Narrative Cinema', *Visual and Other Pleasures*, Macmillan, London, 1989, pp. 14–26.

11 See the special issue, 'Male Trouble', of *Camera Obscura, A Journal of Feminism and Film Theory*, 17, 1988; and Alice Jardine and Paul Smith (eds), *Men in Feminism*, Methuen, New York and London, 1987.
12 'Defining The Postmodern', *Postmodernism*, ICA Documents 4, London, 1986, p. 6.
13 Barbara Creed, 'From Here to Modernity', *Screen*, 28, 2, 1987, pp. 47–67; also in Joseph Netoli and Linda Hutcheon (eds), *A Postmodern Reader*, State University of New York Press, Albany, 1993, pp. 398–418.
14 *Gynesis: Configurations of Woman and Modernity*, Cornell University Press, Ithaca and London, 1985, p. 25.
15 *Ibid.*, p. 62.
16 *Ibid.*, p. 72–3.
17 Bad Object-Choice, *How Do I Look?; Differences, A Journal of Feminist Cultural Studies—Queer Theory*, 3, 1991; Richard Dyer, *Now You See It: Studies on Lesbian and Gay Film*, Routledge, London, 1990; Diana Fuss, *Inside/Out, Lesbian Theories, Gay Theories*, Routledge, London, 1991.
18 *Sight and Sound*, September 1992, p. 32.
19 'Beyond the Sons of Scorsese', *ibid.*, p. 37.
20 Jayne Melville, '*Seduction the Cruel Woman*', *Square Peg*, 13, 1986, p. 33.
21 For an overview of this debate see: Julia Creet, 'Daughter of the Movement: The Psychodynamics of Lesbian S/M Fantasy, *Differences*, 3, 1991, pp. 135–59.
22 *Ibid.*

14 Unequal Partners
Carmel Shute

A much earlier version of this chapter, *Don't Be Too Polite, Girls: Women, Power and the Australian Trade Union Movement*, was presented to the First World Summit on 'Women and the Many Dimensions of Power', Montreal, Canada, 3–8 June 1990. My many thanks must go to the busy people from academia and the labour and women's movements who took time to be interviewed for this chapter and the earlier paper and/or made comments on it: Helen Creed, Kay McVey, Frances Vinycomb, Heather O'Connor, Irene Bolger, Tricia Carswell, Marilyn Lake, Ann Sherry, Ann Byrne, Dominica Whelan, Brenda Forbath, Louise Connor, Jennie George and Peter Love. All errors of fact or interpretation are, of course, mine.

1 William Lane, *The Workingman's Paradise: An Australian Labour Novel*, Edwards, Dunlop and Co., Brisbane, 1892.
2 'A Question of Time' in David McKnight (ed.), *Moving Left: The Future of Socialism in Australia,* Pluto, Sydney, 1986, pp. 140–1.
3 'Aristocracy of Muscle: Meatworkers, Masculinity and Trade Unionism in the 1950s', MA Thesis, La Trobe University, 1991, p. i.
4 Round-table discussion with Tricia Carswell (then Industrial Officer, Victorian Trades Hall Council), Marilyn Lake (Director, Women's

Studies, La Trobe University) and Dominica Whelan (Industrial Officer, Australian Council of Trade Unions), 14 December 1989.

5 Peter Berry, *Can Unions Survive?*, BWIU, Melbourne, 1989, p. 15.
6 Australian Bureau of Statistics (ABS), Catalogue No. 6325.0.
7 *Sydney Morning Herald*, 26 September 1989.
8 *Age*, 29 September 1989.
9 ABS Catalogue No. 6325.0
10 Awards cover about 85 per cent of Australian workers. They are legal documents covering particular industries or jobs, which set down the wages and conditions applying to those jobs.
11 *Workplace: The ACTU Magazine*, Summer 1992–3, p. 5.
12 Ron Callus *et al.*, *Industrial Relations at Work: The Australian Workplace Industrial Relations Survey and Trade Unionism*, Department of Industrial Relations, AGPS, Canberra, 1991, p. 7.
13 *Sydney Morning Herald*, 27 September 1989.
14 Berry, *Can Unions Survive?*, p. 46.
15 *Daily Telegraph*, 27 September 1989.
16 *Brothers*, Pluto Press, London, 1983, p. 34.
17 Round-table discussion with Louise Connor (then Industrial Officer, Australian Journalists' Association, Federal Office), Brenda Forbath (then Industrial Officer, Hospital Employees' Federation, No. 1, Victorian Branch), Ann Byrne (then Co-ordinator, Labour Research Centre), 4 December 1989.
18 Cited in Fay Gale, 'A Comfortable Kind of Unionism', *Australian Quarterly*, Autumn 1990, p. 19.
19 'The Participation of Women in Five Victorian Unions', MA Thesis, La Trobe University, 1991.
20 Gale, 'A Comfortable Kind', p. 19.
21 Felicity Rafferty, 'Pay Equity: An Industrial Relations Anomaly', *Journal of Industrial Relations*, 33, 1, 1990, p. 17.
22 O'Keefe, *Participation of Women*, p. 14.
23 Martina Nightingale, *Facing the Challenge: Women in Victorian Unions*, Victorian Trades Hall Council, Melbourne, 1991, p. 61.
24 'Women Workers in Western Australia: Their Unions, Industrial Awards and Arbitration', in Margaret Bevege *et al.* (eds), *Worth Her Salt: Women at Work in Australia*, Hale and Iremonger, Sydney, 1982, pp. 358–66.
25 Victorian Trades Hall Council, *Action Plan for Women Workers*, VTHC, Melbourne, September 1987, p. 14.
26 *Participation of Women*, p. 14.
27 Gerald Griffin and John Benson, 'Barriers to Female Membership Participation in Trade Union Activities', *Labour and Industry*, 2, 1, 1989, p. 93.
28 Carol O'Donnell and Phillipa Hall, *Getting Equal: Labour Market Regulation and Women's Work*, Allen and Unwin, Sydney, 1988, p. 38.
29 Santina Bertone and Gerald Griffin, *Immigrant Workers and Trade Unions*, Bureau of Immigration Research, AGPS, Canberra, 1992, pp. 97–100.
30 For an historical perspective, see Brandon Ellem, *In Women's Hands: A History of Clothing Trades Unionism in Australia*, University of NSW Press, Sydney, 1989.

31 Bertone and Griffin, *Immigrant Workers*, pp. 100–1.
32 Ibid., pp. 105, 115.
33 R. Till-Retz, cited in Griffin and Benson, 'Barriers to Female Membership', p. 87.
34 O'Donnell and Hall, *Getting Equal*, p. 147.
35 Interview with Jennie George (then former Vice-President, Australian Council of Trade Unions), 7 December 1989.
36 Nightingale, *Facing the Challenge*, and Barbara Pocock, *Women Count: Women in South Australian Unions*, Centre for Labour Studies, and United Trades and Labor Council of South Australia, 1992.
37 Pocock, *Women Count*, p. 14.
38 Paul Rodan, 'Women and Unionism: The Case of the Victorian Colleges Staff Association', *Journal of Industrial Relations*, 32, 3, 1990, p. 402.
39 Nightingale, *Facing the Challenge*, p. 50.
40 *Ibid.*, p. 32.
41 Figures supplied to the author.
42 *Australian*, 29 September 1989.
43 Anna Stewart Memorial Project, *Evaluation Report: 1984–1989.*
44 Round-table discussion with Connor *et al.*
45 *Ibid.*
46 Interview with Jennie George.
47 Pocock, *Women Count*, p. 32.
48 O'Donnell and Hall, *Getting Equal*, p. 12.
49 Rachel Robertson, 'Enterprise Bargaining: Implications for Women', *Work and People* (Department of Industrial Relations), 14, 2, 1992, p. 19.
50 *Age*, 17 December 1992.

15 Women, Paid Work and Social Policy
Lois Bryson

1 E. Ryan and A. Conlon, *Gentle Invaders: Australian Women at Work*, Penguin, Ringwood, Vic., 1989.
2 D. Deacon, 'Political Arithmetic: The Nineteenth-century Australian Census and the Construction of the Dependent Woman' *Signs* 11, 1, 1985, pp. 27–47. For a feminist commentary and critique of official statistics see M. Waring, *Counting for Nothing: What Men Value and What Women are Worth*, Allen and Unwin, Wellington, 1988.
3 E. Ryan, 'Women in Production in Australia' in N. Grieve and A. Burns (eds), *Australian Women: New Feminist Perspectives*, Oxford University Press, Melbourne, 1986.
4 B. Hiatt, 'Woman the Gatherer' in F. Gale (ed.), *Women's Role in Aboriginal Society*, Australian Institute of Aboriginal Studies, Canberra, 1978, p. 12; see also I. M. White 'Aboriginal Women's Status: a Paradox Resolved', *ibid.*
5 'Women in Production', p. 262.
6 K. Buckley and T. Wheelwright, *No Paradise for Workers*, Oxford University Press, Melbourne, 1988, p. 145.
7 Pat Quiggin, *No Rising Generation: Women and Fertility in Late Nineteenth-Century Australia*, ANU Printing Service, Canberra, 1988, p. 90.

8 'Women in Production', p. 267.
9 *Ibid.*
10 *Ibid.*, p. 265
11 'The Sexual Division of Labour: Theoretical Arguments' in Grieve and Burns, *Australian Women*, p. 331.
12 Ryan, 'Women in Production', p. 266.
13 *Ibid.*
14 'Political Arithmetic', p. 46.
15 Buckley and Wheelwright, *No Paradise*, p. 145.
16 Ryan and Conlon, *Gentle Invaders*, p. 63.
17 See also L. Bryson, 'The Proletarianisation of Women: Gender Justice in Australia?' *Social Justice*, 16, 3, 1989, pp. 87–102.
18 See G. Esping-Andersen, *The Three Worlds of Welfare Capitalism*, Polity Press, Oxford, 1990, Part 2.
19 United Nations Development Programme, *Human Development Report, 1990*, Oxford University Press, New York, 1991.
20 B. Cass, 'Rewards for Women's Work', in J. Goodnow and Carole Pateman (eds), *Women, Social Science and Public Policy*, Allen and Unwin, Sydney, 1985, pp. 67–94.
21 Barbara Hobson, 'No Exit, No Voice: Women's Economic Dependency and the Welfare State', *Acta Sociologica*, 33, 3, 1990, pp. 235–50.
22 G. Russell, *The Changing Role of Fathers?*, University of Queensland Press, St Lucia, 1983.
23 Australian Bureau of Statistics (ABS), *Social Indicators Australia 1992 No. 5*, Catalogue No. 4101.0, Canberra, 1992, p. 207.
24 Erica Fisher, *Occupation: Unemployed Trends in Unemployment in Australia 1970 to 1986*, Research Paper No. 36, Department of Social Security, Canberra, 1987, pp. 14–15.
25 *Ibid.*
26 Women's Bureau, Department of Labour and National Service, *Women and the Workforce No. 6: Fact and Figures*, Government Printer, Melbourne, 1968, p. 11.
27 Women's Bureau, Department of Employment, Education and Training, *Women and Work*, Canberra, 1991, p. 12.
28 C. O'Donnell and P. Hall, *Getting Equal*, Allen and Unwin, Sydney, 1988, p. 7.
29 Fisher, *Occupation*, p. 15.
30 Women's Bureau, *Women and the Workforce*, p. 12; Ministry of Labour, *Labour Market and Labour Policy in 1986*, Stockholm, Swedish Government Printing, 1988.
31 Swedish Institute, *Fact Sheets on Sweden: Equality Between Men and Women*, Stockholm, 1989, p. 2.
32 ABS, *Social Indicators*, p. 120.
33 *Ibid.*, p. 129.
34 Department of Employment, Education and Training, 'Higher Education Series—Female Students', *Update*, 1, 1992, p. 1.
35 *Ibid.*, p. 3.
36 Women's Bureau, *Women and the Workforce*, p. 12.

37 Department of Industrial Relations, *Equal Pay Unit Newsletter*, 2, 1992, p. 6.
38 *Ibid.*, p. 7.
39 *Ibid.*, p. 6.
40 Meredith Burgmann, 'Backlash: Women's Wages on the Skids', *Broadside*, 19 August 1992, p. 10.
41 Women's Bureau, Department of Employment, Education and Training, *Pay Equity: A Survey of Seven OECD Countries*, AGPS, Canberra, 1987, p. 66.
42 Hobson, 'No Exit'.
43 O'Donnell and Hall, *Getting Equal*, p. 1.
44 E. Ryan, 'Enterprise Bargaining', *Wel-Informed*, January 1992, p. 4.
45 *Ibid.*
46 Judy Wajcman and Steve Rosewarne, 'The "Feminisation" of Work', *Australian Society*, 5, 9, 1986, p. 16.
47 See e.g. L. Bryson, 'Women and Management in the Public Sector', *Journal of Public Administration*, XLVI, 3, 1987, pp. 259–72.
48 Wajcman and Rosewarne, 'The "Feminisation" of Work', p. 15.
49 O'Donnell and Hall, *Getting Equal*, p. 20.
50. Women's Bureau, *Women and the Workforce*, p. 12.
51 *Ibid.*, p. 12.
52 Wajcman and Rosewarne, 'The "Feminisation" of Work'; Esping-Andersen, *Three Worlds of Welfare Capitalism.*
53 H. Glezer, *Maternity Leave in Australia: Employees' and Employers' Experiences*, Australian Institute of Family Studies, Melbourne, 1988, pp. 3–4.
54 J. Beggs and B. Chapman, 'The Foregone Earnings From Child-Rearing in Australia', Centre for Policy Research, Research School of Social Sciences, Australian National University, Canberra, 1988, p. 40.
55 L. Bryson, 'Women as Welfare Recipients: Women, Poverty and the State', in Cora Baldock and Bettina Cass (eds), *Women, Social Welfare and the State in Australia*, Allen and Unwin, Sydney, 1983.
56 Minister for Employment Education and Training, Media Release: 'JET: Help for Sole Parents', 23 August 1988.
57 Department of Social Security, *Annual Report 1990–91*, AGPS, Canberra, 1991, pp. 275–6.
58 R. Anstie *et al.*, 'Government Spending on Work-Related Child Care: Some Economic Issues', Discussion Paper No. 191, Centre for Economic Policy Research, Australian National University, Canberra, 1988.
59 O'Donnell and Hall, *Getting Equal*, p. 65.
60 R. Ross, 'Child Care for the 1990s', *Newsletter*, 40, 1991, Social Policy Research Centre, University of New South Wales, p. 2.
61 M. Clyde, 'Social and Economic Demands—A Balancing Act?', paper presented to conference, Ensuring our Futures: The Fabric of Childhood in Australia, 15–17 May, Adelaide, 1991.
62 H. Hernes, 'Women and the Welfare State. The Transition from Private to Public Dependence', in Hariet Holter (ed.), *Patriarchy in a Welfare Society*, Universitetsforlaget, Oslo, 1984.

16 'She' Will Mean 'A Complaining Customer'
Beverley Kingston

Unless otherwise stated, references are to *The Retail Trader*, the Journal of the Retail Traders Association of NSW.

1 August 1962, pp. 13–16.
2 September 1944, pp. 4–5.
3 *Ibid.*
4 January 1958, p. 25.
5 February 1960, p. 47.
6 January 1958, p. 2.
7 January 1958, pp. 4–7.
8 August 1958, p. 11.
9 September 1958, pp. 40, 42.
10 May 1958, p. 5.
11 February 1959, p. 18.
12 Peter Spearritt in Wray Vamplew (ed.), *Australians: Historical Statistics*, Fairfax, Syme, Weldon, Broadway, NSW, 1987, p. 167.
13 February 1964, p. 7.
14 August 1954, p. 33; see also Gail Reekie, 'Market Research and the Post-war Housewife', *Australian Feminist Studies*, 14, Summer 1991, pp. 15–27.
15 March 1958, pp. 5, 48.
16 July 1951, pp 38, 40; December 1955, pp. 23–4.
17 October 1958, p. 28.
18 Julie Rigg, 'The Loneliness of the Long-distance Housewife: Mrs Consumer', in Julie Rigg (ed.), *In Her Own Right: Women of Australia*, Nelson, Melbourne, 1969, p. 143.
19 George Patterson Pty Ltd, *The Patterson Report, or Wooing the Australian Woman*, Melbourne, 1972.

17 Ladies to Women: Women in the Professions
Rosemary Pringle

I should like to thank the following for their assistance with this paper: Colleen Chesterman, Michael Chesterman, Reg Graycar, Cas Lawrence, Jenny Mann, Chris Ronalds, Anna Rubbo, Sophie Watson.

1 D. Weisbrot, *Australian Lawyers*, Longman Cheshire, Melbourne, 1990, p. 62.
2 W. Bottero, 'The Changing Face of the Professions: Gender and Explanations of Women's Entry to Pharmacy', *Work, Employment and Society*, 6, 3, 1992, p. 331.
3 12 October 1992.
4 See *Law Society Journal*, March 1992, and *Sydney Morning Herald*, 28 November 1992.
5 *Sydney Morning Herald*, November 1992.
6 See A. Witz, *Professions and Patriarchy*, Routledge, London, 1992.
7 See for example, S. Anleu, 'Women in the Legal Profession', *Law Institute Journal*, March 1992, pp. 162–5; C. Menkel-Meadow, 'The Comparative

Sociology of Women Lawyers: The "Feminization" of the Legal Profession', *Osgoode Hall Law Journal*, 24, 4, 1986; A. May, 'The Impact of the 1970s Women's Movement on the Position of Women in Architecture in Australia, B. Arch. Hons Thesis, University of Sydney, 1988.

8 Bottero, 'The Changing Face'.

9 Weisbrot, *Australian Lawyers*, p. 86.

10 T. Parsons, 'Professions' in D. Sills (ed.), *Encyclopedia of the Social Sciences*, Macmillan, New York, 1968.

11 E. Freidson, *Professional Dominance: The Social Structure of Medical Care*, Aldine, Chicago, 1970; T. J. Johnson, *Professions and Power*, Macmillan, London, 1972, p. 45; E. Willis, *Medical Dominance*, Allen and Unwin, Sydney, 1983.

12 J. and B. Ehrenreich, 'Medicine and Social Control', in J. Ehrenreich (ed.), *The Cultural Crisis of Modern Medicine*, Monthly Review Press, New York, 1978.

13 *Limits to Medicine*, Penguin, London, 1976.

14 *The Birth of the Clinic*, Tavistock, London, 1973.

15 E. Coroneos, 'Different by Design: Interviews with Constructive Women', *Refractory Girl*, 42, March 1992, pp. 22–3.

16 David Silverman explores this in relation to doctor–patient relations, though unfortunately he ignores gender considerations. See his *Communication and Medical Practice*, Sage, London, 1987.

17 A. Yeatman, 'A Vision for Women's Studies', *Women's Studies Journal* (New Zealand), 8, 1992, pp. 30–46.

18 C. Battersby, *Gender and Genius*, Women's Press, London, 1989.

19 E. Partridge, 'Gender Representation and Architecture', B. Arch. Hons Thesis, University of Sydney, 1992, pp. 6–7.

20 See *Professions and Patriarchy*, pp. 60–4.

21 *Four Corners*, 12 October 1992.

22 M. Belgrave, 'Excerpts', in M. M. Maxwell, *Women Doctors in New Zealand: An Historical Perspective, 1921–1986*, IMS(NZ) Ltd, Auckland 1990, pp. 203–16.

23 This has been theorised by Joan Riviere, 'Womanliness as Masquerade' in V. Burgin, J. Donald and C. Kaplin (eds), *Formations of Fantasy*, Methuen, London, 1986.

24 L. Dennerstein *et al.*, 'Practice Patterns and Family Life—A Survey of Melbourne Medical Graduates', *Medical Journal of Australia*, 151, 2 October 1989, pp. 386–90.

25 J. Lawrence, paper presented to conference, Women's Health into the 21st Century, Brisbane, 29–31 August 1990.

26 *Ibid.*

27 E. Smith, 'Career Aspirations of First-year Medical Students—The NSW Survey', paper presented to conference, Women's Health into the 21st Century, Brisbane, 29–31 August 1990.

28 V. Lawson, 'Women and the Law', *Sydney Morning Herald*, 28 November 1992.

29 Weisbrot, *Australian Lawyers*, p. 88.

30 *Ibid.*, pp. 86–7.

31 *Ibid.*, p. 89.
32 C. Falls, 'Women at the Top: What Price Partnership?', *Law Society Journal*, July 1988, pp. 36–8.
33 'Women, Law and Kids', *Law Society Journal*, March 1992, pp. 51–2.
34 Summarised by J. and D. Rand, 'Women Lawyers: Archetype and Alternatives', *Fordham Law Review*, 57, 1989, pp. 933–4.
35 J. Mathews, 'Women in the Law', *Refractory Girl*, 41, Summer 1991, pp. 27–8.
36 Weisbrot, *Australian Lawyers*, p. 263.
37 *Ibid.*, p. 249.
38 *Ibid.*, pp. 249–51.
39 F. Riley, 'The Future of the Legal Profession in New South Wales', *Law Society Journal*, 30, 9, 1992, pp. 50–3.
40 J. Bielski, 'Women in Engineering in Australia', *Refractory Girl*, 35, May 1990, p. 28.
41 Office of the Status of Women, *National Agenda for Women: Implementation Report*, AGPS, Canberra, 1992, p. 42.

18 The Seductive Allure of EEO
Margaret Thornton

1 I have developed a comprehensive critique in *The Liberal Promise: Anti-Discrimination Legislation in Australia*, Oxford University Press, Melbourne, 1990. See also Gretchen Poiner and Sue Wills, *The Gifthorse: A Critical Look at Equal Employment Opportunity in Australia*, Allen and Unwin, Sydney, 1991; Chris Ronalds, *Affirmative Action and Sex Discrimination: A Handbook on Legal Rights for Women*, Pluto Press, Sydney, 1991.
2 See, for example, Regina Graycar and Jenny Morgan, *The Hidden Gender of Law*, Federation Press, Sydney, 1990; Catharine A. MacKinnon, *Feminism Unmodified: Discourses on Life and Law*, Harvard University Press, Cambridge, Mass., 1987.
3 The constitutionality of the legislation is open to question.
4 *Anti-Discrimination Act 1977* (NSW); *Anti-Discrimination Act 1991* (Qld); *Discrimination Act 1991* (ACT); *Equal Opportunity Act 1984* (SA); *Equal Opportunity Act 1984* (Vic.); *Equal Opportunity Act 1984* (WA).
5 *Teed v. Mount Alexander Hospital* (1987) EOC 92–211 (Vic. Equal Opportunity Board). This complaint followed *Chief General Manager, Department of Health v. Arumugam* (1987) EOC 92–195 (Vic. Supreme Court), per Fullagar J., which established that complainants under the *Equal Opportunity Act 1984* (Vic.) had to prove that the respondent *intended* to discriminate. Other Australian jurisdictions accept that a focus on the *effects* of the discriminatory conduct satisfies the legislative provisions. The intent requirement has since been questioned by the High Court in *Waters v. Public Transport Corporation* (1991) EOC 92–390, per Mason C. J. and Gaudron J. (Deane J. concurring).
6 Clare Burton, 'Equal Opportunity Programmes: Issues in Implementation', in N. Grieve and A. Burns (eds), *Australian Women:*

New Feminist Perspectives, Oxford University Press, Melbourne, 1986, pp. 292–304.

7 *Proudfoot v. Australian Capital Territory Board of Health* (1992) EOC 92–417 (Human Rights and Equal Opportunity Commission).

8 See Dorothy Broom, 'Adding Insult to Injury: The Discrimination Case against Women's Health Centres', *Refractory Girl*, 42, 1992, pp. 62–5 and 'With Friends like These', *Alternative Law Journal,* 17, 1992, pp. 142–3.

9 Sandra Fredman, 'European Community Discrimination Law: A Critique', *Industrial Law Journal*, 21, 1992, pp. 119–34, 129.

10 See Pamela L. Berry, 'Two Faces of Disparate Impact Discrimination', *Fordham Law Review*, 59, 1991, pp. 523–94.

11 *Australian Iron and Steel v. Banovic* (1989) EOC 92–271 (High Court).

12 Michael Newcity, 'The Sociology of Defamation in Australia and the United States', *Texas International Law Journal*, 26, 1991, pp. 1–69.

13 *Equal Opportunity at Work: 112 Studies from Major Australian Companies*, Council for Equal Opportunity in Employment, Melbourne, 1990.

14 *Ibid.*, Book 4, p. 42.

15 *Ibid.*, Book 5, p. 24.

16 This figure has remained virtually constant throughout the century. See National Women's Consultative Council, Labour Research Centre, *Pay Equity for Women in Australia*, AGPS, Canberra, 1990, p. 22.

17 Compare Ann Game, 'Affirmative Action: Liberal Rationality or Challenge to Patriarchy', *Legal Service Bulletin*, 9, 1984, pp. 253–7.

18 See Hester Eisenstein, 'Femocrats, Official Feminism, and the Uses of Power: A Case Study of EEO Implementation in New South Wales, Australia', *Yale Journal of Law and Feminism*, 2, 1989, pp. 51–73.

19 Clare Burton, *The Promise and the Price: The Struggle for Equal Opportunity in Women's Employment*, Allen and Unwin, Sydney, 1991, p. 52ff.

20 Margaret Thornton, 'Hegemonic Masculinity and the Academy' *International Journal of the Sociology of Law*, 17, 1989, pp 115–30. It should nevertheless be noted that the female participation rate in higher education has increased markedly in recent years, and reached 52.7 per cent in 1990. See Australian Bureau of Statistics, *Year Book Australia 1992*, Canberra, 1992, p. 317.

21 'More Power to the Powerful: Corporate Management, Mergers and the Implications for Women of the Reshaping of the "Culture" of Australian Tertiary Education', *Australian Feminist Studies*, 15, 1992, pp. 65–89.

22 See report of a University of Sydney proposal, *Australian*, 4 November 1992.

23 Blackmore, 'More Power to the Powerful', p. 81.

24 Australian women earn 83 per cent of the average weekly ordinary-time earnings of men. The approximate comparable figure for the UK is 74 per cent; the US, 70 per cent; Canada, 65 per cent. See Women's Bureau, Department of Employment, Education and Training, *Pay Equity: A Survey of 7 OECD Countries*, AGPS, Canberra, 1987.

25 I have considered the significance of the public–private dichotomy for EEO in 'The Public/Private Dichotomy: Gendered and Discriminatory', *Journal of Law and Society*, 18, 1991, pp. 448–63.
26 Moira Gatens, *Feminism and Philosophy: Perspectives on Difference and Equality*, Polity Press, Cambridge, 1991; Carole Pateman, *The Disorder of Women: Democracy, Feminism and Political Theory*, Polity Press, Cambridge, 1989.
27 Mary E. Becker, 'Needed in the Nineties: Improved Individual and Structural Remedies for Racial and Sexual Disadvantages in Employment', *Georgetown Law Journal*, 79, 1991, pp. 1659–93, 1667 f.
28 I have elaborated on this point in 'Feminism and the Contradictions of Law Reform', *International Journal of the Sociology of Law*, 19, 1991, pp. 453–474.

19 Provoking Comment
Adrian Howe

1 See especially Carol Smart's analysis of the 'sexed subject' of legal discourse in 'Law's Power, the Sexed Body and Feminist Discourse', *Journal of Law and Society*, 17, 2, 1989, pp 31–49.
2 Victorian Law Reform Commission, *Homicide*, Discussion Paper No. 13, Melbourne, March 1988, para 7.2.
3 *Ibid.*, para. 135.
4 *Ibid.*
5 *Ibid.*, para. 140.
6 *Ibid.*, para. 140 and n. 46.
7 Victorian Law Reform Commission, *Homicide*, Report No. 40, Melbourne, 1991, para. 167.
8 *Ibid.*, para. 178.
9 Victorian Law Reform Commission, *Homicide Prosecutions Study*, Appendix to Report No. 40, Melbourne, October 1991, para. 151.
10 *Ibid.*
11 *Ibid.*, para 154. The fact that this research was not carried out is another unsatisfactory aspect of the *Prosecutions Study*.
12 *Homicide*, Report No. 40, para. 165. The numbers given in this final report are slightly different from those given in the *Prosecutions Study*, where it is claimed that in the 53 cases where males who were presented for murder argued provocation, 21 involved a female victim. Of these, 8 (38.1 per cent) resulted in a murder conviction and 12 (57.1 per cent) resulted in a manslaughter conviction. In contrast, only 5 (15.6 per cent) of the 32 cases involving a male victim resulted in a murder conviction, while manslaughter convictions were obtained in 20 (62.5 per cent) cases with male victims: *Prosecutions Study*, para. 156.
13 *Homicide*, Report No. 40, para. 166. Significantly, the commission adds that an assessment of the fact summaries in the *Prosecutions Study* indicates that heavier sentences for the males were generally appropriate. But these fact summaries do not appear in the published report.
14 *Prosecutions Study*, para. 90. The commission notes that this figure understates domestic homicide as it excludes murder–suicide cases, most

of which fall into the domestic category. Police data indicate that 18 per cent of victims were killed by an offender who then suicided (thus evading trial). Of these cases, 90 per cent were domestic in the period from 1 January 1984 to 30 June 1988: *ibid.*, para. 93. When these cases are included in the calculations, domestic homicide rises to 42 per cent of the total homicides in Victoria: *Homicide*, Report No. 40, n. 6.

15 Feminist research in Australia has 'clearly established the link between domestic violence and homicide and revealed the marital relationship as being potentially the most lethal in our society': Julie Stubbs and Alison Wallace, 'Protecting Victims of Domestic Violence' in Mark Findlay and Russell Hogg (eds), *Understanding Crime and Criminal Justice*, Law Book Company, Sydney, 1988, p. 54.

16 *Prosecutions Study*, para. 157.

17 *Homicide*, Report No. 40, para. 168.

18 *Ibid.*, para. 168 and n. 132.

19 The feminist literature in this field is vast. See for example Julie Tolmie, 'Provocation or Self-Defence for Battered Women Who Kill?' in Stanley Yeo (ed.), *Partial Excuses to Murder*, Federation Press, Sydney, 1991.

20 *Homicide*, Report No. 40, para. 5 and n. 6, and para. 89.

21 *Prosecutions Study*, para. 20 and table 35.

22 Once again the literature is vast but see, for example, Carol Smart, 'Law's Truth, Women's Experience' in Reg Graycar (ed.) *Dissenting Opinions: Feminist Explorations in Law and Society*, Allen and Unwin, Sydney, 1990; and Celia Wells, 'Domestic Violence and Self-defence', *New Law Journal*, 140, 1990, pp. 127.

23 See Tolmie, 'Provocation or Self-Defence'; J. Greene, 'A Provocation Defence for Battered Women Who Kill?', *Adelaide Law Review*, 12, 1989, p. 146; Stella Tarrant, 'Provocation and Self-Defence: A Feminist Perspective', *Legal Service Bulletin*, 15, 4, 1990, p. 147; Jill Radford ' "Womanslaughter": A Licence to Kill? The Killing of Jane Asher' in Phil Scraton (ed.), *Causes for Concern: Questions of Law and Justice*, Penguin, Harmondsworth, 1982.

24 Susan Edwards, ' "Provoking Her Own Demise": From Common Assault to Homicide' in Jalna Hanmer and Mary Maynard (eds), *Women, Violence and Social Control*, Macmillan, London, 1987, pp. 152, 161, 163.

25 *Ibid.*, p. 165.

26 As we shall see, the fact that men sometimes kill men in sexual jealousy cases does not negate the argument that provocation operates in these cases as a deeply sexed excuse.

27 (1672) 86 ER 108.

28 (1707) 84 ER 1107.

29 (1835) 168 ER 1133.

30 (1848) 175 ER 342.

31 (1871) 12 *Cox* 145.

32 For example, David Lanham, 'Provocation and the Requirement of Presence', *Criminal Law Journal*, 13, 1989, p. 133. On the evidence of the case law, the statement that 'a confession of adultery might be thought to be one of the strongest cases of provocation occurring in the absence of

the defendant' rests on a masculinist presumption of a male defendant: *ibid.*, 139. Similarly, the view that 'adultery seems to be an even more severe provocation' than physical blows would not be supported on any feminist reading of cases involving battered women who kill: *ibid.*, 141.

33 *Ibid.*

34 Edwards, ' "Provoking Her Own Demise" ', pp. 164, 166. Consider for example, *R v Duffy* [1949] 1 All ER 932.

35 (1981) 28 SASR 321.

36 *Homicide*, Discussion Paper No. 13, para. 55.

37 Bebe Loff, 'The Axe Murder Case', *Legal Service Bulletin*, 7, 1982, pp. 52, 54. The majority found that when viewed against the background of his sexual violations of his daughters, the victim's actions on the night of his death could have constituted provocation. However, the court declined to confer a verdict of manslaughter as urged by the defence, and one of the majority judges declared that the evidence in support of the defendant's provocation claim was 'not strong': (1981) 28 SASR 345. See also Greene, 'A Provocation Defence', pp. 154–6 and Tarrant, 'Provocation and Self Defence', p. 150.

38 R v Duffy, 933–4.

39 (1977) 138 CLR 601; (1979) 21 SASR 356; (1984) 36 SASR 283; (1989) 42 A Crim R. 279.

40 [1983] 1 VR 460; Matthew Goode, 'The Abolition of Provocation' in Yeo, *Partial Excuses*, p. 44.

41 The court held that: 'The jury needed to be told it is the law that, if the applicant approached Shears still suffering from a sudden and temporary loss of self-control, caused by the provocative words of Marino, and whilst out of control killed Shears, a defence of provocation was open to the applicant.' (at 286)

42 For example, *Homicide*, Report No. 40, paras 192–3.

43 (1981) 28 SASR 343.

44 *Moffa*, 606–7. Typically, Moffa's admission at his trial that he had taken some of the photographs (at 615) has escaped comment.

45 (1981) 28 SASR 328.

46 'One Law For All Reasonable Persons?', *International Journal of the Sociology of Law*, 16, 1986, pp. 419, 428.

47 *Ibid.*, p. 429.

20 Women and the Secret Garden of Politics
Marian Simms

I am grateful to Christine Jennett (ANU) and Norma Grieve for their helpful comments on an earlier draft of this paper. Thanks also to Jacky McKimmie for her excellent keyboard skills.

1 See M. Simms, 'Writing the History of Australian Women', *Labour History*, 34, 1978, pp. 93–102; and 'Introduction' in M. Simms (ed.), *Australian Women and the Political System*, Melbourne, 1984.

2 K. McClure, 'The Issue of Foundations: Scientized Politics, Politicized Science and Feminist Critical Practice' in J. Butler and J. W. Scott (eds), *Feminists Theorize the Political*, New York, 1992.

3 New York, 1984. I would wager that most feminists have a copy on their bookshelves.
4 For details see M. Sawer and M. Simms, *A Woman's Place: Women in Australian Politics*, 2nd edn, Sydney, 1993.
5 H. Silverberg, 'What Happened to the Feminist Revolution in Political Science? A Review Essay', *Western Political Quarterly*, 43, 1990, pp. 890–1.
6 *Ibid.*, p. 890.
7 *Ibid.* Silverberg referred to M. Githens, J. Prestage and Virginia Sapiro.
8 See S. M. Lipset, *Political Man*, London, 1964.
9 S. Harding, 'Feminism, Science and the Anti-Enlightenment Critiques' in L. J. Nicholson (ed.), *Feminism/Postmodernism*, New York, 1990, p. 83.
10 *Ibid.*, p. 99.
11 *Ibid.*, p. 100.
12 Nancy Hartsock, *Money, Sex and Power*, Northeastern University Press, Boston, 1983, pp. 163–4.
13 'Oscillation between Power and Denial' in E. Marks and I. de Courtivron (eds), *New French Feminisms*, Amherst, 1980, p. 166.
14 Ithaca and London, 1992.
15 *Ibid.*, pp. 166–7.
16 'Feminist Analysis of Gender: A Critique' in M. Lowe and R. Hubbard (eds), *Woman's Nature: Rationalizations of Inequality*, New York, 1983, p. 103.
17 These critiques are discussed in Sawer and Simms, *A Woman's Place*, ch. 9.
18 For a survey see *ibid.*
19 See P. Norris, *et al.*, 'Party Selectorates in Australia, Britain and Canada: Prolegomena for Research in the 1990s', *Journal of Commonwealth and Comparative Politics*, 28, 1990, pp. 219–45.
20 J. Hills, 'Life-Style Constraints on Formal Political Participation—Why So Few Women Local Councillors in Britain?', *Electoral Studies*, 2, 1983, p. 41.
21 The principal investigators were A. Ascui, R. Jones, I. McAllister and T. Mughan (1987 Election and Candidates Study) and D. Gow, R. Jones, I. McAllister, E. Papadakis and M. Simms (1990 Election and Candidates Study). For the 1988 State Secretaries Study, M. Simms was the sole researcher. Funding was from a mixture of ARC and university money.
22 For more details on the results of the Candidates Studies see Sawer and Simms, *A Woman's Place*, ch. 3.

21 Boys' Own Stories
Stephanie Bunbury

With thanks to the Australian Film Institute library for help with research, to Adrian Martin for his suggestions, and to Philippa Hawker for her video selections and thoughtful comments.

1 'The World According to Teenpix', *Film Literature Quarterly*, 20, 1, 1992.
2 A teenage girl from California's San Fernando Valley, famous for an idiosyncratic jargon. The term is generally derogatory and denotes a faddish, materialistic and vacuous character.

3 From the theme song of *The Patty Duke Show*, a classic teen TV show of the 1960s.
4 *Men, Women and Chainsaws: Gender in the Modern Horror Film*, BFI Publishing, London, 1992.
5 Gertrud Koch, 'Why Women Go to Men's Films', in Gisela Ecker (ed.), *Feminist Aesthetics*, Women's Press, London, 1985.

22 Can a Boy Be a Girlfriend?
Norma Grieve

I am grateful to the following people who have read and commented on this chapter at various stages: Andrea Allard, Amanda Sinclair, Rosslyn Ives, Anna Grieve and above all my co-editor, Ailsa Burns.

1 Lolles Leon, actor, in the documentary *Pedro Almodovar*, a Channel X Production for Channel 4 Television, 1990: 'He is more than just a film director. He is a film director, a friend, a brother, a mother, a father, a lover, a neighbour, a girl-friend.'
2 *Weekly Telegraph*, 53, p. 22.
3 Clare Burton, 'Equal Employment Opportunity Programmes: Issues in Implementation', in N. Grieve and A. Burns (eds), *Australian Women: New Feminist Perspectives*, Oxford University Press, Melbourne, 1986, pp. 294–5.
4 Martina Nightingale, *Making Affirmative Action Work*, Victorian Trades Hall Council, 1992, p. 15.
5 'Gender as a Social Category', *Developmental Psychology*, 24, 6, 1988, p. 756.
6 Sandra Milligan and Karen Thomson, *Listening to Girls*, Report for the Committee to Review the National Policy for the Education of Girls, conducted for the Australian Education Council, 1991; Margaret Clark, *The Great Divide: The Construction of Gender in the Primary School*, Curriculum Development Centre, Canberra, 1989; Bronwyn Davies, 'The Discursive Production of the Male/Female Dualism in School Settings', *Oxford Review of Education*, 15, 3, 1989.
7 *Social Development*, Harcourt Brace Jovanovich, New York, 1980, p. 217.
8 'Gender as a Social Category', p. 756.
9 Milligan and Thomson, *Listening to Girls*; Clark, *The Great Divide*; Davies, 'Male/Female Dualism'.
10 'Gender as a Social Category'; Eleanor Maccoby, 'Gender and Relationships: A Developmental Account', *American Psychologist*, 45, 4, 1990.
11 Graeme O'Neill, 'Sex on the Brain', *Age*, 21 October 1992, p. 11. Interview with David Williamson on his new play 'Brilliant Lies': 'I think at a very deep level, the sexes do have different agendas which do probably have a biological basis': *Australian*, 2 April 1993, p. 1.
12 O'Neill, 'Sex on the Brain', p. 11.
13 J. Shibley-Hyde and M. C. Linn (eds), *The Psychology of Gender:*

Advances through Meta-Analysis, Johns Hopkins University Press, Baltimore, 1986.
14 Doreen Kimura, 'Sex Differences in the Brain', *Scientific American*, 267, 3, 1992, p. 87.
15 'Gender and Relationships', p. 513.
16 *Ibid.*
17 *Ibid.*
18 *Ibid.*, p. 514.
19 Jeanne Maracek, Introduction, *Psychology of Women Quarterly*, 13, 1989, p. 369.
20 Anne Moir and David Jessell, Mandarin, London, 1989, p. 178.
21 'Sex Differences', p. 87.
22 Wendy Steiner, 'Old-Fashioned Girls: Review of *Brain-Sex: The Real Difference between Men and Women* by Ann Moir and David Jessel', *London Review of Books*, 25 January 1990, p. 22.
23 Maccoby, 'Gender and Relationships', p. 514.
24 L. Serbin, I. Tonick and S. Sternglanz, 'Shaping Cooperative Cross-sex Play', *Child Development*, 48, 1977, pp. 924–9.
25 'Gender as a Social Category', p. 757.
26 R. Aukett, J. Ritchier and K. Mill, 'Gender Differences in Friendship Patterns', *Sex Roles*, 19, 1/2, 1988, pp. 57–66.
27 Maccoby, 'Gender as a Social Category', p. 758.
28 Deborah Tannen, *You Just Don't Understand: Women and Men in Conversation*, Random House, Milsons Point, 1991, p. 217.
29 *Ibid.*, pp. 216–24.
30 Clark, *The Great Divide*, p. 49.
31 Maccoby, 'Gender as a Social Category', citing the work of Charlesworth and Dzur, p. 757.
32 Maccoby, *Social Development*, pp. 215–16.
33 Maccoby, 'Gender and Relationships', p. 516.
34 *Ibid.*, p. 516.
35 Maccoby, 'Gender as a Social Category', p. 756.
36 *Ibid.*, p. 757.
37 Marilyn Poole, 'Choices and Constraints: The Education of Girls', in Grieve and Burns, *Australian Women*, p. 117.
38 Maccoby, 'Gender as a Social Category', p. 758.
39 Maccoby, 'Gender and Relationships', p. 514.
40 Maccoby, 'Gender as a Social Category', p. 756.
41 *The Great Divide*, p. 41.
42 Maccoby, 'Gender as a Social Category', p. 760.
43 'Gender and Relationships: A Reprise', *American Psychologist*, 46, 5, 1991, p. 538.
44 Clark, *The Great Divide*, pp. 42–3.
45 'Gender and Relationships: A Reprise', p. 538.
46 *Learning to Labour*, Gower, Aldershot, 1977, p. 146.
47 Davies, 'Male/Female Dualism'; Clark, *The Great Divide*.
48 'Male/Female Dualism', pp. 234, 238.

49 *The Great Divide*, pp. 32–48.
50 *Ibid.*, p. 34.
51 *Ibid.*, p. 35.
52 *Ibid.*, p. 45.
53 'Gender and Relationships: A Reprise', p. 538.
54 *The Great Divide*, p. 33.
55 'Gender and Relationships: A Reprise', p. 538.
56 Clark *The Great Divide*, p. 42.
57 'Male/Female Dualism', pp. 239–40.
58 D. Ullian, 'The Development of Concepts of Masculinity and Femininity', in B. Lloyd and J. Archer (eds), *Exploring Sex Differences*, Academic Press, New York, 1976.
59 'Family Structure and Feminine Personality', in M. Z. Rosaldo and L. Lamphere (eds), *Woman, Culture and Society*, Stanford University Press, Stanford, 1974, p. 50.
60 Clark, *The Great Divide*, p. 59.
61 *Ibid.*, p. 33.
62 Poole, 'Choices and Constraints', pp. 117–19.
63 Milligan and Thomson, *Listening to Girls*, p. 10.
64 *Ibid.*, pp. 20–1. See also Shirley Sampson, 'Bridging the Gap', *Age*, 21 July 1992, p. 19.
65 *Listening to Girls*, p. 7.
66 Philippa Pattison, 'Gender and Mathematics', in P. Grimshaw, R. Fincher and M. Campbell (eds), *Studies in Gender: Essays in Honour of Norma Grieve*, Committee for Gender Studies, University of Melbourne, 1992, p. 109. See also Helen Keating, *Age*, 16 June 1992, p. 19.
67 Milligan and Thomson, *Listening to Girls*, pp. 22–3.
68 Clark, *The Great Divide*, p. 57.
69 *Ibid.*, p. 32.
70 *Ibid.*, p. 53.
71 *Writing a Woman's Life*, Women's Press, London, 1988, p. 100.
72 Clark, *The Great Divide*, p. 39.
73 Ashley Hay, 'Sex Wars in the Playground', *Independent Monthly*, June 1992, p. 17.
74 *Ibid.*
75 Clark, *The Great Divide*, p. 57.
76 Andrea Allard Di Bretherton and Linda Collins, 'Education, Gender and Conflict: The Effective After-School Learning Program', in Grimshaw, Fincher and Campbell, *Studies in Gender*.
77 Clark, *The Great Divide*, p. 57.
78 Beatrice Whiting and Carolyn Edwards, *Children of Different Worlds*, Harvard University Press, Cambridge, Mass., 1988, p. 276.
79 Drury Sherrod, 'The Bonds of Men: Problems and Possibilities in Close Male Relationships', in H. Brod (ed.), *The Making of Masculinities*, Allen and Unwin, Winchester, 1987, p. 237.
80 Amanda Sinclair, 'Sex and the M.B.A.', paper presented at conference, the Australian and New Zealand Academy of Management, Sydney, December 1992.
81 Tannen, *You Just Don't Understand*, pp. 235–8.

23 Why Do Women Put Up With the Double Load? Ailsa Burns

1 See chapters by Lois Bryson and Rosemary Pringle, in this volume.
2 See for example M. Barrett and M. McIntosh, *The Anti-social Family*, Verso, London, 1982; L. Bryson, 'The Australian Patriarchal Family' in S. Encel *et al.* (eds), *Australian Society*, Longman Cheshire, Melbourne, 4th edn, 1984.
3 See chapters by Bryson and Pringle.
4 M. M. Ferree, 'Feminism and Family Research' in A. Booth (ed.), *Contemporary Families: Looking Forward, Looking Back*, National Council on Family Relations, Minneapolis, 1991.
5 M. Bittman, *Juggling Time*, Office of the Status of Women, Canberra, 1991.
6 M. Bittman and F. Lovejoy, 'Domestic Power: Negotiation and Unequal Division of Labour Within a Framework of Equality', paper presented to the Australian Sociological Association, Perth, December 1991; J. J. Goodnow and J. M. Bowes, *Men, Women and Household Work: New Views, New Ways*, Macquarie University, Sydney, 1992.
7 P. Barach and M. Baratz, 'Decisions and Nondecisions: An Analytical Framework', *American Political Science Review*, 57, 1963, pp. 641–51.
8 Bittman and Lovejoy, 'Domestic Power'.
9 A. Komter, 'Hidden Power in Marriage', *Gender and Society*, 3, 1989, pp. 187–216.
10 Ferree, 'Feminism and Family Research'.
11 S. Duck, *Human Relationships*, Sage, London, 1992.
12 See for example H. Glezer, 'Antecedents and Correlates of Marriage and Family Attitudes in Young Australian Men and Women', in Committee of Family Research, *Social Change and Family Policies*, vol. 1, Australian Institute of Family Studies, Melbourne, 1984; Bittman and Lovejoy, 'Domestic Power'.
13 K. Dempsey, *A Man's Town: Inequality Between Men and Women in Rural Australia*, Oxford University Press, Melbourne, 1992.
14 *Ibid.*, p. 50.
15 *Ibid.*
16 *Ibid.*, p. 103.
17 Bittman and Lovejoy, 'Domestic Power'.
18 L. Dennerstein, 'Women and Health Care: Australian Perspectives on Medical Women', in P. Grimshaw, R. Fincher and M. Campbell (eds), *Studies in Gender: Essays in Honour of Norma Grieve*, Committee for Gender Studies, University of Melbourne, 1992.
19 See Rosemary Pringle, in this volume.
20 D. Bair, *Simone de Beauvoir: A Biography*, Vintage, London, 1990, p. 400.
21 J. Osborne, *Almost a Gentleman*, Faber and Faber, London, 1991.
22 Bair, *De Beauvoir.*
23 See for example H. Eisenstein, *Contemporary Feminist Thought*, Unwin, London, 1984; and other chapters in this book.
24 See Norma Grieve, in this volume.

25 Eisenstein, *Contemporary Feminist Thought*; L. Gordon, 'Feminism, Reproduction and the Family', in B. Thorne and M. Yalom, *Rethinking the Family*, Longman, New York, 1982, 1992.
26 P. McDonald, 'The 1980s: Social and Economic Change', *Family Matters*, 26, 1990, pp. 13–181.
27 L. Thompson and A. Walker, 'Gender in Families: Women and Men in Marriage, Work and Parenthood', *Journal of Marriage and the Family*, 51, 1990, pp. 845–69; L. Genevie and E. Margolis, *The Motherhood Report*, Macmillan, New York, 1987.
28 Genevie and Margolis, *The Motherhood Report.*
29 Goodnow and Bowes, *Men, Women and Household Work.*
30 *Ibid.*, p. 7.11.
31 *Ibid.*, p. 7.18.
32 *Ibid.*, p. 5.12.
33 *Ibid.*, p. 7.11.
34 P. Blumenstein and P. Schwartz, *American Couples*, Morrow, New York, 1983.
35 E. Macklin, 'Nontraditional Family Forms', in M. Sussman and S. Steinmetz (eds), *Handbook of Marriage and the Family*, Plenum, New York, 1987, pp. 317–53.
36 M. Schneider, 'The Relationships of Cohabiting Lesbians and Heterosexual Couples: A Comparison', *Psychology of Women Quarterly*, 10, 1986, pp. 243–39; W. Masters and V. Johnson, *Homosexuality in Perspective*, Little Brown, Boston, 1979.
37 P. McDonald, 'The Shift Away from Marriage among Young Australians', *Family Matters*, 30, 1991, p. 50.
38 *Ibid.*
39 H. van de Kaa, 'Europe's Second Demographic Transition', *Population Bulletin*, 42, 1, 1987.
40 *Ibid.*; McDonald, 'The Shift Away from Marriage'.
41 F. Headlam, 'Marital Breakdown: Reactions to Separation and Postseparation Experience of Adults' in *Proceedings of the Australian Family Research Conference, Canberra, November 1983*, Australian Institute of Family Studies, Melbourne; P. Jordan, *The Effects of Separation on Men: 'Men Hurt'*, Family Court of Australia Research Report No. 6, Brisbane.
42 H. Glezer, *Maternity Leave in Australia*, Australian Institute of Family Studies, Melbourne, 1988.
43 B. Hoem and J. Hoem, 'The Swedish Family: Aspects of Contemporary Developments', *Journal of Family Issues*, 9, 3, 1988, pp. 397–424.
44 C. Etzler, *Education, Cohabitation and the First Child: Some Empirical Findings from Sweden*, University of Stockholm Research Reports in Demography No. 34, 1987.
45 Australian Bureau of Statistics, *Family Formation and Dissolution 1982*, Catalogue No. 4411.0, Canberra, 1985; P. McDonald, 'The Rise in Ex-nuptial Births', paper presented to the 2nd Australian Family Research Conference, Melbourne, 1986; S. E. Khoo, 'Living Together as Married: A Profile of De Facto Couples in Australia', *Journal of Marriage and the Family*, 49, 1987, pp. 185–91.

46 H. Glezer, 'To Tie or Not Tie the Knot: Pathways to Family Formation', paper presented at the 4th Australian Family Research Conference, Sydney, 17–19 February 1993; J. Cunningham and J. Antill, 'Cohabitation: Marriage of the Future?', paper presented to the ANZAAS Congress, Auckland, 1979; E. Thomson and U. Colella, 'Cohabitation and Marital Stability: Quality or Commitment', *Journal of Marriage and the Family*, 54, 2, 1992, pp. 259–68.

24 Women's Studies in Australia
Susan Magarey, Lyndall Ryan, and Susan Sheridan

1 Mirna Cicioni, ' "Love and Respect, Together": The Theory and Practice of *Affidamento* in Italian Feminism', *Australian Feminist Studies*, 10, 1989, pp. 71–83.

2 Red Fems, 'The Implications of Technological Change for Women Workers in the Public Sector' in M. Bevege *et al.* (eds), *Worth Her Salt: Women at Work in Australia*, Sydney, 1982, pp. 148–62.

3 E. Windschuttle (ed.), *Women, Class and History*, Melbourne, 1980; Bevege *et al.*, *Worth Her Salt*; Women and Labour Publications Collective (ed.), *All Her Labours*, vol. 1: 'Working It Out'; vol. 2: 'Embroidering the Framework', Sydney, 1984.

4 Gloria Bowles and Renate Klein (eds), *Theories of Women's Studies* London, 1983; Catharine R. Stimpson, *Women's Studies in the United States*, New York, 1986; Sneja Gunew (ed.), *Feminist Knowledge: Critique and Construct*, London and New York, 1990.

5 Cited in M. Boxer, 'For and About Women: The Theory and Practice of Women's Studies in the United States' in N. O. Keohane *et al.* (eds), *Feminist Theory: A Critique of Ideology*, Brighton, Sussex, 1982, p. 238.

6 S. Sheridan, 'Feminist Knowledge, Women's Liberation and Women's Studies' in Gunew (ed.), *Feminist Knowledge*, pp. 45–6.

7 J. Allen, 'Women's Studies in the 1990s: Problems and Prospects', *Australian Universities Review*. 34, 2, 1991, pp. 8–11. On the political nature of knowledges, and on 'trans-disciplinarity' (see below), see also S. Magarey, 'Women's Studies Programme: An Attempt at Interdisciplinary Studies', *ANU Reporter*, 28 November 1980; and 'Women's Studies in Australia—Towards Trans-Disciplinary Learning', *Journal of Educational Thought*, 17, 2, 1988, pp. 162–71.

8 'Women's Studies Courses', *Refractory Girl*, 2, 1973, p. 39; Penny Ryan (ed.), *A Guide to Women's Studies in Australia*, Melbourne, 1973, p. 41; Beverly Walker and Margaret Smith, 'Women's Studies Courses in Australian Universities', *Women's Studies International Quarterly*, 2, 1, 1979, pp. 373–80; S. Sheridan, 'From Margin to Mainstream', *Australian Feminist Studies*, 2, 1986, p. 3.

9 'Women's Studies Courses', *Refractory Girl*, 1, 1972–3. p. 39.

10 Editorial, *Refractory Girl*, 10, 1976, p. 2.

11 A. Neale, 'The Philosophy Strike: Feminism Bypassed at Sydney'. *Refractory Girl*, 3, 1973, pp. 28–9.

12 G. Poiner, 'Report on Women's Studies at Macquarie University', unpublished paper (1992), appendix 3.

13 'Women's Studies Courses', *Refractory Girl*, 2, 1973, p. 39.
14 J. J. Matthews and D. Broom, 'Orphans of the Storm: The Attrition of the ANU Women's Studies Program', *Australian Universities Review*, 34, 2, 1992, pp. 12–14.
15 See L. Ryan, 'Women's Studies in Australian Higher Education: Introduction and Brief History', *Australian Universities Review*, 34, 2, 1992, pp. 2–7.
16 See 'A Directory of Women's Studies in Australian Universities', in Gender Theory Group, Curtin University of Technology, *Women's Studies in Australian Universities: A Directory*, Nepean, 1992.
17 Magarey, 'Women's Studies in Australia', p. 163.
18 Debates on this issue are canvassed in S. Reinharz, *Feminist Methods in Social Research*, New York and Oxford, 1992, pp. 12–14 *et passim*.
19 S. Magarey, opening paper, HRC Conference on 'Feminist Enquiry as a Transdisciplinary Enterprise', Research Centre for Women's Studies, Adelaide University, August 1986.
20 Paper presented at the 1990 Women's Studies Conference, University of Melbourne, and published as 'Women's Studies in the 1990s', p. 11 (see note 7 above).
21 E. Grosz, 'A Note on Essentialism and Difference' in Gunew, *Feminist Knowledge*, pp. 332–44.
22 For example, T. de Lauretis, 'Eccentric Subjects: Feminist Theory and Historical Consciousness', *Feminist Studies*, 16, 1, 1990, pp. 115–50.
23 For example, D. Haraway, 'A Manifesto for Cyborgs', *Australian Feminist Studies*, 4, 1987, pp. 1–42.
24 Liz Flanagan and Kat Felton, paper presented at the *Lilith* Conference on Women and Difference, University of Melbourne, November 1992.
25 See for example gay and lesbian journals *Burn* and *Cargo*, as well as the journal *Australian Lesbian Feminist Studies*, started in 1991.
26 See for example C. Bulbeck, *One World Women's Movement*, London, 1988.
27 For example, S. Brodribb, *Nothing Mat(t)ers: A Feminist Critique of Postmodernism*, Melbourne, 1992.
28 M. Morris, 'Introduction' and 'Bibliography', *The Pirate's Fiancée: Feminism, Reading, Postmodernism*, London, 1988, pp. 1–23.
29 Chilla Bulbeck, Panel on Women's Studies at Australian Women's Studies Association Conference, University of Sydney, October 1992.
30 Sue Himmelweit, *ibid.*
31 T. de Lauretis, 'Eccentric Subjects', p. 138.

Index